BTEC Level 2 Firsts in
SPORT

Rob Commons, Michala Swales, Ian Wood, Ray Barker, Gez Rizzo and Darrel Barsby

OXFORD
UNIVERSITY PRESS

OXFORD
UNIVERSITY PRESS

Great Clarendon Street, Oxford OX2 6DP

Oxford University Press is a department of the University of Oxford.
It furthers the University's objective of excellence in research,
scholarship,and education by publishing worldwide in

Oxford   New York

Auckland   Cape Town   Dar es Salaam   Hong Kong   Karachi
Kuala Lumpur   Madrid   Melbourne   Mexico City   Nairobi
New Delhi   Shanghai   Taipei   Toronto

With offices in

Argentina   Austria   Brazil   Chile   Czech Republic   France   Greece
Guatemala   Hungary   Italy   Japan   Poland   Portugal   Singapore
South Korea   Switzerland   Thailand   Turkey   Ukraine   Vietnam

Oxford is a registered trade mark of Oxford University Press
in the UK and in certain other countries

British Library Cataloguing in Publication Data

Data available

ISBN 978-1-85008-515-7

FD5157

10 9 8 7 6 5 4 3

Printed by Bell & Bain Ltd, Glasgow.

Paper used in the production of this book is a natural, recyclable product
made from wood grown in sustainable forests. The manufacturing process
conforms to the environmental regulations of the country of origin.

Series design: Rosa Capacchione
Page layout: Planman Technologies
Picture research: Hardwick Studios
Artwork: Planman Technologies
Cover design: Rosa Capacchione
Front cover image: Mark Shearman Sports Photography

Mixed Sources
Product group from well-managed
forests and other controlled sources
www.fsc.org   Cert no. TT-COC-002769
© 1996 Forest Stewardship Council

Contents

Unit 1: Fitness Testing and Training

Components of fitness

A person is considered to be physically fit if they are able to carry out all of their daily tasks easily and without becoming fatigued. However, being 'fit for sport' requires a much higher level of fitness than that needed for activities such as walking the dog or gardening.

Fitness for sport can be broken down into eleven individual components, grouped under two main headings: physical fitness and skill-related fitness. A good level of both physical fitness and skill-related fitness is needed to be successful in most sports, but the relative importance of each component is dependent upon the sport chosen. A component that may be vitally important for one sport may be much less important for another. Elite athletes need a thorough understanding of all the components in order to be successful, so that training sessions can be tailored to their individual needs.

Physical fitness

Aerobic endurance: This is a measure of how well you are able to keep your muscles supplied with oxygen. It relies on a strong heart muscle to keep blood pumping around your body and a good pair of lungs to keep supplying the blood with fresh oxygen. Aerobic endurance is sometimes called cardiovascular endurance.

Marathon runners and distance cyclists require a high level of aerobic endurance to be able to keep working over a long period of time in a race.

Your cardiovascular endurance can be improved by taking part in aerobic training.

Muscular endurance: You have a good level of muscular endurance if your muscles can keep exerting force for a long time. This can mean that they are able to contract many times, for example, when running a marathon, or it can mean that they can sustain one contraction for a long period of time, for example, when pulling in a tug of war. Muscles need a good supply of oxygen (see aerobic endurance) **and** a good supply of energy in the form of glycogen, a type of sugar that is broken down to release energy.

Professional footballers need a high level of muscular endurance to keep them moving around the pitch for 90 minutes.

Muscular endurance can be improved by taking part in weight training activities, by running or by regularly performing exercises such as sit-ups and press-ups.

Physical fitness

Body composition: This is a measure of how much of your body is made up of muscle compared with how much is made up of fat. It is important to have a good balance of the two but sports players usually have a greater proportion of muscle.

Some sports performers, such as rowers, require a large muscle mass to give them lots of power and strength, but others, such as marathon runners, require a lower muscle mass so that they don't have to carry 'extra' body mass as they are running. Some sports performers, such as sumo wrestlers, even require quite a large mass of body fat to be successful.

Everyone is born with a predisposition to a particular body composition, although small changes can be made by varying your diet and the amount/type of exercise that you take part in. The important thing is to have the correct body composition for your sport.

Flexibility: This is the range of movement possible at a joint. Flexibility is determined by how elastic the ligaments and tendons are at a joint, how strong the muscles are that pull against the joint and the shape of the bones that form the joint. Most joints are designed to give either strength or flexibility, so the shape of the bones is usually the most important factor in determining flexibility. For example, the shoulder joint is made up of a ball-shaped bone (the end of the humerus) and a cup-shaped bone (the end of the scapula), allowing lots of movement in many directions.

Gymnasts have to be flexible so that they can twist their bodies into different shapes when performing routines or vaults.

Flexibility can be improved by taking part in lots of stretching exercises on a regular basis.

Speed: This is how fast a muscle can contract, once or repeatedly, in a given amount of time. For example, in order to be good at the 100m sprint, the muscles in your legs and arms have to contract over and over again as quickly as possible. The faster they contract, the more speed you have.

Speed is important in many team sports to help players beat their opponents. For example, netballers need speed so that they can get into spaces more quickly than their opponents and rugby players need speed to be able to beat their opponents to the try-line.

Speed is often said to be something that we are born with, although some improvements can be made by taking part in strength training and sprint training.

Strength: This is the amount of force that can be generated by a muscle when it is contracting. There are lots of different types of strength but the main two are:

- Explosive strength, the amount of force that can be exerted in one quick, powerful contraction, which is useful in sports such as the javelin and the high jump. It is closely linked to power.
- Dynamic strength, the amount of force that can be exerted repeatedly by a muscle, which is useful when completing sit-ups or when cycling. It is closely linked to muscular endurance.

Strength can be increased by taking part in weight training. Smaller weights are lifted lots of times to improve dynamic strength and heavier weights are lifted fewer times to improve explosive strength.

BRONZE

1. Choose five sports and, for each one, **describe** the three most important components of physical fitness.

SILVER

2. Choose five sports and, for each one, **explain** the three most important components of physical fitness.

3. Rank the components of physical fitness, in order, from the most important to the least important, for each of the following sports performers: a footballer, a cyclist taking part in the Tour de France and a swimmer in the 50m freestyle. Give reasons to justify your rankings.

Skill-related fitness

Skill-related fitness

Agility: Agility is the ability of a sports player to move and change direction quickly and under control. For example, a basketball player has to change direction quickly when dribbling and driving towards the basket. Training has little or no effect on improving agility.

Balance: Balance is the ability to keep the body stable, when still or moving, by keeping the centre of gravity over the base of support, for example, when performing a handstand or a cartwheel. An individual's overall level of balance is not really something that can be trained, although the ability to perform a particular type of balance, such as a headstand, can be improved through practice.

Coordination: Coordination is the ability to use two or more parts of the body at the same time. Even simple acts such as walking require a degree of coordination but a much higher level of coordination is required when playing a tennis shot. Again, an individual's level of coordination cannot be improved through training, although the ability to perform a particular task can be improved through practice.

Power: Power is the ability to combine strength with speed, to perform a strong contraction very quickly. Power is very closely linked to explosive strength. Power is needed in most sports, although it is more obvious in some. For example, boxers need power to able to punch hard and fast, whilst golfers need power in order to hit the ball over a greater distance.

Reaction time: This is the time it takes to respond to a stimulus, such as a ball coming towards you when fielding in cricket. The shorter the amount of time it takes to respond, the quicker the reactions of the performer. Reaction time is incredibly important in events such as the 100m because the sprinter who responds fastest to the sound of the gun has a better chance of winning the race. Reaction time cannot be improved through training, although the time taken to respond to a simple stimulus like the starting gun can be improved through practice. It is likely, though, that this is more about anticipating the gun than responding to it.

Fitness training methods

Fitness training is much more technical than simply going for a jog each day. Each of the components of fitness has to be trained in a different way and different training methods will develop some components more than others. Because all sports require a mixture of the components of fitness, they require participants to take part in a range of training methods. Indeed, overusing one particular training method is likely to lead to injury in the long term and, for this reason, all sports performers should try to vary their training schedule on a regular basis.

The training pyramid

The training pyramid is a way of calculating how hard you need to train and how long each training session should be. Each section of the pyramid represents a different training zone and the higher the zone, the harder you need to work. The width of the zone represents the amount of time that you need to train in that zone. So, if you are working in the aerobic training zone you would work for longer and have longer but fewer rest periods than you would if you were working in the speed zone, because the aerobic zone takes up a wider section of the pyramid.

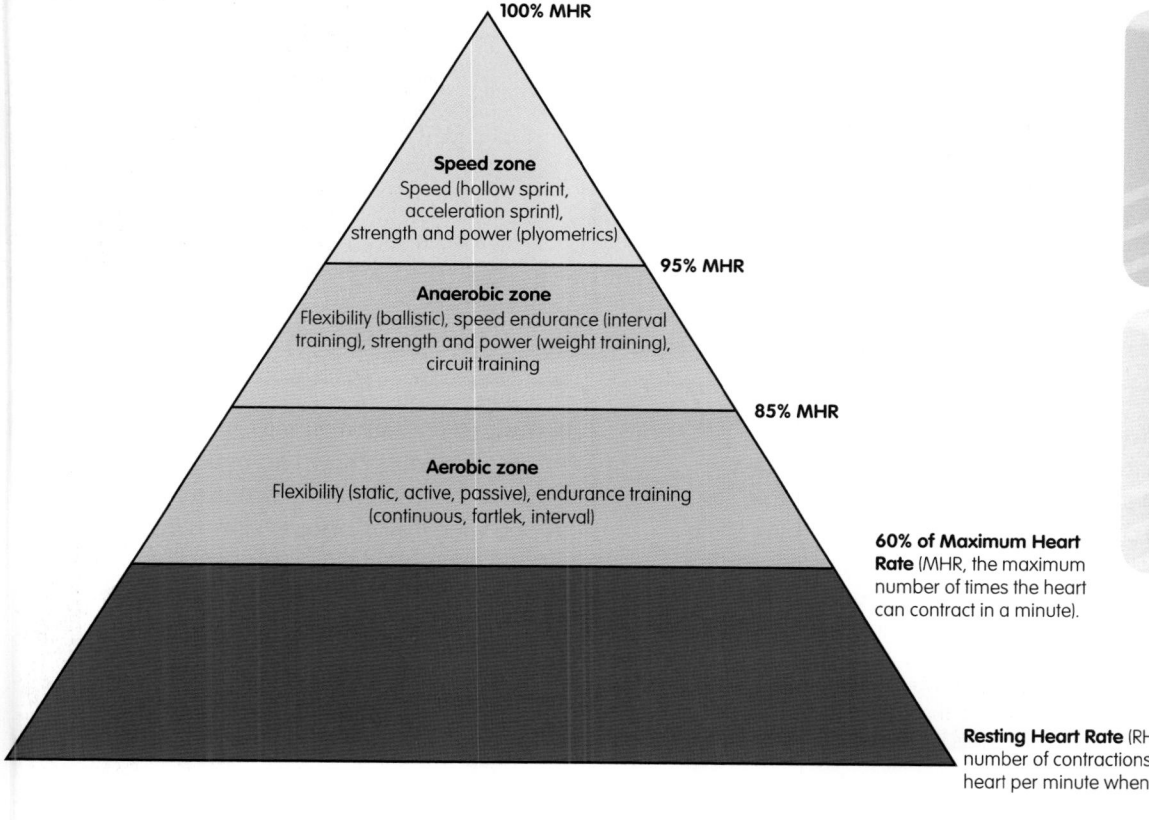

100% MHR

Speed zone
Speed (hollow sprint,
acceleration sprint),
strength and power (plyometrics)

95% MHR

Anaerobic zone
Flexibility (ballistic), speed endurance (interval training), strength and power (weight training), circuit training

85% MHR

Aerobic zone
Flexibility (static, active, passive), endurance training (continuous, fartlek, interval)

60% of Maximum Heart Rate (MHR, the maximum number of times the heart can contract in a minute).

Resting Heart Rate (RHR, the number of contractions of the heart per minute when resting).

Maximum Heart Rate for men = 220 – age
Maximum Heart Rate for women = 226 – age

So a 15-year-old male's MHR = 220 – 15 = 205bpm (beats per minute)

From this we can calculate the training zones. The aerobic zone = 60 per cent of 205 to 85 per cent of 205 = 123 to 174bpm

Therefore, a 15-year-old male who wishes to undertake continuous training should work hard enough to make their heart contract between 123bpm and 174bpm. Slower than 123bpm would have little or no training effect and above 174bpm would cause the performer to become fatigued too quickly.

BRONZE

1. Suggest a suitable training zone for a 20-year-old male javelin thrower.

2. Suggest a suitable training zone for a 20-year-old female marathon runner.

SILVER

3. Apart from the difference in heart rates, what other differences would there be in the training schedules of the javelin thrower and the marathon runner? Why?

Flexibility training

Most sports performers undertake flexibility training as part of their regular training programme. Some, such as dancers and gymnasts, do so in order to enable them to stretch further and perform more complex and difficult actions. Others, such as footballers, use flexibility training as a way of preventing injuries such as torn muscles and ligaments. There are four types of flexibility training:

- static stretching
- passive stretching
- active stretching
- ballistic stretching.

Static stretching

Here, there is no movement and the stretch is held for 10–16 seconds. An example would be leaning against a wall to stretch the muscles in the lower leg.

Active stretching

Here the performer moves slowly into the stretch to apply extra force to the muscle. An example would be taking slow, small steps and rising up on tiptoes to stretch the muscles of the lower leg with each step.

Passive stretching

Here the force of the stretch is applied by a partner, while the performer tries to relax. The most common form of passive stretching is the hamstring stretch, where the performer lies flat on the floor and a partner lifts a leg, trying to raise it to an angle of 90 degrees or further.

Ballistic stretching

This is sometimes known as 'bounce stretching', because the performer tries to use extra force by bouncing the muscles to stretch them further. A good example is the high kick action which is often performed by hurdlers before a race.

BRONZE

1. Try to perform each type of flexibility training to see how it feels. Then, suggest a sports performer that would benefit from each type of training and a sports performer who would gain little or no benefit from each type of training.

Circuit training

Circuit training consists of a series of exercises arranged in order and designed to develop general fitness, physical fitness, and/or skill-related fitness specific to a particular sport, depending on the exercises chosen.

The great advantage of circuit training is that, depending on the exercises chosen, it can be used to develop strength, power, muscular endurance, agility, aerobic endurance and anaerobic endurance (the ability to work without burning oxygen for an extended period of time; top class 800m runners can work anaerobically for approximately 90 seconds) in a limited time and limited space. It can also involve large numbers of participants in a relatively small space, and participants of different fitness levels can train together.

To improve a component of fitness it is necessary to 'overload', to work harder than your body is used to working normally. Overload is achieved in circuit training by:

- reducing target times (the time taken to complete a given number of repetitions)
- increasing exercise resistance (increasing the difficulty of the exercise)
- increasing repetitions (increasing the number of times the exercise is repeated, possibly in a given time)
- increasing circuits (increasing the number of times the circuit is completed).

There are a number of things to think about when designing a circuit:

- Decide on the fitness requirements of the people completing the circuit and choose the exercises accordingly. Do they want to develop general fitness, physical fitness and/or skill-related fitness for a specific sport or physical activity?
- The number of participants.
- The current level of fitness of the participants.
- The time, space and equipment available.

And, don't forget the golden rule: the same body part should not be exercised consecutively. For this reason, it is important to alternate between exercises designed to work the upper body and exercises designed to work the lower body.

BRONZE

1. Design a circuit training session for a sport of your choice. Explain why you have included each of the exercises you have chosen.

SILVER

2. Explain how you would adjust your circuit to accommodate participants of varying fitness levels.

Strength and power training

Weight training

An effective way to improve strength is to use weight training. Here, a combination of free weights and resistance machines are used to put the muscles under stress. As a muscle works the individual fibres in the muscle tear and, as they repair themselves over the next 24 hours or so, they become stronger and bigger. Over time this leads to an overall increase in the size and strength of the muscle.

In general, resistance machines are much safer than free weights. They can usually be used when working alone, whereas free weights often require a 'spotter', a partner who is there to help set up and keep the performer safe. Resistance machines are also much better at working individual muscles and there are a range of machines available, each targeted at a specific muscle group. This gives them a distinct advantage over free weights, which are often inappropriate for training certain muscles.

Each time a performer completes a lifting or moving action they are working against a 'resistance' (an amount of force or weight that must be lifted or moved). Each lift is known as one repetition or 'rep'. A set is the name given to the number of repetitions a performer completes without a rest. For example:

Strength	**Power**
8 reps	8 reps (performed at speed)
3 sets	3 sets
Heavy weight (load)	Heavy weight (load)

Plyometrics

This is designed to improve strength and power. It involves the performer jumping down off a box and then immediately back up onto another box, or something similar. On hitting the ground, the quadriceps muscle lengthens to act as a brake. By immediately jumping back upwards the quadriceps is forced to shorten quickly, thereby producing more power. You can see how this works by stretching an elastic band between your fingers. You will find that the further you stretch the elastic band, the more powerfully it contracts back.

Using free weights.

Using a resistance machine.

Plyometrics training.

BRONZE

1. Try to perform each type of strength and power training to see how it feels. Then, suggest a sports performer that would benefit from each type of training and a sports performer who would gain little or no benefit from each type of training.

2. Design a training session for a performer who wants to develop muscular power.

Endurance training

Endurance training requires the sports performer to work for an extended period of time, often longer than the actual event for which he or she is training. For example, Paula Radcliffe will often train upwards of four hours at a time, even though her event (the marathon) is usually over in less than two-and-a-half hours. Endurance training should take place largely in the aerobic training zone of the training pyramid and the work to rest ratio should be in the region of 3:1. This means that if you work for 30 minutes you should follow it with a ten-minute rest and then repeat the session again. There are three types of endurance training:

- continuous training
- fartlek training
- interval training.

Continuous training
Continuous training involves performing an activity – such as jogging, swimming, cycling, walking or rowing – for an extended period of time (usually longer than 20 minutes) without rest. To improve aerobic fitness you should complete three to four sessions of continuous training per week.

Fartlek training
Fartlek training, also known as 'speed play', is a form of road running or cross-country running in which the runner, usually running alone, varies their pace significantly during the run. It is usually regarded as an advanced training technique for an experienced runner who has been using interval training to develop speed and to raise their anaerobic threshold. However, the 'average' runner can also benefit from a simplified form of fartlek training, to develop self-awareness and to introduce variety into the training programme.

Endurance training is crucial to the success of athletes such as Paula Radcliffe and Lance Armstrong.

Fartlek is similar to interval training in that short, fast runs are alternated with recovery periods of slow running or jogging. The vast majority of the running takes place in the aerobic zone but the short, fast sprints push the performer to work anaerobically for short periods at a time. However, with fartlek training you are running on the road or in a park and there is no predetermined schedule to follow. Instead the athlete sets the length of the intervals and their pace in response to how they are feeling. An advantage of fartlek training is that the athlete concentrates on feeling the pace and their physical response to it, thereby developing self-awareness and pace-judgement skills. Also, the athlete is free to experiment with changes of pace and endurance, making it an excellent component of a distance runner's training programme. However, it is primarily a technique for advanced runners because it requires honesty to ensure a demanding workload, and maturity to avoid overdoing the pace or length of the intervals.

Interval training
Interval training consists of alternating intervals of running over a specific distance in a set time (fast running in other words), with recovery periods that are specified in terms of duration, distance or both. Interval training can improve endurance when the work period is longer than 20 minutes and the rest period is one third of the work period. Training sessions will focus on specific race demands.

Interval training is similar to fartlek training, except that it is much more rigid. You decide before you start how long to run for, at what speed, and how long and often your rest periods will be. It is more suitable for the inexperienced athlete, as it does not require the same level of honesty and decision making as fartlek training.

This type of training is a component of a balanced training programme that will include recovery days and a range of other running activities, depending on the goals of the individual. Mixing interval training with running a range of distances, and different types of running (such as, cross-country running and hill running), can contribute to overall fitness and the capacity to engage in successful competitive running.

BRONZE
1. Try to perform each type of endurance training to see how it feels. Then, suggest a sports performer that would benefit from each type of training and a sports performer who would gain little or no benefit from each type of training.

2a) Design a training session for a distance runner.

b) Based on the performer's ability, suggest ways of changing the session if they were running at school, county, regional, national and international level.

3. List the benefits of fartlek training for an elite international athlete.

Speed and speed endurance training

Speed training is a way of developing a performer's speed over short distances. This is useful in almost all sports because speed can often be the difference between winning and losing. For example, footballers need to be able to cover a distance quickly to beat an opponent to the ball and tennis players need to be quick to reach the ball during a rally. Speed training should always be carried out in the speed zone of the training pyramid. It is of a very high intensity, so work periods should be short and frequent, and interspersed with lots of short rest periods. This makes speed training a type of interval training. It is generally accepted that a work to rest ratio of 1:6 is desirable. This means that a performer should work at a maximum level for a very short period, usually up to about 15 seconds, and then follow this with a rest period that is six times longer, repeating the sequence several times. There are two types of speed and speed endurance training:

- hollow sprints
- acceleration sprints.

Hollow sprints

These are similar to interval training, in that a period of work is broken up by a 'hollow' period of either rest or lower level work. A typical hollow sprint session would look something like this:

50m	Sprint	(6–7 secs)
50m	Jog	(25 secs)
50m	Sprint	(6–7 secs)
50m	Walk	(30 secs)
50m	print	(6–7 secs)
150m	Walk	(90 secs)

This is repeated five times before a longer, ten-minute rest period.

Acceleration sprints

As the name suggests, the aim here is to improve acceleration from a starting position. This equates to the first five to ten metres of any race, such as a 100m sprint or a race to a loose ball in rugby. Training is usually designed to match the demands of a particular sport. For example, rugby players may start the sprint by lying on the ground to simulate a ruck, whereas footballers may start with their back to the direction of the sprint to simulate turning away from a defender and sprinting into a space. A typical session may look something like this:

American sprinter Tyson Gay works on improving his speed in training.

10 x 5m sprint (walk back to start each time)
30-second rest between each sprint.

BRONZE

1. Try to perform each type of speed and speed endurance training to see how it feels. Then, suggest a sports performer that would benefit from each type of training and a sports performer who would gain little or no benefit from each type of training.

Speed training for footballers often involves turning away from a defender.

SPOTLIGHT on fitness and training requirements

BRONZE

Completing these activities will help you to achieve a **Pass** in your assignment.

1. Complete the table below :

Sport	Type of strength	Example of this type of strength in action
Rugby	Explosive	
Gymnastics	Explosive	Vaulting
Football		
Hockey		Penalty flick
Netball		
Rowing	Dynamic	
100m sprint		

2. What is meant by 'cardiovascular endurance'? Name five sports where cardiovascular endurance is important.

3. Name two sports where muscular endurance is important and, for both, suggest which muscle groups the competitors should concentrate on improving.

4. Describe three fitness training methods that could be used by basketball players.

SILVER

Completing these activities will help you to achieve a **Merit** in your assignment.

5. Name three sports in which flexibility is important. Compare and contrast the different types of flexibility training and decide which would be most appropriate for each of the sports you have chosen.

6. Explain the major differences between interval training and continuous training. Under which circumstances would a marathon runner choose to train using the interval method?

7. Write a paragraph to justify the following statement: 'International footballers need a much higher level of strength, endurance and flexibility than international rugby union players'.

8. Explain how knowledge of the training pyramid can be used to improve the quality of a fartlek training session.

The effects of lifestyle on sports training and performance

To perform at your best, you need to be in peak physical condition. A common mistake is to assume that peak physical condition comes merely as a result of completing hours, days and weeks of training. There is, however, another factor that is far more important – lifestyle.

Lifestyle factors account for failure amongst top athletes far more often than poor training. Too little or too much sleep, stress at home, medical history and diet all play a major role in the physical condition of both amateur and professional sports performers. For a person to perform at his or her best, their lifestyle factors and the training must all come together at the crucial time.

Stress

Stress can be both good and bad for a person engaged in a sporting event. Good stress can improve performance, whereas bad stress can cause them to underperform.

The body's response to stress is to change the biochemistry in the blood, by releasing adrenalin. This gives the body an energy boost. The muscles become tighter and prepared for exertion. The senses become more attuned. For example, pupils dilate to allow more light to enter the eye and improve eyesight. This response is known as the 'fight-or-flight' response.

If too much adrenalin is released, the performer suffers from a lack of control; their hands will shake and their muscles will contract with too much power. This can lead them to mistime a tackle in football or overstep the throwing line in an athletics event. If there is not enough adrenalin present, the performer will suffer from a lack of energy in training or competition, and will be too lethargic to be competitive.

Stress is a crucial part of ensuring peak performance in any sport. Attaining the perfect level of stress for the individual at the right time is often harder than attaining peak physical condition. Having knowledge of a person's stress levels, and knowing how to manage and alter these levels, is the only way to improve this aspect of an individual's condition.

Diet

Eating well is an important part of improving sporting performance, and a winning diet is not just for Olympic hopefuls. Athletes of all ages and levels benefit from eating well.

There isn't a magic eating plan that works for everyone. Eating well is specific to you, your individual nutritional needs, and your training and competition schedule. It is also important to match your diet to the demands of your sport. For example, endurance athletes, such as distance runners, need to consume large amounts of carbohydrates because these contain lots of energy for aerobic performance. Athletes relying on strength, on the other hand, need lots of protein to help build muscle bulk and power. The key is to make sure that you are eating the right foods, at the right times and in the right quantities.

Lifestyle

Alcohol

Alcohol affects the body's ability to turn food into energy, slows down reaction times, increases body heat loss and reduces endurance. For example, if you have alcohol 24 hours before exercising you are more likely to develop muscle cramps.

The relaxant properties of alcohol can affect your sporting ability long after you've finished drinking. Alcohol slows down the information processing ability of the brain. This, in turn, affects your reactions, coordination, accuracy and balance – all the things that are important for staying on top in any sport.

After exercising the body needs to be rehydrated. It's not helpful to drink alcohol straight after a match or event as this will continue to dehydrate the body further.

Medical history

Culture

Gender

Smoking

Smoking interferes with the body's ability to function in a number of ways. Firstly, tobacco smoke affects the lungs so that they work less efficiently and can't pick up the amount of oxygen the body needs when it is working hard. Secondly, tobacco smoke contains a chemical called carbon monoxide, which gets into the bloodstream and inhibits it from picking up oxygen. It also contains other chemicals that affect the circulation of blood. They make the blood vessels smaller so that they are less able to carry oxygen when your body is burning up large amounts of energy. In short, if you smoke your body has less fuel and the fuel it does have is transported less efficiently to those areas that need it when you are taking part in sport. Because of this, smokers tend to have less energy and also find it harder to maintain high levels of fitness than non-smokers.

Weight

Sports participation and level of activity

Drugs

As sport becomes more competitive some people are tempted to cheat to improve their chances of winning. People who cheat by abusing medicines may be banned from sport if they are caught. They are also risking their health. Some athletes have died because they have abused medicines.

To discourage cheating, sports authorities have banned certain medicines. Some medicines are banned in some sports, but not in others. Athletes also need to be careful about what they take because some of the banned medicines, such as cold and flu remedies, can be bought from a pharmacy without a prescription. Depending on their sport, some athletes who need treatment for problems such as diabetes or asthma may also need to get permission to take their medication in order to ensure they aren't breaking any rules.

Drugs can be classified into three groups: socially acceptable, socially unacceptable and performance-enhancing.
- Socially acceptable drugs, such as cigarettes and alcohol, are rarely banned in sport, but they do have a negative effect on performance.
- Socially unacceptable drugs include substances such as cannabis and ecstasy. Not only are these substances banned in sport but it is illegal to carry, consume or supply them.
- Performance-enhancing drugs include anabolic steroids (which build muscle strength), stimulants (which reduce tiredness), and narcotic analgesics (which relieve pain). These substances are almost always banned in sport because they give a competitor an unfair advantage. They can also be extremely dangerous.

Demands of work

Many sports performers have to juggle training and competition with a normal 'day' job. This often leads to conflicts where there isn't enough time to do both properly. This is even more so for sportsmen and women who are parents. If a sports performer commits insufficient time to training their physical fitness will decrease. If the sports performer commits insufficient time to their work or family life this is likely to lead to an increase in stress levels, which will affect physical performance. The important thing is to achieve a healthy balance, where the demands of work and family fit easily into a daily routine that also allows enough time for training.

Sleep

Getting the right amount of sleep is crucial to sporting success. Sleep impacts on performance in three main ways:
- Too much or too little sleep can cause a decline in the performance of the brain which, in turn, causes problems with focus, concentration, flexibility, decision making and information processing.
- Very deep sleep helps consolidate activities, tasks and skills undertaken during the day. It is indispensable for helping motor learning and skill acquisition.
- Sleep stimulates the release of growth hormones, the body's natural agent for cell growth and reproduction. This increases muscle mass and also stimulates the immune system. Sleep deprivation raises the level of stress hormones, which interfere with tissue repair and growth, and have a negative effect on performance.

BRONZE

1. Choose one of the lifestyle factors that aren't explained on this page – medical history, weight, gender, culture, and sports participation and level of activity – or find out how it affects sports participation and performance.

2. Research four different performance-enhancing drugs and produce a presentation that could be used to inform younger students of their dangers.

The effects of psychological factors on sports training and performance

Being physically trained to perfection does not guarantee success. To win, athletes also have to be able to cope with the psychological demands of their competition. This involves being able to cope with losing as well as winning, and being able to draw the positives from a poor performance. In the same way that physical skills cannot be developed overnight, psychological preparation needs to be developed over a long period of time in order to be effective. A performer who is physically **and** psychologically prepared is much more likely to succeed.

Motivation

Put simply, motivation is what gives a performer the energy to accomplish something, and it can come from both internal and external sources. Internal or 'intrinsic' motivation comes from within the sports performer, whereas external or 'extrinsic' motivation comes in the form of more obvious rewards. The table below gives some examples of each type of motivation:

Intrinsic motivation	Extrinsic motivation
Personal pride	Financial reward
The will to win	Public acclaim
A need to be a winner	A better lifestyle
Wanting to be the best	A cup or a trophy

Whatever your motivation, be it intrinsic or extrinsic, it will be related to achieving success; and the greater the level of motivation, the more likely you are to succeed (up to a point – see 'Arousal').

Jenson Button holds aloft the trophy presented to him for winning the Formula 1 Grand Prix in Bahrain in 2009.

Many sports coaches believe that intrinsic motivation is more important than extrinsic motivation. This is because a person who has a desire to succeed for themselves is more likely to continue to want to improve, even when they have achieved their initial goal. They may set themselves a more difficult challenge as a result. In contrast, a person who is largely motivated by extrinsic factors will often become bored once they have reached their initial goal.

Sports coaches will always try to look for the positives in a performance and use this as a way of maintaining intrinsic motivation. For example, if a tennis player loses a match, their coach may try to establish the positives by saying something like: 'Your opponent was better than you today but you still played some fantastic shots. If you continue to improve and work hard, I'm sure you'll beat him next time.' It is this positive reinforcement from the coach that will enable a player to keep working hard in training, maintaining their level of motivation and thus ensuring that they continue to work towards their goals.

Arousal

'Arousal' is a term used to describe a person's state of mind and covers a continuum stretching from deep sleep through to extreme excitement. It is very closely linked to motivation, and controlling both motivation and arousal is often the key to achieving sporting success. A player's arousal level describes their level of enthusiasm or interest, and commentators will often talk about players being 'in the zone' or conversely 'away with the fairies'.

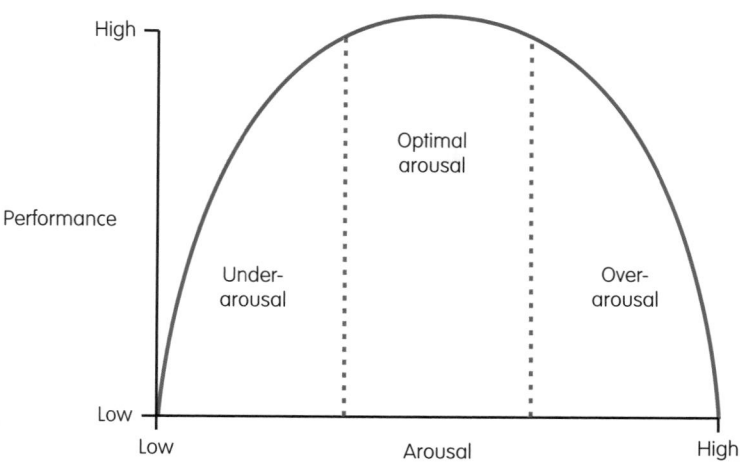

The most common understanding of arousal is based on the Inverted-U hypothesis, as shown in the diagram above. When a player is under-aroused their level of performance will often be too low, and they may show a lack of interest and enthusiasm. If they are over-aroused, their performance level may also deteriorate because they are trying too hard and, therefore, making mistakes. Optimal arousal facilitates the best performance levels.

Anxiety

Anxiety is the term used to describe feelings of worry, concern and apprehension. It can be classified as 'trait anxiety', where a person is anxious at all times and in everything they do, or 'state anxiety', where a person's level of apprehension fluctuates according to the situation. Of these two types, 'state anxiety' is more likely to exist in a sporting situation.

Anxiety usually exists because the performer feels unable to cope with a situation. This is most often because they feel that their opponent is better than they are, but it can also be caused by other factors such as the size of the crowd or the importance of the event. For example, a young footballer may feel extremely anxious when making their debut for the first team; asking themselves, 'Am I good enough?', 'How will the crowd react to me?' and 'What will my teammates think if I make a mistake?'

Coaches often try to reduce a player's feelings of anxiety by using the following techniques:

- **Imagery:** The player is asked to close their eyes and imagine being in a peaceful environment or performing well in the forthcoming event.
- **Thought stopping:** The coach will stop the player from verbalizing any negative thoughts.
- **Positive talking:** A player will be told to repeat phrases such as 'I am the best' and 'I can do this' over and over again before an event.
- **Muscular relaxation:** A player is given a relaxing massage before an event, in an attempt to remove the tension which can tighten muscles.

Overall, a small amount of anxiety is a good thing because it can help performers to focus on the forthcoming event and can be used to motivate them. However, too much anxiety inevitably leads to over-arousal which, in turn, can lead to a poorer performance (see 'Arousal').

Jimmy White is unable to hide his anxiety.

Personality

'Personality is the sum total of an individual's characteristics which make him unique' (Edwin P. Hollander)

Everyone is unique and different, but people generally fall into one of two broad categories:

- **Introverts** are characterized by being shy, timid, reserved, happy in their own company and self-sufficient.
- **Extroverts** are characterized by being adventurous, confident, sociable, enthusiastic and happiest in group situations.

Andy Murray must try to avoid being distracted by noise or movement in the crowd during a match.

Coaches should use their knowledge of a player's personality type to motivate them towards achieving their goals. For example, an extrovert is often at risk of becoming over-aroused and so a coach may use something such as calming music to help them to relax. On the other hand, an introvert may be at risk of being under-aroused and so could have their level of arousal increased, for example, by listening to a different style of music.

Concentration

A performer requires concentration to focus on the most relevant cues and to ignore those cues that are irrelevant. Many sports psychologists believe that mistakes made by professional players are more likely to be due to a lack of focus, rather than a problem with technique. For example, when Andy Murray serves a double fault, it is unlikely that it is due to poor physical technique but the fact that it has happened could imply a lack of concentration.

Coaches will often help prepare a player for a competitive fixture or tournament by encouraging them to use 'selective attention'. Practice often takes place in a noisy, busy environment, with various other cues thrown in to confuse the performer, which helps them learn to focus their attention on the things that really matter, such as the flight of the ball or the movement of opposition players. Once the competitive fixture takes place, the performer is ready to focus on the important cues and discard the things that are not important.

BRONZE

1. Give three examples from sport where high levels of arousal are important and three examples from sport where low levels of arousal are important.

2. Write down four words which you think describe your personality. Try to be honest! Now discuss your choice of words with a partner. Do they agree with you?

SILVER

3. What is the most common type of motivation for an amateur sports player? How does this differ from a professional competitor?

4. Think of a sporting situation in which you felt anxious. Try to pinpoint the reasons why and then suggest techniques that you could have used to reduce your anxiety levels.

GOLD

5. Name three sports that would be more suited to introverts and three sports that would be more suited to extroverts. Justify your choices.

6. Explain the Inverted-U hypothesis using a well-known incident from the Olympic Games or other worldwide sporting event.

Unit 1 assignment, part one

Background

As part of a government initiative to tackle decreasing levels of physical activity in young teenagers, you have been employed by the local authority as a fitness consultant. Your role is to visit schools around your local area and:

a) raise awareness of the strong links between sporting excellence, psychological well-being, lifestyle and levels of physical fitness

b) demonstrate to your audience how to use different methods of fitness training to achieve sporting excellence.

Task

Design a presentation that can be delivered to multiple audiences. Your presentation needs to be informative and engaging and must include the following:

GRADING CRITERIA TO BE ASSESSED
P1, P2, P3, P6
M1, M3
D2

PASS

A description of the fitness requirements for achieving excellence in a selected sport (P1).

A description of three different fitness training methods used to achieve excellence in a selected sport (P2).

A description of four different lifestyle factors that can affect sports training and performance (P3).

A description of the effects of psychological factors on sports training and performance (P6).

MERIT

An explanation of the fitness requirements for achieving excellence in a selected sport (M1).

An explanation of the effects of psychological factors on sports training and performance (M3).

DISTINCTION

An analysis of the effects of psychological factors on sports training and performance (D2).

Tackling the assignment

This assignment is best approached by creating a presentation, such as a PowerPoint® presentation, although a simple written piece of work which could be delivered as a speech would also suffice. The key is to make sure it is informative and engaging without being too lengthy or 'wordy'. It is important to cover all of the criteria for a Pass but if you are aiming for a Merit or a Distinction you could cover the relevant criteria in the same presentation by simply adding more information to each slide and providing evidence to support your explanation.

Meeting the Pass criteria

BTEC Level 2 Firsts in Sport

Unit 1 assignment, part one   Julie Khan

I have chosen to meet the Pass criteria for the assignment by producing a written piece of work, which will be delivered as a speech to my audience.

Sport: Cycling – Tour de France
Competitors in the Tour de France are elite athletes. As such, they have to be at the peak of their fitness when taking part, and this means that they have to know which components of fitness are important for long-distance cycling. As it is an endurance event, the two most important components of fitness are cardiovascular endurance and muscular endurance. Together, these two components can enable a cyclist to keep working for an extended period of time without running out of energy. This is important because competitors can spend up to six hours a day for three weeks in the saddle. Cardiovascular endurance helps keep the muscles supplied with blood and, therefore, oxygen, and muscular endurance means that the muscles can convert all of the oxygen into energy.

One method of achieving high levels of fitness in both types of endurance is through fartlek training. This involves the cyclist training for long periods of time (4–7 hours each session), working in both the aerobic zone and the anaerobic zone of the training pyramid. Most of the session is spent working aerobically but, at times, the cyclist will push himself and begin to work anaerobically. This means the cyclist gets used to switching between zones, which prepares his body for parts of the race such as the hill climbs and the sprint finishes.

> Julie has made a good start to this assignment but needs to further develop her description of the fitness requirements for cycling to fully achieve P1. For example, she has not mentioned power, which is important for acceleration and hill climbing, or speed, which is essential for making the pedals – and therefore the wheels – turn at a fast rate.

> Julie's information on endurance is both accurate and informative. I particularly like the way she has linked the fartlek training session to parts of the race, showing that she understands that the training undertaken needs to be specific to the event. As yet, though, she has only mentioned one type of training, so has not met the criteria for P2, which clearly states that three types of training should be covered. However, if Julie develops her description to cover two other types of training she will meet the criteria for P2.

Meeting the Merit criteria

BTEC Level 2 Firsts in Sport

Unit 1 assignment, part one   James Char

Sport: Football

Arousal

Arousal can be defined as:

a state of mind which runs from deep sleep to being extremely excited or agitated

under-arousal — poor performance because the player is not 'up for it'

optimal arousal — best performance because the player is 'in the zone'

over-arousal — poor performance because the player is 'trying too hard'

> James has begun to explain how arousal affects performance and I am sure over the next few slides he will also explain the effects of other psychological factors, such as motivation and personality. This slide on its own, however, does not really develop the explanation far enough.

> I would like to see James linking his understanding of arousal specifically to his chosen sport of football. For example, he could take the idea of a player taking a penalty in a World Cup Final and show how different arousal levels might contribute to the success or failure of the kick.

> As yet, I am not confident that James has shown enough understanding to meet the criteria for M3, although he has met the criteria for P6.

Meeting the Distinction criteria

BTEC Level 2 Firsts in Sport

Unit 1 assignment, part one | **James Chan**

Sport: Football

Arousal

Arousal is about being excited, keen, and ready for an event or activity.

Under-arousal

Optimal arousal

Over-arousal

Cristiano Ronaldo UEFA Champions League Final 2009

Many pundits agree that Ronaldo did not perform at his best in the above event. Many believe that this is because he had already decided to leave Manchester United to sign for Real Madrid and that this meant he was unable to motivate himself for the game.

Roy Keane UEFA Champions League Semi-Final (2nd Leg) 1999

Manchester United were 2-0 down to Juventus and were going to be out of the cup. Keane received a yellow card which meant he would miss the Final anyway. Instead of giving up, he reached a point of optimal arousal, and went on to score and lead his team to a 3-2 win. His performance has been voted by some as 'Best ever' in European football.

Roy Keane Manchester derby 2001 (tackle on Alf-Inge Haaland)

Keane admitted in his autobiography that his tackle on Haaland was premeditated and that he had wound himself up before the game. As a result, his performance in the game was below par and his actions led to a series of bans/fines.

James has now linked his understanding of arousal to concrete evidence from his chosen sport of football. Had he used three different sports or three different players from the same sport, I would have classed this as an explanation and would have been happy to award M3. However, because he has used the same player (Roy Keane) in two of his explanations, it not only shows that James **understands** the concept of arousal, but also that he is able to **critically analyse** its effects on sporting performance. As such, I would be happy to award D2 (assuming, of course, that he continues in this manner for other psychological factors, such as motivation and personality).

Conducting fitness tests

Sports participants should regularly undertake fitness testing so that the effects of their training can be evaluated. After all, there's no point in continuing with a training schedule that is no longer working! But, before carrying out fitness testing, there are a number of pre-test procedures that should be considered.

1 Checking the equipment

It is important to check the equipment to make sure that it is safe and working properly. This includes calibrating machines and, where necessary, checking that they are recording data accurately.

2 Informed consent

It is extremely important to ensure that you have informed consent from all participants who are going to take a test. No one should be asked to undertake a fitness test without first completing a consent form.

3 Reliability and validity of fitness tests

Reliability and validity are two of the major problems with using fitness tests. Reliability refers to the degree to which repeated measurements give the same result, and validity refers to the honesty of the test or, to put it another way, the degree to which the assessment method measures what it is intended to measure.

The reliability of a test is often called into question because the same person gets different results each time they complete it. This can be for a number of reasons:

- Is the test being conducted properly?
- Has the person suffered an injury since they last took the test?
- Is the equipment damaged in any way?
- Is the person using the same amount of effort each time? (Something that it is very difficult to determine.)

The results of a fitness test are more likely to be valid if the test uses expensive, specialized equipment which has been designed specifically for the purpose of carrying out the test. If the test uses cheaper, everyday items, such as a stopwatch and a ruler, it is likely to be less valid.

The validity of a test is much less uncertain – either the test measures what it is supposed to measure or it doesn't. Perhaps the best example of a test providing results that are not valid is the multistage fitness test. As you will see later on, this test has been designed to measure cardiovascular endurance (the ability to use oxygen effectively over a period of time). According to the rules of the test, the higher the level of the test reached, the higher the level of cardiovascular endurance. However, there are two serious flaws with this method:

- The test is supposed to measure cardiovascular endurance but a high degree of agility (to turn quickly each time), power (to push off each time) and speed (to maintain the required pace between bleeps) are also required. For this reason, a swimmer may have a very high level of cardiovascular endurance but not return good results because they aren't a very good runner. The test might, therefore, give invalid results.
- Towards the higher levels of the test, the performer may well be working anaerobically (without oxygen) and, as a result, would get a very high score even though their cardiovascular endurance was surpassed before the end of the test. In this case, the results would again be invalid.

This is not to say that the test should not be used. It does give a good **indication** of an individual's cardiovascular fitness. It is also cheap to carry out and can be administered to lots of participants at the same time. The key with any fitness test is to understand how useful the results are going to be and to make sure that it is carried out properly, according to the protocol (rules) of the test, to ensure that the results are reliable and valid.

Informed Consent for Exercise Testing

I hereby voluntarily give consent to engage in a fitness test. I understand that the cardiovascular fitness test will involve progressive stages of increasing effort and that at any time I may terminate the test for any reason. I understand that during some tests I may be encouraged to work at maximum effort and that at any time I may terminate the test for any reason.

I understand there are certain changes that may occur during the exercise test. They include abnormal blood pressure, fainting, disorders of heartbeat, and very rare instances of heart attack. I understand that every effort will be made to minimize problems by preliminary examination and observation during testing.

I understand that I am responsible for monitoring my own condition throughout testing, and should any unusual symptoms occur, I will cease my participation and inform the test administrator of the symptoms. Unusual symptoms include, but are not limited to: chest discomfort, nausea, difficulty in breathing and joint or muscle injury.

Also, in consideration of being allowed to participate in the fitness tests, I agree to assume all risks of such fitness testing, and hereby release and hold harmless _____, and their agents and employees, from any and all health claims, suits, losses, or causes of action for damages for injury or death, including claims for negligence, arising out of or related to my participation in the fitness assessments.

I have read the foregoing carefully and I understand its content. Any questions which may have occurred to me concerning this informed consent have been answered to my satisfaction.

Name	Date
Witness	Date

The fitness tests

Over the next few pages you will see a range of tests that can be used to measure an individual's level of fitness. There are also suggested results that you would expect from various levels of performer. It should be remembered that these are only some examples of fitness tests and that there are several others that can be used as well. It should also be stressed that the expected results are given only as a guide.

BRONZE

1. Undertake each of the following fitness tests, recording the results accurately.

SILVER

2. Accurately administer each fitness test for your peer group.

GOLD

3. Comment on the reliability and validity of each fitness test that you have undertaken.

Flexibility

Sit and reach test

What do you need?
A box and a measuring tape
or
A sit and reach table

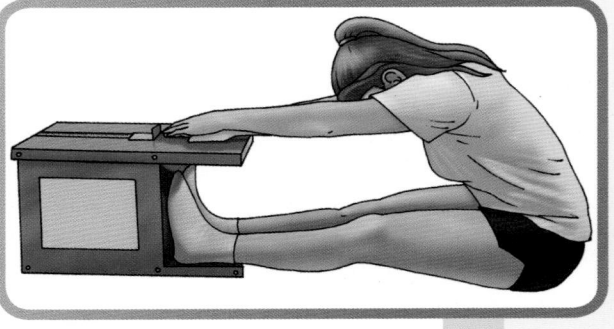

How do you do the test?
- Sit comfortably on the floor with your legs straight out in front of you.
- Place the measuring tape, with 0cm level with your feet, parallel with your legs. If you are using a sit and reach table, the measurements are already marked.
- Put the soles of your feet, shoulder width apart, against the box/table.
- Make sure your knees are locked/straight, as this is what determines hamstring flexibility. If your knees bend during the test, the results will be inaccurate.
- With your hands stretched towards your feet, lean forward and reach as far as possible with your fingertips. If possible, reach beyond the end of your toes and over the top of the box. You must make sure, however, that there are no jerky movements while doing this and that you are able to hold the reach for at least two seconds.
- You get three chances to stretch forward and then the fourth is measured.
- The distance that your fingers touch on the tape measure/sit and reach table will be your score. If you don't make it to your toes then you will get a negative score, showing the distance you were from 0cm.

Expected level	Male footballer	Male gymnast
Regional	7–10cm	10–12cm
National	9–13cm	13–17cm
International/professional	>15cm	>18cm

	Male	Female
Average 16–19 year old	7–10cm	7–11cm

(Source: Davis, B. et al. *Physical Education and the Study of Sport*, Mosby Publishing, 2000)

Goniometers
Another way to measure flexibility is to use goniometers. These are like a pair of compasses in that they are used to measure the angles at a joint. The wider the angle, the greater the level of flexibility.

Goniometers being used to measure the flexibility of the finger joints.

Strength

One-repetition maximum (1RM)

What do you need?
A weight bench
A series of 'free' weights
A partner

Remember:

You must make sure you have warmed up properly before performing a 1RM test or you will increase your chances of injury.

How do you do the test?
- Set 1: Begin with ten reps of a light weight. Rest for 60 seconds.
- Set 2: Do three to five reps with a weight that will not allow you to perform a sixth repetition. Rest for two minutes.
- Set 3: Do two to three reps with a weight that will not allow you to perform a fourth repetition. Rest for three minutes.
- Set 4: Add 20 per cent more weight and try to perform a single rep. If you can manage more than one repetition, rest for another three minutes, load the bar with slightly more weight and try again. Remember, your goal is to progress to a weight where you can perform only one rep.
- All repetitions should be performed under control and without cheating. Your partner is on hand in case you can't manage the weight, not to help you complete a rep.

It is very difficult to give expected levels for this test, as the results will vary dramatically from player to player and from performer to performer. For example, Peter Crouch's results will differ dramatically from Wayne Rooney's because of their difference in body size and composition.

Grip dynamometer

What do you need?
A grip dynamometer

How do you do the test?
- Use a grip dynamometer to measure grip strength.
- Record the maximum reading from three attempts using the dominant hand. Allow a one-minute recovery between each attempt.

Expected level	Male footballer	Female footballer
Regional	> 40kg	> 28kg
National	> 45kg	> 32kg
International/professional	> 50kg	> 36kg

	Male	Female
Average 16–19 year old	30–35kg	22–26kg

Aerobic endurance

Multistage fitness test

What do you need?

A multistage fitness test CD
A CD player
Cones
A 15/20m marked area

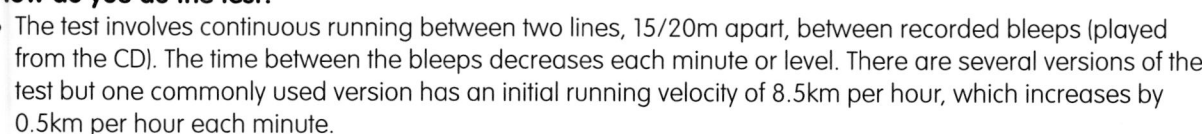

How do you do the test?

- The test involves continuous running between two lines, 15/20m apart, between recorded bleeps (played from the CD). The time between the bleeps decreases each minute or level. There are several versions of the test but one commonly used version has an initial running velocity of 8.5km per hour, which increases by 0.5km per hour each minute.
- You must always ensure that you have one foot on or beyond the 15/20m marker at the end of each shuttle run.
- If you reach the marker before the next beep, you should wait there until you hear it before resuming running.
- If you do not manage to reach the end of the shuttle run before the beep sounds then you are given two or three more attempts to catch up with the pace before being stopped.

Expected level	Female footballer	Female gymnast
Regional	Level 9	Level 8
National	Level 10	Level 9
International/professional	Level 12+	Level 10

Chester step test

This is a variation of a stepping-type fitness test which is commonly used in the UK.

What do you need?

A step
A heart-rate monitor
A Chester step test CD
A CD player
A perceived exertion scale

How do you do the test?

- Choose the correct step height (from 0.15 to 0.30m) for your age and history of physical activity.
- Follow the stepping rate set by the metronome and instructions on the CD. The initial step rate is 15 steps per minute and, every two minutes, the tempo increases by five steps per minute.
- Stop and rest when you reach 80 per cent of your Maximum Heart Rate (MHR).

Expected level	Male footballer	Male boxer
Regional	12 RPE*	11 RPE*
National	15 RPE*	13 RPE*
International/professional	17 RPE*	15 RPE*

* RPE = Rating of Perceived Exertion, as calculated from the level reached in the test using the conversion table which comes with the CD.)

Speed

40m sprint

The objective of this test is to monitor the athlete's level of sprint fatigue.

What do you need?
A 40m marked section in a traight line, preferably on a running track
Starting blocks
A stopwatch
An assistant

How do you do the test?
- Sprint 40m from a standing start/sprint start using the blocks.
- Allow a 30-second recovery while walking back to the start.
- Repeat the sprint five times, completing a total of six sprints.
- Record the time for each sprint.

At the present time, there is no data on expected levels available for this test, although it is generally accepted that a difference of less than 0.8 seconds between the first sprint and the last sprint represents excellent performance.

Power

Vertical jump test

What do you need?

A wall
Chalk
A measuring tape
A partner

How do you do the test?
- Stand side-on to a wall and reach up with the hand closest to the wall. Keeping your feet flat on the ground, the point of the fingertips is marked or recorded by a partner. This is called the standing reach.
- Stand away from the wall and jump vertically as high as possible using both your arms and your legs to help you project your body upwards. Touch the wall at the highest point of the jump and have this marked or recorded.
- The difference in distance between the standing reach height and the jump height is the score. The best of three attempts is recorded.

Expected level	Male footballer	Male basketball player
Regional	55–64cm	65–74cm
National	65–74cm	75–84cm
International/ professional	> 75cm	> 85cm

	Male	Female
Average 16–19 year old	40–49cm	36–46cm

(**Source:** www.brianmac.co.uk)

Wingate test

What do you need?
A mechanically braked bicycle ergometer (an arm ergometer can also be used)
A stopwatch
A partner

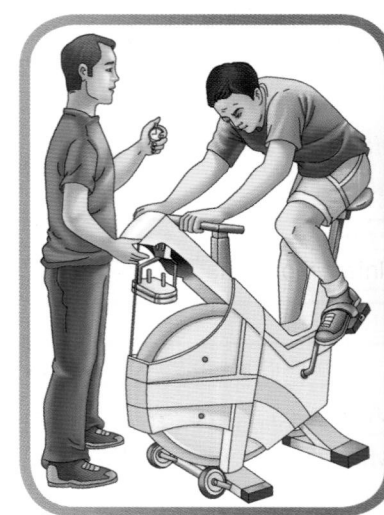

How do you do the test?
- Complete a three- to five-minute warm-up.
- On a signal from the person administering the test, begin pedalling for 30 seconds at an 'all out' pace with no resistance. Within three seconds, the predetermined fixed resistance is applied to the flywheel and remains there for the duration of the test. A counter will record the revolutions of the flywheel at five second intervals.
- Complete a one- to two-minute recovery cool-down.

At the present time, there is no data which can be used to compare performance against regional, national and international/professional performers.

Muscular endurance

One-minute press-up test

What do you need?
A stopwatch
A partner

How do you do the test?
- Take up the starting position, with your arms straight, elbows locked, body straight, hands placed slightly wider than shoulder-width apart (with fingers pointing forward) and both feet on the floor.
- From the starting position, on the command 'go', start the press-up by bending your elbows and lowering your body until the shoulders drop below the level of the elbows. Then return to the starting position. Pausing to rest is permitted only in the starting position.
- Your partner should count how many full press-ups are completed in one minute or up to the point where the performer retires from the test.

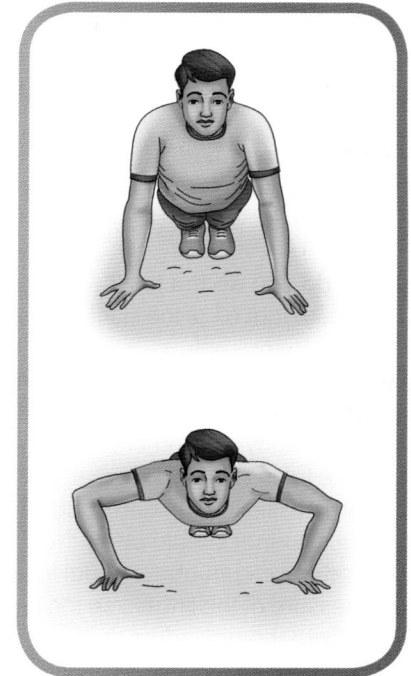

Expected level	Male footballer	Male swimmer
Regional	45	50
National	55	55
International/professional	65+	60

One-minute sit-up test

What do you need?
A stopwatch
A partner

How do you do the test?
- Lie on a carpeted or cushioned floor with your knees bent at approximately right angles and your feet flat on the ground. Your hands should be resting on your thighs.
- Squeeze your stomach, push your lower back flat and raise your upper body high enough for your hands to slide along your thighs to touch the tops of your knees. Don't pull with your neck or head, and keep your lower back on the floor. Then return to the starting position.
- Your partner should count how many full sit-ups are completed in one minute or up to the point where the performer retires from the test.

Expected level	Female rower	Female gymnast
Regional	40	30
National	45	35
International/professional	50	40

	Male	Female
Average 16–19 year old	20–25	15–20

Source: Davis, B. et al., *Physical Education and the Study of Sport*, Mosby Publishing, 2000)

Body composition

Skinfold callipers test

There is a layer of subcutaneous fat beneath the skin, and the percentage of total body fat can be estimated by taking a measure of the 'skinfold' at selected points on the body with a pair of callipers.

What do you need?

Skinfold callipers
A partner

How do you do the test?

- Ensure that all of the skinfold measurements are taken on the right side of the body in millimetres.
- Measurements should be taken at the following sites: triceps, sub-scapula (just below the scapula), supra-iliac (between the pelvis and the ribcage at the side of the body), abdomen, front thigh, chest (men only), rear thigh (women only).
- Take each skinfold between your thumb and index finger so as to include two thicknesses of skin and subcutaneous fat.
- Your partner should apply the callipers about one centimetre from the fingers and at a depth about equal to the thickness of the fold. Very slightly release the pressure of the fingers so the greater pressure is exerted by the callipers.
- Repeat the procedure three times (as the measurement may vary) at each site and then take an average.
- Add the results of each measurement to get a total value in millimetres.

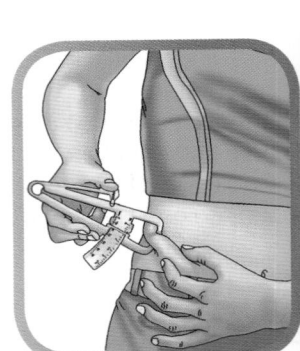

Expected level	Male footballer	Male cyclist
Regional	61–80mm	56–75mm
National	51–60mm	45–55mm
International/professional	40–50mm	30–45mm

Body mass index test

Your body mass index (BMI) provides a way of calculating whether or not your body is of an ideal weight. A BMI test is designed for men and women over the age of 18, and although people under the age of 18 can use it, their results should not be taken to have any significant meaning.

What do you need?

Weighing scales marked in kilograms
A tape measure
A calculator
A partner

How do you do the test?

- Measure your weight in kilograms.
- Measure your height in metres (so 182cm is actually 1.82m).
- Calculate your BMI using this formula below:

$$BMI = \frac{weight\ (kg)}{height\ (m) \times height\ (m)}$$

NHS Direct (UK) provides the following assessment of BMI measurements:

- If your BMI is less than 18.5 you are underweight for your height.
- If your BMI is 18.5 to 24.9 you are an ideal weight for your height.
- If your BMI is 25 to 29.9 you are over the ideal weight for your height.
- If your BMI is 30 to 39.9 you are obese.
- If your BMI is over 39.9 you are very obese.

It is important to remember, however, that muscle weighs more than fat, so bodybuilders and trained athletes will often have a BMI in excess of 25 without being overweight.

Bioelectrical impedance analysis

Another way to measure body fat is to use bioelectrical impedance analysis, where electrodes are attached to the wrist and the ankle, and an electrical current is passed from one to the other. Body fat restricts the flow of the electric current, so the more current that is needed, the greater the percentage of body fat the person has.

Unit 1 assignment, part two

Background

As part of a government initiative to tackle decreasing levels of physical activity in young teenagers, you have been employed by the local authority as a fitness consultant. Your role is to visit schools around your local area and:
a) engage students in a range of fitness tests aimed at measuring different components of fitness
b) enable students to compare their results with normative data, suggesting areas of strength and weakness.

Task

Produce a series of handouts that show how to conduct four different fitness tests. Each test should measure a different component of fitness and each handout should contain data that allows users to compare their results against a set of standard scores. Complete the tests and include your own results on each handout, along with guidance on what your results communicate about your level of fitness. You must make sure that you have:

GRADING CRITERIA TO BE ASSESSED
P4, P5
M2
D1

Carried out four different fitness tests for different components of fitness, recording the results accurately (P4).

Interpreted your test results and personal level of fitness (P5).

Explained your test results and personal level of fitness, identifying strengths and areas for improvement (M2).

Evaluated your test results and personal level of fitness, considering the level required to achieve excellence in a selected sport (D1).

Tackling the assignment

This assignment is relatively straightforward – you carry out the tests using the correct protocols and then record your results. The difficulty arises when it comes to **interpreting** your results to achieve a Pass, **explaining** your results to achieve a Merit and **evaluating** your results to achieve a Distinction.

To achieve P5 it would be acceptable to record your results in a table alongside normative data (data showing average results for a particular age group and/or expected results for regional, national and professional athletes) and to note whether your scores are above or below the expected values.

This would be strengthened if the table was extended to allow comparisons with other members of your peer group.

To achieve M2 it would be necessary to make informed comments on the data in terms of your personal level of fitness and then to suggest which areas are strengths and

which are weaknesses, always remembering to suggest reasons to support your judgements.

In order to achieve D1 it is necessary to mention the validity and reliability of the test results. For example, you may have identified that, as a swimmer, you would expect to have high levels of cardiovascular endurance but your test results from the multistage fitness test show poor levels of endurance. You could argue that the test is not valid for swimmers because it tests running ability and not swimming ability. You could also argue, for example, that the results are not reliable because the floor was slippery which made it difficult to turn effectively. This level of analysis would show that you are able to not only conduct the tests and record the results, but that you are also able to critically evaluate the data produced. You would also need to evaluate your personal level of fitness in terms of where you are in relation to the level required to achieve excellence in your selected sport.

Unit 2: Practical Sport

Types of sports

Sports can be broadly grouped into two categories: team sports and individual sports.

Team sports

Water
Team sports that take place in or on water, including water polo and synchronized swimming.

Team sports

Invasion
Sports in which you invade the other team's territory and attempt to outwit them so that you can score goals or points, including association football, basketball, hockey, lacrosse, netball, rugby union and rugby league.

Adapted team sports
Team sports that have been adapted so they can be played by people with specific disabilities, including wheelchair basketball, goal ball, and football for the blind or partially sighted.

Striking and fielding
Sports where players strike a ball to deceive or avoid the fielders, and then run between wickets or around bases to score runs/points. These include cricket, rounders and softball.

Net/wall
Sports in which one team tries to ensure a ball or other object lands in a target area that the opposing team is defending, including volleyball, badminton and tennis.

Individual sports

Water
Individual sports that take place in or on water. Including swimming, diving and sailing.

Martial arts
Forms of unarmed combat or self-defence performed as a sport. Including karate, judo and tae kwon do.

Target
Sports where you aim an object at a target. Including golf, archery, fencing, darts, shooting and boccia.

Individual sports

Athletics
Sports in which you improve your personal best in relation to speed, height, distance and accuracy. Including running at all distances, hurdles, javelin, shot-put, hammer, discus, high jump, triple jump and pole vault.

Net/wall
Sports in which a competitor tries to ensure a ball or other object lands in a target area that their opponent is defending. Including tennis, table tennis, badminton and squash.

BRONZE

1. To achieve a Pass in this unit you must complete a series of practical sessions for a team sport and a series of practical sessions for an individual sport. The sessions must be led by a qualified instructor. Find out which team and individual sports you can take part in locally – at school, college or at local clubs – and choose one of each to follow.

Skills, techniques and tactics

All sports have a range of skills, techniques and tactics that need to be developed in order for participants to be successful.

What is a skill?

A skill is something that often requires practice many times in order for someone to become proficient in it or able to carry it out consistently, again and again.

For example, when you learn to play badminton one of the first, and most important, skills you learn is the serve. As you practise the serve over and over again, your delivery is likely to become more effective and you may find that you do not have to think about it as much as you did when you first started. When you watch professional badminton players you can see that the years of practice really do make a difference, because they rarely fail to place the serve almost exactly where they want it to go.

Some skills are sport-specific but many can be transferred from one sport to another. For example, the skill of passing a ball by throwing it between members of the same team is used in basketball, netball and rugby.

What is a technique?

A technique is the way in which you perform a particular skill. There are many different parts to a badminton serve and when you put all the parts together you are performing a skill; the way in which you put them together is your technique. Two people might be able to perform a skill equally effectively but one might have a much better technique than the other.

These images show a student completing four of the seven stages that make up a successful badminton serve.

What are tactics?

Tactics can be thought of as the plan of action set to outwit your opponent and gain an advantage. A coach may work with a badminton player during practice sessions to put together a game plan or series of tactics for the next game. The coach may point out weaknesses that are known about the opponent and how certain shots may be used to take control of the court as a result.

It is important to remember that tactics can be changed throughout a game, if things are not going as planned. For example, you often see coaches and managers shouting instructions, making substitutions and changing the formation being used during football matches.

BRONZE

1. Plan a way of gathering evidence of the different skills, techniques and tactics that you will develop in both your chosen team and individual sports. You could keep a diary, a logbook or a portfolio; a record of witness testimonies, feedback sheets or an observation record; and use audio or video equipment.

Unit 2 assignment, part one

Background

Your school has recently become a specialist Sports College and is creating a 'Leadership academy' for students. The academy is looking for energetic, well-motivated and able students to work alongside staff from the sports development team to plan and lead a variety of sports festivals and competitions for primary school children. You have decided to apply to become a member of the Leadership academy and need to prepare for the interview. You have been asked to bring along something to demonstrate your knowledge and understanding of sports activities.

Task

Collect and then present evidence that you regularly take part in different physical activities. Your presentation, which should last about 10–15 minutes, needs to:

> GRADING CRITERIA
> TO BE ASSESSED
>
> P1, P2
> M1
> D1

 **PASS**

Demonstrate the use of practical skills, techniques and tactics appropriate for one team sport (P1).

Demonstrate the use of practical skills, techniques and tactics appropriate for one individual sport (P2).

 **MERIT**

Describe the use of tactics appropriate for one team and one individual sport (M1).

 **DISTINCTION**

Justify the use of tactics appropriate for one team and one individual sport, identifying areas for improvement (D1).

Tackling the assignment

There are a number of different ways that you could approach this assignment but a good one is to produce a video diary showing you in action both in one team and one individual sport. The video diary should demonstrate your level of practical ability, and illustrate the skills, techniques and tactics that you have learnt and use regularly in training and game situations.

If you are aiming for a Merit, you could add a voice-over or text on screen describing how tactics could be correctly applied to some of the situations in the video diary to improve performance. If you are aiming for a Distinction, you need to go a step further and justify how and when specific tactics should be used, and how applying tactics in the right situation can improve performance.

Rules, regulations, scoring systems and officials

Understanding the rules, regulations and scoring systems of the sports you participate in, as well as the roles and responsibilities of the officials involved, will help make you a more competent performer.

Rules, regulations and scoring systems

Matin Atkinson awards a direct free-kick.

Each sport generally has a national or international governing body that sets out specific rules or laws to ensure that a sport is played fairly by all competitors. These rules will cover everything from how a game will be started to when a free kick may be awarded in a rugby game, for example. Each sport also has a set of regulations. These generally control how the sport will be played or conducted, including what surface it will be played on and what safety standards need to be met in order to help prevent injuries.

Each sport has its own scoring system, from scoring three points in basketball for a shot outside the three-point arc to winning a point in badminton. Each sport also has its own methods or requirements for victory. Scoring systems form part of the rules that govern how a sport is played.

The roles and responsibilities of officials in sport

Umpire Aleem Dar signals the fall of a wicket.

Every sport has one or more officials to oversee the running of a game, match or competition to ensure that all rules and regulations are followed by competitors and that the scoring systems are applied correctly. If sports did not have officials it would be difficult to ensure that rules and regulations were applied fairly, and competitions would descend into chaos with opposing teams arguing.

BRONZE

1. Research the rules, regulations and scoring systems for one of your chosen sports.

2. Understanding the roles and responsibilities of the officials involved in the sports you have chosen will help you to improve as a sportsperson. Complete the table on the right, for either your team sport or your individual sport, listing all the officials involved along with their roles and responsibilities. Don't forget to include officials who aren't on the pitch or court throughout the match or game; some officials are out of sight but still have an important role to play. An example from football has been completed for you.

Official's role (for example, their title)	Official's responsibilities	Training or qualification required	Level of fitness required	Age restrictions
Fourth official in football	Assisting the referee before, during and after a match, including the announcement of how much added time there will be, and advising the referee of a case of mistaken identity or misconduct that has occurred outside the view of the referee.	They need to be a qualified referee to be a fourth official. First, they need to pass a Basic Referee's Course and then progress to the level required to officiate at the desired standard of football. For example, to be an official in a semi-professional league they would need to have reached Level 3.	Good level of fitness required, in case they need to replace the active officials during a game.	In England, retirement is usually imposed at 49 years of age (although in most other countries the age limit is 45).

Unit 2 assignment, part two

Background

Your school or college has decided to hold an open evening to celebrate its success. It has invited local primary school students to take part in some of the different activities that are available. You have been asked to help plan and lead this event, and to ensure that all visiting students leave the open evening with some information about the different sports on offer and how they are officiated and regulated.

Task

Produce an information leaflet for visiting students that will cover two sports, one team sport and one individual sport. The leaflet should include:

GRADING CRITERIA TO BE ASSESSED
P3, P4, P5, P6 M2

A description of the rules, regulations and scoring systems for one team sport (P3).

A description of the rules, regulations and scoring systems for one individual sport (P4).

A description of the main roles and responsibilities of officials in one team sport (P5).

A description of the main roles and responsibilities of officials in one individual sport (P6).

An assessment, using appropriate examples, of the rules, regulations and scoring systems for one team and one individual sport (M2).

Tackling the assignment

The most obvious way to approach this assignment is to produce one or two leaflets containing all the relevant information. When tackling the Merit criteria, you will need to be more explicit, explaining why the rules and regulations are necessary, and why the scoring systems are as they are.

Meeting the Pass criteria

BTEC Level 2 Firsts in Sport

Unit 2, assignment two   Jodie Meehan

Badminton

Rules, regulations and scoring

For singles matches, the rules include:
- A match consists of the best of three games.
- The player that first scores 21 points shall win.
- The player that wins a rally shall add one point to their score.
- If a score becomes 20–20, the player who scores two consecutive points shall win that game.

Referee and officials' participation

The referee is in overall charge of the tournament. The umpire is in charge of the match. The umpire supports the referee while the service judge calls service faults if they occur. There is also a line judge who indicates whether the shuttle has landed in or out of the court. The officials' decisions are final.

An umpire shall:
- Call a fault or let if either occur.
- Give a decision on any appeal regarding a point of dispute, if made before the next service is delivered.
- Ensure players and spectators are kept informed of the progress of the match.
- Record and report to the referee all matters in relation to continuous play, misconduct and penalties.

> Jodie has presented a detailed leaflet that clearly shows the relevant information in order to meet the Pass criteria of the assignment for an individual sport. The leaflet gives a particularly clear explanation of the new scoring system in badminton and how it is used in singles and doubles play. If Jodie can produce a similar piece of work that covers the necessary details for a team sport, a Pass can be achieved.

Meeting the Merit criteria

BTEC Level 2 Firsts in Sport

Unit 2 assignment, part two   Spencer Smith

Leicester Tigers' Number 8 came from an off-side position around the ruck and interfered with the play. Because the Tigers gained an advantage from this action, the referee blew the whistle and awarded a penalty kick to the opposition.

The laws of rugby state very clearly that the off-side line is directly through the ball, parallel to the try lines. It also states that when a player enters a ruck they must do so from behind the 'hindmost foot'. It was very clear in this incident that the Number 8 had not come from behind the 'hindmost foot' of the ruck and, therefore, the referee was correct in awarding a penalty kick.

> This piece of work begins to meet the Merit criteria. Spencer has applied his knowledge of the rules and regulations of rugby to a specific example within a real-game setting.

> To fully meet the Merit criteria, Spencer needs to explain the rules of the game in more detail. For example, he could have explained that a player must enter a ruck from their own side, from behind the hindmost foot and not at an angle.

Reviewing sports performances

When we watch sports performers we often comment on how well they have performed skills and executed techniques. Understanding how to make accurate observations and constructively review sports performances – your own, your team's and your opponent's – will help you become a better sportsperson.

There are four stages to reviewing a sports performance:

Observation

A lot of information can be obtained about both a performer's skills and techniques, and how well their tactics are working, by observing practical performances. Observations can be live, when the performance is happening and being observed in real-time, or recorded, when the performance has been filmed and is observed later. The latter method is favoured by most coaches and managers because the footage can be played back to different performers as many times as is necessary.

An observation checklist is a very useful tool that helps an observer to focus on important aspects of a performance and to communicate their observations to the performer. An observation checklist will be specific to a particular sport and, to compile one, you need to think about:

- The skills and techniques the performer should be demonstrating.
- The tactics the performer should be demonstrating.
- The data to be collected. This could include information about points scored and conceded; times, distances or heights achieved; passes, interceptions and tackles; or penalties given away and other infringements on the rules.
- The level the performer is at. An observation checklist aimed at performers at club level will be different from one aimed at international performers, because international performers are at a higher level and will therefore be more likely to be working on fine-tuning their skills, techniques and tactics.
- How you are going to record your observations during the performance. Are you going to tick boxes, make notes or score performers against criteria?

Analysis and evaluation

When you have observed a performer you are ready to analyse and evaluate their performance. This involves looking carefully at your observations and highlighting the performer's strengths and weaknesses.

Having a good understanding of the sport you are reviewing is vital if you are going to carry out an effective analysis of a performer. It is important to understand the skills and techniques of the sport, and how these can be applied tactically in different situations, so that the feedback you give to the performer about their strengths and weaknesses is appropriate.

When you are observing, analysing and evaluating a performer, you should also look beyond the performance itself to consider the performer's strengths and weaknesses in other areas that could have an impact on it, including:

- **Application of and respect for the rules and regulations:** Performers who are very knowledgeable about their sport, or understand the rules and regulations and how they can be used to improve their performance, are often successful.
- **Teamwork:** For team sports, how well a performer works with other members of the team is just as important as, if not more important than, their individual skills and techniques. A coach or manager sometimes needs to decide whether a player with outstanding skills should be replaced by someone who has weaker skills but is more of a team player.
- **Discipline:** Good discipline in sport is essential, especially when you are competing at a high level. Good discipline will help keep a sports performer at the peak of their fitness both in terms of general fitness and also sport-specific fitness. An elite sports performer will need to keep up with their training schedule, even when times get tough or the weather is quite challenging.
- **Preparation:** All performers need to adequately prepare for an event, be it a 'friendly' game or part of a competition. An observer can quickly determine how well a performer understands the benefits of preparation and what impact it might have on their performance.
- **Health and safety:** A performer's knowledge of health and safety, and how they apply this knowledge to a competitive setting (to ensure they don't pose a risk to themselves or others), is very important.

Review

When you have analysed and evaluated a performance, and identified a performer's strengths and areas for improvement, you need to communicate your findings to the performer. It is important that you make sure your feedback is constructive and positive and, above all, that it motivates the performer.

One successful model for constructive feedback works like this:

- Ask the performer how they feel it went.
- Tell the performer how you think it went.

- Ask the performer what they think they did well.
- Tell the performer what you think they did well, using specific examples from your observation, analysis and evaluation.

- Ask the performer what they think they could do differently or better.
- Tell the performer what you think they could do differently or better, using specific examples from your observation, analysis and evaluation.

- Agree the next steps together. These could be short-term, medium-term or long-term goals, and could focus on anything from individual skills, techniques or tactics to teamwork or fitness.

Implementation

The next stage is to implement the changes required in order to improve performance. This might be through a training programme, a course or by using technology such as video analysis software. It might also involve a performer seeking help outside their school, college or club if the help or advice needed isn't available there.

This may sound straightforward but when a performer who has done something in a certain way for a long time is then asked to modify their practice, there can be difficulties. Sometimes, performers take a step backwards before making improvements. Their coach or manager needs to be aware of this and encourage them, giving praise when it is deserved and constantly motivating the performer to work hard.

Using video analysis software such as Dartfish™ can make implementing required changes easier. Here, the focus is a sprinter's start.

Unit 2 assignment, part three

Background

As a sports leader in your school or college, you have been given the role of coach for your chosen team or individual sport. You have been asked to review the performance of either the team or an athlete involved with the individual sport, so that specific training can be delivered with maximum effectiveness.

Task

Produce an observation checklist to enable you to review the performance of a team or individual participating in one of your selected sports. Brief the team or individual on the performance review process. Then, use your observation checklist to help you observe, analyse and evaluate their performance. Finally, review their performance during a post-match or post-training debrief session, and agree how the changes required to improve performance will be implemented. You should:

| GRADING CRITERIA |
TO BE ASSESSED
P7, P8
M3, M4

Produce, with tutor support, an observation checklist that could be used to review the sports performance of an individual or a team (P7).

Use the observation checklist to review the sports performance of an individual or a team, identifying strengths and areas for improvement (P8).

Independently produce an observation checklist that could be used to review the sports performance of an individual or a team (M3).

Explain the strengths and areas for improvement of an individual or a team, in one individual sport or one team sport, justifying recommendations for improvement (M4).

Tackling the assignment

When planning this assignment, you need to think carefully about what it is you are trying to find out. Most people can observe a performance and comment on something that is good or not so good, but your observation and analysis needs to be more detailed than this. Essentially, you need to look at each part of the performance: the individual skills used, how successfully the skills are applied, and the performer's knowledge and understanding of rules and regulations. Try to break down the information you want to find out; you may find producing a mind map is a useful starting point. Then, once you have a list of ideas, you can begin to group them together to form your checklist.

Remember:

If you are aiming for a Merit then it is important that you produce your observation checklist without support from your teacher or tutor.

Meeting the Pass and Merit criteria

BTEC Level 2 Firsts in Sport

Unit 2 assignment, part three   Abi Edwards

Observation checklist

Observation grade	Total observation grade	Player's overall performance
5 = Excellent	15–25	Poor
4 = Very good	26–36	Not very good
3 = Good	37–50	Good
2 = Not very good	51–65	Very good
1 = Poor	66–75	Excellent

Place the grade you think the player is performing at next to each skill in the table below.

Player's name: Janice Shaw	**Sport:** Badminton

	Observation grade
Physical abilities	
Has the player got good balance?	3
Is the player physically fit?	3
Mental abilities	
Is the player always concentrating?	3
Has the player got the determination to win or come back from behind?	2
Footwork/positioning	
Is the player in the centre of the court when attacking?	3
Does the player stand in a side-on position?	4
Ability to attack	
Does the player use a range of attacking shots?	3
Does the player place the shuttlecock where it's hard for the opponent to hit it?	4
Ability to defend	
Does the player use a range of defensive shots?	3
Does the player drive the opposition into a defensive position?	2
Shot selection	
Does the player perform the correct shots at the right time?	3
Does the player serve correctly depending on where the opposition is situated in the service box?	3
Tactical awareness	
Do the strokes played make the opposition move to the front and back of the court?	3
Application of skill	
Can the player perform a range of different shots?	4
Is the player comfortable playing difficult shots, such as the backhand drop shot?	2

Strengths	**Areas to develop**
On the whole, the player observed is of a good standard, consistent with her game, and generally successful in both attacking and defending situations. The player is able to select and apply appropriate shots with success for the majority of the time.	More work needs to be done on driving the opposition into defensive positions, such as moving the opponent to the back of the court or forcing the opponent to play a backhand shot.

This observation checklist clearly shows that different areas of the performance are being observed. The framework allows skills and other factors, such as physical and psychological factors, to be observed. If the checklist was produced with some tutor support, Abi will achieve P7. If it was produced without tutor support, she will achieve M3.

At it stands, this piece or work would achieve P8 because the performance has been reviewed, and strengths and areas for improvement have been identified. To achieve M4, Abi would need to explain the strengths and areas for improvement, and not just describe them. To do this, she would need to make links between the observation grades and her analysis, and recommend things that the observed player could do to improve.

Unit 2 assignment, part four

Background

As part of your ongoing development in your team or individual sport, it is important that you are able to review your own performance. This helps you to understand how it feels to have your performance reviewed, which will make you better at reviewing the performances of others. Identifying your strengths and weaknesses, and implementing the changes needed to improve your performance, will also make you a better athlete. As part of your role as a coach you have been asked to deliver a presentation showing how self-analysis is a very important part of development in sport.

Task

Using yourself as a case study, create a presentation that illustrates how you can use an observation checklist to analyse performance and how the findings can be used to identify areas for improvement. You should:

GRADING CRITERIA TO BE ASSESSED
P9
M5
D2

Use the observation checklist to review your own sports performance in an individual sport or team sport, identifying strengths and areas for improvement (P9).

Explain your own strengths and areas for improvement in an individual sport or team sport, providing recommendations for improvement (M5).

Analyse your own strengths and areas for improvement in an individual sport or team sport, justifying recommendations for improvement (D2).

Tackling the assignment

There are a number of different ways that you could approach this assignment but a good one is to produce a DVD showing you in action either in one team sport or one individual sport. The DVD should demonstrate the skills, techniques and tactics that you use regularly in game situations. You can then use your observation checklist to observe your performance, and your findings to review your performance.

Unit 3: Outdoor and Adventurous Activities

What are outdoor and adventurous activities?

Outdoor and adventurous activities, often called OAAs, usually take place outside, and involve the participant competing against the environment, on land, water, snow or a combination of all of these. This makes them risky, but it also makes them challenging and exciting. If a participant combines knowledge and skill then they can successfully, and safely, take part in some of the most exhilarating sports in the world.

Orienteering

Sailing

Caving

Snowboarding

Rock climbing

Kayaking

The organization and provision of outdoor and adventurous activities in the UK

Just like other sports, outdoor and adventurous activities are well organized through national governing bodies, and there are opportunities to take part at local and national level.

The organization of outdoor and adventurous activities in the UK

National governing bodies

All of the recognized OAA sports have a national governing body, including:

- British Bobsleigh Association
- British Canoe Union
- British Caving Association
- British Orienteering Federation
- Royal Yachting Association
- Snowsport England, Snowsport Scotland and Snowsport Wales, for all snowsports including skiing and snowboarding
- British Water Ski and Wakeboard.

Each governing body is responsible for the provision of that sport in the area that they govern. For example, all ski slopes in England are affiliated to Snowsport England and all canoe clubs in the UK are affiliated to the British Canoe Union. As part of their role, each national governing body offers recognized coaching and leadership awards specific to their sport. It is usually a legal requirement for coaches to have these qualifications before they can teach or coach the sport. For example, Snowsport England administers a licensing scheme for those who wish to teach on artificial slopes, develop performers, lead groups or become an official, and snowsport clubs will not allow anyone to coach within their facilities unless they hold a valid certificate. Similarly, the British Canoe Union (BCU) offers a range of coaching courses aimed at developing leaders within their sport and practising coaches must be licensed by the BCU. Details of the coaching awards available are usually accessible on the appropriate national governing body's website.

Clubs

National governing bodies hold details of all their affiliated clubs, and this should be the first point of contact for anyone wishing to take part in an outdoor and adventurous activity. Some sports have to take place at specific locations, for example, there are only a limited number of ski slopes throughout England, whereas others, such as orienteering, can take place almost anywhere. Members of the British Canoe Union, for example, are issued with a licence which allows them to paddle on over 4000km of Britain's waterways.

Most participants in OAAs choose to join a local club because it often enables them to meet like-minded people, and can provide them with access to recognized competitions and events.

Working in outdoor and adventurous activities

Outdoor and adventurous activities have enjoyed a huge increase in popularity over the last 25 years, and there are more and more clubs opening up each week, all looking for coaches. However, jobs in this sector are incredibly popular and much sought after. This means that there is strong competition for jobs, and only the very best coaches and instructors are able to make it a full-time vocation. Most OAA coaches fit their coaching in around their main employment, usually in the evenings or at weekends, and a large proportion work on a voluntary basis. As with most things involving OAAs, the first point of contact for anyone seeking employment in this sector should be the national governing body of the relevant sport.

BRONZE

1. Find out about other outdoor and adventurous activities, which aren't mentioned on this page, making a list of six activities and their national governing bodies.

2. Choose two outdoor and adventurous activities that you don't already take part in and find your local club for each one.

SILVER

3. Compare and contrast – or describe the similarities and differences between – the local provision for each of the two sports you found out about for Activity 2.

The provision of outdoor and adventurous activities in the UK

Local provision

The local provision of facilities for outdoor and adventurous activities is primarily a matter for local authorities, although many private businesses also run facilities. Exactly what is provided is largely determined by the terrain of an area. This means that there will be geographical differences in provision, with provision in the Peak District being very different from that in inner city areas. For example, mountainous activities are very popular in Wales due to the topography of the land, whilst skiing is more popular in Scotland because of the weather. However, in recent years, the development of artificial facilities has meant that many inner-city areas are now able to offer local people the opportunity to take part in outdoor and adventurous activities such as climbing and skiing.

National provision

On a national scale, there are various organizations that safeguard the natural environment and contribute towards the provision for outdoor and adventurous activities, and in most cases these organizations work with local authorities.

Natural England advises the government on the natural environment, providing practical advice on how best to safeguard England's natural wealth for the benefit of everyone. It exists to secure a healthy natural environment for people to enjoy, where wildlife is protected and England's traditional landscapes are safeguarded for future generations.

BRONZE

4. Create a map of the UK with the location of the national sports centres clearly marked. For each centre, produce a list of the main sports for which it caters.

SILVER

5. Using the map you created for Activity 4, justify the choice of the location for the national provision for outdoor and adventurous activities in the UK.

Sport England is the government agency responsible for building the foundations of sporting success by creating a world-leading community of clubs, coaches, facilities and volunteers in England. It coordinates the work of the national sports centres, which provide top-level facilities. For example, Plas y Brenin in Wales specializes in outdoor and adventurous activities, running a year-round programme of mountain sports courses, including rock climbing, mountaineering, scrambling, hill-walking, orienteering, mountain biking, skiing, kayaking and canoeing. Also, the National Water Sports Centre at Holme Pierrepont in Nottingham has become the focal point for water sports in the UK.

Securing the London 2012 Olympic and Paralympic Games has led to the development of many more national centres in and around the capital, but it is not yet known what long-term effect this will have on the provision for outdoor and adventurous activities in the UK.

There are 15 National Parks in the UK, incorporating mountains, meadows, moorlands, woods and wetland. These are areas of protected countryside, which everyone can visit, where people live, work and shape the landscape. Each National Park is run by an organization that works with others to look after the landscape and wildlife, and helps people to enjoy and learn about the area. Access to all the National Parks is free, and outdoor and adventurous activities are very popular within these parks.

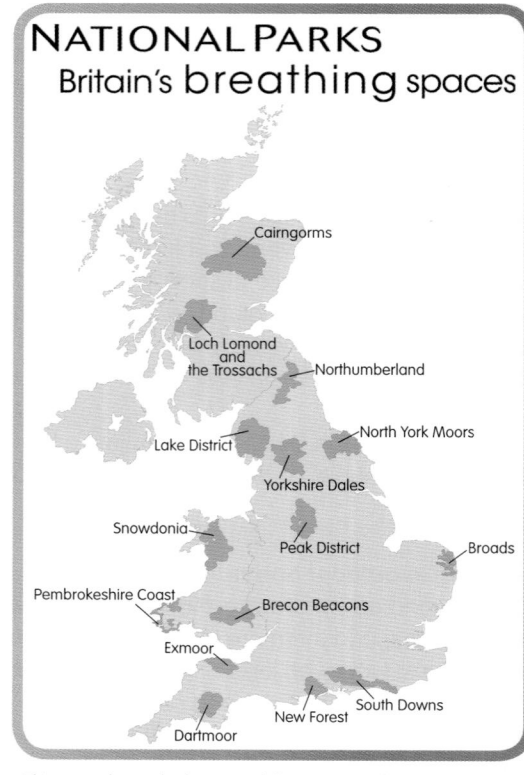

This map shows the location of the 15 National Parks in the UK (www.nationalparks.gov.uk).

Unit 3 assignment, part one

Background

As a university tutor of outdoor and adventurous activities, your role is to prepare future OAA leaders to work with young people. To do this, you must provide them with the skills, knowledge and experience that will enable them to take responsibility for young people in an outdoor environment. In practice, this means providing them with knowledge of the issues surrounding health and safety, risk assessment and the impact of OAAs on the environment, as well as the more obvious skills required to lead specific activities.

Task

Produce a series of web pages that detail the local and national organization and provision for two outdoor and adventurous activities. Your web pages should:

GRADING CRITERIA TO BE ASSESSED
P1
M1

Describe the organization and provision of two outdoor and adventurous activities (P1).

Compare the organization and provision of two outdoor and adventurous activities (M1).

Tackling the assignment

This assignment should be approached by following the instructions given and producing a series of web pages. It is important to keep to the brief and only include the information you have been asked for, because it can be very easy to go overboard and spend a lot of time including things that are not really relevant to the assignment. Remember to ensure that you include both the organization of **and** provision for the activities chosen, and that you do this at a local **and** at a national level.

Meeting the Pass criteria

- Home page
- Local provision
- National provision
- British Mountaineering Council
- Getting involved
- Equipment
- Contact us

Local provision

It is possible to take part in rock climbing outdoors without any instruction. Just turn up, set up and climb. However, I would always recommend using a qualified instructor as a guide to the rock face. He or she will be able to deal with any injuries of difficulties, will know which areas are safe and which to avoid, as well as have a knowledge of the likely weather conditions for the locality.

(Indoor)
The Edge, Sheffield, 0114 275 8899
www.sheffieldclimbing.com

(Outdoor)
Peak District, John White, 01768 486 731
www.mountainguides.co.uk

I am concerned that Kamil has only attempted to describe the organization and provision for one OAA. There do not appear to be any links to another activity. Even if Kamil makes the changes described in the comment below, he will not be able to achieve P1 unless he repeats the process for a second activity.

Kamil has made a good start to this assignment but needs to develop his web pages further. He has given a clear indication of where climbers can go to take part in climbing in the local area but he has not described the provision that is available. I would have liked to see more detailed descriptions of the facilities available at each of the locations, including an idea of the costs involved.

Meeting the Merit criteria

Rock climbing and Skiing by Kitty Commons

- Home
- The activities
- Local organization
- Local provision
- National organization
- National provision
- Further information
- Contact

Local provision

There is a marked difference in the local provision for skiing and rock climbing. To put it bluntly, skiing is relatively inaccessible, whereas rock climbing is readily available.

Within 50 miles of my home town, there are 12 indoor climbing centres and over 100 outdoor rock faces which are regularly used for climbing. In contrast, there are only two skiing centres (one artificial outdoor dry slope and one indoor slope with artificial snow).

Because of this, skiing is very expensive when compared with rock climbing. Two hours of skiing costs over £30 and two hours of instruction costs £75, not including transport, clothing and equipment. Climbing, on the other hand, starts at £3.50 for two hours or £18 for two hours with an instructor.

At least five local climbing centres can be accessed using the local bus service and the journeys cost under £2, but you really need a car to get to the nearest ski slope. You can get there by public transport, but it is an expensive and time-consuming journey involving three buses and a train.

Clearly, the local provision for climbing is significantly better than the local provision for skiing. This is probably explained by the relative costs involved with running the two types of centre.

Kitty's web page for local provision contains all the necessary information but, crucially, it also compares and contrasts each relevant point. By using the sentence in bold at the bottom of the page, Kitty has also clearly shown that she understands the task and has made an effort to carry out thorough research. At this stage, I am confident that Kitty will achieve M1, although I would need to see all of the web pages to give a final decision.

Kitty has adopted a very sensible approach towards this assignment, and by producing a separate web page for each section (one for local organization, one for local provision, one for national organization and one for national provision) she has made it very obvious that she has attempted to cover all of the relevant parts of the criteria.

Health and safety for outdoor and adventurous activities

Regardless of whether you are taking part in outdoor and adventurous activities at a competitive level or simply enjoying them as a pastime with friends and family there are rules, regulations and legislation in place to protect you from injury.

Rules and regulations

Put simply, rules are statements of what you are and are not allowed to do in a given situation. Rules can be formal or informal. Formal rules, for example, rules that are set down by a governing body of a sport, are often called regulations.

Golden Rules from the British Canoe Union

- **Be able to swim at least 50m:** You do not need to be able to swim vast distances but the ability to remain confident in and under the water, without panicking, is vital.
- **Use a buoyancy aid:** This should be worn whenever you get into your boat.
- **Stay with the boat and, in the unfortunate event that you do capsize, stay with the upturned canoe:** A canoe is easier to spot than a swimmer's head and its in-built buoyancy will help you to remain afloat.
- **Never paddle alone:** If anything does go wrong it is vital to have someone else along; it's also friendlier.
- **Make sure you are properly equipped for the water and weather conditions you expect to encounter.**
- **Attend a qualified first-aid course and get qualified.**
- **Practise. Keep your skills sharp and be prepared.**

(www.bcu.org.uk)

Of course there are other things to be taken into consideration but common sense and reading the relevant sections of the *Canoe and Kayak Handbook* published by the British Canoe Union will give you much more help with maintaining personal safety whilst canoeing.

In addition to the guidelines set by governing bodies, individual clubs will have their own rules. These rules will be specific to the location in which the club operates. For example, they may require you to sign a document stating that you have been made aware of the tide times of the waterway you are using or advise you that a certain area of a rock face should not be used for climbing because erosion is causing debris to fall in the path of climbers.

The important thing to remember is that such rules are always set to ensure safety and failure to follow them could put your life – and the lives of others – in danger!

Legislation

Legislation is the name given to rules and regulations that have been made into law by the government of a country. Mostly, these relate to protecting the safety of participants and ensuring that neither the participants nor rescue teams are put in unnecessary danger. Failure to comply with legislation can lead to the prosecution of an individual, a group of people or a club.

In the UK, there are two main organizations that are responsible for overseeing legislation surrounding outdoor and adventurous activities, and for licensing organizations that deliver outdoor and adventurous activities to under-18s in return for payment:

1. The Adventurous Activities Licensing Authority (AALA), which is a role undertaken by the Health and Safety Executive (HSE).
2. The Adventure Activities Licensing Service, which is contracted by the Health and Safety Executive to deliver licensing on a day-to-day basis.

According to the AALA, 'Adventure activities licensing ensures that activity providers follow good safety management practices. These should allow young people to experience exciting and stimulating activities outdoors without being exposed to avoidable risks of death or disabling injury.' In practice, this means that the Adventure Activities Licensing Service inspects clubs and organizations to ensure that they are taking safety seriously, that they have adequate insurance cover, and that leaders and coaches are suitably qualified.

Examples of activities which need a licence include:

Climbing	Water sports	Trekking	Caving
• Rock climbing • Abseiling • Ice climbing • Gorge walking • Ghyll scrambling • Sea level traversing	• Canoeing • Kayaking • Dragon boating • Wave skiing • White-water rafting • Improvised rafting • Sailing • Sailboarding • Windsurfing	• Hillwalking • Mountaineering • Fell running • Orienteering • Pony trekking • Off-road cycling • Off-piste skiing	• Caving • Pot-holing • Mine exploration

Activities such as pony trekking must be lead by an organization or leader with the appropriate licence.

BRONZE

1. Choose two outdoor and adventurous activities and find out ten rules or regulations set by the governing body of each sport.

2. Contact two local OAA clubs and obtain their rules and regulations relating to health and safety.

SILVER

3. Compare and contrast the information you obtained for Activities 1 and 2. Do both activities have robust rules and regulations, or do the rules of one governing body and club seem more stringent than the other?

GOLD

4. Analyse how the information you obtained for Activity 1 will affect people taking part in the activities in question. For example, does the need for expensive equipment make the activity inaccessible to some people?

Risk assessment

Getting hurt while taking part in outdoor and adventurous activities is not a pleasant subject to think about. However, the reality is that every year in the UK people die taking part in outdoor and adventurous activities, and thousands of non-fatal injuries also require treatment. The mistake is to believe that these things happen in exceptional circumstances and will never happen to you. This is not the case but it doesn't mean that you should avoid all dangerous activities. Carrying out a risk assessment beforehand can prevent many accidents from happening.

What is risk?

The *Oxford English Dictionary* defines risk as 'the possibility that something unpleasant will happen'. If we apply this to an OAA context, we could say that risk is 'the possibility that an injury to one or more participants will happen'.

Most people would agree that preventing an injury from occurring makes more sense than dealing with it once it has happened and this is where risk assessment comes in. By assessing the dangers that could occur, participants and leaders can take steps to remove some of the hazards. A risk assessment is a careful examination of what, in your activity, could cause harm to the participants. It is a simple, practical exercise that requires little more than common sense.

Carrying out a risk assessment before an OAA can reduce the chance of participants sustaining serious injuries.

Why should we carry out a risk assessment?

- Carrying out a risk assessment is a good way to work out how risky something is. It makes you think of everything that could be risky, not just the obvious things.
- Part of completing a risk assessment is putting plans in place to minimize the risks you have identified. It is unlikely that you will be able to eliminate the risks altogether, but a risk assessment does play an important part in reducing the likelihood of the risks you have identified, and therefore in minimizing the risk of injury.
- Completing a risk assessment promotes the safety and welfare of all involved, including participants, club members, spectators, and members of the general public who you might come into contact with while engaged in your sport or activity.
- Risk assessments should be regularly reviewed to ensure that a safe environment is continually maintained.
- If an accident does happen everyone wants to avoid liability at all costs, both in terms of criminal prosecutions and civil claims for compensation. Carrying out a risk assessment shows good practice, and all governing bodies of outdoor and adventurous activities (and their insurance policies) insist that clubs and other organizations carry out such assessments.

Not all risks are this obvious.

The six-step process for carrying out a risk assessment

There are six stages to producing a formal risk assessment document. Failure to complete any of the six stages could lead to someone being seriously injured.

6. Review your decisions regularly and make changes if necessary: Hazards change on a regular basis, so the risk assessment must be reviewed to keep it up to date. This is even more important for OAAs due to changes in the environment, such as the weather, so risk assessments must be dynamic.

1. Identify the hazards: Have a good look around at all the equipment, venue and participants, and decide what could cause harm, no matter how minor. For example, a broken piece of equipment would be a hazard.

5. Record your findings and implement them: By law, the risk assessment findings must be written down. It is also important to put in place the control measures you have decided on. For example, making someone responsible for checking the equipment on a weekly basis.

2. Decide who might be harmed and how: Decide whether it is the participants, the leader or the general public who might be harmed. Then decide what may happen to them. What injuries could they sustain? Might they even die? For example, climbing on an eroding cliff face could lead to a fall that would result in serious injuries or death.

4. Decide how to prevent or reduce the level of risk: Practical solutions to reduce the level of risk, called 'control measures', must be found. For example, checking all equipment once a week to make sure it is not broken, and therefore dangerous, and making a commitment to replace or repair damaged items.

3. Identify the level of risk: Decide how likely it is that the potential accidents you have identified will occur. For example, damaged climbing equipment would represent a high level of risk.

BRONZE

1. Get into two teams and hold a debate, one team arguing for the statements below and one team arguing against the statements below:

'It is impossible to completely eliminate risk from an outdoor and adventurous activity.'

'Outdoor and adventurous activities would be more fun if there was no danger or risk.'

2. Place the following sports on the continuum below, according to the potential risk of injury:

Safe ⟷ Dangerous

a) Rock climbing on a climbing wall.
b) Rock climbing on a remote rock face.
c) Skiing on an artificial or indoor slope.
d) Skiing off a piste in the French Alps.
e) Canoeing on an open waterway.
f) Caving in an artificial practice cave.

3. Compile a list of ten risks that you take between the end of this lesson and the start of the next lesson.

4. Using the example on page 112 (Unit 5) as a guide, create a risk assessment form that you can use to assess the risks present in taking part in an OAA of your choice.

5. Use the risk assessment form you have created to identify all the hazards in an outdoor sporting space in your school. This could, for example, be the playground, a climbing wall, or the field.

Unit 3 assignment, part two

Background

As a university tutor of outdoor and adventurous activities, your role is to prepare future OAA leaders to work with young people. To do this, you must provide them with the skills, knowledge and experience that will enable them to take responsibility for young people in an outdoor environment. In practice, this means providing them with knowledge of the issues surrounding health and safety, risk assessment and the impact of OAAs on the environment, as well as the more obvious skills required to lead specific activities.

Task

Produce a document, which can be handed out to future leaders, detailing the health and safety considerations for two outdoor and adventurous activities of your choice. The document should contain a formal risk assessment for one of the two activities you have chosen. The document should also:

GRADING CRITERIA TO BE ASSESSED
P2, P3
M2
D1

Describe the health and safety considerations associated with participation in two outdoor and adventurous activities (P2).

Produce a risk assessment for a selected outdoor and adventurous activity (P3).

Explain health and safety considerations associated with participation in two outdoor and adventurous activities, identifying precautions and actions that can be taken, or used, in relation to them (M2).

Explain precautions and actions that can be taken, or used, in relation to health and safety considerations associated with participation in two outdoor and adventurous activities (D1).

Tackling the assignment

If you are aiming for a Pass, you could produce a poster or an information booklet to accompany your risk assessment. If you are aiming for a Merit or a Distinction and decide to produce a poster, it should probably be accompanied by a small booklet to make sure that you have enough space to cover all the relevant information.

You can use the example on page 112 as a template to help you structure your risk assessment, but you can amend it or produce your own document if the example doesn't meet your needs.

Meeting the Pass, Merit and Distinction criteria

BTEC Level 2 Firsts in Sport

Unit 3 assignment, part two   Michael Foster

Canoeing

Canoeing is a potentially lethal activity and, as such, everyone taking part must have a working knowledge of the health and safety aspects of the activity.

Health and safety considerations

The following points must be considered before, during and after any canoeing activity takes place:

- The people.
- The environment.
- The equipment.

The people involved are the most important consideration, and nothing else should be decided until the competency and experience of the group is known. Group size should also be carefully considered, because beginners will need much more attention than experienced canoeists.

The environment is the second most important consideration, and should be chosen based on the ability and experience of the participants. For example, it would be unwise to take beginners out on a fast-flowing river, while more experienced canoeists would gain little or no benefit from canoeing on flat, open water. Therefore, once the ability of the participants is known, an appropriate environment should be chosen. Another environmental consideration that should be taken into account is the prevailing weather conditions and the likelihood of changes in the weather. Even experienced canoeists will sometimes cancel a trip if the weather conditions make the activity dangerous.

Health and safety precautions

Accidents will happen in all activities from time to time, but applying basic health and safety precautions will ensure accidents are reduced in both frequency and severity. Before undertaking any activity with a group, the leader should take the following precautions:

- Research likely hazards and complete a risk assessment.
- Confirm group experience and capabilities (where possible).
- Check environmental conditions, including the weather forecast, river levels and tidal patterns, where appropriate.
- Carry out headcounts before departure and throughout the activity.
- Be alert to changes in the physical and psychological condition of the group.
- Control the pace of the activity to suit the group.

By researching the likely hazards and completing a risk assessment before meeting with the group, the leader is able to take control of the situation from the very start; a key role of any leader is to lead by example. Hazards should be explained to the group at the outset and should be reinforced throughout the activity.

The final two points are perhaps the most important but can be the most difficult to apply. Young participants tend to want to push themselves and 'paddle before they can float', and this can lead to accidents occurring. The leader needs to constantly assess the performance of the group and their levels of fatigue. By attempting to control the pace the leader can ensure that everyone sticks together, because if students are allowed to travel at their own pace, the group can quickly become separated and this is a recipe for disaster! However, the leader must be careful not to travel too slowly as some members of the group could become bored and this can lead to a lack of concentration, which in turn leads to accidents. Creating a pace where everyone is safe and everyone is able to push themselves a little is a delicate balancing act. It is a skill which can only be developed through experience.

Michael has listed the key considerations from a health and safety perspective and has described the people-related and environment-related considerations. His description here is very basic and would benefit from a bit more detail, but it does begin to meet the criteria for P2. Michael now needs to describe the equipment-related considerations in the same way, and to consider the health and safety considerations for a second OAA, to fully achieve P2.

Michael is providing more detail here and is therefore working towards meeting the criteria for M2. He not only describes the environmental considerations, linking the type of water to the participants' ability, but he also develops his thinking to include general weather conditions and even explains what should happen if the weather is poor. He now needs to explain the other health and safety considerations for canoeing in a similar amount of detail and then go on to do the same for a second OAA.

In addition to explaining the health and safety considerations of two OAAs, Michael also needs to identify the precautions and actions that should be taken to prevent accidents happening in order to fully meet the criteria for M2. There is no requirement here to explain these precautions and a simple list, like the one Michael has produced here, will suffice.

In this paragraph Michael is working at Distinction level because he is explaining the health and safety precautions and actions that should be taken to prevent accidents from happening. He has suggested both some benefits of controlling the pace at which the group is working, as well as the potential pitfalls. To fully meet the criteria for D1, Michael will need to examine the other precautions in the same depth, and do the same for a second OAA.

The environmental impact of outdoor and adventurous activities

Everyone who uses the countryside should be concerned about looking after it and making sure that it remains the way it is for others to enjoy. We call this conservation. Because outdoor and adventurous activities usually take place outside they can easily have a detrimental effect on wildlife, and can cause pollution and erosion. Therefore, everyone taking part in an OAA needs to know exactly how to look after the countryside, because doing the wrong thing can often do more harm than doing nothing at all.

Wildlife

Wildlife is the most wonderful feature of the great outdoors, and includes both plants and animals. These can be protected by following a few very simple rules:

- Guard against all risks of fire and, when you light a fire, do so in a suitable area, making sure that it is fully extinguished before you leave.
- Leave all gates exactly as you find them. Close them again if they were closed before and leave them open if they were already open.
- Avoid contact with animals whenever possible.
- Do not remove anything, including plants, rocks and shells, from their natural habitat.
- Keep to public footpaths and bridleways.
- Use gates and stiles to cross fences and walls, rather than climbing over them.
- Do not make any unnecessary noise.
- Take all of your litter home with you. It spoils the countryside for others and can cause injury to wild animals.

Erosion

Natural erosion takes place all of the time. You only have to look at the way Britain's coastline has changed over the last century to realize that erosion is a natural process. However, we shouldn't make the situation worse. Erosion can be reduced if we stick to footpaths as much as possible and many of Britain's National Parks now have gravelled walkways across remote areas to make this easier. Motor vehicles should only be driven on proper roads, and not on tracks, except in an emergency. The erosion of rock faces can be reduced by avoiding climbing in areas where earth and rocks could be displaced. By following these simple steps we can reduce erosion and preserve the countryside for future generations.

Pollution

The biggest polluter as far as outdoor and adventurous activities are concerned is the use of cars, vans and minibuses to gain access to the countryside. Whilst it is difficult to stop this, we can reduce the impact of vehicles on the environment. For example, using public transport whenever possible, and wearing appropriate clothing for the weather before you set off so that you don't need to sit in the car with the engine and heater running on a cold day.

Waste products, such as those produced when cooking or going to the toilet, can also pollute the environment, particularly fresh stream water. Wherever possible, take everything you brought with you home and, if you need to go to the toilet, bury your waste well away from sources of fresh water.

Construction of facilities

Some OAAs require facilities to be built in remote areas. There are, for example, many hostels in areas which are almost inaccessible by road. The key thing is to ensure that building programmes in the countryside are kept to a minimum. One way to do this is to convert existing buildings, rather than building new ones. For example, many of the hostels in the Peak District National Park are actually converted cattle sheds and are just a room with a roof, without drinking water or toilets. Where new buildings do have to be erected, they should be built using natural materials that are sympathetic to the surrounding environment wherever possible. For example, the mountain restaurants in many ski resorts are usually built from trees which have been felled on site.

BRONZE

1. Design a poster that informs people how to protect the natural environment.

2. Choose two contrasting outdoor and adventurous activities, and list ten ways in which each activity works with the environment. Then try to list ten ways in which the activities can harm the environment.

SILVER

3. Choose one item from the list of ways in which the activities can harm the environment that you created for Activity 2 and explain how it affects the environment negatively.

GOLD

4. Explain what could be done to minimize or remove the negative effects on the environment that you explored in Activity 3.

Unit 3 assignment, part three

Background

As a university tutor of outdoor and adventurous activities, your role is to prepare future OAA leaders to work with young people. To do this, you must provide them with the skills, knowledge and experience that will enable them to take responsibility for young people in an outdoor environment. In practice, this means providing them with knowledge of the issues surrounding health and safety, risk assessment and the impact of OAAs on the environment, as well as the more obvious skills required to lead specific activities.

GRADING CRITERIA TO BE ASSESSED
P4
M3
D2

Task

Create a poster or a leaflet which shows the impact of outdoor and adventurous activities on the natural environment. You should use written sections to support any drawings or photographs, and your poster or leaflet should also:

Describe environmental impacts associated with participation in two outdoor and adventurous activities (P4).

Explain the environmental impacts associated with participation in two outdoor and adventurous activities, identifying precautions and actions that can be taken, or used, to reduce them (M3).

Explain precautions and actions that can be taken, or used, to reduce the environmental impacts associated with participation in two outdoor and adventurous activities (D2).

Tackling the assignment

If you are aiming for a Pass or a Merit then you could choose to produce either a poster or an information booklet. If you are aiming for a Distinction then it would be best to create an information booklet, because it allows you to expand your ideas and gives you room to explain what can be done to reduce the environmental impacts of outdoor and adventurous activities.

Meeting the Pass and Merit criteria

The Environmental Impact of Outdoor & Adventurous Activities

By Chloe Tate

Litter causes irreparable damage to the environment. Litter dropped and left when camping can catch fire and also be harmful to wild animals. Litter dropped when canoeing can have disastrous consequences because it can pollute the water, making it unsafe to drink for humans and wildlife. In addition, ring-pulls from cans can cut wildlife and small animals can become tangled in plastic bottle ties.

When trekking it is easy to stray away from official footpaths and walk on fresh grass. This leads to loss of plant cover, which leads to soil erosion.

Campfires can be a problem when camping and trekking. The most obvious impact occurs when a fire burns out of control, particularly in remote wooded areas, which can be inaccessible to the fire service.

Even small fires have an environmental impact because they damage vegetation and can damage soil in such a way that it can take years to recover.

Travel to and from a place of activity for canoeing or camping often has a greater environmental impact than the activity itself. Cars pollute the atmosphere and have been linked to climate change.

A more immediate impact is the erosion caused by the car when driving to and from remote areas, particularly if the access route takes the car across non-tarmac roads or, worse, across farmland and farm tracks.

> Chloe's poster works well because it clearly covers two different outdoor and adventurous activities (camping and canoeing), and it can be difficult to combine information about two different activities in one place.

> In places, Chloe has met only the Pass criteria (P4). For example, she has described the fact that soil erosion is an impact of camping, but has not explained the effects of this erosion and why it is bad for the environment. If Chloe had added this extra detail, she would have met the Merit criteria (M3). In other places, Chloe has given more information and has explained the environmental impacts. Her explanation of the problems caused by litter is a good example of where she is achieving M3.

> I would have liked to see Chloe consider other environmental impacts of camping and canoeing, such as the spread of campsites in rural areas and the potential destruction of habitats caused by canoe landing sites.

> To fully meet the criteria for M3, Chloe also needs to identify things that campers and canoeists can do to minimize or completely remove the environmental effects of their activities.

Meeting the Distinction criteria

Reducing the environmental impacts of outdoor and adventurous activities
Tomas Pawelski

Trekking impacts on the environment in many ways, including:
- Trampling and cutting-off vegetation (page 1).
- Escapes from campers' fires (page 2).
- Expansion of campsites (page 3).
- Outbreaks of gastroenteritis (page 4).
- The rapid deterioration of walking tracks (page 5).

Trampling and cutting-off vegetation
The impact of trampling and cutting-off vegetation can be vastly reduced if users of the countryside follow some simple rules:

- **Stay on the track even if it's rough and muddy:** Walking on the track edges and cutting corners on steep 'zigzag' tracks increase damage, erosion and visual scarring, as well as causing confusion about which is the right track.
- **Spread out in open country where there are no tracks:** Spreading out, rather than following in each other's footsteps, disperses impact. A plant stepped on only once has more chance of survival than if trampled on by the whole party.
- **Avoid sensitive vegetation:** Cushion plants and other sensitive vegetation are easily destroyed by trampling. Stay on rocks and hard ground whenever possible.

- **Keep the wilderness wild:** Cutting new tracks is illegal in some areas, and marking tracks with rocks, cairns, tape or other material is unsightly and can confuse other walkers.
- **Choose a different route** each time you visit a track-less area and camp at different sites whenever possible. This reduces erosion and gives vegetation in areas that have been used time to recover.
- **Walk softly:** Choose appropriate footwear for the terrain. Solid but lightweight walking boots are best. Sand-shoes can be used on most tracks on the mainland in summer and should be worn around campsites. This type of footwear spreads weight over a larger area and therefore causes less damage to vegetation.

Overall, the key message is to 'leave no trace', which means that other walkers should not know that you have been in the area. By following the simple guidelines above, it is possible to maintain the countryside for future generations.

> Tomas' work shows real depth of thought. He has not only identified the precautions and actions that can be taken when trekking (M3), he has also explained each precaution (D2). A good example of this can be found in his last bullet point, where he explains how the use of a special type of footwear can help to spread 'weight over a larger area' and therefore cause less damage.

> Although only one page is visible here, it is clear, from the references to other pages, that Tomas has considered a range of other environmental impacts of trekking and the precautions and actions that can be taken to reduce them. However, he has failed to fully meet the criteria so far because he has only considered one OAA. So, even though this piece of work is at Distinction level, Tomas would fail to achieve even a Pass in this part of the assignment if he has not considered another OAA in the later pages of his work.

Skills, techniques and tactics

All sports, including outdoor and adventurous activities, have a range of skills, techniques and tactics that need to be developed in order for participants to be successful.

What is a skill?

A skill is something that is usually practised many times in order for someone to become proficient in it or able to carry it out consistently, again and again.

For example, when you begin to learn to climb, one of the first things to learn is how to tie a figure-eight knot. This takes practice at first but experienced climbers can tie the knot blindfolded.

Some skills are activity specific but others can be transferred from one activity to another. For example, the skills of communication and interaction between group members are important in all OAAs. These skills can be developed through trekking, but then used in climbing and canoeing as well.

What is a technique?

A technique is the way in which you perform a particular skill. For example, when tying the figure-eight knot, many climbers tend to think of it in three stages, with each stage producing a little part of the total knot. Although everyone follows these three stages, some people complete them more accurately and can be said to have a better grasp of the technique.

Skills, techniques and tactics can involve the use of specialized equipment.

What are tactics?

Tactics can be thought of as the plan of action set to outwit your opponent and gain an advantage. In OAAs it is more accurate to say that tactics are a way of beating your environment. This may be a way of tackling a climbing wall or the route to cover for an orienteering course. Essentially, the tactics are a plan of action but the plan should not be set in stone. Changes in the environment (weather, loose rocks or injury) may mean that the tactics have to be changed in order to succeed.

BRONZE

1. Plan a way of gathering evidence of the different skills, techniques and tactics that you have developed in your chosen outdoor and adventurous activities. You could keep a diary, a logbook or a portfolio, a record of witness testimonies, feedback sheets or an observation record, and use audio or video equipment.

Reviewing your performance

It is important for people taking part in outdoor and adventurous activities to review their performance regularly so that they can become a better sportsperson. If a skill, technique or tactic is unsuccessful for any reason, the performer can work to improve it. Equally, if something worked really well, this method can be used again in the future.

When reviewing your performance it is important to gather information from everyone involved, including other participants, leaders and observers, to build an accurate picture of how it went. You might want to ask people about:

- **Strengths:** What was good about your performance?
- **Areas for development:** What could you have done better?
- **Health and safety:** Was the performance safe? Did it follow the guidelines set down by the national governing body of the activity? If anything did go wrong, did you respond to problems efficiently and effectively?

It is easiest to review a performance if everyone involved is asked the same questions, in the same format. The most common way of doing this is to use a questionnaire that includes a series of simple, open-ended questions, which allow participants to express their opinions effectively.

Setting targets for improvement and development

After you have reviewed your performance, you should set yourself targets for improvement and development. These should be SMART targets:

SPECIFIC: Targets should be specific; they should set down precisely what you want to achieve. For example, 'I want to progress from climbing walls rated "severe" to those rated "very severe".'

MEASURABLE: Targets should be measurable so that you can work out if you have achieved them. For example, it is better to say that your target is to climb three different walls rated 'very severe' than it is to say that you want to climb more difficult walls.

ACHIEVABLE: Targets should be set appropriate to the fitness and skill levels of the performer. They should be close enough for us to see but not so far away that we can't touch them.

REALISTIC: It is important that we set targets that we have the capacity to achieve. All targets need to be challenging so that you have to work hard to achieve them, but they must also be realistic in order for them to serve their purpose and motivate you.

TIME-BOUND: Targets should have a time limit on them. For example, 'I want to climb three walls rated "very severe" by the end of the season.' If your long-term goals rely on you achieving your short-term goals, then you need to set time limits on your short-term goals in order to reach your long-term goals.

Having decided on your targets, you can create a development plan summarizing both your short- and long-term goals, and ways in which you can achieve them. For example, you might mention training courses that you would like to attend or coaching opportunities you would like to experience.

BRONZE

1. Create a questionnaire that you can use to gather feedback on your performance.

Unit 3 assignment, part four

Background

As a university tutor of outdoor and adventurous activities, your role is to prepare future OAA leaders to work with young people. To do this, you must provide them with the skills, knowledge and experience that will enable them to take responsibility for young people in an outdoor environment. In practice, this means providing them with knowledge of the issues surrounding health and safety, risk assessment and the impact of OAAs on the environment, as well as the more obvious skills required to lead specific activities.

Task

GRADING CRIT
TO BE ASSESSE

P5, P6, P7
M4, M5
D3

Take an active role in at least two different outdoor and adventurous activities. Whilst taking part, you will need to keep a record of your own performance and the performance of one of your peers. Afterwards, you must review your own performance and the performance of one of your peers. You must:

PASS

Demonstrate techniques and skills appropriate to two outdoor and adventurous activities (P5).

Review the performance of another individual participating in two outdoor and adventurous activities, identifying strengths and areas for improvement (P6).

Carry out a review of your own performance in outdoor and adventurous activities, identifying strengths and areas for improvement (P7).

MERIT

Review and justify your choice of techniques demonstrated in outdoor and adventurous activities (M4).

Explain identified strengths and areas for improvement in your own performance in outdoor and adventurous activities, making recommendations for further development of identified areas for improvement (M5).

DISTINCTION

Justify recommendations relating to identified areas for improvement in your own performance in outdoor and adventurous activities (D3).

Tackling the assignment

This assignment has to be approached in two stages. Firstly, you must take an active role in two different outdoor and adventurous activities. Then you must complete two separate reviews: one of your own performance and one of the performance of a member of your peer group. The reviews must cover your performance and a peer's performance in **both** activities.

Proof that you have taken part, of your practical performance, can take the form of photographs, film footage or a witness statement from your teacher, tutor or coach. Evidence for the reviews could be in the form of a written statement or a film.

Meeting the Pass and Merit criteria

Climbing skills: a practical demonstration and review

by James Kershaw

Within climbing, the most important skills are setting up a harness and tying suitable knots. Failure in either of these areas could have severe consequences and lead to serious injury or worse. The photos below show my demonstrations of fitting a harness correctly and of tying a figure-eight knot.

There are many different types of harness available but the most common style was used in my demonstration. As for the tying on, I chose to demonstrate a figure-eight knot. This is the most common type of knot and is much easier to learn than some other styles. Moreover, it is easy to check if this knot has been tied correctly (because the end result should look like the number eight), which means that my peers were able to check their own knots and their partners', and I was able to see quickly if any mistakes had been made. Other knots (Alpine Butterfly, Prusik Knot, Italian Hitch and so on) are often used by more advanced climbers but everyone should be taught the figure-eight knot to begin with.

> This extract is short and to the point. It is an excellent demonstration of how to meet the assignment criteria simply and effectively. By using photographs as evidence, James makes it clear that he has demonstrated the skills needed in climbing, thereby proving he is working at a Pass level, although evidence of more climbing skills and techniques, and a second outdoor and adventurous activity would be needed to fully meet the requirements for P5.

> James' explanation and justification for his use of the figure-eight knot show that he is beginning to meet the criteria for M4. However, before awarding James a Merit for this piece of work, I would like to see him justify some of the other skills and techniques he used when climbing, as well as a complete review of his second outdoor and adventurous activity.

Meeting the Distinction criteria

Skiing: A review of my performance

Gabriella Williams

Having skied several times, I would class myself as a solid intermediate skier. I know that there are areas I can improve upon but there are several areas that I could comfortably class as strengths.

Strengths	Areas for development
Snowplough (both for stopping and turning)	Carving
Stem turn	Unweighting the skis
Parallel stop	Parallel turns
Use of lifts	Controlling jumps

It is my aim to become an advanced level skier, so I need to work hard on my areas for development.

Unweighting the skis: This is a key area in my development and one that I currently struggle with. The process of taking weight off the skis allows turns to become much sharper and more controlled, and for this reason I will not be able to perform parallel turns until I master this skill. Parallel turns allow speed to be controlled much more quickly and this is vital when travelling across moguls. At present I tend to avoid bumps and moguls because I am not confident that I will be able to control my speed, and a mistake could lead to a serious injury. The following diagram shows how an improvement in unweighting the skis ultimately leads to being able to ski on moguls.

Unweighting the skis ➔ parallel turns ➔ speed control ➔ travelling across moguls.

> Gabriella's review of her performance is very honest, and she has clearly analysed her own strengths and weaknesses in detail. She begins by identifying (P7) her strengths and weaknesses in the table. Her paragraph about unweighting the skis shows a real depth of understanding and she justifies (D3) why this development is necessary by outlining the benefits that can be gained from improving this technique. If Gabriella analysed her other areas for development in this way and completed a similar review for her second OAA, I would be happy to award her the criteria for D5.

Unit 4: Anatomy and Physiology for Sport

The skeletal system

The skeleton is the framework of the body and gives a person their shape. It consists of 206 bones, which are held together by ligaments at the joints. The bones are divided into four main types and each has a special function.

The major bones of the body

In order to understand the skeletal system, it is important to remember the names of all the major bones of the body.

Clavicle: also known as the collar bone, the clavicle supports the shoulder and connects the upper arm to the main part of the body. The clavicle is a **flat** bone.

Scapula: situated at the back of the body, connecting the arm to the central skeleton. The scapula is a **flat** bone.

Skull: made up of 28 bones, eight of which form the cranium, which protects the brain. These are **flat** bones.

Radius: one of the bones in the lower arm. It rotates around the ulna to allow movement. The radius is a **long** bone.

Humerus: also known as the 'funny bone', the humerus is situated in the upper arm. It is a **long** bone.

Carpals: found in the wrist and glide across one another to enable the wrist to move in multiple directions.

Ulna: situated in the lower arm. It rotates around the radius to allow movement. The ulna is a **long** bone.

Sternum: a flat bone which lies in the centre of the chest and has ten pairs of ribs attached to it.

Ribs: there are 12 pairs of ribs, which are all joined to the vertebrae. Ten of these pairs of ribs are also attached to the sternum. The ribs are **flat** bones. They form a cage, which surrounds the heart and lungs to provide protection.

Patella: also known as the knee cap, this is a small bone situated between the upper and lower leg. The patella is not connected to any other bones. It is an **irregular** bone.

Pelvis: also known as the hip, the pelvis connects the legs to the body and provides protection for the lower internal organs. It is a **flat** bone.

Fibula: the smaller of the two lower leg bones. The fibula is a **long** bone.

Tibia: also known as the shin bone, this is one of the two bones situated in the lower leg and is the larger of the two. The tibia is a **long** bone.

Femur: the longest bone in the body, the femur is situated in the upper part of the leg and is a very strong bone. It is a **long** bone.

Different types of bones

Bones are divided into four types: long, short, flat and irregular.

- **Long bones:** These are found in the arms and legs. They are greater in length than they are in width. They are hollow with bone marrow inside them. They are lightweight but strong.
- **Short bones:** These are found in the ankles, feet, wrists and fingers. They are cube shaped and are light but strong.
- **Flat bones:** These are strong, flat plates which provide protection for major organs such as the brain, heart and lungs. They also provide attachment for muscles.
- **Irregular bones:** These bones don't fit into any other category. They support and protect joints, such as the patella at the knee joint.

The vertebral column

The vertebral column, also known as the spine, consists of 33 vertebrae. The vertebrae form a hollow column, called the vertebral column, which contains and protects the spinal cord. It is also flexible to allow the body to bend and twist. Each vertebra has a hole in the centre which allows the spinal cord to pass through. The vertebrae are irregular bones and are separated by discs of cartilage, which act as shock absorbers. The vertebral column is made up of five sections:

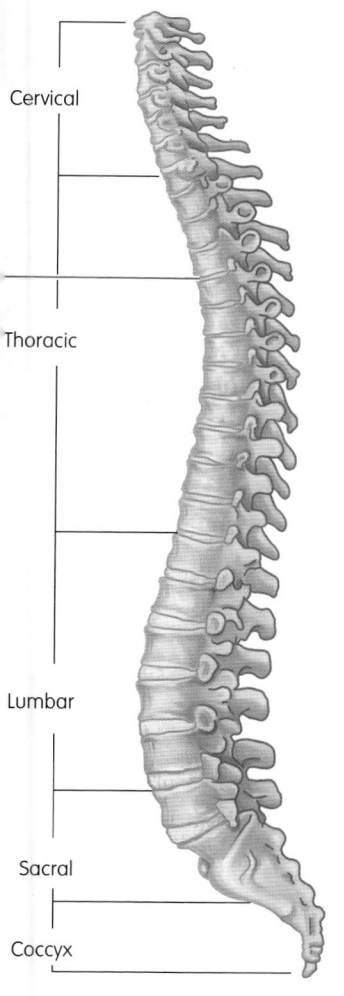

Cervical

Thoracic

Lumbar

Sacral

Coccyx

BRONZE

1. Copy the names of the major bones onto pieces of scrap paper. Then close this book and, in pairs or small groups, stick the labels in the appropriate places on a volunteer. When you have finished, check to see how many you got right.

2. Copy and complete the table below, identifying what type of bone each one is. Is it long, short, flat or irregular?

Bone	Type
Clavicle	Flat
Ulna	
Femur	
Patella	
Cranium	
Tibia	

3. Which sport-related occupations do you think require knowledge of the skeleton and bones? Try to come up with as many ideas as you can.

Functions of the skeletal system

The skeleton not only gives the body its shape, it performs five very important functions. These are: protection, movement, shape, support and blood production.

Protection

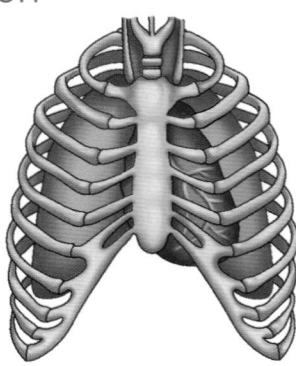

Some parts of the body are delicate and can be damaged easily. The skeleton helps to protect them by providing a shield around them. Examples of this are the ribcage and sternum, which protect the heart and lungs.

Movement

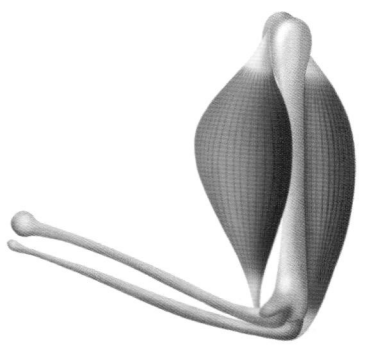

The bones of the skeleton give the muscles something to attach to. Muscles work by contracting and as they get shorter they pull on the bones. This action allows the body to move in a range of directions, particularly if the joint that attaches the bones is freely moveable.

Shape and support

Without the rigid framework that the skeleton provides, the body would be a mass of soft tissue. It gives the body its shape and also provides support, holding vital organs in place. For example, the shape of the vertebral column gives the body height and the ribcage supports the lungs.

Blood production

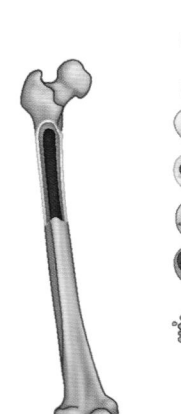

Some of the larger bones contain bone marrow. Red and white blood cells and platelets are formed in the marrow cavities. Some of the bones where this process takes place include the humerus, ribs and femur.

Remember:

FACT: The most delicate part of the body is the brain. The skull protects the brain and the vertebral column protects the spinal cord.

QUESTION: Male skeletons tend to be bigger than female skeletons but females usually have wider hips. Do you know why this is?

BRONZE

1. Design a poster illustrating the functions of the skeleton in relation to a sporting situation. It could show, for example, how the skull protects the brain during a rugby tackle.

Types of joint

A joint is a point where two or more bones meet. There are over 100 joints in the human body and they are classified by the amount of movement they allow. The three types of joint are: fixed, slightly moveable and freely moveable.

Where two or more bones meet, there is a layer of smooth cartilage that prevents them from rubbing against one another. Tough, fibrous straps, called ligaments, hold the bones at a joint in place. Ligaments are elastic to allow movement at the joints.

Fixed joints
Fixed (fibrous) joints, also known as immoveable joints, are located in areas of the body where movement is not beneficial. For example, the bones in the skull have fixed joints. The bones in fixed joints usually link together or overlap and are held together by tough connective tissue. Other examples of fixed joints are the pelvis and the fused joints in the sacrum.

Freely moveable, or synovial, joints
Freely moveable (synovial) joints are the most common type of joint found in the human body. They allow the bones at the joint to move freely.

Slightly moveable joints
Slightly moveable (cartilaginous) joints allow a small amount of movement. They are held together by tough ligaments and are connected by cartilage. The pads of cartilage between the vertebrae make the joints slightly moveable as they prevent the bones from jolting when a person runs or jumps. The joints between the ribs and sternum are other examples of slightly moveable joints.

A freely moveable or synovial joint, such as the knee joint, has the following main components:

Cartilage: there is a layer of smooth (also known as 'articular') cartilage that covers the ends of bones to form a cushion, which prevents the bones from rubbing.

Joint capsule: this is made of fibrous tissue and protects the joint by holding the bones together.

Connective tissue: such as tendons and ligaments. Tendons attach muscles to bones and ligaments are thick straps of tissue that hold bone to bone.

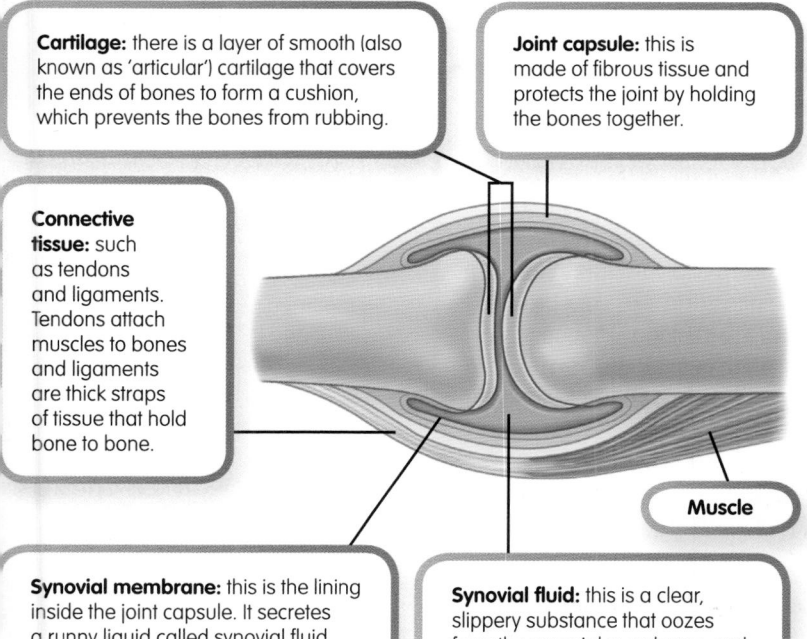

Muscle

Synovial membrane: this is the lining inside the joint capsule. It secretes a runny liquid called synovial fluid, which lubricates the joint.

Synovial fluid: this is a clear, slippery substance that oozes from the synovial membrane and oils the joint, preventing friction.

BRONZE

1. Copy and complete the paragraphs below, filling in the missing words using the words underneath:

There are _____ types of joint in the human body. _____ joints, also known as immoveable joints, allow no movement between the bones. Slightly moveable joints, such as those between the _____, allow sm\all movements.

_____ _____ joints, also known as synovial joints, are the most common joint found in the body and they allow _____ _____ in one or more directions. Synovial joints are unique as they consist of several components, including the synovial _____, which lines the joint _____. There is also a slippery substance called _____, which lubricates the joint to prevent friction.

synovial fluid	**capsule**	**three**	**movement**
membrane	**fixed**	**vertebrae**	**freely moveable**

SILVER

2a) How do synovial joints differ from other joints?

b) Identify the six most commonly used synovial joints in the body and name a sporting action that involves the use of each of them.

c) Choose one of your sporting actions and explain how the joint moves during the three phases of the action, during preparation, execution and follow-through. For example: When preparing to perform a chest pass in netball, the elbow joint is 'flexed'. The humerus is close to the radius and ulna in preparation for passing the ball horizontally. When executing the chest pass and releasing the ball the elbow 'extends' and the radius and ulna move away from the humerus. During the follow-through phase the elbow extends further as the ball is pushed away from the body and towards its intended target.

Synovial joints

The majority of joints in the body are freely moveable or synovial. There are several types of synovial joints in the body, allowing a range of movement possibilities. For example, the shoulder joint can move in more directions than the knee joint, yet they are both synovial joints. The range of movement depends on the shape and size of the bones at the joint and the ligaments that keep them in place.

Gliding joint: this type of joint allows a small amount of movement in all directions because the ends of the bones are flat and move in a gliding motion over each other. This type of joint is found in the small bones of the hands and feet.

Ball and socket joint: this is the most moveable joint in the body. The wide range of movement is made possible by a round-headed bone, which fits into a socket. Examples of this type of joint are the hip and the shoulder.

BRONZE

1. Research the six main types of synovial joint and provide an illustrated description of each one.

Condyloid joint: this joint has one bone that has a rounded bump on the end which fits into a hollow cavity on the other. Movement at this type of joint is similar to the movement that takes place at saddle joints. Examples of condyloid joints are those in the wrist and at the base of the skull.

Saddle joint: as the name of this joint suggests, the ends of the bones are shaped like saddles and they fit closely together. The movement range at this type of joint is forward and backward, and side to side. An example of this type of joint is the thumb.

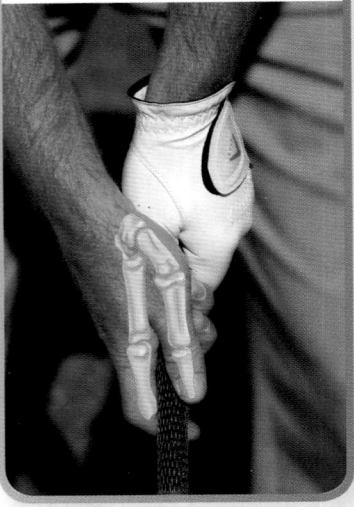

Hinge joint: this type of joint can only move in one direction and works in a similar way to a hinge on a door. The bones can move towards and away from each other as one bone has a pulley-shaped end that fits into a hollow in the other bone. Examples of this type of joint are the elbow and the knee.

Pivot joint: this joint only allows rotation. It consists of a cylindrical surface at one end, which rotates within a ring-like structure made of bone and ligament. This is similar to a wheel rotating around its axis. Examples of pivot joints in the body are the atlas and axis vertebrae in the neck, and the joint that attaches the radius to the ulna in the lower arm

SILVER

2. Choose two synovial joints. For each, draw or download images of four physical activities that require movement at that joint and then explain what is happening. Remember to:

- name the articulating bones
- name the type of synovial joint
- describe the movement that is taking place
- explain the ways in which the joint allows the movement to take place.

Movement at the joints

There are six different types of movement possible at joints.

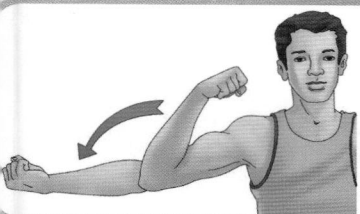

Flexion: This is when a joint is bent and the two bones either side come towards each other.

Extension: The joint is fully stretched out or straightened when it is extended.

Abduction: This is a sideways movement where a part of the body is taken away from the centre line of the body.

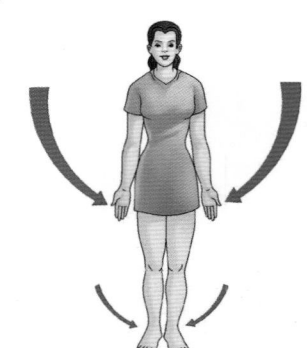

Adduction: This is the opposite of abduction, when a body part is moved towards the centre line of the body.

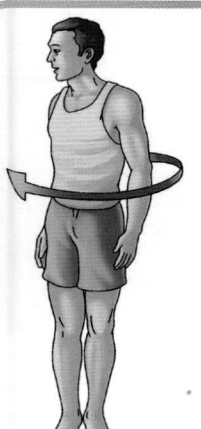

Rotation: This is a spinning or turning movement, where part of the body rotates around an imaginary axis.

Circumduction: This is when a bone or bones rotate fully around an axis to complete a full circle of movement

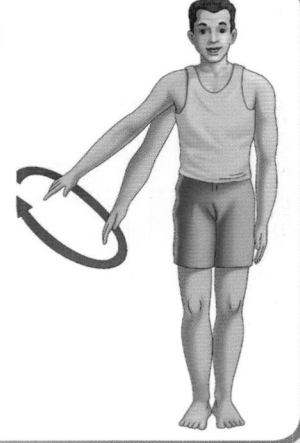

BRONZE

1. Copy and complete the table below, which shows the types of synovial joints in the left-hand column and the six different ways that joints can move across the top. Tick the appropriate boxes to show which movements occur at which joints.

	Flexion	Extension	Abduction	Adduction	Rotation	Circumduction
Ball and socket						
Hinge						
Pivot						
Saddle						
Condyloid						
Gliding						

SILVER

2. Add a sporting example to each box in the table above where you have a tick. For example, the front crawl arm action requires flexion (and extension) of the hinge joint at the elbow.

Remember:

Abduct means to take away from the centre line of the body.

Adduct means to bring toward the centre line of the body.

65

SPOTLIGHT on the skeletal system

BRONZE

Completing these activities will help you to achieve a **Pass** in your assignment.

1. Design a poster illustrating the different types of bones and their functions within the body.

2. Create a PowerPoint® presentation about the three main types of joint. Highlight the differences in the structure, location and movement possibilities of each type.

SILVER

Completing this activity will help you to achieve a **Merit** in your assignment.

3. Create a booklet about four different types of physical activity and the movement that takes place at two synovial joints during each.

The muscular system

Muscles come in a range of different shapes and sizes. The muscular system refers to **all** the muscles in the body; from the large muscles of the legs, to the small muscles of the hands and even the tongue (the only muscle in the body which is only attached at one end!).

The major muscles of the body

The major muscles of the body are used to produce the movements needed in sport, such as kicking a ball, running and throwing a javelin. All sportsmen and women should have a knowledge of the most important muscles in the body, and these are shown in the diagram below.

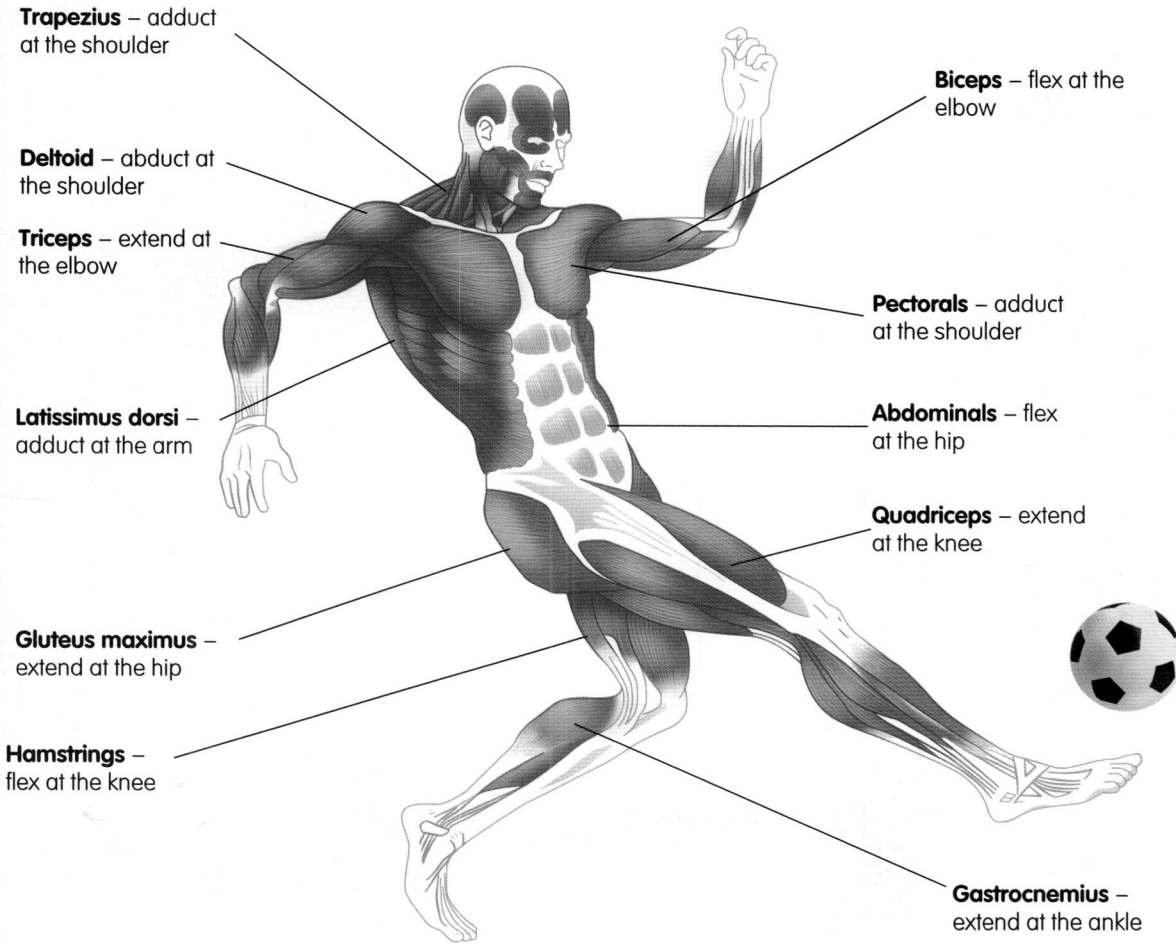

Trapezius – adduct at the shoulder

Deltoid – abduct at the shoulder

Triceps – extend at the elbow

Latissimus dorsi – adduct at the arm

Gluteus maximus – extend at the hip

Hamstrings – flex at the knee

Biceps – flex at the elbow

Pectorals – adduct at the shoulder

Abdominals – flex at the hip

Quadriceps – extend at the knee

Gastrocnemius – extend at the ankle

BRONZE

1. Copy the names of the major muscles onto pieces of scrap paper. Then close this book and, in pairs or small groups, stick the labels in the appropriate places on a volunteer. When you have finished, check to see how many you have right.

2. Design a circuit training session incorporating 12 stations, one for each of the major muscles in the human body. For example, you could use a triceps dip station to develop the triceps muscles.

3. Create a poster of a sportsperson in action, such as a gymnast performing a handstand, and label all the muscles that are working.

Types of muscle

Muscle tissue is made up of individual fibres and the characteristics of these fibres determine the type of muscle. You will, no doubt, be familiar with one type of muscle – skeletal muscle – but you may not have heard of the other two types: cardiac muscle and smooth muscle.

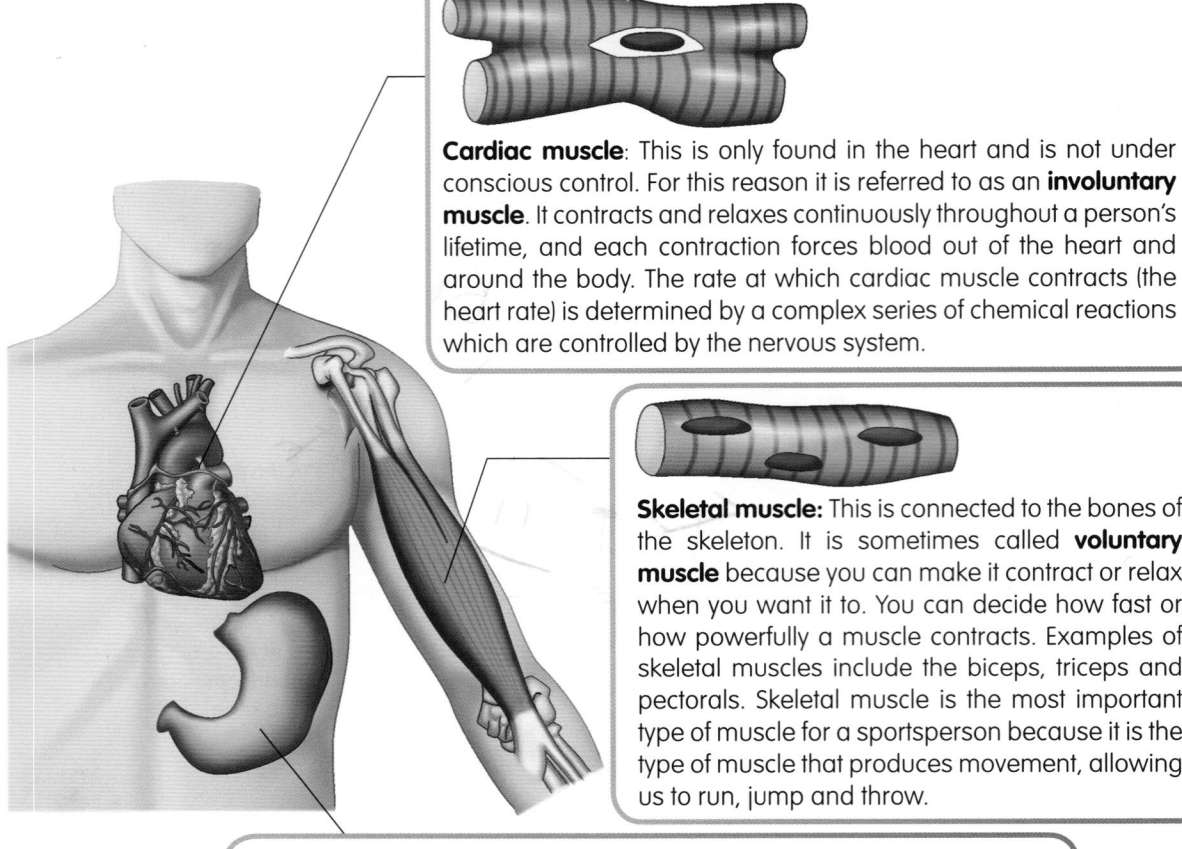

Cardiac muscle: This is only found in the heart and is not under conscious control. For this reason it is referred to as an **involuntary muscle**. It contracts and relaxes continuously throughout a person's lifetime, and each contraction forces blood out of the heart and around the body. The rate at which cardiac muscle contracts (the heart rate) is determined by a complex series of chemical reactions which are controlled by the nervous system.

Skeletal muscle: This is connected to the bones of the skeleton. It is sometimes called **voluntary muscle** because you can make it contract or relax when you want it to. You can decide how fast or how powerfully a muscle contracts. Examples of skeletal muscles include the biceps, triceps and pectorals. Skeletal muscle is the most important type of muscle for a sportsperson because it is the type of muscle that produces movement, allowing us to run, jump and throw.

Smooth muscle: This is found within the walls of hollow internal structures, such as blood vessels and throughout the intestines of the digestive system. It is also classified as **involuntary muscle** because, like cardiac muscle, we have no conscious control over it. Smooth muscle contracts like a wave pushing substances along, such as food through the intestines.

BRONZE

1. As an aspiring fitness trainer, you need to know about the different types of muscle so that you can design effective fitness training programmes for your clients. You have a basic knowledge of the names and locations of some of the muscles within the body, but you have decided that you need to develop your knowledge of the different types of muscle. Design a poster, which you can show to your clients, that:

- describes the three types of muscle
- gives an example of each type of muscle
- explains how each type of muscle is controlled.

2. Create a list of ten jobs that require knowledge of the three types of muscles. For example, a cardiologist.

Muscle fibre types

Muscles contract at different speeds depending on the movement required. For example, the quadriceps will contract quickly when sprinting and slowly when jogging. This change in the speed of the contraction is possible because each muscle is made up of hundreds (and sometimes thousands) of different fibres that can be divided into two categories: fast twitch muscle fibres and slow twitch muscle fibres. Sports coaches and other professionals in sport need to understand the difference between the two types of muscle fibre, so that they can help sportspeople to train correctly, and avoid fatigue and injury.

Slow twitch muscle fibres

Slow twitch muscle fibres are used in endurance events, such as the marathon or when jogging in football. They work aerobically, which means they need oxygen to produce energy. The oxygen is used to break down a substance called adenosine triphosphate (ATP), and this process releases the energy needed to make the muscle move. Myoglobin, a substance within the muscles, collects oxygen from the blood and transports it to the mitochondria, the engine rooms of the muscle fibres, where ATP is broken down.

Slow twitch muscle fibres:

- contract at a slow speed
- work aerobically and use oxygen to produce energy
- work at a constant pace for a long period of time
- become fatigued less quickly than fast twitch muscle fibres
- are red in colour.

Fast twitch muscle fibres

Fast twitch muscle fibres are suited to fast, explosive activities such as the 100m sprint and weightlifting. They are also needed in team sports when explosive power is required, for example, when jumping for a rebound in basketball. They work anaerobically, which means they do not require oxygen to produce energy. Instead, ATP is broken down by a substance called phosphocreatine (PC) which is stored inside the muscle cells. However, after a period of time a substance called lactic acid builds up, and this causes pain and stops the muscle working properly.

Fast twitch muscle fibres:
- contract at a high speed
- work anaerobically and do not need oxygen to produce energy
- produce very powerful contractions for a short period of time
- become fatigued very quickly
- are white in colour.

Each person has a mixture of both fast and slow twitch muscle fibres. However, some people have more of one kind of muscle fibre than the other, making them more suited to certain kinds of physical activity than others.

BRONZE

1. Compile a list of ten famous sportsmen and sportswomen. Rank them, placing the person you think will have the highest percentage of fast twitch muscle fibre at the top and the person you think will have the highest percentage of slow twitch muscle fibre at the bottom.

SILVER

2. As a fitness coach you need to be able to identify the predominant twitch muscle fibres used in different physical activities so that you can direct people to the activities that are most suited to their physiology. Copy and complete the following table, listing five activities that fit into each column, based on the predominant twitch fibre used for that activity. One example has been completed for you:

Fast twitch muscle fibres	Slow twitch muscle fibres	A mixture of fast and slow twitch muscle fibres
		Football

3. The government has expressed concern that not enough people are taking part in physical activities to maintain and/or improve their health. Design a circuit-training session that can be used to develop both of the twitch fibre types.

Muscles and movement

Our skeletal muscles contract to create movement but this movement is created by groups of muscles, not individual muscles, because muscles can only pull, not push. When several muscle groups contract in a coordinated pattern, the result is movement such as running, jumping and throwing that we see in sport.

Muscles working in pairs

When a muscle contracts it shortens in length and when it relaxes it gets longer. As a muscle shortens it pulls against the bone it is attached to, causing that bone to move. For example, as the biceps muscle shortens it pulls against the bones in the lower arm, creating movement at the elbow joint. This movement is known as a biceps curl. Then, because the biceps muscle is unable to straighten the elbow, the straightening movement is created by the triceps muscle, which contracts, shortens and pulls against the bones in the lower arm to straighten the arm again.

When a muscle pulls to create movement, it is called the **agonist** muscle or the **prime mover**. The partner muscle is called the **antagonist** muscle. In the example on the right, the biceps is the agonist when the elbow is bending and the triceps is the antagonist. When the elbow is straightening, the triceps becomes the agonist and the biceps the antagonist.

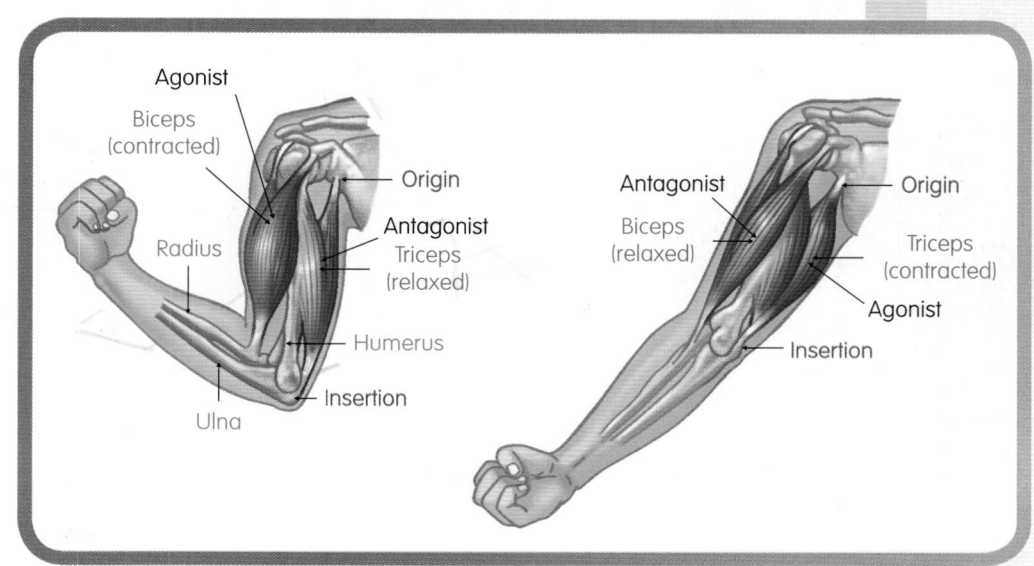

Agonist and antagonist muscles.

Types of muscle contraction

There are two different ways in which a muscle can work – **isometrically** and **isotonically** – and all movements in sport require a combination of both types of contraction.

Isometric contractions

Isometric contractions occur when a muscle that is working stays the same length. A good example of this takes place during a tug of war (assuming that the teams are evenly matched). The muscles of the arms, legs, back and shoulders are all working to pull the centre of the rope, and the opposing team, past the winning line; but because the other team is trying to do the same, the muscles in the body are working really hard without producing any movement. Try pushing against a wall and see how the muscles in your upper arms contract.

An example of isometric contractions.

71

Isotonic contractions

Isotonic contractions occur when a muscle changes length as it works. When a muscle shortens this is called a concentric contraction and when the muscle lengthens it is called an eccentric contraction. For example, when performing a press-up, the triceps muscle shortens as you push up from the floor – a concentric contraction takes place – causing the elbow to extend. As you lower yourself to the floor, with gravity pulling you down, the triceps muscle lengthens under tension and an eccentric contraction takes place. If the triceps muscle didn't contract in this way you would hit the floor face first! An eccentric contraction only occurs when the movement is being caused by an outside force, such as gravity or another person.

Remember:

When a muscle shortens it is called a **concentric contraction**.

When a muscle lengthens it is called an **eccentric contraction**.

A concentric contraction takes place in the triceps.

An eccentric contraction takes place in the triceps.

BRONZE

1. Group the main muscles of the body together in pairs. Look back at page 67 if you need to remind yourself of what these are.

2. Describe how the muscles move during a biceps curl. You may want to perform a biceps curl with your bag in your hand to help you feel the contractions. Remember to use the following words in your description:

- contracts
- relaxes
- shortens
- lengthens
- biceps
- triceps
- agonist/prime mover
- antagonist
- isotonic concentric contraction
- isotonic eccentric contraction
- isometric contraction.

SILVER

3. Copy and complete the table below, listing three physical activities for each type of muscle contraction and the muscles involved:

Muscle contraction	Physical activity	Muscles contracting
Isometric		
Isotonic concentric		
Isotonic eccentric		

SPOTLIGHT on the muscular system

BRONZE

Completing these activities will help you to achieve a **Pass** in your assignment.

1. Create a poster, to be displayed in a PE classroom, highlighting the major muscles in the body. You should ensure that the poster has a front and back view of the body.

2. Create a PowerPoint® presentation that describes the different types of muscle and the different ways that muscles move. You should include examples of physical activities with labelled pictures to support your text.

SILVER

Completing this activity will help you to achieve a **Merit** in your assignment.

3. Design a web page containing information on the muscular system. You should include a section about the three different types of muscular contraction and give an example of each contraction taking place in a different physical activity. Use pictures and diagrams to make your web page visually interesting.

GOLD

Completing this activity will help you to achieve a **Distinction** in your assignment.

4. Choose four different physical activities, such as a racket sport, a team sport, an athletics event and a gymnastics event. Then, for each activity, analyse the movements occurring at four different synovial joints, such as the shoulder, elbow, hip and knee joints. Try to make comparisons and explain differences between the four activities. For example, you might say that the flexion occurring at the elbow when throwing a javelin is similar to, but less pronounced than, the flexion of the elbow joint which takes place during a short throw-in in a football match. This is because the javelin throw requires more power.

Unit 4 assignment, part one

Background

As a physiotherapist at a Premier League football club you are responsible for ensuring that the players are always at their peak of physical fitness. You are often asked anatomy and physiology questions by the younger players and the club's manager has asked you to deliver a presentation on the skeletal and muscular systems after the next training session.

GRADING CRITERIA TO BE ASSESSED
P1, P2, P3, P4
M1, M2
D1

Task

Produce a presentation that can be delivered to a group of young sports players, which doesn't have to focus exclusively on football. Your presentation needs to cover all of the areas listed below.

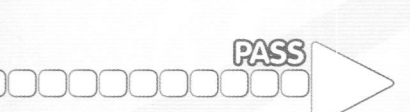

A description of the structure and function of the skeletal system (P1).

A description of the **three** different types of joint and movement possibilities (P2).

The names, types and locations of the major muscles (P3).

A description of the different types of muscle and how muscles create movement in the body (P4).

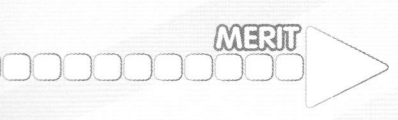

An explanation of the movement occurring at **two** synovial joints during **four** different types of physical activity. Use the same two joints for each of the four activities (M1).

Examples of **three** different types of muscular contraction relating to **three** different types of physical activity (M2).

An analysis of the musculoskeletal actions occurring at **four** synovial joints during **four** different types of physical activity (D1).

Tackling the assignment

The most obvious way to approach the task is to use an ICT presentation package such as PowerPoint®. However, if you do not have access to the necessary computer facilities, you can still put together an interesting presentation using large sheets of paper and card. The key is to be imaginative because your presentation needs to be engaging in order to encourage your audience to listen to what you are saying. You may even decide to ask someone to help you by demonstrating the various actions you refer to in your presentation.

That said, above all, it is important that you concentrate on the content of your presentation. There is no point having an interesting and engaging presentation if it fails because of a lack of appropriate content! Focus first on meeting the Pass criteria. Once these have been achieved, move on to the Merit criteria. Only once you have achieved the Pass and the Merit criteria should you move on to the Distinction section of the assignment.

Meeting the Pass criteria

BTEC Level 2 Firsts in Sport

Unit 4 assignment, part one　　　　　　　　　　　　　　**Lottie Commons**

> Clearly, Lottie has taken a sensible approach to meeting the criteria for the assignment. However, this piece of work does not yet fully meet the criteria for P1. It is missing some vital information because it does not describe the functions of the skeletal system (protection, movement, shape/support and blood production). With a little more effort and time, the piece of work could easily be developed to cover all of the criteria for P1.

STRUCTURE AND FUNCTION OF THE SKELETON

Number of bones in the skeleton

Types of bone:
- Long
- Flat
- Short
- Irregular

(The information below will accompany a series of headline slides such as that on left . I don't want my audience to be bored by too much reading.)

The human skeleton consists of 206 bones and the points at which these bones meet are called joints.

There are four types of bone in the body and these are classified according to their shape. They are long, flat, short and irregular (a term that is used to classify any bone that won't fit into the other three types). Each bone has a specific function:

Long: Used as levers to produce movement (such as the femur).

Short: Used for strength and weight bearing (such as the tarsal bones).

Flat: Used for protection (such as the ribs, which protect the lungs).

Irregular: Used to support and protect joints (such as the patella at the knee joint).

Meeting the Merit criteria

BTEC Level 2 Firsts in Sport

Unit 4 assignment, part one　　　　　　　　　　　　　　**Zak Johnson**

Notes:

When the body goes down towards the ground in a press-up, there is flexion at the elbow. The triceps contract eccentrically and the humerus moves toward the radius and the ulna.

The movement at the knee joint is different from the elbow, as the knee is fully extended throughout the movement to allow the legs to support the upper body as the press-up is completed. The quadriceps and the gastrocnemius contract isometrically as there is no movement of these muscles during a press-up, but they are still contracting.

> If Zak goes on to explain the movements occurring at two synovial joints in three other types of physical activity, he will have met the criteria for M1 because he has identified the main movements and muscular contractions that occur within this phase of a press-up.

	JOINTS	MUSCLES	CONTRACTION	MOVEMENT
PRESS-UP (Downward phase)	Elbow	Triceps	Eccentric	Flexion
	Knee	Quadriceps/ gastrocnemius	Isometric	Extension

> Zak could further improve his grade if he begins to explain which bones are articulating at each of the joints involved in the movement and gives a more detailed account of the muscular contractions that are taking place. This would enable him to work towards achieving D1.

Meeting the Distinction criteria

BTEC Level 2 Firsts in Sport

Unit 4 assignment, part one

Mary Jones

	JOINTS	BONES ARTICULATING	MUSCLES	CONTRACTION	MOVEMENT
PRESS-UP (Downward phase)	1. Elbow 2. Knee 3. Shoulder 4. Ankle	1. Humerus, radius, ulna 2. Femur, tibia, fibula 3. Scapula, clavicle, humerus 4. Tibia, fibula, tarsals	1. Triceps 2. Quadriceps, gastrocnemius 3. Deltoids, pectorals, trapezius 4. Peroneals (peroneus longus/ peroneus brevis)	1. Eccentric 2. Isometric 3. Eccentric 4. Isometric	1. Flexion 2. Extension 3. Abduction 4. Slight flexion
PRESS-UP (Upward phase)	1. Elbow 2. Knee 3. Shoulder 4. Ankle	1. Humerus, radius, ulna 2. Femur, tibia, fibula 3. Scapula, clavicle, humerus 4. Fibula, lateral malleolus, calcaneus	1. Triceps 2. Quadriceps, gastrocnemius 3. Deltoids, pectorals, trapezius 4. Peroneals (peroneus longus/ peroneus brevis)	1. Concentric 2. Isometric 3. Concentric 4 Isometric	1. Extension 2. Extension 3. Adduction 4. Slight flexion

Notes:

The four joints involved in the three phases of a press-up are the elbow, knee, shoulder and ankle. The elbow joint is a hinge joint, as is the knee, and the range of movement that is possible at each of these joints is flexion and extension only. The shoulder joint is a ball and socket joint at which there is a much greater range of movement, including abduction, adduction and circumduction. The ankle is a gliding joint, which has a wide range of movements. In fact, the ankle can perform all movement possibilities within a small range.

During the downward phase of a press-up, the elbow joint flexes, to lower the torso to the ground. This is controlled by an eccentric contraction of the triceps. During this phase, the angle between the humerus and the radius/ulna is decreased. The eccentric contraction (lengthening under tension) of the triceps is necessary to overcome the force of gravity pulling the body downwards.

During the upward phase of a press-up, the elbow joint extends (straightens) and this is caused by a concentric (shortening) contraction of the triceps. This increases the angle between the humerus and the radius/ulna, thereby lifting the body away from the floor.

Mary has successfully analysed the musculoskeletal actions occurring in one physical activity. She has explained, in detail, the muscles, bones, joints and types of contraction involved in the sporting action, and has also demonstrated a good understanding of the workings of the human body during this activity. If Mary was to provide another three examples to the same standard as the first one, she would achieve D1.

The cardiovascular system

There are three main components of the cardiovascular (CV) system:
- The blood: the medium for moving oxygen, nutrients and waste products around the body.
- The heart: the pump that forces blood to flow through the blood vessels.
- The blood vessels: the pipes through which the blood flows.

The heart

The heart is about the size of a closed fist and lies within the chest cavity just left of centre. The left-hand side of the heart is bigger than the right-hand side. The left-hand side needs to pump blood all the way around the body, whereas the right-hand side only pumps blood to the lungs, which are relatively nearby.

The heart is made up of four chambers. The top two chambers are called the **atria** and the bottom two are called the **ventricles**. The two sides of the heart are separated by the **septum**.

The heart contains valves that play an important role in preventing blood flowing backwards. On the right-hand side of the heart, situated between the right atrium and the right ventricle, is the **tricuspid valve**. On the left-hand side of the heart, the **bicuspid valve** is situated between the left atrium and the left ventricle. When the heart contracts and blood is ejected from the ventricles, it also passes through the **semilunar valves**. The semilunar valves are situated at the openings of the pulmonary artery and the aorta, which deliver blood to the lungs and the rest of the body, respectively.

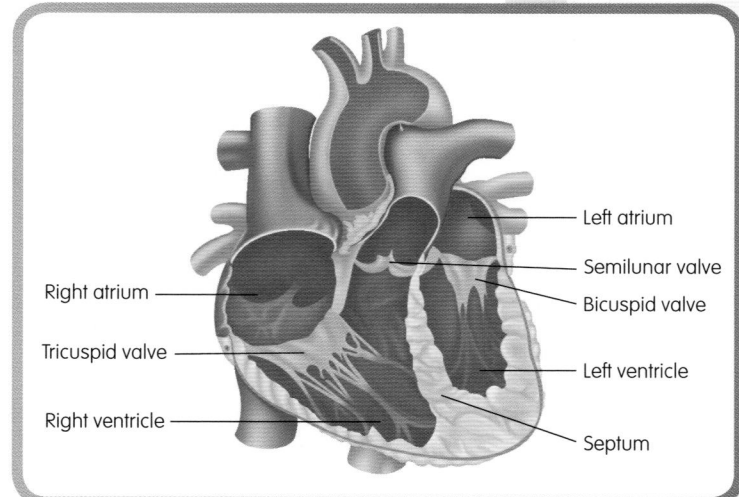

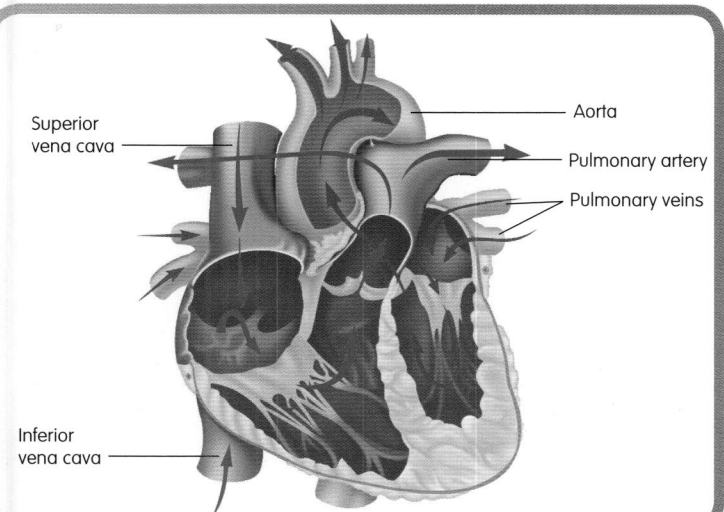

Essentially, the heart has four main blood vessels that link it to the lungs and the rest of the body. These four blood vessels allow the heart to operate as a dual-action pump that keeps a constant supply of oxygen entering the body and provides a way of expelling carbon dioxide. The four main blood vessels are:

- The **pulmonary veins** deliver oxygenated (oxygen rich) blood from the lungs to the left atrium of the heart. They are the only veins in the body that carry oxygenated blood; all the other veins carry deoxygenated blood.
- The **aorta** is the largest artery in the body and delivers oxygenated blood from the heart to the rest of the body.
- The **venae cavae** (superior and inferior) are the largest veins in the body and carry deoxygenated blood from all over the body to the right atrium of the heart.
- The **pulmonary artery** carries deoxygenated blood from the heart to the lungs. It is the only artery in the body that carries deoxygenated blood; all the other arteries carry oxygenated blood.

BRONZE

1. Present the information about the heart on this page in a more visual and interesting format. You could create diagrams, rhymes or even a rap. But, whatever you decide on, make sure you include the following:

- the anatomical make-up of the heart, the chambers
- the valves contained within the heart
- the major blood vessels leading to and from the heart.

Blood vessels

The structures of the three main blood vessels found in the body are different because they each carry blood under different conditions.

Arteries and arterioles

An artery has three layers: an outer layer of tissue, a muscular middle layer, and an inner layer of epithelial cells. Arteries are tough on the outside and smooth on the inside. They carry oxygen-rich blood away from the heart to all parts of the body, under high pressure and at high speed, so they have thick walls which can cope with this pressure. Arteries have a pulse, which allows us to monitor our heart rate. Arterioles are smaller versions of arteries that branch off to form a link between arteries and capillaries.

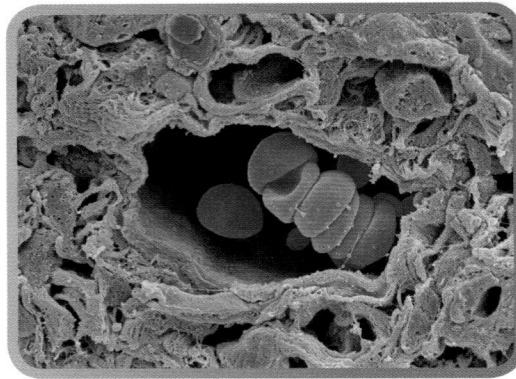
Red blood cells in an arteriole.

Veins and venules

Veins are similar to arteries but, because they transport blood at a lower pressure and at a slower pace, they are not as strong. Like arteries, veins have three layers: an outer layer of tissue, a middle layer of muscle, and a smooth inner layer of epithelial cells. However, each of these layers are thinner than those found in arteries. Veins transport deoxygenated blood back to the heart. They have valves to prevent blood flowing backwards, unlike arteries which do not have any valves. Venules are smaller than veins and provide a link between the capillaries and the veins.

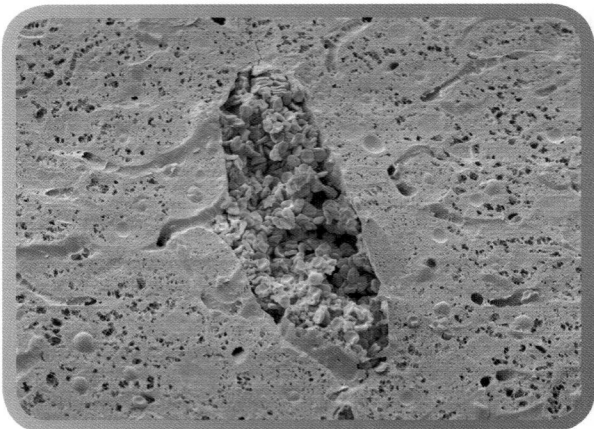
A vein in the liver, filled with red blood cells.

Capillaries

Unlike the arteries and veins, capillaries are very thin and fragile. They are only one cell thick and blood cells can only pass through them in single file. The exchange of oxygen and carbon dioxide takes place through the thin capillary wall. The red blood cells inside the capillary release their oxygen which passes through the wall and into the surrounding tissue. Meanwhile, the tissue releases its waste products, such as carbon dioxide, which pass through the capillary wall and into the red blood cells. This means that capillaries deal with both oxygenated and deoxygenated blood.

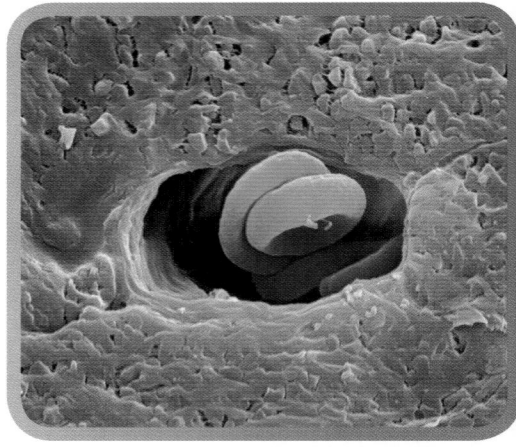
A capillary near the heart containing red blood cells.

BRONZE

1. Using the information on this page, draw a diagram showing the structure and function of the three main blood vessels. Your diagram should show why the arteries, veins and capillaries have different wall thicknesses and include information about the specific jobs that they do.

The function of the cardiovascular system

The main role of the cardiovascular system is to transport oxygen and nutrients to all the tissues in the body, and to remove waste products, such as carbon dioxide, from them.

The dual-action pump

The heart works as a dual-action pump, receiving blood and then forcing it into two different circulatory systems: the systemic circulatory system and the pulmonary circulatory system. Every time your heart beats it is completing one pump; one cycle of receiving and ejecting blood. When a doctor listens to your heart with a stethoscope they hear a 'lub–dub' sound for each beat, or pump, of your heart.

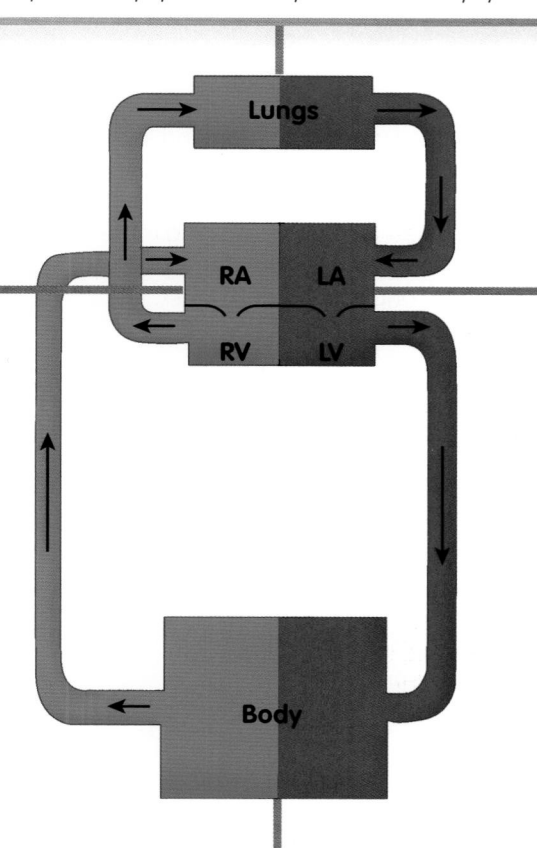

4. When the deoxygenated blood arrives at the lungs the capillaries, again, facilitate gaseous exchange but this time the carbon dioxide is passed from the blood to the lungs, and the oxygen is passed from the lungs to the blood. The capillaries are also therefore the point at which blood moves from the pulmonary circulatory system to the systemic circulatory system.

3. The **pulmonary circulatory system** deals with deoxygenated blood. It collects blood from which the oxygen has been used from around the body. It takes this blood to the right-hand side of the heart, and then on to the lungs where it unloads the carbon dioxide that it was carrying and picks up more oxygen. The veins and venules are part of the pulmonary circulatory system.

1. The **systemic circulatory system** deals with oxygenated blood. It moves blood that has been oxygenated by the lungs to the left-hand side of the heart and then from the heart to the rest of the body. The arteries and arterioles are part of the systemic circulatory system.

BRONZE

1. Devise an active, engaging and practical activity that your classmates can carry out to help them understand how the heart works as a dual-action pump. For example, you could mark out a diagram of the heart and the major blood vessels with cones, and ask your classmates to act as blood cells moving around the diagram.

2. When the oxygenated blood arrives at the body, the capillaries facilitate gaseous exchange. This is the name given to the process by which oxygen is passed from the blood to the organs, and carbon dioxide is passed from the organs to the blood. The capillaries are therefore the point at which blood moves from the systemic circulatory system to the pulmonary circulatory system.

Thermoregulation

The cardiovascular system is also responsible for helping to control the body's temperature. It does this by regulating the flow of blood to certain blood vessels. This process is known as thermoregulation.

Vasoconstriction

When you are cold, blood vessels adapt in order to retain warm blood deeper inside the body. This reaction, called vasoconstriction, is caused by smooth muscle around the blood vessels leading to the skin's surface. These muscles contract and thus restrict the amount of blood flowing to the skin's surface, where heat is lost from the body quite easily through conduction and convection. Your body cannot stop you from losing body heat in cold weather but it can use methods such as vasoconstriction to reduce the amount of heat lost.

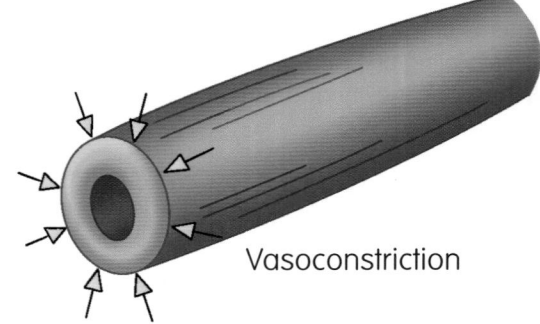
Vasoconstriction

Vasodilation

Vasodilation is the opposite of vasoconstriction and takes place when it is hot, to stop the body's temperature rising too high. The smooth muscles surrounding the blood vessels leading to the skin's surface relax, allowing more blood to reach its destination, so that heat in the blood can escape through conduction and convection.

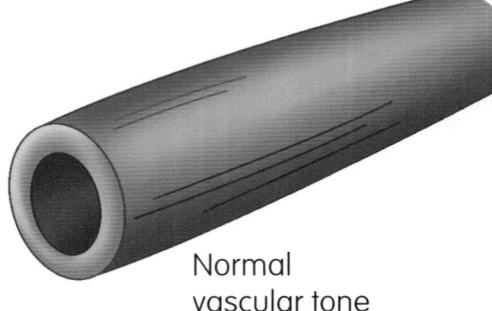
Normal
vascular tone

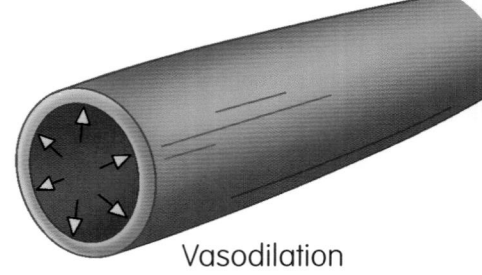
Vasodilation

BRONZE

1. Plan a five-minute presentation to describe the process of thermoregulation. Remember to mention:

- vasoconstriction
- vasodilation
- smooth muscles
- blood vessels
- the skin's surface.

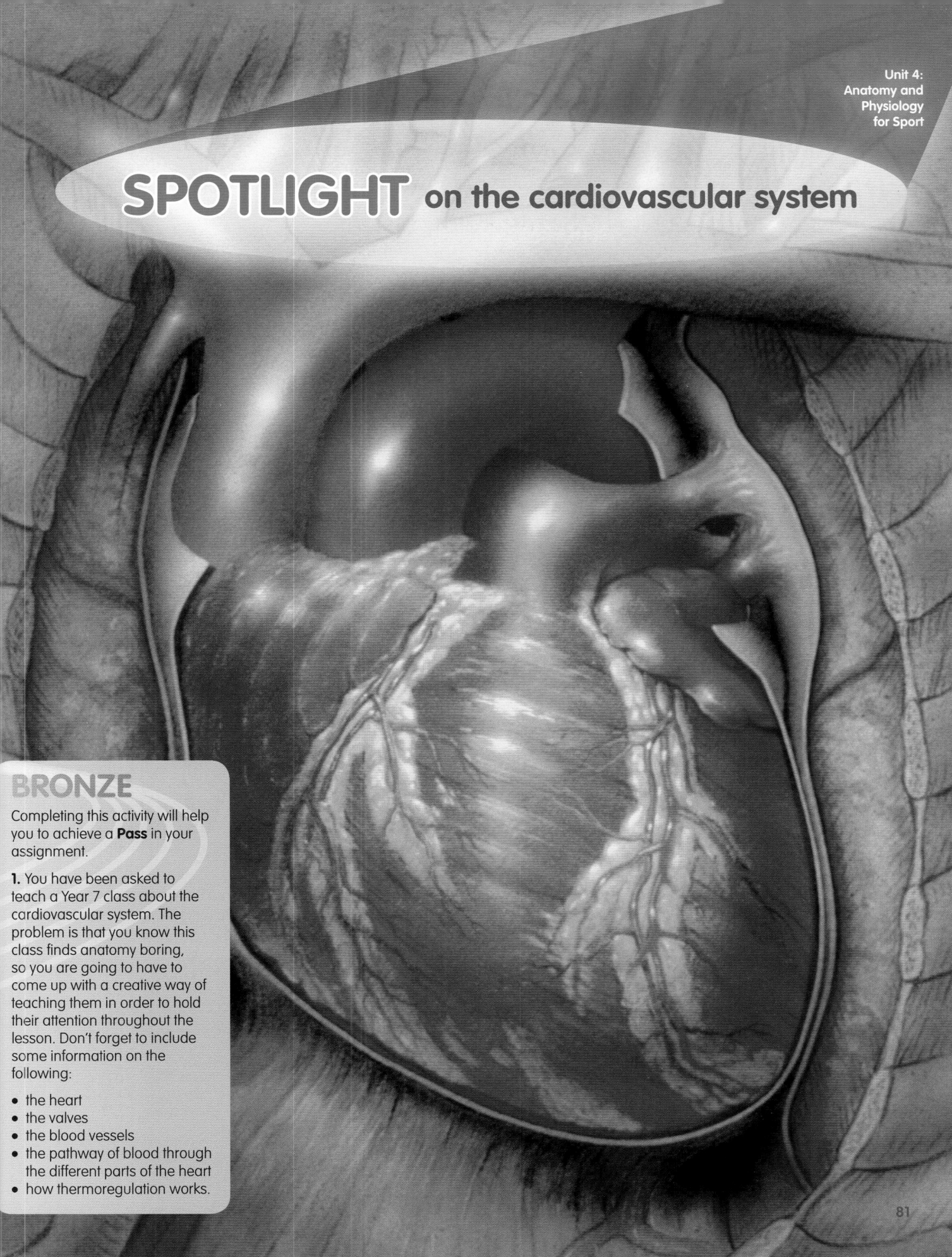

SPOTLIGHT on the cardiovascular system

BRONZE

Completing this activity will help you to achieve a **Pass** in your assignment.

1. You have been asked to teach a Year 7 class about the cardiovascular system. The problem is that you know this class finds anatomy boring, so you are going to have to come up with a creative way of teaching them in order to hold their attention throughout the lesson. Don't forget to include some information on the following:

- the heart
- the valves
- the blood vessels
- the pathway of blood through the different parts of the heart
- how thermoregulation works.

The respiratory system

The respiratory system works to bring about the actions in the body that we call 'breathing'. Breathing is the means by which oxygen from the air is brought into the body.

The structure of the respiratory system

The **trachea**, which is also known as the windpipe, carries the air we breathe towards the next part of the respiratory system, the bronchi.

The **epiglottis** is a flap of cartilage lying behind the tongue and in front of the entrance to the larynx (also called the voice box). This is the entrance to the respiratory system. It allows air to enter the respiratory system but stops food and liquids from doing so.

The **bronchi** are smaller tubes that branch off the trachea and carry the air towards the bronchioles.

The **lungs**.

The **bronchioles** are tiny tubes that are spread across the entire surface of the lungs. They carry the air towards the alveoli.

The **intercostal muscles**, found between the ribs, contract and relax during the breathing process.

The **diaphragm** is a sheet of muscle dividing the chest cavity and the abdominal cavity.

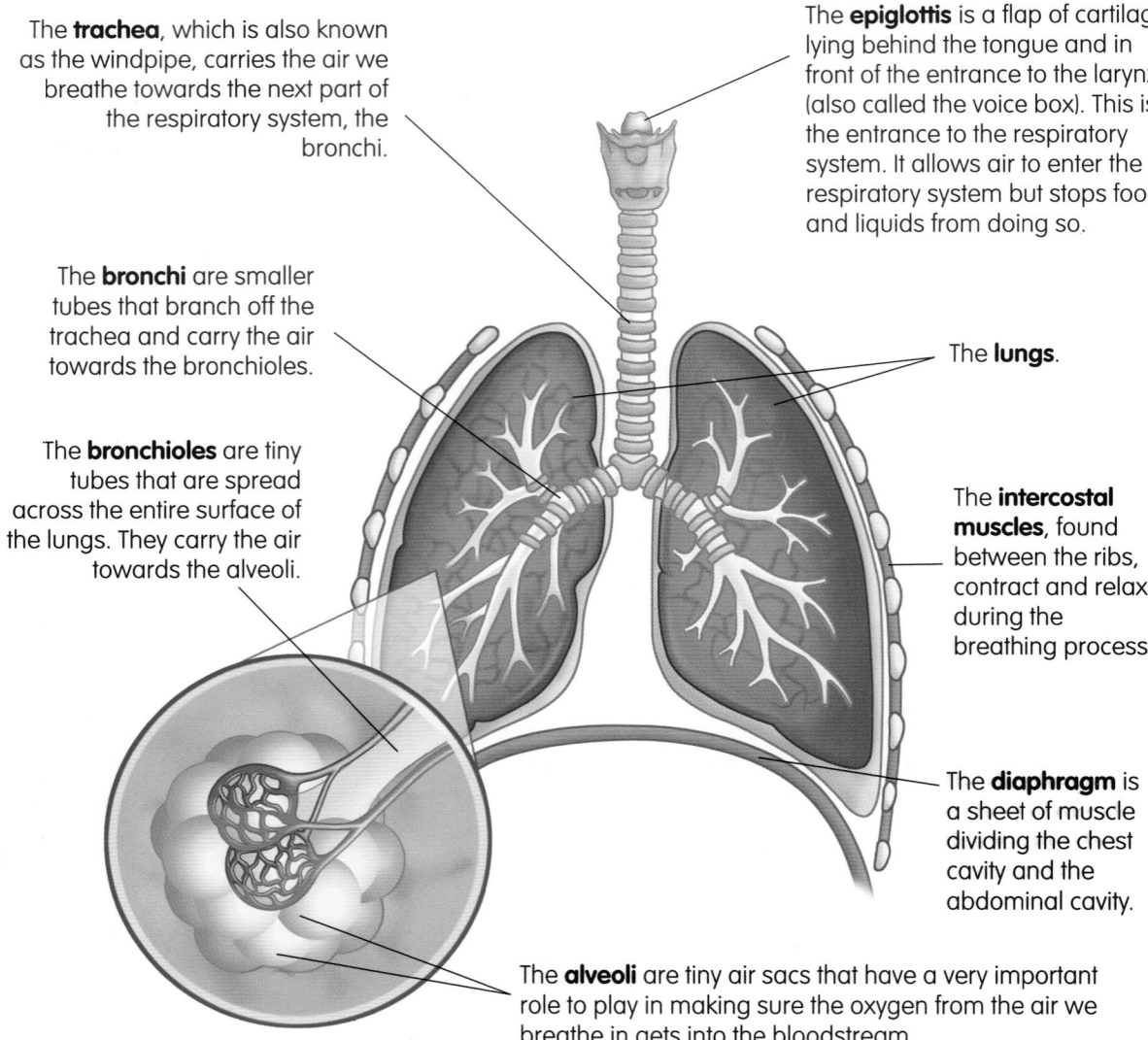

The **alveoli** are tiny air sacs that have a very important role to play in making sure the oxygen from the air we breathe in gets into the bloodstream.

BRONZE

1a) Explore your respiratory system by identifying the parts of your anatomy that allow you to breathe. Breathe in and out slowly, and write down what you can feel.

b) Compare your findings with a partner's. What similarities and differences have you noticed?

2. The respiratory system is often compared to an upside down tree. Draw a diagram to illustrate this comparison. Think about the different thicknesses of branches on a tree and what you find at the end of branches.

3. Read about the mechanics of breathing and gaseous exchange on page 83 and then:

a) Imagine you are an oxygen molecule. Using all your knowledge and understanding about the structure and function of the respiratory system, describe your journey from the air to the blood of a human.

b) Now imagine you are a carbon dioxide molecule and describe your journey from the blood of a human to the air.

The mechanics of breathing

When we breathe in our ribcage rises. This is because the intercostal muscles contract and lift the ribs upwards and outwards. At the same time as this is happening, the diaphragm – a large sheet of muscle separating the abdomen and chest area – contracts and flattens out. These two actions make the volume of the chest cavity bigger, reducing the amount of pressure in the lungs. The pressure in the air around us is now greater than the pressure in the lungs and air rushes into the lungs to equalize the pressure. We call this **inspiration**.

When the air pressure in the lungs is the same as the air pressure in the air around us, both the intercostal muscles and the diaphragm relax. This reduces the volume of the chest cavity and increases the pressure in the lungs. The pressure in the lungs is now higher than the pressure in the air around us and, therefore, air pushes out of the lungs to equalise the pressure. In other words, we breathe out. We call this **expiration**.

Gaseous exchange

We breathe so that gaseous exchange can take place. Gaseous exchange ensures that we get the oxygen which feeds our working muscles and organs into our blood. At the same time, it removes the carbon dioxide, which the blood has carried from the working muscles and organs, from our bodies. Gaseous exchange takes place at the alveoli in the lungs. There are millions of alveoli in the lungs; so many, in fact, that if you flattened them all out you would cover the area of half a tennis court!

The alveoli have capillaries running across them. These are the part of the cardiovascular system where the exchange of oxygen and carbon dioxide takes place. Because the walls of the alveoli are so thin, oxygen and carbon dioxide can move between the alveoli and the capillaries; that is, between the respiratory system and the cardiovascular system.

Diffusion is the term used to describe how molecules move from an area of higher concentration to an area of lower concentration. Oxygen and carbon dioxide can move between the alveoli and the capillaries because of diffusion.

- The concentration of the oxygen in the alveoli, which has just been breathed in, is higher than the concentration of the oxygen (in the blood) in the capillaries, which has been circulated around the body. Therefore, the oxygen molecules move from the alveoli to the capillaries; from the area of higher concentration to the area of lower concentration.
- The carbon dioxide moves in the opposite direction. The concentration of the carbon dioxide in the capillaries is higher than the concentration of the carbon dioxide in the alveoli, and so the carbon dioxide molecules move from the capillaries to the alveoli; from the area of higher concentration to the area of lower concentration.

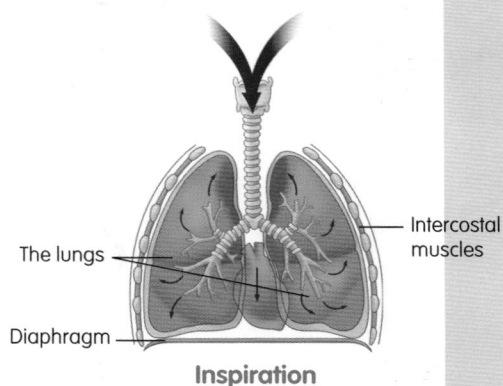

The lungs

Intercostal muscles

Diaphragm

Inspiration

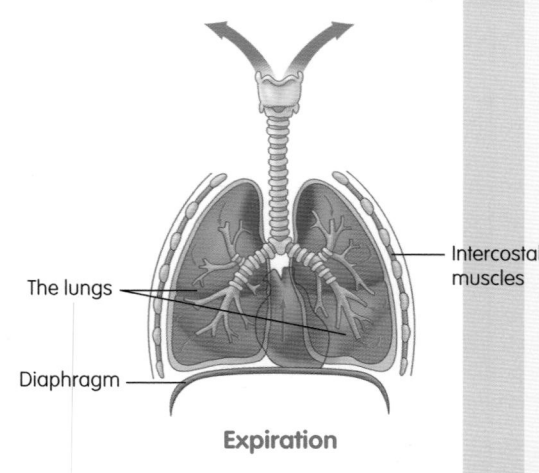

The lungs

Intercostal muscles

Diaphragm

Expiration

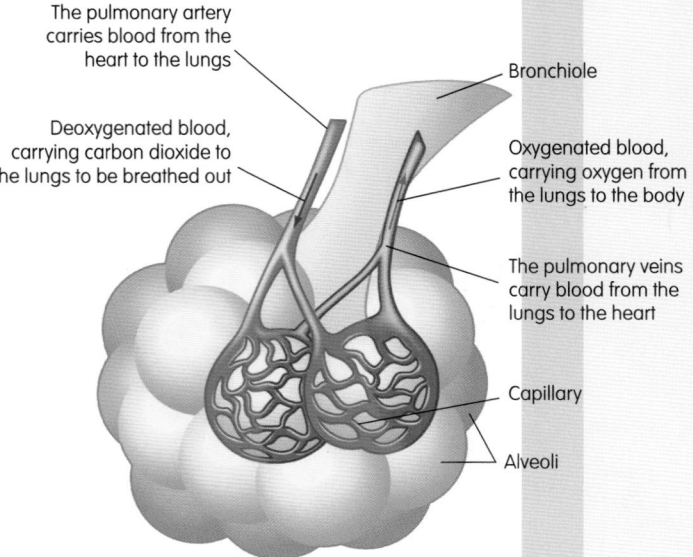

The pulmonary artery carries blood from the heart to the lungs

Deoxygenated blood, carrying carbon dioxide to the lungs to be breathed out

Bronchiole

Oxygenated blood, carrying oxygen from the lungs to the body

The pulmonary veins carry blood from the lungs to the heart

Capillary

Alveoli

The bronchiole and alveoli

SPOTLIGHT on the respiratory system

BRONZE

Completing this activity will help you to achieve a **Pass** in your assignment.

1. Build a model of the respiratory system. It should show:

- the structure of the respiratory system
- how we breathe
- how gaseous exchange takes place.

SILVER

Completing this activity will help you to achieve a **Merit** in your assignment.

2. In pairs, decide which of you is going to take on the role of the cardiovascular system and which of you is going to take on the role of the respiratory system. Then, using your hands and any other objects that you think might help you, show how the two systems work together to supply the body with oxygen.

GOLD

Completing this activity will help you to achieve a **Distinction** in your assignment.

3. The local rugby club has signed up for a six-week training programme at your local fitness centre and the head coach has asked that all players are provided with information on how the body's systems work. You have been asked to assist the fitness instructor by focusing on the cardiovascular and respiratory systems. The coach is very keen that the players understand how these systems operate, how they work together and how they have equally important roles in making them better, more efficient players. To ensure that this happens, you need to include clear, accurate examples in your presentation and run through various exercises that will develop the players' efficiency further. You will need to mention the supply of oxygen and the removal of carbon dioxide.

Unit 4 assignment, part two

Background

As a physiotherapist at a Premier League football club, you are responsible for ensuring that the players are always at their peak of physical fitness. The club's manager is concerned that some of the younger players are not fully aware of the importance of healthy cardiovascular and respiratory systems. He has asked you to produce a game, which can be played by the young players, that will improve their knowledge and understanding of the cardiovascular and respiratory systems.

Task

Produce a game, such as a board game or a quiz, that can be used to improve participants' knowledge and understanding of the cardiovascular and respiratory systems. The game should include:

GRADING CRITERIA TO BE ASSESSED
P5, P6
M3
D2

PASS

A description of the structure and function of the cardiovascular system (P5).

A description of the structure and function of the respiratory system (P6).

MERIT

An explanation of how the cardiovascular and respiratory systems work together to supply the body with oxygen (M3).

DISTINCTION

An evaluation of how the cardiovascular system and respiratory system work together to supply the body with oxygen and remove carbon dioxide (D2).

Tackling the assignment

This task gives you an opportunity to be creative. You may decide to introduce the cardiovascular and respiratory systems into the format of a popular board game, such as 'Monopoly', or a quiz show, such as 'Mastermind' or 'Who Wants To Be A Millionaire?'. Alternatively, you may come up with your own board game or quiz. The key is to ensure that your finished product satisfies all of the relevant criteria, showing the examiner that you understand the cardiovascular and respiratory systems, and not simply that you can produce an interesting game.

Most students find the best way is to develop a stepped approach, where the questions get more and more difficult. This way, early questions can be quite simple (satisfying the Pass criteria), and later questions can require the players to show in-depth knowledge (satisfying the Merit and then the Distinction criteria).

Meeting the Pass criteria

BTEC Level 2 Firsts in Sport

Unit 4 assignment, part two   **Kitty Bond**

Name of game: Hearts

Number of players: Two or more

Aim: To be the first player to make a completed model of the cardiovascular system

What is the model?:   The cardiovascular system model consists of the following components:

- 4 x heart chambers (left and right atrium, and left and right ventricle)
- 1 x body card
- 1 x lungs card
- 1 x aorta
- 1 x pulmonary artery
- 1 x pulmonary vein
- 1 x superior vena cava

Game play: There are three piles of question cards in the middle of the table (one pile on the cardiovascular system, one pile on the respiratory system and one wild card pile). Each player takes it in turns to choose a pile and is asked the question on the uppermost card in that pile. Players cannot choose the same pile twice in a row. If a player answers the question correctly, the card is placed on the bottom of the pile and the player receives a piece of their cardiovascular model. If the player answers incorrectly, the next person can attempt the same question for a bonus piece of the model. This continues around the players until either a player answers correctly or none of the players knows the answer. The winner is the first person to collect all the parts of the cardiovascular model and fit them together correctly.

Cardiovascular card

Name three components within the cardiovascular system other than the heart chambers?   (P)

Answer:

Any three from: veins, venules, capillaries, arteries, arterioles, blood, aorta, venae cavae, pulmonary arteries, pulmonary veins.

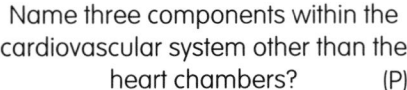

Questions: There are 90 questions in total, 30 for each pile. The cards are random in order, in that some are more difficult than others. The level of difficulty is shown on each card in brackets under the question (P = Pass, M = Merit, D = Distinction).

> The sample question clearly demonstrates the knowledge required to meet P5, although one sample question is not enough for me to award the full mark. To determine whether Kitty has met the criteria for both P5 and P6, I would need to see all the question cards.

> Kitty's work shows an excellent approach to meeting the criteria for the assessment. The game is likely to be enjoyable and competitive for those taking part but will also be very informative for the players, helping them to learn about the cardiovascular and respiratory systems.

Meeting the Merit criteria

BTEC Level 2 Firsts in Sport

Unit 4 assignment, part two   John Pearson

BODY IN SPORT TRIVIA
MERIT QUESTION

Name a site where gaseous exchange takes place and explain how this is an example of the cardiovascular and respiratory systems working together.

> The question is challenging and the answer is explained in enough detail to satisfy the criteria for M3.

BODY IN SPORT TRIVIA
ANSWERS

Gaseous exchange takes place between the alveoli and capillaries in the lungs. Alveoli are tiny air sacs with very thin walls that enable oxygen and carbon dioxide to pass into the capillaries, which also have thin walls that allow gases to pass through them.

The alveoli are part of the respiratory system and the capillaries are part of the cardiovascular system. Therefore, this is an example of how the two systems are working together.

> John will need to add further Merit questions to his quiz in order to fully demonstrate his understanding of how the cardiovascular and respiratory systems supply the body with oxygen.

Meeting the Distinction criteria

BTEC Level 2 Firsts in Sport

Unit 4 assignment, part two   John Pearson

BODY IN SPORT TRIVIA

DISTINCTION QUESTION

How does the cardiovascular system's structure allow it to function effectively with the respiratory system?

BODY IN SPORT TRIVIA

ANSWERS

The obvious point where the cardiovascular and respiratory systems meet is in the lungs, where the alveoli meet the capillaries. Gaseous exchange takes place because the capillaries have a wall thickness of only one cell, which allows gases and nutrients to pass through it. If the capillaries did not have walls one cell thick then gaseous exchange would not be possible.

> To meet the criteria for D2 it is vital that the way in which the cardiovascular system and the respiratory system work together is **evaluated** and not just explained. When you explain something you describe **why** something is like it is. When you evaluate something you **assess** how effective it is and what makes it effective/ineffective. The word 'because' is included in John's answer where he has evaluated what makes the process of gaseous exchange so effective.

> John should be able to meet the D2 criteria although more questions need to be developed that will encourage players to evaluate how the two body systems work together to supply oxygen to the body.

Unit 5: Injury in Sport

Types of injury

People who take part in sport and exercise are at risk of developing injuries. Injuries sustained by sports participants can be categorized into overuse injuries, also known as chronic injuries, and acute injuries.

Overuse injuries

Overuse injuries often occur when a sports performer pushes themselves hard over long periods of time and continuously puts the same muscles, bones and joints under pressure. Examples of this type of injury are:

- **Tendonitis:** The tendon becomes inflamed because lots of pressure is put on it. The tendon can become painful and movement in that area becomes uncomfortable. Tennis elbow and golfer's elbow are common names given to specific examples of tendonitis.

- **Shin splints:** Tiny fractures in the surface of the tibia cause pain and swelling. Shin splints are common in any sport involving running.

Acute injuries

Acute injuries are injuries which reach a crisis quickly. Acute injuries that occur as a result of sport and exercise include:

- **Fractures:** This is the word used to refer to broken bones. There are many types of fracture, but they are generally categorized as 'open' or 'closed'. With an open fracture, a fragment or fragments of bone pierce through the skin causing an open wound. A closed fracture happens when the bone is broken but does not penetrate the surface of the skin, so no wound is visible, other than swelling and bruising around the area.

- **Dislocations:** Two bones become separated or misaligned at a joint, causing deformity, intense pain and swelling.

- **Strains:** Strains occur when a muscle or tendon is overstretched or torn. A strain can cause pain, swelling and muscle weakness.

- **Sprains:** Sprains occur when a ligament is overstretched or torn. Sprains can cause pain, bruising and swelling.

- **Grazes:** A graze happens when a slight abrasion, or rubbing, of the skin causes the surface layer of the skin to come off, leaving the area raw and tender.

- **Bruising:** Bruises occur when the skin is banged or bumped and tiny blood vessels are broken causing the area to become red or purple as it fills with blood.

- **Concussion:** This is a mild brain injury caused by a blow to the skull. Concussion can cause temporary unconsciousness, a headache and a loss of short-term memory. Vomiting and nausea are also common.

- **Spinal injuries:** The spinal cord is damaged, causing reduced movement and sometimes paralysis. Spinal injuries can occur following a blow to the back. For example, a bad fall in gymnastics could result in a spinal injury.

- **Blisters:** Blisters occur when an area of soft skin is rubbed, for example, when rowing. A sac of fluid builds up beneath the surface of the skin, causing pain and discomfort.

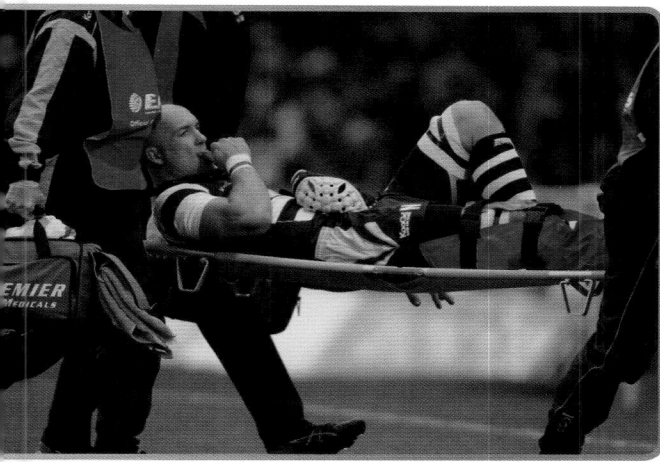

...han Budgett of Bristol is stretchered off with a suspected broken leg in a ...by union match.

French rugby player Yannick Jauzion sporting a bruised eye.

American footballer Michael Lewis is helped from the field while suffering from concussion.

Footballer Kevin Davies looks down at his dislocated finger.

Wales' Lee Byrne receives treatment for what could be a sprained ankle.

BRONZE

1. Discuss, with a partner, which sports performers are most likely to suffer from overuse injuries and why.

2. For each activity in the table below, name an acute injury that participants may suffer:

Sport	Acute injury
Football	
Rugby	
Tennis	
Netball	
Swimming	

Causes of injury

There are many different factors that can cause sports performers to become injured. These factors are often categorized into two types: intrinsic and extrinsic. Intrinsic factors, also known as personal factors, are directly related to the performer. Extrinsic factors relate to the surroundings of the performer.

Intrinsic injuries

Intrinsic injuries occur when an athlete becomes injured as a direct result of taking part in sport. Typical intrinsic injuries include both acute injuries (such as sprains, strains, grazes, bruising, blisters and fractures) and overuse injuries (such as tendonitis and shin splints) because they can either happen suddenly or build up over a period of time.

Intrinsic injuries can be caused by sports performers overusing their bodies during training or in competition. Overuse often takes place when an athlete puts too much pressure on themselves by suddenly increasing the frequency or duration of their training.

Ensuring that the intensity of the activity being undertaken is suitable for the athlete is vital in preventing injury. A performer should make sure that the intensity of their training sessions increases slowly, 'loading' the body according to the pressure it can handle. However, injuries can occur if an athlete 'overloads' their body and puts it under intense pressure; for example, a sprinter who normally works at 50 per cent of their maximum speed suddenly increases to 80 per cent of their maximum speed. Performers are likely to overload when they return to sport after a forced break, for example, if they have been ill. They do not realize that their body has taken a step backwards in terms of fitness and train too hard, too soon on their return.

It is important for sports performers to have good alignment because poor alignment can put a strain on the body and can lead to intrinsic injuries. If an athlete has poor balance, they may put more weight on one foot than they do on the other, causing discomfort and eventually injury. Therefore, it is important that an athlete maintains good posture when training and performing, making sure that they keep a straight back to avoid injuries and/or strains.

In order for part of the body to move, the relevant muscles and bones need to work together as a series of levers. A lever consists of the following three components:
• The pivot (or fulcrum): the point about which the lever rotates.
• The load: the force applied by the lever.
• The effort: the force applied by the user of the lever system.

If the lever is not balanced, for example, if the load is too heavy or the effort is not great enough, an intrinsic injury such as a sprain, strain or even a fracture may occur.

Gravity, the force exerted on the body by the Earth, and resistance, the force that resists the movement of an object, can also have a negative impact on the body when taking part in sports activities. Both can put undue pressure on the joints and muscles, which may result in an intrinsic injury.

Preventing intrinsic injuries

There are ways in which sports performers can try to avoid intrinsic injuries. These include:

- Warming up before training or competition. A warm-up is a vital part of preparing the body for exercise and should consist of three phases: pulse raising, stretching and joint mobilization.
- Following a training schedule designed specifically for the sports performer, which is appropriate to their age, ability, gender and medical condition. Children, in particular, should not be overloaded when training because their bodies are not yet fully developed.
- Ensuring that they wear the correct clothing and footwear for their sport. For example, football boots are worn to prevent a player from slipping because they help to grip the ground as the player moves around.

Warming up properly and wearing the correct clothing are crucial to preventing intrinsic injuries.

Extrinsic injuries

Extrinsic injuries are caused by external factors and not by the sports performer themselves. For example, an extrinsic injury may occur if a force, caused by an opponent or a piece of equipment, comes into contact with a performer. The impact of the force can cause many different injuries, including fractures, concussion, dislocation and spinal injuries.

Tackling in sports such as rugby often leads to extrinsic injuries.

Preventing extrinsic injuries

There are ways in which sports performers can prevent extrinsic injuries. These include:

- Adhering to the rules. Some rules are designed to prevent injuries from occurring and if participants adhere to these rules the risk of injury will be greatly reduced.
- Using the correct equipment. Some equipment is designed to help prevent injuries from occurring, particularly in contact sports where collisions are more likely to happen. For example, shin pads help to minimize the risk of lower leg and ankle injuries in football.
- Ensuring that risk assessments have been carried out. These are a preventative measure, to assess the potential hazards of any given activity or location. Once it has been assessed, plans can be put into place to make the activity or area safe.

Types of illness

When participating in sport it is important that performers recognize the potential threat posed by illness. Not only are some illnesses associated with sports participation but careful consideration should also be given to what effect illness may have on a performer should they become unwell during training or competition.

The following illnesses are associated with sports participation and should be monitored closely when sport or exercise is undertaken:

- **Asthma:** Asthma is a respiratory disorder that affects the lungs. When someone suffers an asthma attack the air passages to the lungs become narrow and normal breathing becomes difficult. Symptoms of asthma include shortness of breath, wheezing, coughing and chest tightness. Asthma attacks can be very mild but they can also be life-threatening.

- **Heart attack:** Heart attacks occur when the blood vessels that supply the heart with blood become blocked. This can be caused by a build up of cholesterol, which makes it difficult for the blood to pass through. Symptoms of a heart attack often include chest pain, sweating and shortness of breath.

- **Viral infection:** A viral infection, such as flu, is caused by the presence of a virus in the body. Any part of the body can be affected by a viral infection and most antibiotics do not help with the symptoms. These symptoms can vary but may include a high temperature, nausea and tiredness.

- **Hypoglycaemia:** Hypoglycaemia occurs when there is a low blood sugar level in the body. People who suffer from diabetes can also suffer with hypoglycaemia. Symptoms include sweating, weakness and confusion.

Fact:

Although some sports, such as swimming, are said to be beneficial for asthma sufferers, this is not the case with one particular type. Exercise-Induced Asthma, or EIA, is a condition that can occur after several minutes of vigorous aerobic exercise. People who suffer from EIA should ensure that they warm up before they exercise and gradually increase the intensity of their activity.

BRONZE

1. Discuss the possibilities of the illnesses above occurring as a result of physical activity. Which people are most at risk of suffering from these illnesses during physical activity?

SILVER

2. What does EIA stand for and how can this affect a sports performer? What should people who suffer from EIA do to ensure that it does not affect their performance?

SPOTLIGHT on injury and illness

SILVER

Completing this activity will help you to achieve a **Merit** in your assignment.

2. Select one of the injuries you researched for Question 1, and create a poster describing the injury and how it can be caused in a sporting context.

BRONZE

Completing these activities will help you to achieve a **Pass** in your assignment.

1a) Choose two injuries and one illness associated with sports participation, and find out as much as you can about them.

b) Find a partner and act out the injuries and illnesses you have chosen. Your partner has to guess what they are.

Risks and hazards

A hazard is different from a risk. A hazard is anything that could potentially cause harm or injury to a person. A risk is the likelihood of harm or injury actually occurring. When planning a sports session, the teacher, coach or leader needs to ensure that all hazards are kept to a minimum and, if any minor hazards cannot be eliminated, that they are pointed out to participants. They must also assess the risk of injury or harm coming to the participants, and do everything they can to reduce that risk. Teachers, coaches and leaders should make every effort to keep participants safe from harm and injury.

BRONZE

1a) Look at the picture above and identify as many hazards as you can. There are ten to find.

b) Categorize each hazard you have identified, as to whether there is a high, medium or low risk of it causing harm or injury to the players.

2. Identify the hazards and risks associated with a sporting area in your school or college. It could be an indoor basketball court or a synthetic pitch.

Risks and hazards from people

Risks and hazards from people are those created by the participants taking part in a sport or physical activity. They include:

Inappropriate warm-up or cool-down: Failing to warm up or cool down properly increases the risk of a performer sustaining an injury. A warm-up should include three phases: a cardiovascular phase that raises the heart rate and gets the blood flowing quicker, a stretching phase that improves the flexibility of the muscles, and a joint mobilization phase that loosens and increases the range of movement at the joints. A cool-down should have two phases: a gentle aerobic phase, which gives the heart a chance to gradually slow down before returning to its resting rate and the muscles a chance to relax, and a stretching phase, which stops the build up of lactic acid in the muscles and helps to prevent immediate cramping or soreness the following day.

Physical fitness: Being physically fit can help reduce the risk of injury because the body is better prepared for any high impact or strenuous demands placed on it during physical activity.

Physique

Overtraining

Arsenal's Eduardo suffered a horrific leg break following this tackle from Martin Taylor of Birmingham City in February 2008.

Alcohol: Drinking alcohol before taking part in sporting activities can be very dangerous for the participant and others. It can have many negative effects that include:
- loss of control, including the ability to concentrate, react quickly and maintain good balance
- increased fatigue, which in turn affects the level of performance
- masking pain that may be indicating that injury is taking place
- increased heat loss.

Food: Eating food during physical activity is not generally advisable because it can cause a decline in performance, and may lead to indigestion, a stitch or even choking.

Chewing gum: Gum should not be chewed during physical activity because it could be swallowed and cause choking.

Jewellery: Jewellery should not be worn when taking part in sporting activities because it can potentially cause injury to the wearer and others around them. For example, if a basketball player is wearing a bracelet an opposing player could get their finger caught in it while attempting to steal the ball.

Technique and skill level: Participants with poor technique and a low skill level are more likely to suffer from injuries than participants with good technique and a high skill level, particularly in higher risk sports such as climbing and skiing. Poor technique when taking part in activities such as weightlifting can also result in injuries like back problems, sprains and strains.

Behaviour of other participants: When a sporting activity involves other people, for example, when you are playing a team game, it is important that the other participants do so responsibly and safely. Injuries can be sustained when opponents perform dangerous tackles or behave in other inappropriate ways.

BRONZE

1. Carry out research and then write two short paragraphs describing why 'physique' and 'overtraining' present a risk and a hazard to people.

Risks and hazards from equipment

Risks and hazards from equipment are the risks and hazards related to something we are using or wearing during sporting activity.

- **Inappropriate clothing and footwear:** Wearing the wrong clothing and footwear, or clothing or footwear that doesn't fit properly, can dramatically increase the risk of injury in many sports. For example, in football, wearing the wrong studs on wet surfaces can result in serious – but avoidable – injuries if players slip and fall into one another.

- **Lack of protective clothing or equipment:** Failing to wear the correct protective clothing or to use the correct protective equipment can make a participant vulnerable to injury. In football, shin pads protect the tibia, which can be on the receiving end of significant kicks and blows because tackling is one of the main methods of intercepting the ball.

- **Playing surfaces:** Playing surfaces must be checked prior to a sporting activity to make sure that play is safe, the surface hasn't been damaged, there is nothing for participants to trip over or slip on, and that there are no other dangerous objects – such as stones – that could come into contact with the participants and injure them. It is more important to check outdoor playing surfaces carefully but indoor playing surfaces should also be checked every time they are used.

- **Faulty or damaged equipment:** All equipment must be checked before it is used. If it is faulty or damaged it can cause serious injury to the participant using it or any people nearby. For example, playing with a tennis racket that doesn't have a suitable grip can injure a player's hand, as the racket could slip around causing blistering, and it can injure people nearby if it flies out of the player's hand and hits a spectator.

SILVER

1. Carry out research into the protective clothing and equipment used in a sport of your choice. Then, write no more than 200 words explaining why it minimizes the risks and hazards involved with taking part in that sport.

Risks and hazards from the environment

Risks and hazards from the environment are those risks and hazards that are all around us.

- **Cold weather:** During cold weather it is important that participants try to stay warm and dry because heat loss increases when we are cold and damp. Several layers of thin clothing are better than one thick heavy one, and are also easier to add or remove when exercising. The thin layers help trap heat in and reduce the amount that escapes. In very cold weather it is also advisable to wear a hat because as much as 50 per cent of total body heat can be lost from the head and neck. If the body's core temperature drops below an acceptable level you will suffer from hypothermia, which, if not treated, can lead to death.

- **Rain:** Rain can lead to flooding and muddy pitches, which increase the risk of slipping and, therefore, the risk of injury.

- **Hot weather:** Taking part in sporting activities in hot weather can increase the risk of injury to the performer. It is harder for the body to cool itself down in hot weather, which can lead to heat stroke or heat exhaustion and even death. Participants are also at risk of sunburn. Taking in lots of fluids is essential in hot weather and staying out of the midday sun is advisable.

There are many different risks associated with climbing in cold weather.

GOLD

1. This page details some of the risks and hazards associated with the environment but there are others. Research another environmental hazard and give a detailed account of why participants are at risk from this whilst taking part in sport.

Rules, regulations and legislation

Whether you are taking part in sport at a competitive level or simply enjoying sport as a pastime with friends, there are rules, regulations and legislation in place to protect you from injury.

Put simply, rules are statements of what you are and are not allowed to do in a given situation. Rules can be formal or informal. Formal rules, for example, rules that are introduced by a governing body of a sport, are often called regulations. Legislation is the name given to rules and regulations that have been made into law by the government of a country.

Organizational rules

Organizational rules are rules that are specific to a particular sport, location or venue that is being used. For example, the rules of rugby say that a player must not jump a tackle being made because this could lead to injury for both the player jumping and the player making the tackle. Similarly, if playing on certain surfaces, such as AstroTurf®, participants may not be permitted to wear many types of football boots. This is because wearing studded boots on a surface that does not safely cushion the studs can injure the wearer and can also damage the playing surface, which is extremely costly to repair.

Legislation

The Health and Safety at Work Act 1974
All workers have a right to work in places where risks to their health and safety are properly controlled. Your employer is responsible for health and safety, for making sure you aren't hurt while you are doing your job and that you don't get ill because of your job, but it is also your responsibility to look after your own health and safety.

Management of Health and Safety at Work (Amendment) Regulations 1994
These regulations require employers, including self-employed people, to ensure that risk assessments have been carried out so that employees and people associated with a business or a place of work are adequately protected. These regulations cover a wide range of scenarios, including those relating to young people and expectant mothers, and imminent or serious dangers.

Control of Substances Hazardous to Health (COSHH) 2002
Using chemicals or other hazardous substances at work can put people's health at risk, so this law requires employers to control exposure to hazardous substances and protect both employees and others who may be exposed to them to prevent ill health.

Health an[d]
What

All workers have a right to work in
controlled. Health and safety is abov
Your employer is responsible for hea

What employers must do for you

1 Decide what could harm you in your job and the precautions to stop it. This is part of risk assessment.

2 In a way you can understand, explain how risks will be controlled and tell you who is responsible for this.

3 Consult and work with you and your health and safety representatives in protecting everyone from harm in the workplace.

4 Free of charge, give you the health and safety training you need to do your job.

5 Free of charge, provide you with any equipment and protective clothing you need, and ensure it is properly looked after.

6 Provide toilets, w and drinking wa

7 Provide adequate facilities.

8 Report injuries, dangerous incide our Incident Cor
0845 300

9 Have insurance in case you get h or ill through we hard copy or ele the current insu where you can e

10 Work with any o or contractors sh workplace or pre employees (such workers), so that health and safety

Your health and safety representatives:

Other health and safety contacts:

HSE

Health and Safety (First-Aid) Regulations 1981
These regulations require employers to provide adequate and appropriate equipment, facilities and personnel to enable first aid to be given to employees if they are injured or become ill at work. These regulations apply to all workplaces, including the self-employed and those with fewer than five employees.

Safety of Sports Grounds Act 1975
Following a number of major accidents at sports grounds it became clear that the structure and management of these venues needed to be controlled. This Act placed the control with local authorities and the Fire Safety and Safety of Places of Sports Act 1987 made it a duty of local authorities to enforce the Act.

The Children Act 2004
This Act supports the government's Every Child Matters programme, which was designed to ensure that all organizations involved in safeguarding children – including district councils, Primary Care Trusts, Youth Offending Teams and schools – work together to improve the well-being of all young people.

ed to know

eir health and safety are properly
hurt at work or ill through work.
must help.

If there's a problem

1 If you are worried about health and safety in your workplace, talk to your employer, supervisor, or health and safety representative.

2 You can also look at our website for general information about health and safety at work.

3 If, after talking with your employer, you are still worried, phone our Infoline. We can put you in touch with the local enforcing authority for health and safety and the Employment Medical Advisory Service. You don't have to give your name.

HSE Infoline:
0845 345 0055
HSE website:
www.hse.gov.uk

Fire safety
You can get advice on fire safety from the Fire and Rescue Services or your workplace fire officer.

Employment rights
Find out more about your employment rights at:
www.direct.gov.uk

Following the Hillsborough disaster, various new rules, regulations and legislation were introduced.

BRONZE
1. Choose a sport or physical activity that you take part in regularly. Then, write down as many rules and regulations as you can think of, which have been designed to control the way you behave and protect you from injury.

SILVER
2. The Hillsborough disaster occurred on 15 April 1989, when 96 Liverpool fans were crushed to death on the terraces of Sheffield Wednesday's stadium. Find out as much as you can about the Hillsborough disaster, and the Taylor Report that followed, and explain the health and safety rules, regulations and legislation that were introduced as a result.

SPOTLIGHT on risks and hazards in sport

BRONZE

Completing these activities will help you to achieve a **Pass** in your assignment.

1a) You are leading a 30-minute lesson for a lower-attaining Year 7 class. Decide what activity the students will do and produce a checklist of the risks and hazards associated with the activity.

b) Which rules, regulations and legislation relating to health, safety and injury in sports participation should you make sure you are following during the lesson?

SILVER

Completing this activity will help you to achieve a **Merit** in your assignment.

2. To achieve a Merit it is important not just to describe or list information but to explain how or why it is relevant. Revisit your answer to Activity 1 and make sure that:

• you have explained why the risks and hazards you have identified might cause injury

• you have explained how the rules, regulations and legislation you have listed apply during the lesson.

GOLD

Completing this activity will help you to achieve a **Distinction** in your assignment.

3. Design an information leaflet for new students at your school, detailing why participants in sporting activities are at risk of injury, what is done by teachers and what can be done by students to minimize the risk of hazards.

Unit 5 assignment, part one

Background

Your school or college is due to hold a sports day for Year 6 students from the local primary schools and you have been asked to assist in the preparations for the event. Planning such events needs to be done very carefully as health and safety is of paramount importance. Everybody involved in the planning and delivery of the sports day needs to be aware of the potential hazards, common injuries and any preventative strategies that can be used, as well as the rules, regulations and legislation that apply to the event.

Task

Prepare an informative document to be given to the teachers from the local primary schools that clearly identifies the potential hazards, common injuries and any preventative strategies that can be used at the sports day, as well as the rules, regulations and legislation that apply to the event. Your document can be presented in any format you wish and should include:

> GRADING CRITERIA
> TO BE ASSESSED
>
> P1, P2, P4, P5
> M1, M3, M4
> D1

PASS

A description of four different types of injuries associated with sports participation and their underlying causes (P1).

A description of two types and signs of illnesses related to sports participation (P2).

A description of six risks and hazards associated with sports participation (P4).

A description of four rules, regulations and legislation relating to health, safety and injury in sports participation (P5).

MERIT

An explanation of why certain injuries and illness are associated with sports participation (M1).

An explanation of the risks and hazards associated with sports participation (M3).

An explanation of four rules, regulations and legislation relating to health, safety and injury in sports participation (M4).

DISTINCTION

A detailed account of why participants are at risk of injury whilst taking part in sport (D1).

Tackling the assignment

One way to approach this assignment is to create a web page that illustrates the risks and hazards associated with a school sports day. You could include links to video footage of hazardous situations (making sure you include two people-related risks and hazards, two equipment-related risks and hazards, and two environment-related risks and hazards), with information about how to prevent injuries from occurring in each situation. Your web page should also include a section on the rules, regulations and legislation that apply to the event, and the ways in which participants can ensure that they are followed.

Meeting the Pass criteria

BTEC Level 2 Firsts in Sport

Unit 5 assignment, part one   Caroline Walker

People factors

Inappropriate warm-up and/or cool-down

If students do not warm up or cool down properly they are at risk of injury and that is a hazard. They could pull a muscle or even break a bone if their body is not coping or is straining because they have not stretched properly. A good warm-up consists of mobility, flexibility and cardiovascular exercises. A cool-down needs to be very slow and simple, for example, an easy jog and a few stretches.

Physical fitness

Students who are not physically fit or prepared are more likely to get an injury. Students need to be aware that they should only push their bodies as far as their physical fitness will allow. For example, your body will not be able to cope with the intense training required to play a full season of football if you did not train in the break between the end of the last season and the beginning of the new season.

Physique

A student's physique has an impact on how well they perform in different sports. For example, if somebody has quite a big build then they are probably more suited to shot-put or discus, and if they have a much smaller build they may be better at sprinting or long-distance running.

> The web page shows a sound understanding of what risks and hazards are associated with people, but P4 does require a description of six risks and hazards associated with sports participation, and there is also no mention of risks and hazards associated with either the environment or equipment. So more work is needed for Caroline to meet P4.

> Using a table to meet the criteria for P4 is a very good way of setting out the work because the description is clearly given next to each risk factor identified.

> More attention could be given to linking the risks and hazards closely with the scenario, and also the specific effects of the risks and hazards mentioned on the students that are taking part in the Year 6 sports day.

Meeting the Merit criteria

BTEC LEVEL 2 FIRSTS IN SPORT

Unit 5 assignment, part one   Luke Norton

Commentary

As you can see from this footage, the students overseeing the long jump have not fully taken into account the risks that the participants are vulnerable to. As competitor number one begins the run up, there are two students walking across the run-up track. This is a people-related hazard because they may cause the competitor to trip or fall as he runs past them. Also, at the pit end of the run-up track, the students overseeing the event have not moved the rake to a safe distance away from the landing area. This could result in a serious injury if a competitor landed on the rake. It is also important to remember that anyone taking part in the long jump could sustain an injury because the event involves taking off with great force, travelling through the air and then landing, and an awkward landing is highly possible.

> Luke has started this piece of work off very well. The video clips show clear practical scenarios that capture the risks and hazards, which are then explained through the commentary.

> A little more work is needed to ensure the work is of Merit standard, especially when it comes to explaining the common injuries that may be sustained. Luke has explained why long-jumpers might sustain injuries but not described what those injuries might be. To achieve a Merit, the link between the injury and the sporting activity needs to be made clearer.

Meeting the Distinction criteria

BTEC Level 2 Firsts in Sport

Unit 5 assignment, part one   Kaushil Khimasia

Environment hazards

Lightning is a serious hazard and can result in dreadful consequences. Unless football is being played at professional level, most matches take place in the middle of a field. If there is a storm during a match, everyone, including the spectators, is at great risk of getting struck by a bolt of lightning because they could be the first things it will strike. Being struck by lightning is very rare, but it does occur and can result in critical injury and death. Usually, all football matches are abandoned if a storm begins, for the safety of the players, managers and spectators.

Heavy rain can be hazardous. It makes the football pitch wet and slippery, which can cause the players to fall and injure themselves. If the rain is torrential, matches can be abandoned because the pitch can develop big puddles that stop the ball being played along the ground. Also, visibility becomes poor, which can result in players running into each other and poorly timed tackles. These conditions can easily result in players getting injured. It's not often a football match gets abandoned but, if it is, heavy rain is often the cause.

Injuries

There are many injuries that can be sustained while playing football but the most common are as follows:

- **Cuts, bruises and grazes:** These are the most common injuries and you rarely come off the pitch without at least one of them. Anything from tackling, marking or being hit by the ball can result in a cut, a bruise or a graze. They aren't very painful and can be treated easily. These injuries can be sustained at any level in football.
- **Pulled muscles:** Pulled muscles can easily be sustained if an appropriate warm-up has not been done. If the muscle has not been warmed up or stretched properly and you play a physical sport like football, it can put too much pressure on the muscle, which causes it to pull and makes you feel pain. Not doing an appropriate warm-up isn't the only cause of a pulled muscle but it does make the injury more likely. Pulled muscles can be sustained at any level in football.

> Kaushil's detailed account is starting to demonstrate his in-depth knowledge and understanding.

> Increased attention could be given to linking the risks and hazards more closely with the scenario. He should also describe the specific effects of the risks and hazards mentioned on the students that are taking part in the Year 6 sports day.

> Kaushil has demonstrated that he is able to produce a detailed account of how a poor warm-up can result in a pulled muscle but, in order to meet the criteria for D1, he needs to add to this information. He needs to explain how certain actions in sport can bring about injuries to specific parts of the body. For example, a hamstring injury can be sustained if a sprinter does not warm up adequately and then attempts to run the 100m sprint.

Procedures and treatment

Anyone who takes part in sport is at risk of becoming ill or injured. It is, therefore, important that all participants are equipped to deal with any situation should it arise. They should be aware of who to contact in the event of an accident or emergency, and how to protect both themselves and the casualty when something happens.

Procedures for dealing with minor injuries or illnesses
Minor injuries or illnesses can be dealt with on-site by a qualified first aider. If there is no qualified first aider on-site, the casualty should be made comfortable, kept warm and advised to see a first aider or GP at their earliest convenience.

Assess the situation
In any accident or emergency situation there are always risks and hazards to consider. So, before approaching an injured person you must survey the surrounding area for potential dangers. Do not, under any circumstances, put yourself in danger to help someone else as you may end up as a casualty too and that isn't helping anyone! However, if you see that there is something you can safely do to minimize further risk to the casualty and other people in the nearby area, do it. Then, when it is safe to approach the injured person, do so.

Assessing the injury or illness
Before implementing the correct procedure you need to assess the injury or illness. Is it a minor injury or illness, like a sprain, strain, cut or stomach upset? Or is it a major injury or illness; is the casualty unconscious or dehydrated?

Procedures for dealing with major injuries or illnesses
Major injuries or illnesses should be initially assessed by a qualified first aider, who will call an ambulance. The paramedics may then decide to take the casualty to hospital, where they will be seen by a triage nurse and then, if necessary, a doctor or even a surgeon.

Methods of providing reassurance

It is vital that a casualty is constantly reassured and that the first aider and other people on the scene remain calm. Even if the casualty is unconscious, they should be spoken to and told that help is on its way. The casualty should be made as comfortable as possible and encouraged to remain calm themselves. A positive, firm and comforting attitude will reassure an injured or ill person without causing them further distress. Again, the casualty should be kept warm until help arrives. If the casualty is under 16, the parents should be contacted to make them aware of the events that have occurred.

Reporting the incident

Following an accident or injury, it is important to complete a clear and accurate record of the events. The list below summarizes what is typically needed on an accident report form:

1. Who the casualty is and their personal details.
2. The location, date and time of the incident.
3. Details of the incident, including any injuries sustained.
4. The treatment or recommended treatment for the casualty.
5. The personal details of the person completing the form.

Dialling 999 or 112

The emergency services need to know detailed information about the incident and the casualty. When you speak to them:

1. Specify which emergency service you require: ambulance, fire brigade, police or coastguard.
2. Give the name and contact number of the person making the call.
3. Tell them where the incident happened.
4. Give details of the person affected and explain exactly what happened.
5. It may also be useful to give directions and information about how the site of the incident can be reached.

Different types of casualty

An important factor in being able to deal with a situation is being capable of identifying and catering for the particular needs of the casualty. Casualties usually fit into one of three possible categories and should be treated accordingly:

- Adult: an adult is a person who is over the age of 18. You do not need to obtain consent from anyone other than the adult themselves to treat an adult for an illness or injury.

- Child: a child is someone who is under the age of 18. Parental consent is usually required before a child is treated for injury or illness.

- Person with specific needs: this type of casualty will have their own individual requirements depending on their existing disability or illness. Examples of a person with specific needs include someone with diabetes, epilepsy, or a physical or mental disability.

Minor injuries

The following injuries may be classified as 'minor'. It is unlikely that they will require emergency medical attention and can, therefore, usually be treated at the scene of the injury by a qualified first aider.

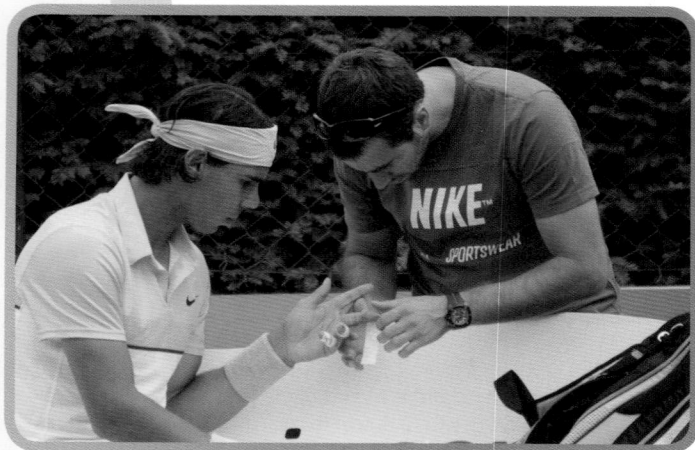

Rafael Nadal receives treatment for a finger injury.

- **Bruise:** Apply a cold compress, such as an ice pack, to the bruised area immediately after the injury is sustained. After 48 hours, a warm compress may then be applied to help the discolouration to fade.
- **Graze:** Wash the affected area with clean water to remove any dirt and then dry it with a clean, sterile pad. If the graze is bleeding, this can be stopped by applying pressure to the wound. Grazes usually heal quite quickly and no further treatment is required.
- **Sprain/Strain:** Sprains and strains are both treated using the 'RICE' method:
  R = REST (Rest the injured area.)
  I = ICE (Apply an ice pack to the affected area.)
  C = COMPRESSION (Apply gentle but substantial pressure to the injury.)
  E = ELEVATION (Raise the injured body part above the level of the heart.)
- **Cramp:** Muscle cramps occur when the muscle has been overstretched or the person has lost a lot of fluid, possibly as a result of sweating. The treatment for muscle cramp is to rest the affected muscle(s), apply an ice pack to the area and perform gentle stretches.
- **Shin splints:** This overuse injury can be treated by applying ice to the affected area and resting the leg. The leg may also be raised to allow the blood to flow away from the site of the injury.

Minor illnesses

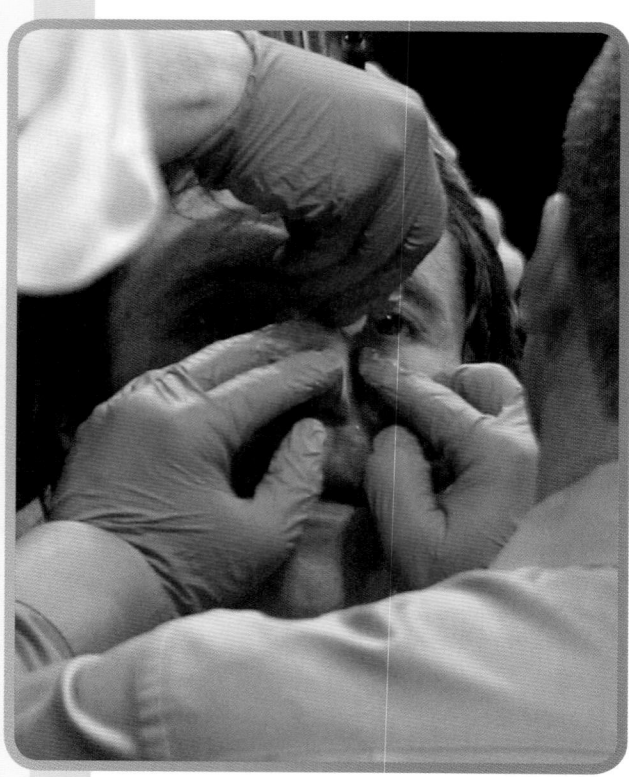

Steve Nash of the Phoenix Suns receives treatment for a nosebleed during an NBA game.

Many minor illnesses do not require medical attention and can be treated by the individual themselves. However, it is important that you do not take part in sport or physical activity if you are suffering from a minor illness, because you could make the condition worse.

- **Cold and flu:** There is no cure for the common cold or flu, but the symptoms can be eased by drinking lots of fluids, consuming plenty of vitamin C and taking paracetamol to help keep your temperature low.
- **Hayfever:** Hayfever is an allergy to certain particles, such as dust mites, pollen and pollutants. The symptoms of this can be eased by taking an antihistamine. People who suffer from hayfever should avoid contact with the irritants that cause them to feel unwell.
- **Nose bleed:** This type of bleeding usually stops quickly without any treatment. However, the flow of blood can be slowed if the person sits down, leans forward with their mouth open and pinches their nose just below the bone for approximately ten minutes. If the bleeding doesn't stop, this process can be repeated for another ten minutes. If the bleeding still doesn't stop, medical advice should be sought.
- **Stomach upset:** Often referred to as diarrhoea and sickness, a stomach upset usually clears up after a few days. In the meantime, drink plenty of fluids and avoid eating until your stomach has settled.

Major injuries

The following injuries are classed as major injuries and generally require the casualty to seek urgent medical assistance.

- **Head, neck and spinal injuries:** Any delay in dealing with head, neck and spinal injuries could result in permanent damage to the brain or nervous system.
- **Unconsciousness:** When you are unconscious you may still be able to hear noises around you, so it is vital that a casualty is reassured while waiting for an ambulance.
- **Airway obstruction:** If the brain is starved of oxygen, even for a short period of time, the cells begin to die. This could result in permanent brain damage or even death.
- **Fractures and dislocations:** Hospital treatment is required for fractures and dislocations. Some broken bones will need to be placed in a cast to aid recovery and, if a joint is dislocated, the bones will need to be put back into place by a suitably qualified medical professional.

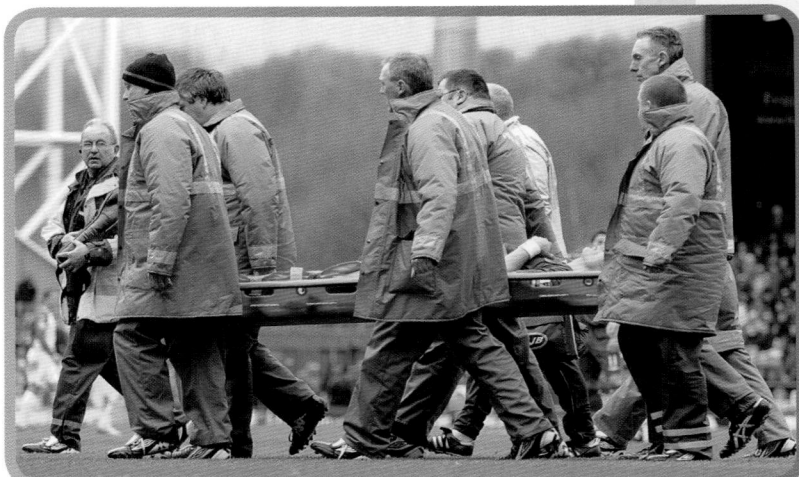

Erik Edman of Wigan Athletic is stretchered off with cruciate ligament damage in March 2008.

- **Uncontrolled bleeding:** When an artery is severed, the blood that escapes is pumping out at an immense speed. The bleeding may be stemmed by applying pressure to the area and raising the body part above the level of the heart while you wait for the ambulance.
- **Respiratory problems:** Severe breathing difficulties caused by an injury to the lungs or ribcage must be dealt with quickly and efficiently. Injuries such as a punctured lung can occur as a result of sports participation and the casualty may need an operation to repair the damaged organ.

Major illnesses

Major illnesses require urgent medical attention and include:

- **Heart attacks:** A heart attack occurs when one of the blood vessels supplying the heart becomes blocked. It is vital that this blockage is removed as soon as possible in order for the casualty to recover.
- **Strokes:** A stroke can happen suddenly if the supply of oxygen to the brain is interrupted. People who suffer from a stroke will need hospital treatment, so it is essential that an ambulance is called as a matter of urgency.
- **Severe asthma attacks:** On occasions, the rescue inhalers that asthmatics use are not sufficient and an asthma attack may become more severe. In such cases, sufferers will need hospital treatment.
- **Hypothermia:** A person may suffer from hypothermia if they are subjected to extremely cold or wet weather.
- **Heat exhaustion/heat stroke:** High temperatures can be very bad for our bodies. Heat exhaustion can occur when the body temperature rises above 37°C and the symptoms are headaches, sweating, vomiting, tiredness and light-headedness. Cold drinks and rest in a cool, shaded area will usually help a casualty to recover

A man with hypothermia is rushed to hospital after completing the Maldon Mud Race in 2003.

from heat exhaustion. However, heat exhaustion can quickly become heat stroke if it isn't treated. Without medical attention, heat stroke can cause organ failure, brain damage and even death.

- **Dehydration:** When the body loses one per cent or more of its weight in fluid, dehydration may occur. It can be mild, moderate or severe depending on the amount of fluid lost. Someone who is suffering from dehydration may feel thirsty, tired and dizzy. Severe dehydration should be treated in hospital.

SPOTLIGHT on procedures and treatment

BRONZE

Completing these activities with support from your tutor will help you to achieve a **Pass** in your assignment.

SILVER

Completing these activities without support from your tutor will help you to achieve a **Merit** in your assignment.

1. Work with a partner to role-play the scenarios below. Take it in turns to be the casualty.

a) You are playing football in the school playground at lunchtime and your friend sprains his ankle. What do you do?

b) A boy collapses after colliding with an opponent in a game of rugby. His leg hurts very badly and he cannot stand up. What do you think is wrong? What will you do to help?

c) You are part of a netball team and you have an important match this afternoon. Your friend, who is a very good player and a vital part of the team, arrives at your house so that you can travel to the match together. She has a temperature, is shivering and has a headache, but is determined to play. What do you think is the matter with her and what do you do?

d) You are playing golf on a very hot day. You have been out on the course for several hours and your opponent has started to complain that they are thirsty and dizzy. What is the matter with them and what should you do?

Unit 5 assignment, part two

Background

Over the course of a term, three students are injured or become ill at your school:

1. During a game of football a boy has fallen close to a goalpost and is now lying on his side, not moving. He is wearing a goalkeeper's shirt and there is a football nearby. There is no response when you call out to him but also no visible signs of injury.
2. A girl collapses while warming up for her sprint event at sports day. She is conscious, but gasping for air and unable to speak. Her face is red and she is wheezing.
3. During a competitive game of tennis, a boy trips when running backwards to reach and return a shot. He falls awkwardly and yells in pain. There is a bone sticking out of his leg just beneath the knee.

Task

Imagine that you were there when each of the scenarios described above happened. What do you do? You need to:

GRADING CRITERIA TO BE ASSESSED
P3
M2

Demonstrate how to deal with casualties suffering from three different injuries and/or illnesses, with tutor support (P3).

Independently deal with casualties suffering from three different injuries and/or illnesses (M2).

Tackling the assignment

One way to approach this assignment is to act out three role plays and video them. You should ensure that the role play is as realistic as possible and that you calmly consider the options at each stage. You will need to assess the situation and then the injury or illness. Are you faced with a minor injury or illness, or a major injury or illness? Who should you contact for help and what should you do while you are waiting for help to arrive? How do you report the incident after it has happened?

What is a risk assessment?

Getting hurt or becoming ill through playing sport is not a pleasant subject to think about. But, the reality is that every year people lose their lives taking part in sport in Great Britain. In addition, around 250,000 non-fatal injuries require treatment each year. The mistake is to believe that these things happen in highly unusual or exceptional circumstances, which will never apply to you or your sport. This is not the case. Carrying out a risk assessment beforehand could often have prevented these things from happening.

What is risk?

The *Oxford English Dictionary* defines risk as 'the possibility that something unpleasant will happen'. If we apply this to a sporting context, we could say that risk is 'the possibility that an injury to one or more players will happen'.

Dare Busst suffers a freak leg-break which could not have been presented.

A spectator puts himself and the cyclists at risk during the Tour de France in 2009.

Most people would agree that trying to prevent an injury from occurring makes more sense than simply dealing with it once it has happened, and this is where risk assessment comes in. By assessing the dangers, players, coaches and managers can take steps to remove some of these hazards. A risk assessment is a careful examination of what, in your sport, could cause harm to people. It is a simple, practical exercise that requires little more than common sense.

Why should we carry out a risk assessment?

1. Carrying out a risk assessment is a good way to work out how risky something is. It makes you think of everything that could be a hazard, not just the obvious things.
2. Part of completing a risk assessment is putting plans in place to minimize the risks you have identified. It is unlikely that you will be able to eliminate the risks altogether but a risk assessment does play an important part in reducing the likelihood of these risks occurring and therefore reduces the risk of injury.
3. Completing a risk assessment promotes the safety and welfare of all involved, including participants, club members, spectators, and members of the general public who you might come into contact with while engaged in your sport or activity.
4. Risk assessments should be regularly reviewed, ensuring that a safe environment is continually maintained.
5. We must comply with the legal requirements that are enforced through Acts of Parliament and European Directives.
6. If an accident does happen everyone wants to avoid liability at all costs, both in terms of criminal prosecutions and civil claims for compensation. Carrying out a risk assessment demonstrates good practice as most sports' national governing bodies strongly advise (and insurance policies insist) that clubs and other organizations do so.

BRONZE

1. Get into two teams and hold a debate, with one team arguing for the statements below and one team arguing against the statements below:

'It is impossible to completely eliminate risk from a sporting activity.'

'Sport would be more fun if there was no danger or risk.'

2. Compile a list of ten risks you take between the end of this lesson and the start of the next lesson.

3. Place the following sports on the continuum below, according to the potential risk of injury:

a) Rugby   **b)** Hockey   **c)** Gymnastics   **d)** Rounders
e) Pole vaulting   **f)** Jogging   **g)** Aerobics   **h)** Cycling

Safe ⟵——————————————⟶ Dangerous

Carrying out a risk assessment

Everyone who is involved in sport – from managers to coaches, from groundsmen to reporters, and from players to spectators – has a responsibility to try and prevent other people from getting hurt. Every club, school and venue needs to carry out a formal risk assessment, to prove that they are taking steps to prevent anyone from becoming injured.

The six-step process

There are six stages to producing a formal risk assessment document. Failure to complete any of the six stages could lead to someone being seriously injured.

6. Review your decisions regularly and make changes if necessary: Hazards change on a regular basis, so the risk assessment must be reviewed to keep it up to date.

1. Identify the hazards: Look around at all the equipment, the venue and the participants, and decide what could cause harm, no matter how minor. For example, a broken piece of equipment would be a hazard.

5. Record your findings and implement solutions: By law, the risk assessment findings must be written down. It is also important to put in place the control measures you have decided on. For example, making someone responsible for checking the equipment on a weekly basis.

2. Decide who might be harmed and how: Decide whether it is the players, the coaching staff or the spectators who might be harmed. Then think about what may happen to them and what injuries might they sustain? For example, a broken goalpost could cause a serious head injury.

4. Decide how to prevent or reduce the level of risk: Practical solutions to reduce the level of risk, called 'control measures', must be found. For example:
- Checking all equipment once a week to make sure it is not broken or dangerous, and making a commitment to remove or repair damaged items.
- Ensuring that all the activity-related equipment designed to protect participants is used. For example, the landing mats used in gymnastics activities provide a safe, soft area for gymnasts to land on. These help to prevent neck and back injuries.
- Ensuring that players wear appropriate protective equipment, particularly in game situations, such as gumshields, which are often worn by rugby players and boxers to protect their teeth.

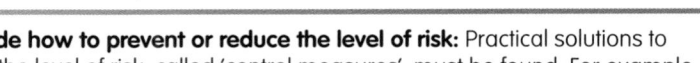

3. Identify the level of risk: Decide how likely it is that the potential accidents you have identified will occur. For example, a broken goalpost represents quite a high level of risk because it is very likely to fall as players and the ball could come into contact with it. Something which is unlikely to happen, such as a badminton post falling over, would represent a low level of risk.

Reporting procedures

When an accident occurs it must be reported. Different organizations have different reporting systems, but generally an accident is reported to the office or administration team by completing a detailed accident/report form containing the following information:
- The personal details of the person involved, including their name, address, contact details and date of birth.
- Details of where the incident occurred, what happened and any injuries that were sustained.
- Information about any witnesses, including their names and what they saw.
- Details of any first aid or medical treatment administered to the casualty.

Contingency plans

All sports leaders should have a contingency plan in case circumstances alter at the last minute. A contingency plan is an alternative plan that can be put into action, if necessary, to ensure an event or session takes place safely. A contingency plan may be required if it is too wet or windy for an activity to take place outside, or if the equipment to be used is not safe or is unavailable at the time that it is needed.

Risk assessment for a school skiing trip

School: St John's Community School	**Leader of visit:** Mr Greig		**Date(s):** 13th March 2010–21st March 2010
Description of location and nature of visit/activity: Skiing in the French Alps		**Year group(s) or ages of students:** Years 10 and 11	

ASSESSMENT OF SPECIFIC SIGNIFICANT RISKS:

Risk	Persons at risk	Control measures/procedures to be in place (include plans for supervision, especially any remote supervision)	Action points/who to be informed (parents/leaders/ students)	Level of risk	Tick if in place
Travel **On coach** Injury; lost or separated student; death	Students/ staff	Students fully informed of expectations of behaviour at service stations. Students to be accompanied by staff at all times during these breaks. All party members informed of hazards specific to travel in a foreign country, namely, travelling on the opposite side of road and use of seat belts.	Staff and students on trip. Parents informed of expectations at parents' information evening.	Low	
At airport terminals Injury; lost or separated student, possible terrorist activity	Students/ staff	Students fully informed of expectations of behaviour at airport terminals. Students to be accompanied by staff at all times during check-in and to be in a minimum group size of four students at all times when using toilets/duty-free shopping areas. Students given a fixed point to meet staff and a staff member to be present at this point at all times. Students informed of specific action to take in case of emergency (meet with staff members at meeting point and follow all airport security announcements).	Staff and students on trip. Parents informed of expectations at parents' information evening.	Low	
On aeroplane Possible disturbance to passengers and crew	Students	NO silly jokes about bombs or other related activity. Students to sit only in seats designated by airline. (These should all be together as the departure time from school should allow for three-and-a-half hours for check-in.)	Staff and students on trip. Parents informed of expectations at parents' information evening.	Low	
At Hotel Glacier Injury; lost or separated student	Students/ staff	Fire drill procedures explained on arrival along with other important safety procedures. These will be led by hotel/Ski-daddle staff. Students informed by Mr Greig of specific 'no-go areas', and areas where trips and falls are more likely (on corner stairs, in bathrooms, and in ski/boot rooms).	Staff and students on trip. Parents informed of expectations at parents' information evening. Also reinforced in resort.	Low to medium	
While wearing ski clothing and boots/ skis Injury; hypothermia or death	Students/ staff	Students will be under the control and supervision of qualified ski instructors and Ski-daddle staff at all times when on the mountain. The only exceptions will be at lunchtime, walking from the hotel to the slopes and while on the ski bus. Students will not be allowed to wear ski boots except in the presence of a ski instructor but have been informed to take a pair of old shoes/trainers, which will be worn at lunchtime, walking from the hotel to the slopes and while on the ski bus.	Staff and students on trip. Parents informed of expectations at parents' information evening. Also reinforced in resort.	Low	
Evening activities (skittles, treasure hunt, quiz, shopping and any free time) Injury; hypothermia or death	Students/ staff	Students to be in minimum groups of four at all times when not in the hotel. Students in groups with a member of staff when going shopping, taking part in the treasure hunt and when playing skittles in the local bowling alley.	Staff and students on trip. Parents informed of expectations at parents' information evening. Also reinforced in resort.	Low	

Alternative plans	In the event of being unable to ski due to poor weather conditions, Ski-daddle will provide alternative activities, which will have been pre-agreed with Mr Greig.
Emergency plan in case of incident or accident	All students and parents will be required to sign a behaviour agreement form before travel. In case of emergency, the Ski-daddle representative will be informed immediately and the company procedures will be followed. In addition, students will be asked not to use mobile phones and Mr Greig will contact the home-based contact who will, in turn, follow the LEA emergency procedures code and inform the head teacher. In case of injury which requires medical treatment (other than that which can be dealt with by the trip's first aider), Ski-daddle will organize transportation for the student and a staff member to the local doctor, pharmacy or hospital. The group is insured through the Ski-daddle insurance (a copy of which is attached).

ASSESSMENT CARRIED OUT BY (NAME): Mr Greig (Visit leader) **SIGNED:** **DATE:**

APPROVED BY HEAD TEACHER AND SIGNED:

SPOTLIGHT on risk assessment

SILVER

Completing this activity will help you to achieve a **Merit** in your assignment.

2. Imagine that you are arranging an inter-school basketball tournament at a venue that you are familiar with. Draw up a contingency plan for the event, considering the venue, the equipment and the participants involved. At each point, explain why you have made the decisions you have.

BRONZE

Completing this activity will help you to achieve a **Pass** in your assignment.

1a) Using the example on the previous page as a guide, create a risk-assessment form that you can use to assess the risks present at a sporting venue.

b) Use the risk-assessment form you have created to identify all the hazards in a sporting area at your school. This could, for example, be the sports hall, the gymnasium, the playground or the field.

c) Complete the risk-assessment form by adding details of the control measures you would put in place to minimize the risks presented by the sporting area.

GOLD

Completing this activity will help you to achieve a **Distinction** in your assignment.

3. Create an advice leaflet detailing the specialized protective equipment used in a sport of your choice. You should explain why the equipment is used, describing the benefits of doing so to the participant.

Unit 5 assignment, part three

Background

Your school or college is due to hold a sports day for Year 6 students from the local primary schools and you have been asked to assist in the preparations for the event. Planning such events needs to be done very carefully as health and safety is of paramount importance. Everybody involved in the planning and delivery of the sports day needs to be aware of the potential hazards, common injuries and any preventative strategies that can be used at the sports day, as well as the rules, regulations and legislation that apply to the event.

GRADING CRITERIA TO BE ASSESSED
P6
M5
D2

Task

Carry out a risk assessment in preparation for the sports day. Focus on the equipment and the venues that will be used. Remember to pay attention to the risks, and identify the control measures that can be put in place to protect the organizers, referees, spectators and other helpers, as well as the participants. You should also consider any contingency plans that may be necessary. You should:

Carry out and produce a risk assessment relevant to a selected sport (P6).

Describe contingency plans that can be used in a risk assessment (M5).

Justify the use of specialist equipment to minimize the risk of injury (D2).

Tackling the assignment

This assignment cannot be attempted until the event has been organized because key questions, such as which activities will be included, will have a direct bearing on the risk assessment procedure. Once such decisions have been taken, then a risk assessment can be completed.

You will need to take a walk around the venues and look at the equipment, asking yourself questions such as, 'How could this cause an injury?' and 'Is this area big enough for the number of people involved?' Make a list of all of your queries. You can then begin to fill in a risk assessment

form and consider the control measures that could be put in place to prevent/reduce the risk of injury. Remember to consider **everyone** who will be present. For a Merit, go on to describe any contingency plans that will be needed if something goes wrong (such as poor weather) and, finally, for a Distinction, justify your ideas on the inclusion of specialist equipment, such as shin pads or gum shields. Remember, justifying the use of the equipment means giving detailed reasons why it is necessary and not simply providing a list.

Meeting the Pass and Merit criteria

BTEC Level 2 Firsts in Sport

Jamilla Khan

Unit 5 assignment, part three

Assessment of Specific Significant Risks:

Risk		Persons at risk	Control measures/ procedures to be in place
Athletics track Glass or other foreign objects	Injury	Students	Organizers to complete a sweep of the athletics track, including the centre and perimeter areas, on the morning of the event. Everyone involved (students, staff and spectators) to be informed that glass bottles should not be brought to the event. Bins to be provided for all litter.
Pot holes/mole hills	Injury	Students	During the sweep described above, mole hills to be flattened and any holes to be filled with soil/sand as appropriate.

Contingency plans

A contingency plan for the sports day is most likely to be needed if it rains. To cope with this, a close eye will be kept on the weather forecast throughout the week leading up to the event and, if rain is likely, either just before or during the sports day, the event will be postponed. If rain occurs unexpectedly during the event or just before the event begins, all staff, students and spectators will be moved inside to the main hall. If the rain passes quickly the event will continue, but if it persists the event will have to be cancelled.

Using a form to meet the criteria for P6 is a good idea and the content is accurate up to a point. However, there needs to be more consideration of the 'Persons at risk' because hazards found on the athletics track would apply to everyone: students, staff and spectators. In addition, Jamilla has not shown any attempt to measure the level of risk posed and this must be included to make the risk assessment complete.

The contingency plans need to be developed further in order to meet the criteria for M5. For example, is it possible to continue the sports day with alternative activities indoors, perhaps in a sports hall, or is there no suitable venue available? Also, Jamilla mentions continuing if the rain lasts for only a short time but this point needs to be expanded. Would some activities, such as the javelin, have to be cancelled because the grass would be slippery or would they continue under alternative rules?

Unit 6: Sports Development

The nature of sports provision

Sport is made up of many different activities. Team sports, such as football, rugby, cricket and netball, often appeal to people who enjoy the social aspects of belonging to a team. In contrast, individual sports, such as tennis, golf and gymnastics, tend to appeal to people who are more motivated by personal achievement. Many people enjoy taking part in both team and individual sports.

Sporting opportunities are provided on a local and national basis and by organizations from the voluntary, public and private sectors.

Sport for all

There are lots of opportunities for people to take part in sport and, increasingly, it is becoming possible to take part in new, challenging and exciting sports. There should be a sport out there for everyone. It is just a case of finding one that you like and are able to take part in.

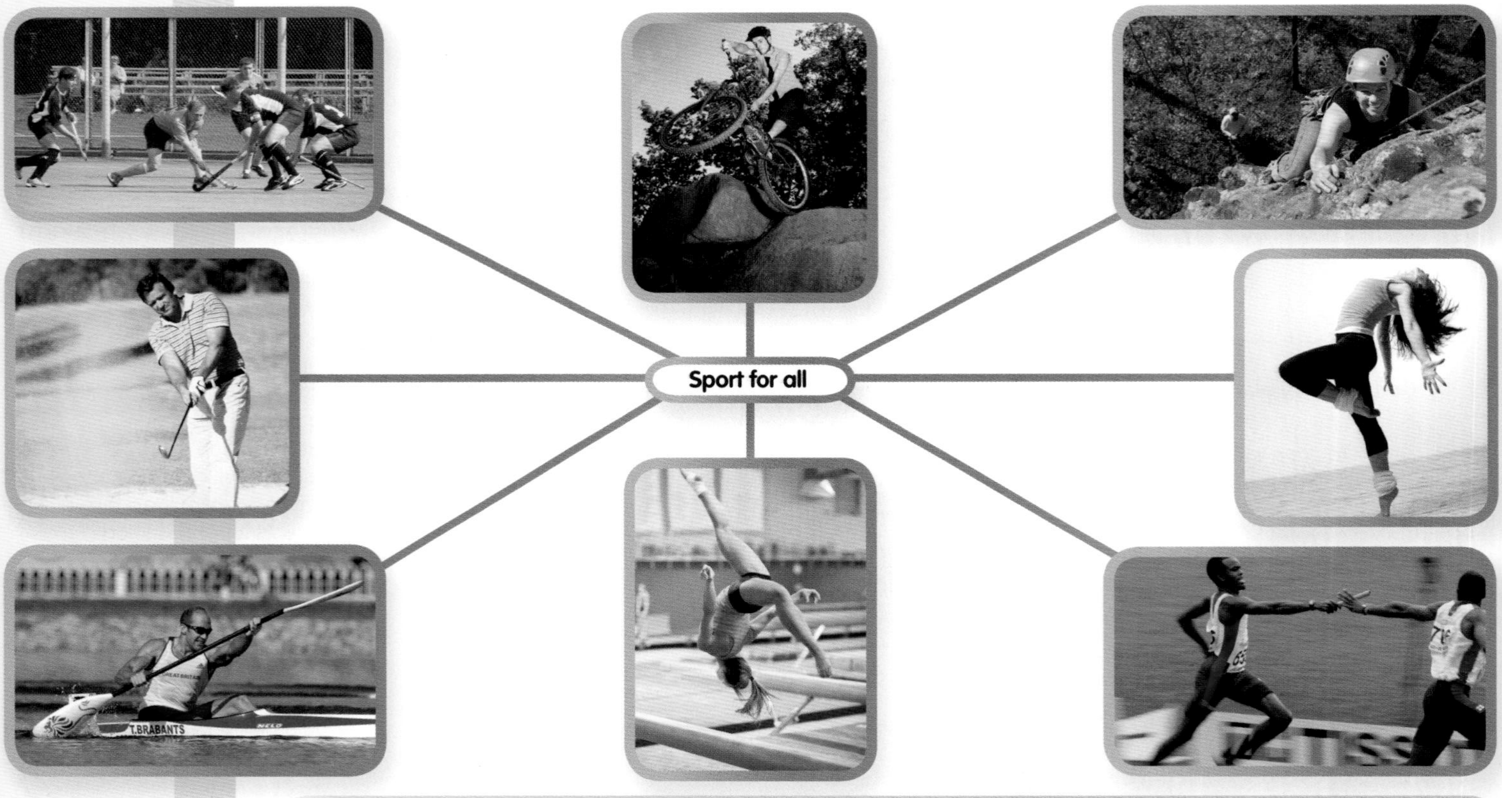

Sport for all

BRONZE

1. Identify your three favourite team sports and note down some of the things that you find most enjoyable about playing them.

2. What about watching sport? Note down some of the things that you enjoy about watching your favourite three sports live or on television.

3. Describe an individual sport to someone who has never heard of it before.

4. Make a list of sports activities that you think would appeal to someone who likes outdoor and adventurous challenges or who would like to take part in activities that are 'a little bit different'.

Local sports provision

Most people who participate in sport do so at a local level, at a local sports centre or by playing for a team near to where they live, for example. These local sporting opportunities are provided by three different types of provider: the voluntary sector, the public sector and the private sector.

The voluntary sector

Voluntary sports clubs provide many, many people with the opportunity to take part in their favourite sport, thanks to the dedication and hard work of the coaches, leaders and administrators. They all help the clubs to function effectively, and many carry out their roles on a voluntary, unpaid basis.

Fact:

In a recent study by Sport England it was calculated that the work volunteers do in providing local sporting opportunities is worth £14 billion per year!

Spondon Cricket Club was established in 1883. It is home to five senior teams who compete in varying divisions within the Derbyshire Cricket League. It also has a thriving junior cricket section, with up to 150 young players (both boys and girls) playing at all levels, from kwik cricket up to under 17s.

Spondon Cricket Club is a designated English Cricket Board Focus Club and has achieved Club Mark status. Club Mark is a national cross-sports quality accreditation scheme for clubs with junior sections. Clubs that achieve Club Mark status operate to a set of consistent and safe standards.

English Cricket Board Focus Clubs are selected by the local County Cricket Board. They are clubs that support the County Cricket Board's strategic development plan and are committed to delivering junior development programmes and/or development activities with specific target groups, such as disabled people, women and girls, and ethnic minorities. Clubs that are designated as a Focus Club are able to access and utilize resources run by the English Cricket Board and the County Cricket Board, as well as local development resources, to support the delivery of their development plan.

The club generates income from a variety of sources including:
• players' fees
• sale of food and drinks at the bar
• local sponsorship deals
• fund-raising events, such as bingo evenings and race nights.

Spondon Cricket Club is run by a committed team of helpers and club officials, including:
• coaching staff
• welfare officer
• treasurer
• club chairperson
• ground staff
• social secretary
• fixture secretary.

Although Spondon Cricket Club is fortunate to own its own facilities – most voluntary sporting organizations use council facilities – the club's organizational structure is similar to many other clubs in the voluntary sector.

Remember:

Most voluntary clubs survive on the fees their members pay to play. Some are fortunate enough to secure sponsorship or obtain grants from their local authority or their national governing body, but for the majority it is a constant struggle to make ends meet.

BRONZE

5. Think of a voluntary club that you have been (or still are) a member of and make a list of the different roles people have within the club. For example, is there a head coach?

6. Read about Spondon Cricket Club on the previous page and think about the local voluntary clubs in your area. What similarities can you identify between the way they are structured and the way they are funded?

The public sector

The public sector also plays an important role in providing sporting and physical activity opportunities at a local level. The level of provision varies from local authority to local authority, but as a general rule the facilities provided by the public sector include:

- playing fields
- sports centres
- swimming pools
- athletics tracks
- tennis courts.

Public sector facilities are funded at a local level by local authorities, who receive income from central government grants, council tax (which is collected at a local level), redistributed business rate revenue and money generated by visitors to sports centres.

Admission fees to local authority facilities are usually kept at a level that allows as many local people to participate in sport as possible. Often, discounted rates are available for senior citizens, people with disabilities and those who are out of work and receiving benefits.

An aerobics class at a local authority leisure facility.

The private sector

Over the past few years there has been a tremendous increase in private sector sports facilities, as more and more people become aware of the importance of having a healthy lifestyle. Private sector facilities range from small businesses, such as a dance studio owned and run by an individual person, through to a multinational chain of health clubs, such as David Lloyd or Virgin Active.

Remember:

As a rule, membership fees and the price of activities at private sector facilities are higher than at public sector facilities.

The money to run private sector facilities comes predominantly from membership fees, sales of goods and services, personal or company savings, and financing initiatives such as bank loans. In recent years, in an effort to increase investment and improve efficiency at public sector facilities, many local authorities get private companies to run their facilities for them, in return for an agreed management fee.

Fact:

There are over 330 private sector companies currently operating public sector sport and leisure centres, investing over £30 million a year.

National sports provision

Everyone has to start somewhere, and footballers such as Wayne Rooney and athletes like Jessica Ennis often start their sporting careers at voluntary clubs. Then, once they are identified as having potential, they move on to clubs, academies or centres of excellence where their talent can be developed and their potential for success maximized. Although these opportunities can be provided at a local level – at a nearby professional football club or top athletics club – more often than not provision for elite performers is found at a national level.

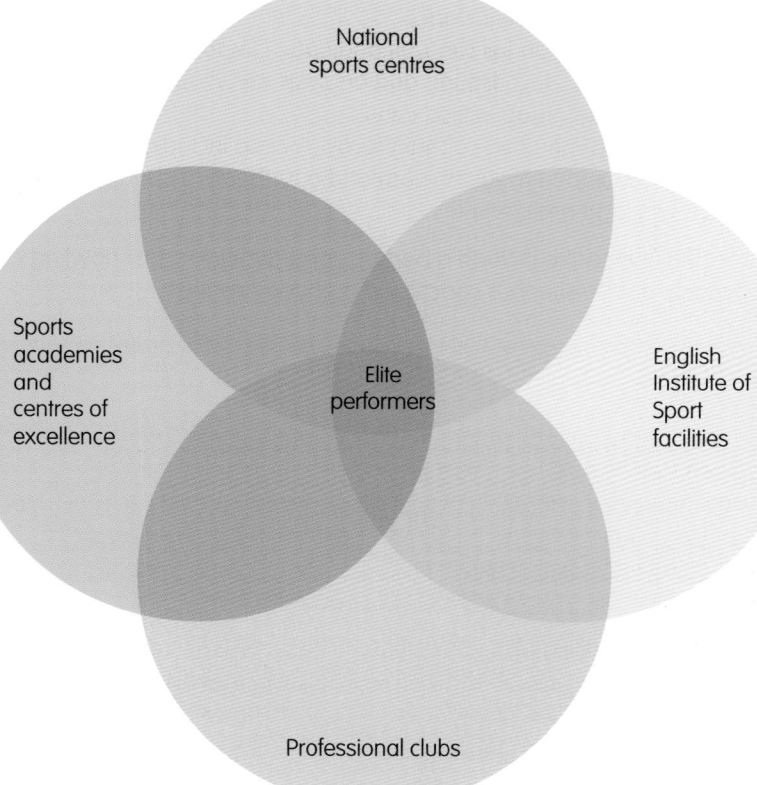

A map showing the location of the four national sports centres.

National sports centres

There are four national sports centres. They are managed by Sport England and provide national- and international-standard training and competition facilities for a range of sports and their national governing bodies.

119

The National Cricket Performance Centre, a centre of excellence

The ECB National Cricket Performance Centre is based at Loughborough University and cost £4.5 million to build in 2002. The facility incorporates all England squads (men and women, disabled and age-groups), with a philosophy to identify and select the most talented cricketers, and develop them through excellent coaching and support services in outstanding facilities.

The centre works in partnership with Loughborough University, which offers a range of world-class training, medical and sports science facilities concentrated together on one site. The cricketers therefore have the benefit of training alongside many of the country's best athletes from a variety of other sports.

Facilities at the centre include:
- six net lanes, with full run-ups and space for the wicketkeeper to stand back
- the latest high-tech filming and analysis resources, including the Hawkeye tracking system
- a fitness and rehabilitation centre
- a changing room with a main recovery area including hot and cold spa baths
- a fully equipped medical room and a further two changing rooms servicing the outdoor cricket ground
- access to 18 grassed nets.

Staff at the centre include a performance director, a fast bowling coach, a batting coach, a fielding coach, a wicketkeeper coach and a physiotherapist.

BRONZE

10. Choose one of the four national sports centres and find out as much as you can about it. For example:

- Where is it?
- What facilities does it have?
- Which national governing bodies use it?

- Who operates it?
- What community use does it encourage?
- Does it work with any partners?

Present your findings in a format that can be shared with your classmates.

11. Find out what provision at local, regional and national level is provided for elite performers in your favourite sport. You may want to think about the following questions while you are carrying out your research:

- Who runs the facility or scheme?
- What standard do performers have to reach to be accepted?

- What is the coaching setup?
- What support services, such as dieticians and physiotherapists, are on offer to performers?

SILVER

12. Using the information you have collected for Activity 11, suggest ways in which provision for elite performers in your favourite sport could be improved. Make sure that your suggestions are feasible and that they are fully backed up with reasoned arguments.

Unit 6 assignment, **part one**

Background

As a Sports Development Officer employed by your local authority you are excited when you hear that provision for sport in your area may be increased in the near future. A firm of consultants has been asked to look at the feasibility of increasing provision locally by bringing it more in line with what is available nationally and has started to investigate the current situation. They have asked you to help them.

Task

Produce a presentation to establish the current sporting provision in your local area and how it compares with national provision. Your presentation should:

GRADING CRITERIA
TO BE ASSESSED

P1, P2
M1
D1

Describe local voluntary, public and private sector sports provision for three different sports (P1).

Describe three different types of national sports provision that support elite performance (P2).

Compare local and national sports provision, identifying areas for improvement (M1).

Evaluate local and national sports provision, explaining ways in which provision could be improved (D1).

Tackling the assignment

Choose three sports that interest you, making sure that you cover the opportunities provided by all three sectors in your local area. You also need to include material covering three different types of national sports provision that supports elite performance. You could create your presentation in PowerPoint® or produce a series of fact sheets, which you support verbally. It would be great to add graphics to your presentation, as this may help you get the information across more effectively.

Remember:
- When you **describe** something you need to paint a picture in words, making sure you include sufficient detail so that someone else can see the picture you are painting.
- A **comparison** requires you to identify similarities and differences, strengths and weaknesses, and **explain** (or give reasons why) these exist.
- An **evaluation** requires you to examine strengths and weaknesses, commenting, for example, on the quality or importance of something or the impact a suggested improvement might have.

Meeting the Pass criteria

Unit 6 assignment, part one   Bobby Smith

A description of local voluntary, public and private sector sports provision for three different sports

My first sport is swimming. There is a wide range of provision in my local area, the main one being the three swimming pools run by the local council. Two of the pools are traditional ones, where you can swim up and down, and the other is a modern fun pool with a slide and wave machine.

At all the pools there are activities such as public swimming, lessons, aqua aerobics, etc.

> Good start, but where are the pools, what size are they, and so on?

There is also a 25m pool as part of the private health club situated on the outskirts of the town. It is a members-only club but the elite swimming squad based in the city uses the club for early morning training three times per week. Again, lessons take place at this pool.

There are no voluntary sector swimming pools in my area but there are four voluntary clubs. The top club is for the top swimmers in the city, who have to reach county standard to swim for the club. Two are competitive clubs and the final one has a water polo team and synchronized swimming section.

> Bobby's work is promising, but he needs to go into more detail to paint a really good picture of local provision and give the consultants a clear vision of what is in place. We need to know where the clubs train, how many members they have, what competitions they compete in, and so on.
>
> Bobby also needs to go into the same detail for two other sports to achieve P1, and the same detail for national sports provision for elite performers to achieve P2.

Meeting the Merit criteria

Unit 6 assignment, part one   **Mary Malone**

Although the provision for sport in my local area is good, it doesn't compare with what is provided nationally, although we do have a BMX cycling circuit that is used for national events.

I have looked at a selection of the most popular sports:

Football

There is a mix of public, private and voluntary sector provision in my local area that I would expect to see repeated in other areas of a similar size (see my earlier description).

However, we don't have a large stadium (such as a premier league team might have) because our local club are a non-league side. Nor do we have a large indoor five-a-side centre because there is one in the town 15 miles away, which some people from our area use.

The Football Association use the national sports centre at Lilleshall for some of their development work and the England football team play their international matches at Wembley. You would not expect to see these sorts of facilities at a local level.

> This is good. There is no need to repeat information that you have already provided.

> Mary has started well and makes some good points, but she needs to compare the provision for the other two sports she selects **and** make some suggestions about how provision could be improved in order to meet the criteria for M1. For example, she could suggest that an AstroTurf pitch is needed locally and that the FA National Football Centre at Burton-on-Trent needs to be completed.

Meeting the Distinction criteria

Unit 6 assignment, part one	Troy Taylor

I have evaluated local and national sports provision in the form of a table, commenting on the strengths and weaknesses of sports provision and explaining ways in which it could be improved.

Local provision: Gymnastics

Strengths	Weaknesses	Improvements
• There are excellent opportunities for beginners. The local authority runs five one-hour sessions per week and there are three after-school clubs based at primary schools. • There are two voluntary clubs who have well-qualified coaches and healthy membership numbers. • The clubs are located in the centre of town, which makes access relatively easy via public transport or car.	• The voluntary clubs have long waiting lists. • The local authority sessions take place in general activity areas and the standard of equipment is poor. • There is no provision for higher level gymnasts as the clubs only cater for beginner and intermediate levels. Those with potential have to travel over 17 miles to the nearest club with suitable facilities and experienced coaches.	There needs to be support for more voluntary clubs or the existing clubs need to expand in order to take on extra members. This will need investment from both the local authority and the national governing body for gymnastics, British Gymnastics. The money is needed to train more coaches, develop volunteers and make more facilities available for training and competition.

Using a table is a good way to summarize his ideas, and Troy could build on this information verbally if required.

Troy is definitely on the right lines. His examination of local gymnastics provision is taking shape and the one improvement he has explained is clearly linked to a weakness in provision that he has identified. He has a way to go before he fully meets the criteria for D1, because he needs to mention two other sports and look at national provision, but he has made a very encouraging start.

How people participate in sport

People participate in sport in many different ways, and not all of them involve getting hot and sweaty!

Performer

Most people have taken part in some form of sport at some point in their lives but the level at which they perform varies considerably. For example, a professional footballer will train most days, play a match once or possibly twice a week, and will get paid for doing so. In contrast, an amateur player may train once a week, try and keep fit at the gym, and play a match most weekends. In most cases, amateur players have to pay for the privilege of training and playing through their subs and travel costs.

Consumer

A consumer is anyone who buys sports-related goods, such as sportswear, sports equipment, sports magazines or dietary supplements to help with their training.

Retailer

Sports retail is big business. There are countless independent and national chains of shops selling sportswear and sports equipment, and many sell goods over the Internet.

Administrator

Administrators can be involved in many different ways. For example, they may organize fixtures, look after a club's accounts or perform the really important role of welfare officer and be the first point of contact for anyone with concerns about the way things are run at the club.

The different ways in which people participate in sport

Spectator

Thousands of people up and down the country watch sport every weekend, following their favourite rugby team live or on television from the comfort of their own home, or watching their children play a tennis match in the local park.

Sports development

Many people are involved in developing sport. They include professional sports development officers working for local authorities or national government bodies, as well as voluntary staff with a responsibility for developing provision within a local club.

Medical staff

Physiotherapists are an example of sports-related medical staff. They work in a wide variety of settings, such as hospitals, sports clubs and gyms. They specialize in maximizing human movement and may work with a performer after injury. As with many other sports-related medical staff, they are starting to play an ever-increasing role in sport.

Leader

Leaders are different from coaches. They tend to organize and supervise activity sessions, rather than develop someone's skill and proficiency in a sport like a coach does. They still play an important role though.

Coach

Coaches work with performers of all levels, from beginners to elite athletes, helping them to improve their performance. Many coaches are volunteers, but there are also lots of professional coaches, who are paid for their work.

Official

Officials are needed at all levels of all sports to make sure that they run smoothly and the rules are followed. Most officials work on a voluntary basis, but professional sports rely on highly trained and well paid officials.

BRONZE

1. Look at the different ways people can participate in sport and identify a real person for each of the roles, noting down a few words about each person. For example, for 'spectator' you could write: 'My uncle loves rugby and watches Leicester Tigers home and away each week. He hasn't missed a home game for three years!'

Why people participate in sport

It is estimated that approximately 75 per cent of people in the UK aged between 16 and 24 take part in some form of physical activity, and although this percentage decreases with age, sport is still a major pastime for over-55s. In fact, statistics indicate that over 40 per cent of the UK population exercises to some degree. So why are sport and physical activity so popular?

Health and fitness benefits

For lots of people, sport is great way to help them stay fit and healthy. Regular participation in physical activity:

- Benefits every part of your body, including the mind. This in turn helps your body stay in good working order so that you can cope with everyday tasks that involve physical exertion.
- Helps you look better and feel more positive about yourself.
- Helps you lose weight and lowers the risk of some diseases, including high blood pressure and heart disease.
- Helps you age well, keeping your bones strong and your joints mobile as you grow older.

It is important to keep exercising as you get older.

Social benefits

Participating in sport is not only good for the body. It also has social benefits:

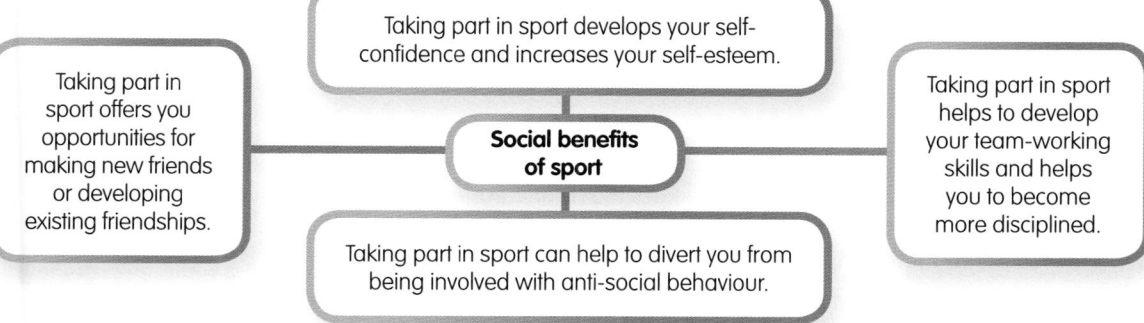

Taking part in sport offers you opportunities for making new friends or developing existing friendships.

Taking part in sport develops your self-confidence and increases your self-esteem.

Social benefits of sport

Taking part in sport helps to develop your team-working skills and helps you to become more disciplined.

Taking part in sport can help to divert you from being involved with anti-social behaviour.

Personal development

Sport is a great way to develop many of the personal qualities and skills required for life. Sport can help an individual:

- build character and develop resilience if things aren't going well
- develop their ability to think strategically
- think analytically
- set goals and targets
- learn and use leadership skills
- take calculated risks
- develop the motor skills needed to perform many day-to-day tasks.

BRONZE

1. Look at the ways in which sport develops personal qualities and skills required for life. Think of an example of when an individual would apply each quality or skill in a sporting context, and an example of when they would apply them in day-to-day life away from sport.

2. Conduct a survey amongst your friends and family to find out why they participate in sport. If they don't participate in sport, why don't they?

Factors that affect participation in sport

Although many people may want to participate in sport, whether they do or not is often influenced by many factors.

Barriers to participation

Disability

The opportunities for people with a disability to take part in sport have increased over the years, but having a disability can still be problematic for some participants. It can still be difficult to find facilities that are modified for disabled use, with easy access, user-friendly changing and suitable equipment. It can also be difficult to find coaches or leaders with the correct training and sufficient confidence to help participants with disabilities.

Provision

Access to a wide range of facilities varies greatly across the UK, and depends on the investment made in sport by the local authority and the willingness of the private sector to build and run facilities in that particular area. Also, many public-sector facilities were built during the 1970s, so although an area may appear to be well served with sports provision, it is often in poor repair or is suffering from a lack of investment.

Cost

The cost of taking part in sport can have an impact on someone's level of participation, especially if the cost of participation is high and their income is relatively low. Many local authorities have concessionary schemes in place at public-sector facilities, offering discounts to people with low incomes, to address this problem. Similarly, many voluntary sports clubs try to keep their membership costs low to encourage participation, often with the support of grants from local authorities and governing bodies. Generally, the private sector only caters for those in the community who can afford their prices.

Location

Facilities may exist, but can you get to them? Location is critical and can often have a significant impact on the opportunity a person has to participate in sport. For example, are the facilities accessible via public transport? If participants do have a car, is parking provision adequate? Do people living in rural communities have to travel great distances to participate? Do elite performers have to travel to access the appropriate facilities or coaching?

Age

Although many people over 55 do take part in sport and physical activity, age can affect participation. Participation rates generally decrease as people get older for a variety of reasons, including:
* reduced mobility and other health problems
* less money to spend on physical activity after retirement
* problems accessing facilities using public transport.

Ethnicity

There are many people from ethnic minority communities in the UK who want to participate in sport but have to overcome significant barriers in order to do so. Reasons put forward for not participating include limited access to facilities and racist incidents. One initiative that hopes to address this is Sporting Equals.

Gender

Gender has often been a barrier, particularly for women due to their traditional involvement in childcare at home and the image portrayed by many sports that they are for males only. This often resulted in fewer sporting opportunities for women, although this is now changing at schools and in sport in general.

Sporting Equals

Promoting ethnic diversity across sport & physical activity

Sporting Equals was set up in 1998 by Sport England in partnership with the Commission for Racial Equality. It is now an independent body that aims to create an environment in which:

- People from black and minority ethnic (BME) communities can influence and participate in all aspects of sport and physical activity.
- National governing bodies and providers of sport and physical activity recognize and value a fully integrated and inclusive society.
- Ethnic diversity is recognized and celebrated.

Sporting Equals has three objectives:

- To raise awareness and understanding of the needs of BME communities within the sports and health sector in order to change attitudes and increase participation in sport and physical activity.
- To empower individuals and communities to play a part in this change, and achieve their full potential through playing sport and being active.
- To advise and support policy-makers and delivery bodies to be inclusive.

Sport in the community events held by organizations such as 't.a.a.rget' aim to reduce barriers to participation and make sport more accessible for everyone.

But it isn't all gloomy …

Sport England's Active People survey, conducted between October 2005 and October 2006, found that 21 per cent of adults took part in at least three, moderate intensity 30-minute sessions of sport and physical activity every week. It also discovered that:

- Walking is the most popular recreational activity for people in England. Over 8 million adults aged 16 and over (20 per cent) had done a recreational walk lasting at least 30 minutes in the previous four weeks.
- 5.6 million people (13.8 per cent) swim at least once a month.
- 4.2 million people (10.5 per cent) go to the gym.
- 4.7 per cent of the adult population (1.9 million people) contribute at least one hour a week to volunteering in sport.

Over time there appears to have been an increase in participation rates because:

- People now have more leisure time than they did in the past, and many spend this time taking part in sport and physical activity.
- People also have more disposable income than they did in the past, and many spend this extra money on enjoying sport.
- There has been an increase in funding for sport, mainly as a result of National Lottery grants, and as a result more facilities have been developed.
- There has been a significant increase in the number of people who understand the benefits of leading a healthy, active lifestyle.
- Sport is now seen as fashionable and becoming a professional performer or a high-profile coach is viewed as a way to potentially earn a good income. Many sportswear manufacturers, such as Nike and Adidas, also spend millions of pounds securing top sports stars to promote their products.

However, an economic downturn may affect the growth in participation. When people lose their jobs they have less money to spend on sport and physical activity. Local authorities and central government also have to make cuts to their budgets and have less money to spend on sport in a recession.

BRONZE

1. Identify at least two ideas to help a person overcome each barrier to participation.
2. What initiatives are in place in your local area to encourage participation by BME communities, and what specific barriers do they aim to overcome?
3. Choose a sports facility in your local area and investigate its provision for participants with disabilities.

Walking in the countryside is free, so cost doesn't have to be a barrier to participation.

Unit 6 assignment, part two

Background

Your role as a Sports Development Officer is varied and exciting. You are currently working with a local primary school that is actively trying to increase participation levels in sport and physical activity by their Year 5 and 6 students. They have asked if you could attend a morning assembly and talk to the students.

Task

Prepare a presentation about how and why people take part in sport and the factors that affect participation. Your presentation should:

GRADING CRITERIA
TO BE ASSESSED
P3, P4

Describe the ways in which people participate in sport and the reasons for participation (P3).

Describe the factors that affect participation in sport (P4).

Tackling the assignment

You need to plan your talk with the target audience in mind, engaging the children and using language and examples they can easily understand. It may be a good idea to structure your talk around a visual presentation (such as a series of PowerPoint® slides, a poster or a flipchart presentation) and prepare a series of crib cards to prompt you while you are speaking.

Meeting the Pass criteria

Unit 6 assignment, part two

Samantha Bond

Planning sheet

I am going to use a range of methods to support my presentation to students, including a PowerPoint® presentation that I will make very visual to grab the students' attention.

I will describe the **reasons** that people participate in sport, such as the health and fitness benefits, and use examples the students can relate to, such as not having time off school.

I will also go through a list of **ways** in which people participate, giving examples that students will have heard of, such as Wayne Rooney, to help them understand what a professional sportsman is, and so on.

It is very important to make a presentation to Year 5 and 6 students visual, so it is good to see that Samantha is planning to do this.

This is an excellent example. The students will be able to relate to it, helping them to understand the reasons more clearly.

Samantha has made an excellent start in her planning. She is thinking very clearly about the target audience and is working methodically through the criteria for P3 and P4. She now needs to follow up this positive start with a concise presentation that reinforces the messages she is going to deliver verbally, and these PowerPoint® slides are great.

Ways in which people participate in sport

Performer

Ways in which people participate in sport

Coach

Ways in which people participate in sport

Official

Strategies to encourage participation

A strategy is a plan of action that is put in place to achieve a particular goal. For example, an organization might have a strategy to increase physical activity participation rates for over-55s by 2 per cent over the next three years. There are so many strategies in place to encourage participation in sport that it would be impossible to discuss them all here. However, some of the most high profile ones are well worth investigating in some detail, including national schemes that encourage mass participation, sport-specific programmes and the role of sports development officers.

National strategies

There are numerous national strategies in place to increase the number of people taking part in various sports and physical activities. They all form part of the drive to make the nation healthier and share common themes, such as creating capacity and providing funding, and they are generally target driven.

The School Sports Strategy

The Youth Sport Trust and Sport England are working with the Department for Children, Schools and Families (DCSF) and the Department for Culture, Media and Sport (DCMS) in the delivery of the PE and Sport Strategy for Young People to help schools offer all young people aged 5 to 16 the opportunity to participate in five hours of high quality physical education and sport a week.

Active women

Sport England distributes National Lottery funding to projects that help women in disadvantaged communities and those looking after children under 16 to participate in more sport and physical activity.

Research from the Women's Sport and Fitness Foundation indicates that there are many emotional barriers to sporting participation for women in both these target groups, the most prominent one being low levels of body confidence and the desire to lose weight.

Sportsmatch

The Sport England Sportsmatch programme increases investment in community sport by matching new sponsorship money pound for pound. It supports the development of grassroots sport in England, making awards to organizations that run projects aimed at increasing participation in sport at community level.

Free swimming

The Department for Culture, Media and Sport (DCMS), working with local authorities, is supporting a £140m scheme to offer free swimming pool use to all people aged 16 and under and all people aged 60 or over in England, in an attempt to get two million people more active by the time London hosts the Olympics and Paralympics in 2012.

BRONZE

1. Take a look at what the national governing body for your favourite sport is doing to encourage people to take part in their sport. Identify one initiative and find out:

- who it is aimed at
- its aims and objectives
- what funding it attracts
- where it is taking place
- how its success is being measured
- anything else you think is important.

SILVER

2. Now that you have completed Activity 1 and have a good understanding of one sport-specific initiative, write down as many reasons as possible why it is needed and expand your understanding of how it is being implemented.

GOLD

3a) Now that you have completed Activities 1 and 2, identify and explain the strengths and weaknesses of the initiative.

b) Use your views on the strengths and weaknesses of the initiative to make recommendations about how this particular initiative or any similar schemes in the future could be improved.

Sports development officers

One of the most important occupations in increasing participation levels in sport is a sports development officer, also known as an SDO. There has been a significant increase in the number of SDOs over the years, some focusing specifically on a particular sport and some working to increase overall activity levels. The two job advertisements below should give you a flavour of the kind of work that SDOs do.

Sports development officers are crucial to the challenge of increasing participation in sport.

BRONZE

4. Devise a person specification for both of the job adverts below. A person specification describes the knowledge, skills and attributes that are essential to perform a job and the knowledge, skills and attributes that are desirable to perform a job.

PROJECT/YOUTH WORKER: TRENT BRIDGE COMMUNITY SPORTS TRUST

Positive Futures is a national social inclusion programme using sport and leisure activities to engage with disadvantaged and socially marginalized young people.

The programme aims to have a positive influence on young people's lives by widening horizons and providing access to new opportunities within a culturally familiar environment.

Using sport and leisure activities as a catalyst to encourage project participation, young people are steered towards education, training and employment.

This is a newly-created two-year fixed-term contract for a part-time position, as part of a joint partnership between the Trent Bridge Community Sports Trust, Rushcliffe Borough Council and the Football Foundation.

You will need to be a qualified youth worker with experience of engaging young people in a youth and/or sporting environment, in particular working with young people at risk of anti-social behaviour.

The successful candidate for this post will be a flexible worker, willing to work evenings, with a hands-on approach, strong organizational and IT skills, and an ability to seek out and respond positively to development opportunities as they arise.

Swimming Coordinator: Amateur Swimming Association

London Swimming, in partnership with Total Swimming, is delivering a pioneering 'mobile pools' programme across the capital and is looking to recruit a Swim 21 Coordinator to help work on the cutting edge Mayoral Pool Programme.

If you have not seen the mobile pools in action then look at some of the press coverage with high profile deployments in Lambeth and Brent.

The successful Swim Coordinator should have a Level 2 teacher qualification or equivalent and will need an understanding of adhering to health and safety standards and experience of working in diverse communities.

In addition you will need excellent administration skills and be proficient in Microsoft® Office applications. You also need to have excellent customer service skills with an ability to manage a varied work programme.

CRB checks will be taken up as part of the employment as this role involves significant access to children. The project will follow guidelines set down in the ASA's Child Protection Policy.

The role of local and national organizations in the development of sport

There are numerous local and national organizations responsible for the development of sport. Some, like Sport England and the Youth Sport Trust, are national organizations that encourage mass participation in sport. Others, like School Sport Partnerships and County Sport Partnerships, also want to get as many people involved with sport and physical activity as possible, but they work at a local and regional level. National governing bodies are concerned with developing one particular sport.

Sport England

Sport England work in partnership with UK Sport, which has responsibility for elite success, and the Youth Sport Trust, which focuses on physical education and school sport. Sport England is accountable to Parliament through the Department for Culture, Media and Sport, and is responsible for building the foundations of sporting success, by creating a world-leading community sport system of clubs, coaches, facilities and volunteers.

The Youth Sport Trust

The Youth Sport Trust is a registered charity that aims to build a brighter future for young people by enhancing the quality of their physical education and sporting opportunities. It wants to help young people to live healthy and active lives and to be the best they can be. It is a high profile organization that plays a major role in many sports development strategies. One of its key responsibilities is to support School Sport Partnerships.

School Sport Partnerships

School Sport Partnerships (SSPs) involve groups of schools working together to develop Physical Education and sporting opportunities for all young people in their local area.

A typical partnership consists of:
- A partnership development manager (PDM) who manages the partnership and works closely with other sports-related organizations in the locality. They are often based at a Specialist Sports College where there is additional expertise available to help develop a range of PE and sport programmes.
- School Sport Coordinators (SSCos) who are based in each secondary school in the partnership. They develop and support after-school sport and inter- and intra-school competitions in their school and their partner primary schools.
- Primary Link Teachers (PLTs) who are based in the partner primary schools. Their main role is to improve PE and school sport within their own school.

A School Sport Partnership may look like this.

A recent addition to the SSP programme is the role of Further Education Sports Coordinators (FESCos). They have a similar role to SSCos, but work in further education colleges.

BRONZE

1. Investigate the involvement your current or previous school has with their School Sport Partnership. You may want to find out:
- How many days a week your SSCo spends on SSP activities.
- What SSP initiatives your school is involved with.
- The increase in inter- and intra-school activity since your SSP came into existence.
- The links your school has developed with local voluntary sports clubs to help students continue with sport outside school.

Local authority Sports Development Departments

Local authority Sports Development Departments are key providers of sporting opportunities across the local area they serve. They work with local and regional partners to develop an infrastructure that enables people to fulfil their potential in a chosen sport or to take part in physical activity for health-related or social reasons.

County Sports Partnerships

There are currently 49 Country Sports Partnerships (CSPs) in England and their role is to provide leadership, direction and support for local organizations involved in the delivery of sport. They work closely with local authorities, national governing bodies, clubs, schools and School Sport Partnerships, and Primary Care Trusts. The Lancashire Sport Partnership is an example of a County Sports Partnership.

Lancashire Sport Partnership

Lancashire Sport Partnership is funded by Sport England, by other local agencies, by local authorities in their area and by private sponsorship. It plays an important part in the government's drive to develop a 'single sports delivery system' across England, and is an important link between local and regional sport networks. Its vision is to increase long-term participation in sport and to widen participation in physical activity for all.

Its key roles are to:
- take the lead in helping organizations within the partnership work together to deliver sport and physical activity effectively within the county
- increase participation in, and widen access to, sport and physical activity
- work with partners to support club, coach and volunteer development throughout the county.

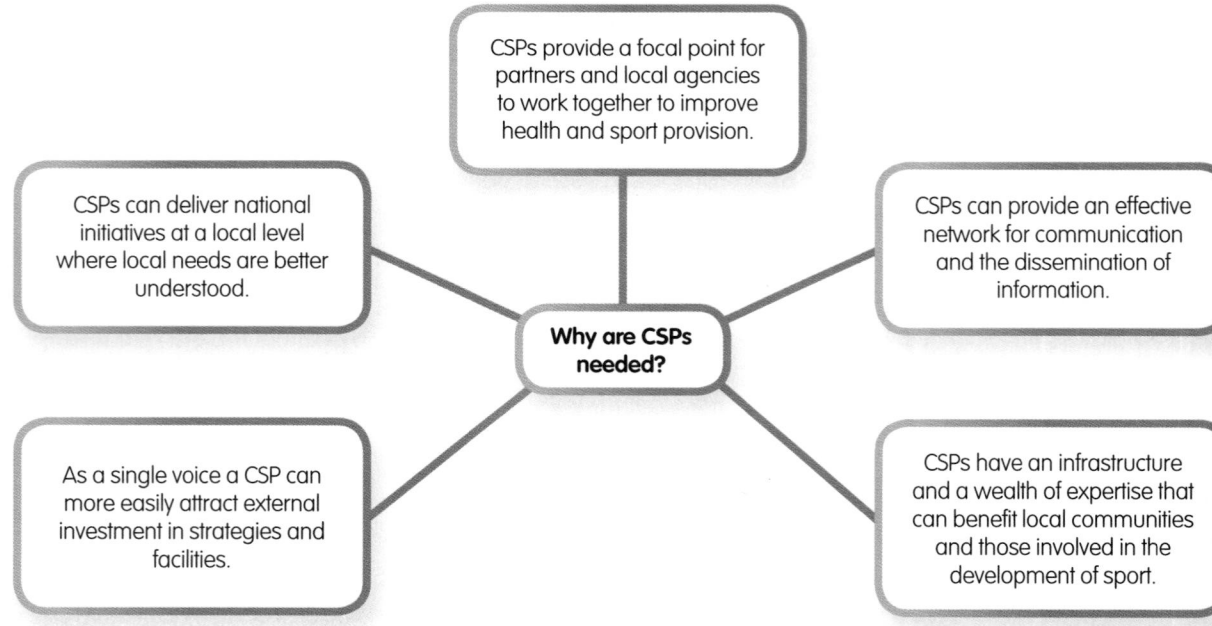

CSPs provide a focal point for partners and local agencies to work together to improve health and sport provision.

CSPs can deliver national initiatives at a local level where local needs are better understood.

CSPs can provide an effective network for communication and the dissemination of information.

Why are CSPs needed?

As a single voice a CSP can more easily attract external investment in strategies and facilities.

CSPs have an infrastructure and a wealth of expertise that can benefit local communities and those involved in the development of sport.

SILVER

2. Your County Sports Partnership plays an important role in supporting the development of sport in your area. It would therefore improve your understanding of sports development if you had a good look at what they do and why they do it. See if you can arrange an interview with a member of the CSP team to find out more about them.

National governing bodies

Whereas organizations such as the Youth Sport Trust and County Sports Partnerships support the development of a range of sport provision, national governing bodies (NGBs) focus on their own particular sport. The main roles of an NGB are to:
- increase participation
- develop talent
- deliver success at elite level.

NGBs oversee the vision for their sport and many have a strategy in place, often called their 'Whole Sports Plan', which outlines this vision and explains in detail how their aims and objectives will be met. NGBs are responsible for:
- Providing national direction for their sport and a structure for it to function effectively.
- Providing support and insurance to those clubs that affiliate with the NGB.
- Increasing the quality and quantity of coaches, volunteers and officials.
- Organizing and/or providing information on competitive opportunities at all levels.
- Assisting with the development of sport-specific facilities.
- Providing information and advice on funding opportunities.
- Providing guidance for clubs and individuals to support the development of their sport.

Many national governing bodies form part of an international structure. The international governing body decides the rules of the game in close consultation with NGBs around the world, and these rules are then implemented at a national level by the NGBs. Here is an example of how this works in practice:

International governing body: FIFA
FIFA is the governing body of football. Its primary objective is to grow the game of soccer and ensure that the game continues to develop. FIFA decides the rules of the game in consultation with the continental bodies that govern their respective areas of the globe.

European governing body: UEFA
UEFA is comprised of 53 national football associations and is recognized by FIFA as one of six continental federations.

National governing body: The FA
The FA is the governing body of football in England and is responsible for developing and regulating the game at all levels, from grassroots voluntary clubs to the international squad. It is committed to making football accessible, enjoyable and safe for everyone, regardless of race, religion, gender, sexuality, background or ability.

BRONZE

3. Choose an NGB to research. You may want to choose the NGB that oversees your favourite sport or to find out about one that you know very little about. Whichever you choose, you need to explore their role in sufficient detail so that you have a good understanding of their aims and how they achieve their objectives.

Unit 6 assignment, part three

Background

Your local Sports Development Department regularly provides work placement opportunities for National Diploma and university students studying sport. All those on a placement are given a series of fact sheets about the Sports Development Department. However, the Senior Sports Development Officer thinks they are in need of a thorough overhaul.

GRADING CRITERIA TO BE ASSESSED
P5, P6
M2, M3
D2

Task

You have been asked to prepare a series of fact sheets about the strategies used to encourage participation in sport and the aims, objectives and roles of local and national organizations in the development of sport. The fact sheets should:

Describe the strategies used to encourage participation in a selected sport (P5).

Describe the role of one local and one national organization responsible for the development of sport (P6).

Explain the strategies used to encourage participation in a selected sport (M2).

Explain the role of one local and one national organization responsible for the development of sport (M3).

Evaluate the strategies used to encourage participation in a selected sport, making recommendations for future strategies (D2).

Tackling the assignment

The first part of the task – P5, M2 and D2 – is a great opportunity to look in detail at your favourite sport, exploring the strategies it uses to get people involved at all levels. The fact sheets should be in sufficient detail to give the reader a good insight into two or more strategies. They should include a description of their aims and objectives and your thoughts on whether they will have the intended effect on future growth in the sport, as well as information about how the strategies are organized (staffing, funding, promotion, and so on). For M2, you need to give clear reasons why the strategies are needed – for example, is there a lack of officials, declining numbers of people participating or a need for better quality coaching – and outline any successes that have already been achieved. And for D2, you need to provide an in-depth account of

the strengths and weaknesses of the strategies, as well as recommendations for future strategies that relate directly to the strengths and weaknesses you have already highlighted.

The second part of the task – P6 and M3 – requires you to provide the reader with clear and concise information about a local **and** a national organization, describing, for example, how they are structured, how they increase participation and how they liaise with partner organizations. Remember to mention aspects of each organization that may be unique, such as groups they are particularly targeting or their methods of working. Again, for M3 you need to give clear reasons why the organizations work as they do.

Meeting the Pass criteria

Unit 6 assignment, part three

Zia Abhas

Go-Ride (British Cycling)

Go-Ride is British Cycling's Club Development Programme, aimed at improving young riders and the clubs that they ride for.

The scheme focuses on volunteers and young members, improving coaching standards and increasing the number of young riders with access to coaching activities.

Go-Ride helps riders link up with clubs so that they have a supply of new young members.

> This is a good start by Zia. More detail like this and she will achieve P5.

Meeting the Merit criteria

Unit 6 assignment, part three

Carrie Cousins

High Fives: Netball

High fives is a modified version of the game of netball that is played in primary schools. It is fun and skilful, and players rotate their positions and adapt skills to play in a variety of roles.

> This is more of a description than an explanation. Carrie needs to give some reasons **why** the sport has been modified, why it is aimed at the primary school age group and why the players rotate positions. At the moment, if Carrie continues like this, she will achieve a Pass. To achieve a Merit she must start explaining each point she makes.

Meeting the Distinction criteria

Unit 6 assignment, part three

Rhys Williams

The Newcastle Football Development Scheme was launched in 1987. It has indoor and outdoor facilities at the Newcastle Football Centre in Benwell and at high-quality venues across Newcastle upon Tyne and North Tyneside.
The strengths of the programme are:

- Many players have come through the scheme and progressed to professional clubs.
- They have introduced weekly coaching sessions for those who want to focus on specific areas of the game.
- Coaches from junior clubs can improve their skills there through the coach education programme.

> Rhys has made a good start by explaining the strengths of the programme, but he needs to build on this by detailing any weaknesses of the scheme and, taking these weaknesses into account, making recommendations for future strategies.

Issues and their impact on the sports industry

If there is one thing that can be said about the sports industry, it is that it is never dull! There is always something happening, whether it is a drugs scandal, a famous England win, poor behaviour by a footballer or a fantastic performance by an athlete at the Olympic Games. And all these events have impacts on the sports industry, some of which are positive and some of which are negative.

Sky Sports: a television revolution!

sky SPORTS HD

British Sky Broadcasting has had a significant impact on sport in the UK since the early 1990s, most notably encouraging the Premier League to break away from the Football League in 1992. As a result of its influence, football in England has changed beyond recognition, sometimes for the better and sometimes for the worse.

Positive impacts	Negative impacts
Huge influx of income into the English game.	Many lower league teams are in financial difficulties because bigger clubs now buy more players from abroad instead of from football league clubs.
Helped top clubs buy the best European and world players.	Matches have been moved away from the traditional 3pm Saturday kickoff so that they can cater for larger television audiences, thereby maximizing advertising revenues.
Helped clubs build bigger and safer stadiums.	The BBC and ITV cannot compete financially with Sky Sports, so many matches are not on terrestrial television and people have to pay to watch them.
Helped The FA redevelop Wembley Stadium.	Top players' wages are now 'sky' high, and many people think of them as overpaid prima donnas.
Helped the FA develop many grassroots initiatives.	If Sky Sports pulled out of their current deal with the Premier League, the FA and the Premier League clubs would be in serious financial difficulties.

The personal becomes public: Tiger Woods

Many events, when they first happen, only appear to have an impact on an individual or a small group of people. But, on closer inspection, the impacts can sometimes have much more far-reaching effects. The problems encountered by the golfer Tiger Woods, when he crashed his car in 2009 and his problems at home emerged, are a good example of this. Initially, it looked like the impact of his actions would be limited to himself and his immediate family – but is that really the case?

Tiger Woods after winning the BMW Championship in September 2009. What shape will his future career take?

The impact of Tiger's behaviour	
On Tiger • It may affect his performance. • It may affect his sponsorship deals. • It may affect his popularity amongst golf spectators.	**On golf** • The image of golf has been affected. • The popularity of the sport may be affected. • Television and sponsorship income may decrease. • The spotlight moves away from golf and focuses on just one player.
On future players • Fewer young people may take up the sport, deciding that other sports have a better image. • They may copy Tiger's behaviour.	**Other impacts** • All the good work Tiger has done in raising the profile of black golfers may be undone.

The growing obesity problem

It is a well researched fact that there is a growing obesity problem in the UK, which is regularly featured in television, radio and newspaper reports. Here are some key facts from the NHS:

• In 2006, 24 per cent of adults (people aged 16 or over) in England were classified as obese. This represents an overall increase from 15 per cent in 1993.
• In 2006, 16 per cent of children aged two to fifteen were classed as obese, an overall increase from 11 per cent in 1995. However, despite the overall increase since 1995, the proportion of girls aged two to fifteen who were obese decreased between 2005 and 2006, from 18 per cent to 15 per cent. There was no significant decrease in the number of boys aged two to fifteen classed as obese over the same period.
• In 2006, boys were more likely than girls to be obese, with 17 per cent of boys classed as obese compared to 15 per cent of girls.

So, what impact is this growth in obesity having? Perhaps surprisingly, there are some positives:
• Levels of physical activity in schools are increasing steadily due to greater investment and focus on school sport.
• School dinners are now more in line with the requirements of a healthy diet.
• Initiatives such as Free Swimming are emerging, to help introduce young people to physical activity.
• Junk food adverts are banned from some of the most popular children's television programmes.
• Some sports are starting to include healthy eating advice in their coach education programmes.

Many schemes are now in place to help young people develop more healthy lifestyles.

BRONZE

1. What are the negative impacts of the growth in levels of obesity?
2. What are the positive and negative impacts of Great Britain winning the opportunity to host the 2012 Olympic and Paralympic Games? Record your ideas in a table.

More sporting issues and an overview of their impacts

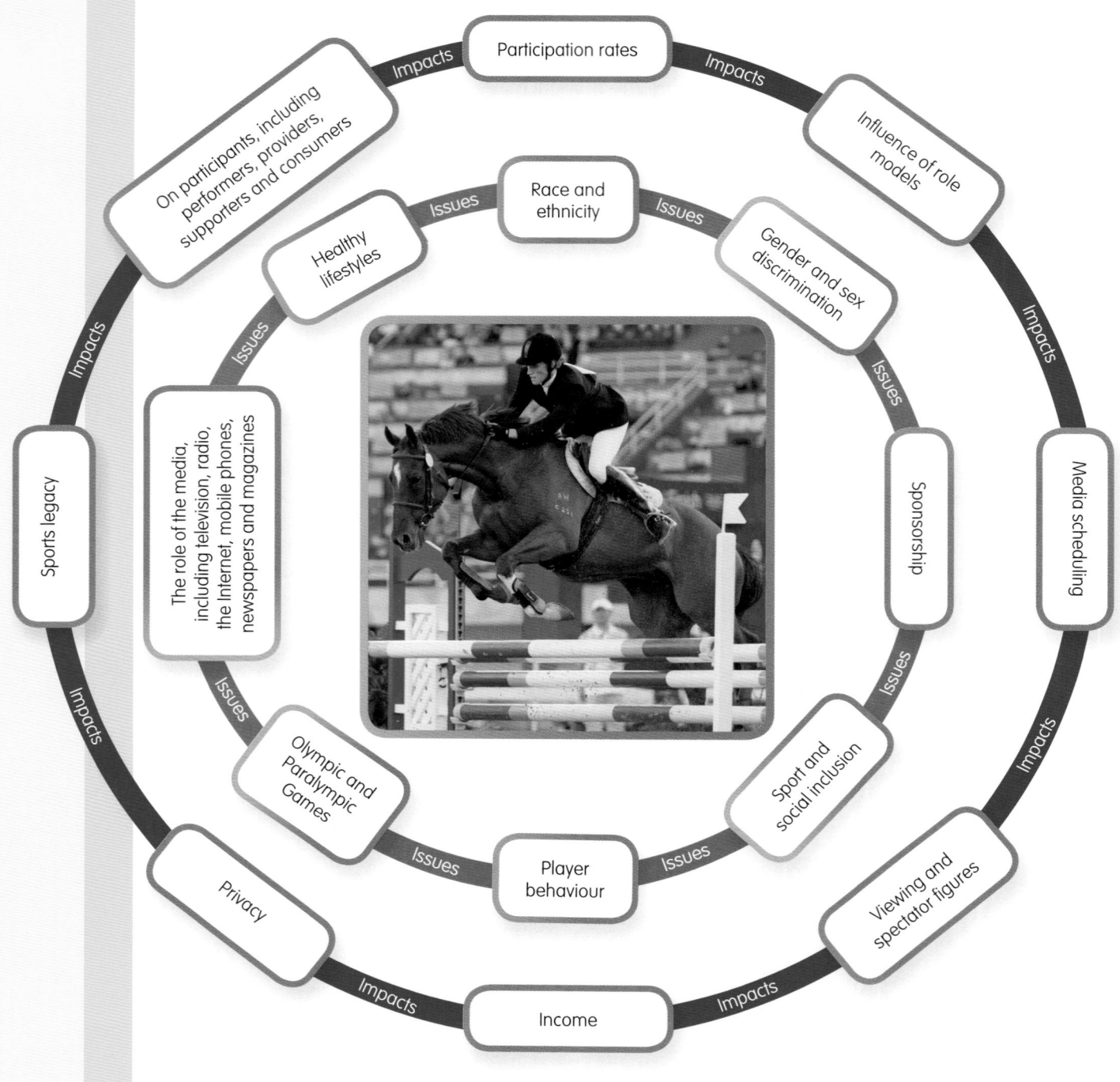

Participation rates

On participants, including performers, providers, supporters and consumers

Influence of role models

Race and ethnicity

Gender and sex discrimination

Healthy lifestyles

The role of the media, including television, radio, the Internet, mobile phones, newspapers and magazines

Sponsorship

Sports legacy

Media scheduling

Olympic and Paralympic Games

Sport and social inclusion

Player behaviour

Privacy

Viewing and spectator figures

Income

Impacts · Issues

BRONZE

3. Choose one issue relating to the sports industry that you would like to investigate in more detail and collect a range of reference material, including newspaper cuttings and information from websites, to help you develop your understanding.

SILVER

4. Having completed Activity 3 you should be much more familiar with the issue you have chosen, so it is time to explain the impact it has had on sport. Think carefully about the positive and negative impacts and, most importantly, the reasons **why** you think the impacts are as you describe them.

Unit 6 assignment, part four

Background

Your team of sports development officers has a full team meeting every month, in which a range of internal and external matters are discussed. 'Key issues and their impact on sport' is a recent introduction to the agenda because the Senior SDO thinks the team needs to be more aware of what is happening in the world of sport. You are looking forward to this element of future meetings and volunteer to kick off proceedings with a presentation.

Task

Prepare a presentation looking at four key issues and explaining their positive, negative and future impacts on the sports industry. Your presentation should:

GRADING CRITERIA TO BE ASSESSED
P7
M4

Describe four key issues in sport and identify their impact on sport (P7).

Explain the impact of four key issues on sport (M4).

Tackling the assignment

There is so much happening it might seem hard to decide which four issues to choose, but try to focus on current issues because there will almost certainly be more information easily available about these.

You need to imagine that the team you are presenting to have a little knowledge of the issues you are going to address, so your **description** needs to include enough detail to keep them interested, give them a really good insight into the issue, and make sure that they learn something new. Make sure you look at both the positives and negatives, but don't worry if there is an imbalance. Some issues will have far more positives than negatives (and vice versa).

Your explanation of the impacts needs to be just that – an explanation. So don't forget to build on your description with some clear **reasons why**. Remember, a reason often includes the word 'because', so make sure you use it!

Meeting the Pass criteria

Unit 6 assignment, part four   **Courtney Davison**

Notes to support my flip chart presentation

Issue 1: London 2012 Olympics and Paralympics

- The 2012 Olympics and Paralympics are to be held in London.
- A range of new facilities are being built so that the events can take place.
- Many sports are being well funded in the run-up to the Games to try and ensure Team GB wins medals at the Games.
- Many schemes are being developed to ensure participation rates in sport increase in the build up to the Games and after them.

Courtney has started to describe the issue well, but she needs to display more depth of knowledge to meet the criteria for P7. For example, where are the new facilities? What are the funding levels? What sort of schemes are there in place?

Issue 1: Impacts of the London 2012 Olympics and Paralympics

- The profile of sport will be raised.
- Certain sports (where we do well) will possibly gain more participants.
- There will be some excellent facilities for the people of London to use after the Games.

Courtney has started to identify some positive impacts and has made an excellent start, but to fully meet the criteria for P7 she needs to identify some negative impacts too, such as:
- Possible transport problems in London during the Games.
- A possible terrorist threat.
- Money being diverted from grassroots sport to elite sport.

Meeting the Merit criteria

Craig should be encouraged to refer to other areas of the health agenda as well, such as healthy eating, school sport and physical education, to increase the depth of his presentation and broaden his audience's understanding of the issue.

Unit 6 assignment, part four   **Craig Cowdell**

The possible impact of the health agenda on sport

Notes to support my talk:

I am going to use the Free Swimming scheme to look at positive and negative impacts of the health agenda on sport.

Positive:

- More people may take up aquatic activities because they have had the opportunity to use swimming facilities more often. They could have found out that they have a talent for swimming or have been made aware of other water-based activities, such as water polo or diving, that they enjoy but didn't know about before.

Negatives:

- Local authorities may see a drop in income from their swimming pools because the subsidy they are receiving is less than it would be if the Free Swimming strategy was not in place. This could result in less investment in other sports because their overall budget for sport has been reduced.

Craig is on a roll! Including reasons means Craig has explained why this is a negative impact. Again, a few more of these and Craig will achieve M4.

This is clearly a positive impact, which Craig has supported with three reasons. This is a great base to expand on verbally. A few more of these and Craig is well on his way to meeting the criteria for M4.

Unit 7: Planning and Leading Sports Activities

Skills associated with good sports leadership

Leaders and coaches play an important role in sport and exercise, so it is vital that they have the necessary skills to organize and implement training sessions and sporting events successfully.

Communication

Communication is especially important when coaching young children.

Communication is one of the most important skills required for planning and leading sports activities and events. There are two main ways in which a sports leader communicates:

1. **Verbal communication:** This is achieved by speaking to people. A leader should be clear and precise in what they are saying. They should keep the information simple and not use too many words, so there is no confusion and the group remains focused throughout.
2. **Non-verbal communication:** This is achieved using lots of different methods, including hand gestures, body language, tone of voice and facial expressions – anything other than what you actually say to people. Non-verbal communication can be very effective when leading a group, particularly if the environment they are working in is noisy. Some learners also respond better to non-verbal communication (for example, a skill being demonstrated) than they do to verbal communication.

A successful leader also has the ability to listen to their group and deal with any issues or concerns they have about the event or session that is taking place. It is important that the leader is understanding and that members of the group feel that their leader is approachable.

Organization of equipment

Leaders need to make sure the necessary equipment is available before a session begins.

Organization is another key skill when planning a sports session or event. Leaders should be aware of both the facilities and the equipment available, and ensure that they have everything in place prior to the session. They should consider the following:

- **Size of the group:** How many are attending the session? Is more space or equipment needed because the group is large?
- **Condition of the equipment:** Is the equipment safe to use? Has it been maintained to a good standard?
- **Variety of equipment:** Is there something for people of all abilities? Different equipment may be required for people who are disabled or have special educational needs.
- **Return of equipment:** It is important that borrowed equipment is returned in the same condition that it was in when it was taken. This will ensure a positive relationship between the lender and the borrower is maintained and that future hire of equipment is possible.

Knowledge

Perhaps most importantly, sports leaders should have an in-depth knowledge of the skills, techniques, rules and regulations of the sport or activity they are leading to ensure that they give out accurate information.

A leader should also possess detailed information about the people in their group to make sure that they know about medical issues or other special requirements. For example, knowing the age of participants means they can make sure that parental consent is obtained for all children under 16 to take part. This information can be obtained by asking participants to fill in a questionnaire or by talking directly to individuals.

Leaders must also be aware of the health and safety implications of the session taking place, and should have completed or viewed a risk assessment prior to the session. They should also have a basic understanding of first aid and be aware of the emergency action procedure.

Activity structure

Before any session or event can take place, a detailed and accurate plan should be drawn up. The plan should include the following information:

- **Your goal:** You should have a clear idea of what you want to achieve and what you want the group to achieve by the end of the session. For example, one of your aims might be to get more than ten participants to attend your session; another might be to ensure that everyone who attends makes some progress by the end of the session. You might set yourself an objective, such as all group members will be able to dribble a basketball using only their right hand by the end of the session, and decide that an expected outcome will be that some members of the group will be able to do this and others will be able to perform a modified version.
- **Content:** Details of what is going to happen during the session will remind you what needs to be covered and ensure that nothing is missed out. For example, 'a warm-up, followed by passing and shooting skills, followed by a competition, followed by a cool-down'.
- **Timings:** It is vital that timings are linked to the content so that everything can be covered in the session, unnecessary delays are avoided and everyone involved knows what should be happening at all times.
- **Equipment:** A list of the equipment to be used is a useful reminder of what you will need to prepare for the activity. You may also wish to consider any special requirements of people in the group at this point, as different equipment may be required to provide tasks that cater for all abilities.

An example of a plan for a session.

Use of language

The way in which a leader speaks to their group can have an effect on the group's behaviour and their performance. For example, when leading young children, basic, exaggerated instructions with lots of demonstrations will help to make you more easily understood. However, where teenagers and adults are concerned, the information can be more detailed and the terminology more specific.

BRONZE

1. Decide which of the following are examples of verbal communication and which are examples of non-verbal communication:

- telling someone to sit down
- demonstrating an overhead pass
- putting your finger on your lips to quieten the group
- asking someone what their targets are
- pointing to the clock to show someone the time
- saying 'Well done' to your athlete.

2. Try the two games below. What do they teach you about communication skills?

a) Sit back to back with a partner. One of you must describe an object without saying what it is, while the other draws the object being described. Then, name the object and see how accurate the drawing is.

b) Stand back to back with a partner. Recite a nursery rhyme, taking it in turns to say each line. As you are reciting the rhyme, walk away from each other.

3. You are running a session for a group of ten to eleven year-old boys. You want to teach them how to pass a football between them using the 'two-touch' method.

- How many balls do you need?
- What other equipment will you use?
- How much space will you need?
- Will your session run indoors or outdoors?
- What else do you need to consider?

4. You have been asked to plan a sports activity session for a sport of your choice. What points should you consider when putting your plan together?

5. Design a questionnaire to obtain information about the participants in your sports activity session. You need to know how old each participant is, if they have any medical conditions and any other important f... that might have an impact on how you lead the session.

Evaluation

It is important for a sports leader to evaluate sessions that they run to provide them with feedback on their performance. If a session is unsuccessful, for whatever reason, the leader can work on improving things for the next time that they lead an activity. Equally, if something worked really well, they may want to use this method in the future.

When evaluating a session or event it is important to gather information from everyone involved, including the participants, the spectators and the helpers, to build an accurate picture of how it went. You might want to ask people about the following:

- **Planning:** How well was the session/event planned?
- **Content:** How suitable was the content of the session/event for the participants? Was there enough/too much going on?
- **Organization:** How organized was the leader before the event and on the day? Did they remain calm?
- **Health and Safety:** Were the participants safe? Were there any incidents? If anyone was injured or ill, were they treated efficiently?
- **Personal qualities of the leader:** How appropriate was the leadership style employed? How confident/enthusiastic/motivational/friendly was the leader? How good was the leader at communicating?
- **Achievements:** Did the leader achieve the objectives set out for the session/event?
- **Areas for development:** What could have been done better? What should the leader do next time to make the session/event run more smoothly?

BRONZE

6. Write down three SMART targets that you want to achieve in your role as a sports leader. For example, you may want to feel more confident when talking to a group by the end of the term.

7. Find an example of a real-life sports leader for each of the skills associated with sports leadership.

SILVER

8. Choose two sports leaders and list all the skills associated with sports leadership that each of them has. Then, compare the two lists, explaining the differences and similarities.

GOLD

9. Look at your answer to Activity 8. Based on their skills, which, in your opinion, is the best sports leader and why?

Target setting

Targets should be set for participants, particularly if the activity is part of a series of sessions aimed at improving skills or techniques in a given sport. For example, if a coach is leading an individual through a series of training sessions, they may wish to set their athlete the target of recording a personal best performance by the end of the season, or of gaining selection for a particular event or squad. Coaches and leaders can also set themselves targets. For example, they may want to improve their leadership skills, try different teaching styles or work on using different communication skills. Targets should be SMART:

SPECIFIC: Targets should be specific; they should set down precisely what you want to achieve. For example, 'I want to run the 100m in under 15 seconds.'

MEASUREABLE: Targets should be measurable, so that you can work out if you have achieved them. It is also better to make these measures specific, wherever possible. For example, it is better to say that your target is to run the 100m in under 15 seconds than it is to say that you want to run the 100m faster.

ACHIEVABLE: Targets should be appropriate to the fitness and skill levels of the performer. They should be close enough for us to see but not so far away that we can't touch them.

REALISTIC: It is important that we set targets that we have the capacity to achieve. All targets need to be challenging so that you have to work hard to achieve them, but they must also be realistic in order for them to serve their purpose and motivate you.

TIME-BOUND: Targets should have a time limit on them. For example, 'I want to run the 100m in under 15 seconds by the end of the summer.' If your long-term goals rely on you achieving your short-term goals, then you need to set time limits on your short-term goals in order to ensure you reach your long term goals.

Qualities associated with good sports leadership

In addition to all the necessary skills, a sports leader should also possess a range of qualities that make them well suited to working with others in a leadership capacity.

Appearance

A sports leader should always take pride in their appearance and look smart because they are setting an example to the people in their group. They may also be viewed as a role model by some members of their group.

Autocratic (Command).

Leadership style

There are many different leadership styles that sports leaders can use with their groups but the three main ones are:

- **Autocratic (Command):** This is a straightforward leadership style where the leader gives out instructions that the group follows. It can be effective when dealing with large numbers of people because there is less chance of the instructions being misinterpreted.
- **Democratic:** This leadership style is more laid back and, unlike the autocratic approach, the leader involves the group in the decision making. This approach is effective with smaller groups and, as the group members are asked for their opinion, it gives them a sense of responsibility for the session or event.
- **Laissez-faire:** This is a very relaxed leadership style in which the responsibility for decision making is largely given to the group. This method can only really be effective if the group members are responsible and experienced, because incorrect decisions could cause problems.

Democratic.

Personality

Leaders all have their own individual personalities. However, they must possess certain qualities in order to communicate well with the members of their group.

Laissez-faire.

Outgoing and sociable
This is important if they are to get along well with members of the public and communicate with a range of different people.

Understanding
There may be occasions when an individual has a delicate issue, which is affecting their performance, that they wish to discuss.

Leaders should be …

Approachable
This is important if they want their group to have confidence in them and feel able to talk to them about any concerns.

Confident with their authority
Leaders must be able to discipline their group if necessary. This is particularly important when considering health and safety issues.

Enthusiasm

When leading a group or individual, it is vital that the coach or leader is enthusiastic about what they are teaching. In order to motivate the participants and keep them interested, the leader must believe in what they are saying and should try to convey this enthusiasm to their group.

Motivation

It is important for leaders to motivate the members of their group, because a motivated group is usually more interested and keen to succeed. Motivational techniques that coaches and leaders can use include encouragement, praising the positives and setting targets for improvement. Leaders should try to be motivational all the time because what they say and do can have a direct effect on the performance of the sportsperson or team.

Humour

Coaches and leaders should enjoy delivering activities and events, and it is really beneficial to have a good sense of humour. A leader who can joke, be light-hearted and have fun with the group could make their sessions more interesting and stimulating than a leader who is serious all the time.

Confidence

A leader should be confident in their ability. This confidence will be passed on to the participants so that they believe their leader knows what he or she is talking about and, therefore, have faith in what they are being taught. A leader may also be required to speak to large numbers of people at any one time and this takes courage and confidence.

A leader needs to be confident if they are to hold the group's attention and lead an effective session.

BRONZE

1. Which of the following statements show an autocratic leadership style, which show a democratic leadership style and which show a laissez-faire leadership style?

a) Are you warmed up enough now? Would you like to end the warm-up there?

b) Pass the ball and move into a space.

c) Would you like to take a rest now?

d) OK, what would you like to do today then? How about a few stretches to start off with?

e) You must use the correct technique every time if you wish to improve.

2. For each style of leadership, identify a famous sports leader who mainly employs this style.

3. Why is it important for a sports leader to be enthusiastic? Describe the effect that an enthusiastic sports leader could have on a participant. When might participants need an enthusiastic sports leader most?

4. For each of the qualities associated with good sports leadership, find an example of a real-life sports leader who possesses it.

SILVER

5. Choose two sports leaders and list all the qualities associated with sports leadership that each of them has. Then, compare the two lists, explaining the differences and similarities.

GOLD

6. Look at your answer to Activity

7. Based on their qualities, which, in your opinion, is the best sports leader and why?

Responsibilities associated with good sports leadership

When running a session or event, sports leaders are responsible for all the people involved, the venue and the equipment being used.

Responsibilities of a good sports leader

Health and safety: A leader must make sure that their group is safe and well while participating in physical activity. This involves duties such as checking that there is a current risk assessment in place and checking that the equipment is in full working order.

Insurance: It is a requirement that sports leaders have insurance to cover them for any activity that they are leading. This provides reassurance to the participants and their families in case of any accident, and protects the leader should anything go wrong.

Child protection: Sports leaders must make sure that children in their care are safe and not at risk from anyone. It is vital that leaders identify children with problems or those who may be suffering abuse. Children often confide in people that they look up to and, if a child is suffering at home, they may share their burden with their sports coach or leader.

Data protection: Sports leaders should be aware of the Data Protection Act 1998, which sets out rules on how organizations should manage confidential, personal information.

Legal obligations: If you are leading a group of children under 16 years old, you are legally obliged to seek the permission of a parent or guardian before allowing anyone to take part. Also, if your activity is considered a contact sport, such as football or rugby, participants must not take part in mixed gender activities and separate-sex practices should be set up.

Rules and regulations: Leaders should be familiar with the rules and regulations of the sport or activity which they are delivering. They should also ensure that their group members, especially if they are young children, adhere to the rules because this may help to prevent injuries.

Professional conduct: Leaders must behave professionally and responsibly at all times. Young children often look up to their leader and view them as a role model. Therefore, their actions and behaviour must be impeccable in order to have a positive impact on the members of their group.

Equality: Sports leaders should be aware of equal opportunities and try to ensure that all participants are treated with respect regardless of their age, gender, disability, race, nationality, ethnicity or national origin. They should encourage members of their group to be polite and respectful to create a good atmosphere.

Attendance registers: It is the leader's responsibility to ensure that a register is taken at every session. This will show who has regularly taken part in the activities and will give the leader an indication of whether or not participants enjoy them. Taking a register also means that the leader knows who is there in the event of an emergency.

Ethics and values: Good sportsmanship is about being fair and honest. Sports leaders should encourage the members of their group to respect each other and their opponents, and to abide by the rules and etiquette expected in their sport or physical activity.

BRONZE

1. Taking your own experience and qualifications as a starting point, find out about the next leadership qualification that you could take for a sport of your choice.

Sports leadership roles

There are different types of sports leadership roles, depending on the age, experience and qualifications of the individual who is leading. A young sports leader may hold a Level 1 Award in Sports Leadership. This means that they are able to deliver planned sessions to young people but must be supervised by a more experienced leader. If they hold the Level 2 Award in Community Sports Leadership they no longer need to be supervised. School and college teachers and coaches may have sport-specific coaching awards, such as a Badminton Leaders Award. These are often picked up while a teacher is training at university. Local club coaches generally hold Level 1, 2 or 3 coaching awards in their chosen sport(s). National club coaches are usually people who have been coaching for many years.

SILVER

2. Explain the following responsibilities of being a sports leader, giving examples to support your answer.

• A sports leader should ensure that their athlete(s) abides by the rules and regulations of the relevant sport.
• It is the responsibility of the sports leader to ensure that everyone in their group has an equal opportunity to participate.

Unit 7 assignment, part one

Background

You are the manager of the local rugby club and are always looking to recruit new members. At the moment, you are also looking for a suitably qualified coach to lead the under-13 squad. You need someone who can work with children, and who has the right skills and qualities to lead a young side.

GRADING CRITERIA TO BE ASSESSED
P1
M1
D1

Task

Imagine that you are writing an article for the sports section of your local newspaper, which is designed to encourage applicants for a job like the one outlined in the scenario above. The article should be based around an analysis of the skills, qualities and responsibilities of two successful sports leaders. Your article should contain:

A description of the skills, qualities and responsibilities associated with successful sports leadership, using two examples of successful sports leaders (P1).

An explanation of the skills, qualities and responsibilities associated with successful sports leadership, comparing and contrasting two successful sports leaders (M1).

An evaluation of the skills and qualities of two contrasting leaders in sport, commenting on their effectiveness (D1).

Tackling the assignment

To ensure that you produce a detailed analysis of the two sports leaders, the work that you produce must contain a substantial amount of text, although you could also include photographs where appropriate. If you are not confident about commenting on two famous or well-known sports leaders, you may wish to use examples of sports leaders that you are more familiar with, such as your PE teachers or college lecturers.

Meeting the Pass, Merit and Distinction criteria

BTEC Level 2 Firsts in Sport

Unit 7 assignment, part one   **Jamie Hill**

Jose Mourinho	Steve McClaren
Manages Inter Milan.	Manages FC Twente.
Experience with previous clubs: • Chelsea • FC Porto • Uniao Leiria • Benfica.	Previous experience as England manager and manager of Middlesbrough FC.
Achieves victory with his team in competitions. So far, he has won: • Portuguese league two years running • Portuguese cup • UEFA Champions League • UEFA Cup • Premiership two years running • Carling Cup twice.	Led Middlesbrough to win their first trophy, the Carling Cup, in 2004 and took them to the UEFA Cup Final in 2006. Former professional footballer with: • Hull City • Derby County • Lincoln City • Bristol City • Oxford United.
Focused on winning. Self-confident. Motivates players. Ambitious. Self-assured (may be considered arrogant). Is a huge personality, known worldwide. Is respected by his players.	Comfortable under the spotlight. Self-assured as shown through his posture and style. Good communication skills.

Comparing Jose Mourinho and Steve McClaren

Jose Mourinho has a track record of winning major competitions. Under his management, FC Porto won a unique treble, winning the Portuguese league and cup as well as the UEFA Cup in 2003. He also led them to Champions League glory in 2004. While managing Chelsea, he won the English Premiership two years running, and the Carling Cup twice. In 2007 he also took Chelsea to the first FA Cup Final at the new Wembley Stadium and triumphed to add an FA cup medal to his collection.

Many people know him for his self-assurance, maybe even his arrogance, and his pleasure at being the main man. It has done him little harm, as many players and managers worldwide respect him. It sometimes causes great rivalry but this just creates more fame for him. His motivational skills get the best out of his players and he never gives up if things look bleak.

Steve McClaren stepped up to the international stage after being a club manager. After taking Middlesbrough to their first trophy, the 2004 Carling Cup, and the UEFA Cup Final in 2006, he was recognized as a successful coach and was appointed as England manager, where he attempted to take England to their first trophy for over 40 years. His communication skills are excellent, which enables him to get the best out of his players on and off the football pitch. Being an international coach came with huge media responsibility, so to be comfortable under the spotlight, as he was, was essential.

Jose Mourinho enjoys being in the spotlight and thrives on such media attention. Although Steve McClaren does not mind being in the spotlight, unlike Mourinho, he does not go looking for press attention. Both are in the press frequently, but one throws himself in front of the media and the other does not.

> Well done, Jamie! You have made an excellent start to your comparison between the two leaders, highlighting some of their skills, qualities and responsibilities. This begins to meet the criteria for P1 and M1, as you show a good understanding of the two football managers and have begun to point out differences in their style of leading a sports team.

> In order to meet the criteria for D1, you should provide an in-depth analysis of the two leaders you have selected, specifically highlighting their similarities and differences in all aspects of leadership. For example, is their leadership style autocratic, democratic or laissez-faire? You should also offer your opinion on who is the better manager and justify your choice.

Planning and leading an activity session

Planning your session

When planning a session or event, the following aspects must be taken into consideration:

Participants:
- How many people are attending the session? How will you split the group up?
- How old are the people attending the session?
- Are the people attending the session male or female, or will there be a mix of participants? Does your activity require children to work in single-sex groups?
- What ability are the people attending the session? Are they all beginners, or will you have a mixture of experienced and inexperienced participants?
- Do any of the participants have medical or other specific needs? How will you ensure that these are met? Will you need to differentiate the activities?

Aims and objectives: Every session should have clear aims and objectives that are both measurable and achievable. An aim is something general that you are working to achieve by the end of the session or series of sessions, for example, to improve the over-arm bowling technique of participants. An objective is something specific that you are aiming to achieve, for example, 'By the end of this session, participants will be able to bowl a ball to a batsman using an over-arm technique'.

Expected outcomes: Each session should have one or more expected outcomes. These are the things that you expect participants to have achieved by taking part in the session. An expected outcome may vary depending on the experience and/or ability of the participants. For example, the expected outcome for one student may be to dribble a basketball in a straight line and the expected outcome for another may be to dribble a basketball around an obstacle.

Resources:
- What equipment will you need? Can you access all the equipment you need when you need it? Is it safe to use?
- How long is your session? Have you allocated times to the different parts of your session? Can the planned activities be completed within the time allowed for the session?

- Do you have an appropriate venue for the session? Will the venue be accessible to you before and after the session so that you can set up and pack away the equipment?

Setting targets: Make sure you set targets for yourself prior to running an event so that when the event is over you have something to measure your own success against. For example, you may set yourself the target of ensuring that all results are recorded accurately.

Your abilities: Are you able to lead the whole session? Sometimes an activity or skill will require a detailed explanation followed by a demonstration. If you can explain it but are not able to demonstrate it, is there someone reliable that you can ask to demonstrate it for you?

The session:
- Begin with a warm-up activity to set the pace for the rest of the session and help minimize the risk of injury. The warm-up should consist of three phases: the pulse-raising phase, the stretching phase and the joint mobilization phase.
- Introduce the session, telling the group the aims, objectives and expected outcomes so that they know what you expect of them during the session.
- Focus on skill work. Whatever the skill you are teaching, break it down into bite-sized segments and focus on one segment at a time. For example, if you want to teach the long jump, break it down into the run up, the take off, the flight and the landing. Remember, it may take several sessions to teach all of the segments.
- Practise the skills.
- It is usual, at the end of a session, to allow a group to play a modified game or competition. This is important, particularly for young children, who quickly get bored if they just practise a skill and cannot imagine doing it in a 'game situation'.
- It is hugely beneficial for a session to end with a cool-down activity. It may just be a gentle jog and a few stretches, perhaps while seated, but this gives the group a chance to recover from the session and helps to bring both their mind and body back to a resting state.

Leading your session

Don't forget to keep a record of the session. You could keep a diary, logbook or portfolio, record witness testimonies, keep feedback sheets or an observation record, and use audio or video equipment.

Reviewing your session

Having planned and led your session, it is important to celebrate your strengths and identify areas for improvement by reviewing your performance. Detailed guidance on how to review performance is given on pages 37–38.

Setting targets for improvement and development

After you have reviewed your session, you should set yourself targets for improvement and development. Detailed guidance on how to set SMART targets is given on page 146.

Having decided on your targets, you can create a development plan summarizing both your short- and long-term goals, and ways in which you can achieve them. For example, you might mention training courses that you would like to attend, and mentoring or coaching opportunities you would like to experience. A development plan should include aims, objectives, intended outcomes and a timescale.

Unit 7 assignment, part two

Background

You are keen to become a sports leader and, as a favour to you, a local sports coach has given you the opportunity to plan and lead an activity for a group of ten-year-old children. Although the sports coach will be in the vicinity when you are leading your activity, you should create a plan for, prepare and deliver the activity independently.

Task

Plan and lead an activity session for a mixed-ability group of boys and girls aged ten. Your session should last approximately 30 minutes and should include a warm-up, skills section and possibly a modified game. You should ensure that you set aims, objectives and expected outcomes for the young people. On completion of the session, you should also review your performance, commenting on your strengths and areas for development. You should aim to:

GRADING CRITERIA TO BE ASSESSED
P2, P3
M2, M3

Plan and lead a sports activity, with tutor support (P2).

Review the planning and leading of a sports activity, identifying strengths and areas for improvement (P3).

Independently plan and lead a sports activity (M2).

Explain strengths and areas for improvement and development in the planning and leading of a sports activity (M3).

Tackling the assignment

In order to meet the Pass criteria for this assignment, you should create a session plan containing details of your intended activities, with time allocations. Ask your teacher for an example.

Your teacher or lecturer should organize a group of youngsters for you to deliver your session to and, when the session takes place, they may make notes about your performance to feed back to you later. You should then review your performance. This can easily be done using a basic form, summarizing what went well and what could have been done better.

If you intend to achieve a Merit, make sure you create your session plan and deliver your activity independently, without support from your teacher or lecturer. You should also include descriptive information about your strengths and areas for improvement when reviewing your session.

Planning and leading a sports event

Plan

Sports events take many forms, from inter-school competitions to regional and international events. Sports events can also be run for fun or for charity, for example, the Cancer Research UK Race for Life event that takes place every year. In order to successfully plan and lead a sports event, the following factors should be considered:

Your role and responsibilities: As the lead organizer you must ensure that all aspects of the event are organized before it begins. You must also decide what you will be doing on the day. Most event organizers find that it is useful for them to float between activities, so that they are available to deal with any issues that may arise, rather than have an actual job.

The roles and responsibilities of others: You cannot run an event single-handedly, so it is important to get other people involved in planning and leading the event. Anyone who volunteers to help you should be responsible and organized, and will ideally have experience as well as a leadership qualification.

The structure of the event or competition: This may include a list showing the order of activities, details of whose responsibility each activity is, and a map or diagram of where each activity is taking place (if more than one site is being used). If the event includes an actual competition, a timetable of races or matches and a set of rules may also be required.

Health and safety: The safety of those attending should be paramount. A risk assessment should be completed beforehand and potential hazards identified. A contingency plan should be created to cater for all eventualities, including a change in the weather or a problem with the venue or equipment.

Refreshments: Entrants will expect to be given or be able to purchase a drink or snack in between activities. Spectators may also require refreshments.

The venue and equipment: You must book the venue and the equipment, making sure that you have access to it in advance of the event so that you can make the necessary preparations.

Prizes: You may want to award prizes to the winners and/or entrants of the event. Depending on how much money you have and whether or not you have sponsorship, your prizes could be certificates, medals or trophies. Holding one or more presentation ceremonies is usually the best way to celebrate achievements.

First aid: It does not matter whether the first aid is provided by the venue or by the organizer, as long as there are an adequate number of first aiders on site throughout the event.

Entrants and spectators: You must advertise the event and clearly explain who is eligible to attend/enter, when it begins and ends, and where it is taking place, as well as details of prizes, refreshments and so on. You need to decide whether entrants need to sign up in advance or if they can just turn up on the day, as well as considering how entrants will be organized when they arrive. You also need to decide where spectators can go during the event.

Rules and scoring systems: If a competitive activity is involved you will need umpires/referees, scorekeepers and/or timekeepers. You should aim to get experienced people to help you with this so that any data collected is accurate. The rules and scoring systems of the event/activities should be researched beforehand so that they are current. It would also be useful if these were on display for all to see in order to avoid any misunderstandings.

Leading your sports event

Don't forget to keep a record of the event. You could keep a diary, logbook or portfolio, record witness testimonies, keep feedback sheets or an observation record, and use audio or video equipment.

Reviewing your sports event

Having planned and led your event, it is important to celebrate your strengths and identify areas for improvement by reviewing your performance. Detailed guidance on how to review performance is given on pages 37–38.

Setting targets for improvement and development

After you have reviewed your session, you should set yourself targets for improvement and development (see page 146).

Having decided on your targets, you can create a development plan summarizing both your short- and long-term goals, and ways in which you can achieve them. For example, you might mention training courses that you would like to attend, and mentoring or coaching opportunities you would like to experience. A development plan should include aims, objectives, intended outcomes and a timescale.

Unit 7 assignment, part three

Background

You have volunteered to help a local charity organize a fund-raising event. The charity workers believe that to raise the most money it would be beneficial to invite local businesses to take part in the event. You can choose the activities that will take place on the day but they should include something fun, with prizes for the winning team. You have the assistance of the charity workers, so you can share the planning and organization with them.

Task

As part of a small group, assist with the planning, leading and post-event review of an event consisting of a team or individual competition. Ensure that a record is kept of all the stages in the planning process and all communication, such as emails or letters, which you send out. You should also make sure that a detailed review is carried out after the event. It should include information about the roles and responsibilities of each person contributing to the planning and leading, and also their strengths and areas for development. You should aim to meet the following criteria:

GRADING CRITERIA TO BE ASSESSED
P4, P5
M4
D2

PASS

Contribute to the planning and leading of a sports event (P4).

Review own performance whilst assisting with the planning and leading of a sports event, identifying strengths and areas for improvement (P5).

MERIT

Explain strengths and areas for improvement in assisting with the planning and leading of a sports event, making suggestions relating to improvement (M4).

DISTINCTION

Evaluate your own performance in the planning and leading of a sports activity and event, commenting on strengths, and areas for improvement and further development as a sports leader (D2).

Tackling the assignment

In order to meet the criteria for this assignment, you need to work as part of a small group to plan and lead an event. This means that members of the group must divide the tasks equally between themselves and each plan a section of the event, listing their individual responsibilities. In order to provide evidence of the planning procedure, each person in the group should also have a copy of all communication that takes place.

When delivering the actual event, your teacher or lecturer will make notes about your leadership skills. Participants could be adults working in local businesses and you could raise money for a chosen charity. Alternatively, you could run a competition at your school or college.

Each individual must complete their own personal review of the task, referring specifically to their role in the planning, organization and leading of the event.

Unit 8: Technical Skills and Tactical Awareness for Sport

Technical skills and tactical awareness

To be successful in sport, players, coaches and managers have to have a thorough understanding of techniques and tactics. As players compete at a higher level, the technical demands of their sport increase as does the complexity of the tactics involved, and games, matches and competitions are often won or lost on the training pitch.

Technical demands in sport

In recent years, the level of analysis in sports has greatly increased. TV cameras cover almost every tackle, shot, throw and jump, and this enables coaches to study an athlete's performance in depth. Minute corrections to technique can often lead to vast improvements in performance, but before this level of analysis takes place, a coach and a competitor must understand the basic skills underpinning a successful technique.

Skills can be classified in one of three ways:

Discrete skills:

These are skills that have a definite beginning and a definite end, and which happen only once. A good example is the golf swing. It begins with the player addressing the ball, and ends at the point where the club is pointing behind the player (i.e. after the follow through phase). To perform the skill again, the player must make a conscious effort to return to the starting position.

Continuous skills:

These are skills that **do not** have a definite beginning and end, but which appear to be the same technique repeated over and over again. A good example is the leg action in cycling. Once the rider is moving, it is impossible to determine where one rotation ends and the next one begins, but it is clearly the same skill performed repeatedly.

BRONZE

1. List three discrete skills, three continuous skills and three serial skills.

2. Break the serial skills you listed into their component parts. For example, the serial skill of the triple jump can be broken down into the hop, the skip and the jump.

Serial skills:

These are a series of discrete skills performed in sequence. Perhaps the most recognizable example is the triple jump. Here, there are three discrete phases – the hop, the skip and the jump – which are performed in sequence.

Once a coach or a performer has knowledge of the breakdown of a skill, they can isolate and train each phase to improve the athlete's technique, the way in which they perform the skill.

Tactical demands in sport

Tactics are plans that a player or team uses to beat opponents. Often these are devised before a game takes place, and a coach or manager will spend a large amount of time preparing the player or team for a specific match or event. However, the most successful teams, players and managers are able to adjust their tactics throughout a match or competition, in order to react to the tactics employed by their opponents.

When devising tactics, they can be considered as a whole team approach, an attacking approach or a defending approach. Whichever method is used, tactics involve a working knowledge of:

- **Positioning:** This can be the position of the whole team (such as a zone defence in basketball), the position of an individual (such as playing from the baseline in tennis) or the positioning of small groups of players within a team (such as the positioning of the back row in rugby union). Usually, positioning will be considered in two basic situations: positioning when in attack and positioning when in defence. However, at the top level, teams will often use a combination of all these components of positioning.

- **Choice of stroke, shot or pass:** Knowledge of which skill to use in which situation is vital if you are going to beat an opponent. Usually, the decisions are made during the game or match, but in some cases prior knowledge of a teammate's or an opponent's ability will cause a player to use a specific stroke or shot. For example, football teams who have a tall centre forward will often play high balls into the box, knowing that they have an increased chance of winning the ball in the air.

- **Variation:** Using the same tactics over and over again is rarely successful, particularly in professional sport. Opposing coaches, managers, teams and players will quickly work out what is happening, and adjust their own tactics to cope. For example, if a team regularly plays high balls into the box because they have a tall centre forward, the defending team will quickly change their own tactics in an attempt to stop their opponents delivering the high balls. They may do this by shutting down wide players early or by moving their defence higher up the pitch and forcing the centre forward into an offside position. The attacking team then have to vary their tactics in order to be successful.

- **Conditions:** The weather can have a major impact on the tactics employed by a team or player. In high winds, golfers will try to keep the ball low to reduce the likelihood of a ball veering off target. In bright sunshine, rugby teams will kick the ball high towards their opponents so it is difficult for them to see, which increases the chances of a knock-on occurring. The importance of a game or the size of the crowd can also have a major effect on tactics. A tennis player, playing on Centre Court at Wimbledon for the first time, is likely to play to their own strengths and will rarely try to implement new tactics or play unusual strokes.

- **Use of space:** The most common tactic is to create space when attacking and to close down available space when defending. Players who are able to create space also create the time needed to make a decision, which in turn allows them to choose the most appropriate course of action (to decide whether to shoot, pass or dribble in basketball, for example). A player who is denied time and space is much more likely to make a mistake.

BRONZE

3. List five tactics a team or individual player might use when defending and five tactics they might use when attacking in a sport of your choice.

4. Choose three attacking strategies used by a team or player in a sport of your choice, and suggest ways that an opposing team or player could counteract them.

SILVER

5. Explain the difference between the tactics employed by amateur participants and those employed by professionals in a sport of your choice. For example, an amateur tri-athlete will often put maximum effort into each phase – the swim, the cycle and the run – whereas a professional will usually conserve energy in their weakest area, allowing them to work harder in their area of strength.

Analysing performance

All the best sports performers continually analyse their own performances and the performances of their competitors. By doing this, they can identify and work to reduce areas of weakness, and can further develop areas of strength. Whilst self-analysis is useful, the most effective analysis often comes from others: from coaches, managers and teammates.

Performance analysis

Analysis of performance can take place during a match or event, after it or both. Usually, the following methods are employed:

- **Observation:** Data, such as the number of passes and interceptions or the positioning of the player or opponent, are gathered and these are used to analyse performance. At grass roots level, this observation is usually carried out by the team coach and feedback is given orally. However, in professional sport, a significant amount of money is spent on using the latest technology to carry out observational analysis.
- **Use of technology:** This most commonly takes the form of video analysis, where a performance is recorded and then analysed by reviewing the footage produced. This allows a player or a team to observe themselves in action, and often provides a valuable insight into the success or failure of the tactics employed. At a professional level, whole organizations are devoted to analysing performance (see OPTA statistics for the Premier League) and these provide additional information that can be used by managers, coaches and players. Using technology to support performance analysis is much more useful than basic observation analysis, because footage can be reviewed several times and discussed by several different interested parties.
- **Notational analysis:** This is a system used to record information while observing a performance because writing information long-hand takes a long time and it is easy to miss a lot of the action while you are writing. It consists of a series of strokes and symbols that are used to record information which are specific to individual sports. For example, a hyphen with a letter above it may be used to record offside in football, whereas it may symbolize a double fault in tennis or a line out in rugby.

This image shows two amateur cricketers performing an off drive. By filming and then aligning the shots, it is clear to see that the batsman below is performing at a higher level than the batsman above

The analysis model

Sport has developed rapidly over the last 30 years, changing from a pastime to big business. The ways in which performances are analysed have also changed, particularly with the emergence of new technology. Regardless of the method used to analyse performance, however, the way in which the information collected is used has remained the same.

5. Perform again to see if the training plan has worked. For example, another match is videoed and the number of double faults is observed, analysed and evaluated to see if the change in service style has reduced the number of double faults.

1. Observe the performance. For example, videoing a tennis match.

2. Analyse the performance to create data. For example, the observations could be analysed to find out how many double faults were committed in each service box during a tennis match.

3. Evaluate the data to find patterns and to discover reasons for success or failure. For example, you might discover that 4% of serves to the forehand resulted in double faults whereas 12% of serves to the backhand resulted in double faults, because too many of the serves to the backhand hit the net on second service.

4. Plan for future success. For example, a training plan is devised to develop the service to the backhand by changing the style of the service from a top-spin to a sliced serve.

Strengths and areas for improvement

In its simplest form, performance analysis generates information about a performer's strengths and weaknesses. This enables the performer to concentrate on using their strengths in a competitive situation and eliminating their weaknesses during training. However, by itself, performance analysis rarely provides reasons to explain why a particular technique or tactic is classed as a strength or a weakness. Therefore, for performance analysis to be effective, you must have a thorough understanding of the techniques and tactics that constitute a successful performance.

SWOT analysis

One way in which to analyse and evaluate a performer's strengths and areas for improvement is to complete a SWOT analysis. This involves considering the Strengths, Weaknesses, Opportunities and Threats that exist within a performance. Strengths and weaknesses are usually identified before the performance by interviewing the player, and are then added to through observation. Opportunities are chances to improve, by finding extra time to train within an existing training schedule for example. Threats are things that could hinder a performance, such as poor health, damaged or poor quality equipment, lack of sleep or motivation, or inappropriate techniques or tactics. Having made a list under each of the headings, a plan can then be devised to take advantage of the opportunities and strengths, and to reduce the impact of the weaknesses and threats. A SWOT analysis is more commonly used for individual sports rather than team sports.

Performance profiling

One of the most difficult areas to analyse is a performer's state of mind, during and in the lead up to a competition. A player will only perform at their best in the optimum conditions, and anything that could distract them or lead to a loss of motivation is likely to hinder performance. The aim of performance profiling is to ensure that a performer is in the right frame of mind at the right time. The player is asked questions about their state of mind, such as:

- Are you feeling confident?
- Are you thinking of anything other than the competition?
- What motivates you to succeed in this competition?
- Are you enjoying playing at the moment?

Once any problems with a player's state of mind have been established, a psychological training plan can be developed to remove the distractions or enable the performer to cope better with them. Unit 9: Psychology for Sports Performance explains how to develop a psychological training programme.

Elite performance

One of the best ways to develop the skills of analysis is to observe an elite performer in action, including professional players, world record holders, national competitors and Olympic champions. The advantage of observing elite performers is that they will almost always display a technically perfect model. For example, Roger Federer's service shows the perfect model for each of the three phases: preparation, execution and recovery. Watching his serve allows young players to compare their own performance with one that is accepted as perfect. It is even possible with modern technology to record your own performance of a skill and then overlay it on a recording of a professional performing the same skill, so that you can compare their body shape and positioning with your own.

Key

- Possession lost
+ Possession gained
⬇\ Pass backwards complete
⬇/ Pass backwards incomplete
⬆\ Pass forwards complete
⬆/ Pass forwards incomplete
© Shot on goal
©✓ Shot scored

Attacks in match

+ ⬇\ ⬇\ ⬆\ ⬆\ ⬆\ ©

(Unsuccessful shot after five passes, two backwards and three forwards.)

+ ⬆/ - + ⬆\ ⬆\ ©✓

(First pass incomplete, followed by regained possession. Then two forward passes resulting in a goal.)

Notational analysis of two attacks in a football match.

BRONZE

1. Gather evidence of the different skills, techniques and tactics that are used in your chosen sport.

2. Using the format you chose for Activity 1, analyse the performance of one of your peers in your chosen sport.

GOLD

3. Using the data gathered for Activity 2, compare and contrast – describe the similarities and differences between – the performance of your peer with the performance of an elite athlete in the same sport.

Unit 8 assignment, part one

Background

As a professional sports coach, you are responsible for ensuring that players within your club are suitably prepared for competition, both physically and mentally. You must also ensure that they have the technical skills and tactical awareness to compete successfully.

GRADING CRITERIA TO BE ASSESSED
P1, P2, P3 M1, M2, M3 D1

Task

Provide written evidence of your in-depth knowledge of your chosen sport, and produce an analysis of your own and others' performance. You must:

 **PASS**

Describe the technical and tactical demands of a chosen sport (P1).

Assess the technical skills and tactical awareness of an elite performer, identifying strengths and areas for improvement (P2).

Assess your own technical skills and tactical awareness in a chosen sport, identifying strengths and areas for improvement (P3).

 **MERIT**

Explain the technical and tactical demands of a chosen sport (M1).

Assess the technical skills and tactical awareness of an elite performer, explaining strengths and areas for improvement (M2).

Assess your own technical skills and tactical awareness in a chosen sport, explaining your own strengths and areas for improvement (M3).

 **DISTINCTION**

Compare and contrast your own technical skills and tactical awareness with those of an elite performer and the demands of a chosen sport (D1).

Tackling the assignment

This assignment is best approached by producing a word-processed document, perhaps supported by photos and/or diagrams, although these are not strictly necessary. Three pages would suffice if you are aiming for a Pass: a page describing the technical and tactical demands of a chosen sport, a page assessing your own performance, and a page assessing the performance of an elite athlete. Alternatively, you could meet the criteria by submitting video clips, providing the analysis as a voiceover.

If you are aiming for a Distinction, it is important to remember that the elite performer that you analyse to meet the criteria for P2 and M2 must be doing the same sport that you are doing to meet the criteria for P3 and M3. This is so that you can compare and contrast your technical skills and tactical awareness with those of the elite performer.

Meeting the Pass criteria

BTEC Level 2 Firsts in Sport

Unit 8 assignment, part one	Nicola Brown

The Technical and Tactical Demands of Football

Football is a very technically demanding game and the tactics involved become more varied as the level of performance increases. A grass-roots player needs to be able to cope with the basic technical aspects of the game, which means being able to perform each of the following skills:

- passing
- tackling
- shooting
- heading
- marking
- dribbling
- controlling the ball.

The level of technical expertise required for each of the above skills will vary depending on the quality of the opposition and your teammates. For example, an eight-year-old school player would be expected to pass accurately over five metres for two out of five passes or around 40 per cent of the time, whereas an 18-year-old professional youth team player would be expected to achieve a success rate of over 95 per cent in the same skill, and a Premier League player somewhere in the region of 99 per cent accuracy.

Tactically, footballers should have a working knowledge of:

- positioning
- shot and pass selection
- playing conditions and weather conditions
- use of space.

The tactical demands at grass-roots level are fairly basic, and focus on encouraging players to mark a player when the opposition has the ball and to lose their own marker when a teammate has possession. At a professional level, players will need to understand different forms of zonal marking, including how to cope with numerical inferiority and how to exploit numerical superiority.

Nicola clearly plays football and understands the different skills required to play the game, as demonstrated by her bulleted list of the techniques involved. She has also demonstrated her knowledge of football by making clear comparisons between the technical and tactical demands of the sport at different performance levels.

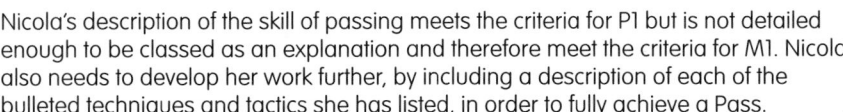

Nicola's description of the skill of passing meets the criteria for P1 but is not detailed enough to be classed as an explanation and therefore meet the criteria for M1. Nicola also needs to develop her work further, by including a description of each of the bulleted techniques and tactics she has listed, in order to fully achieve a Pass.

Meeting the Merit and Distinction criteria

BTEC Level 2 Firsts in Sport

Unit 8 assignment, part one   **Emma Jones**

An explanation of my own volleyball skills and those of an elite performer

My skills

My strength in volleyball is as a specialist setter. This is seen by many as the most important role in the game because it enables the team in possession to set up an attack, increasing their chances of winning the point. Technically, I am able to perform a very accurate set from almost any position on court, although the downside of my set is that the ball often travels too high, which allows opposing teams time to predict what will happen next and organize their defence. I need to develop this skill, although I am also aware that such improvement is of no use if my own teammates are unable to exploit the advantage; if they cannot cope with the reduced amount of time the ball spends in the air and, as a result, they play the ball upwards over the net instead of smashing it downwards.

The skills of Karch Kiraly, a professional volleyball player

Karch Kiraly is arguably the best volleyball player of all time. He has won three Olympic gold medals. Having watched him play on film, I have learnt several things from his performance. One of his greatest skills was setting the ball accurately, time and time again. He very rarely played a poor set and his team often won points on the back of his setting skills. He was also able to set from seemingly impossible positions; I have seen him set from a diving position on several occasions. Also, the ball generally travelled along a low trajectory, meaning that it spent only a short time in the air. Karch Kiraly was also able to play other positions on court and he possessed a devastatingly powerful serve. He was often able to retrieve points that seemed lost, by playing the ball when it was only inches from the ground. Perhaps his greatest strength, however, was in anticipating opposition attacks and positioning himself to play a block, often winning points in the process.

A comparison of my skills with those of Karch Kiraly

Clearly, Karch Kiraly was a better volleyball player than I will ever be. His set accuracy was much greater than mine and they travelled along a much lower trajectory than my sets do. However, I believe that with practice and experience, my setting skills will greatly improve, although they will never be anywhere near as good as those of my idol. The biggest difference between the two of us is that I am really only effective in one position, as a setter, while Karch Kiraly could play effectively in all six positions on court. In addition, both his serve and his block were major strengths, whereas I struggle in each of these areas.

Emma has produced a piece of work that goes some way to meeting both the Merit and the Distinction criteria for this assignment. She has clearly assessed her own strengths and weaknesses, and explained her areas for improvement to meet the criteria for M3. This is seen most clearly by her acknowledgement of the weakness of her setting skills. However, although she has assessed the strengths of an elite performer, she has failed to note any weaknesses or identify any areas for development for the elite performer, so has not met the criteria for M2. Using a SWOT analysis to structure the assessment of her own technical skills and tactical awareness against the technical skills and tactical awareness of an elite performer would have helped Emma to ensure that she had fully met these criteria.

By comparing her own skills with that of an elite performer, Emma has begun to meet the Distinction criteria for this assignment (D1). However, while her comparison of setting skills shows a depth of understanding, she has not fully covered other areas, such as serving, blocking and smashing the ball. To be fully deserving of a Distinction, her answer would need to be expanded.

Planning and reviewing a training programme

Once a performance has been analysed, the next step is to design a training programme to develop the performer's strengths and improve the areas that have been identified as weaknesses. There are many factors to consider, including which key techniques must be developed and which areas of tactical awareness need to be improved. Once the training programme has been completed, it should be reviewed and further goals for development identified.

Aims and objectives

Aims and objectives give a training plan its focus. They are, essentially, the long-term goals for the plan and describe what you want to have achieved by the end of the six-week training programme, as identified by the performance analysis. They may relate to tactical awareness, such as developing a more detailed working knowledge of the offside system in football or improving your ability to mark man-to-man in basketball. Or they may relate to technical skills, such as improving stick control in hockey or a more accurate high serve in badminton. Long-term goals should be discussed and agreed between a performer and their coach or manager.

Whatever the long-term goals are, they need to be SMART:

*S*PECIFIC: such as improving the accuracy of overhead clears in badminton.

*M*EASURABLE: such as improving the number of overhead clears landing inside the back court tramlines.

*A*CHIEVABLE: such as achieving more than 75% of overhead clears landing inside the rear tramlines in a conditioned practice situation.

*R*EALISTIC: such as achieving more than 75% accuracy in a practice and **not** 100% in a game.

*T*IME-BOUND: such as achieving more than 75% accuracy in a practice and **not** 100% in a game, over three months.

Training

Each training session must be:

- **Planned:** Planning each training session carefully will ensure that it is successful and that the aims and objectives of the training plan are met. Establishing SMART short-term goals for each training session is one way of ensuring that training is properly planned.

- **Structured:** Each training session must be structured and will generally follow the same basic format so that the performer understands what is required from them and can focus. A typical training session will begin with a series of drills aimed at developing technical ability or tactical awareness. The performer will then be placed in a conditioned competitive situation to enable them to practise what has been learnt.

- **Safe:** It is important to begin each training session with a suitable warm-up, and to conclude each training session with a suitable cool-down. Failure to complete either of these routines is likely to lead to injury, which can have a detrimental effect on the training programme.

Technical and tactical development

Technical improvements are brought about through the continual use of drills that focus on specific skills that have been identified as weak. These drills begin with basic concepts and become increasingly difficult, usually by reducing the time available for decision making or by requiring greater accuracy, or both. Essentially, the aim is to increase the difficulty of the drills until they resemble a competitive situation. Many top tennis players, such as Andy Murray and Roger Federer, train with each other because they struggle to find training partners who are capable of replicating a competitive situation.

Similarly, tactical development is brought about by conditioned training practices which are specifically designed to work on one particular area, such as a zone defence in basketball or shooting tactics in netball.

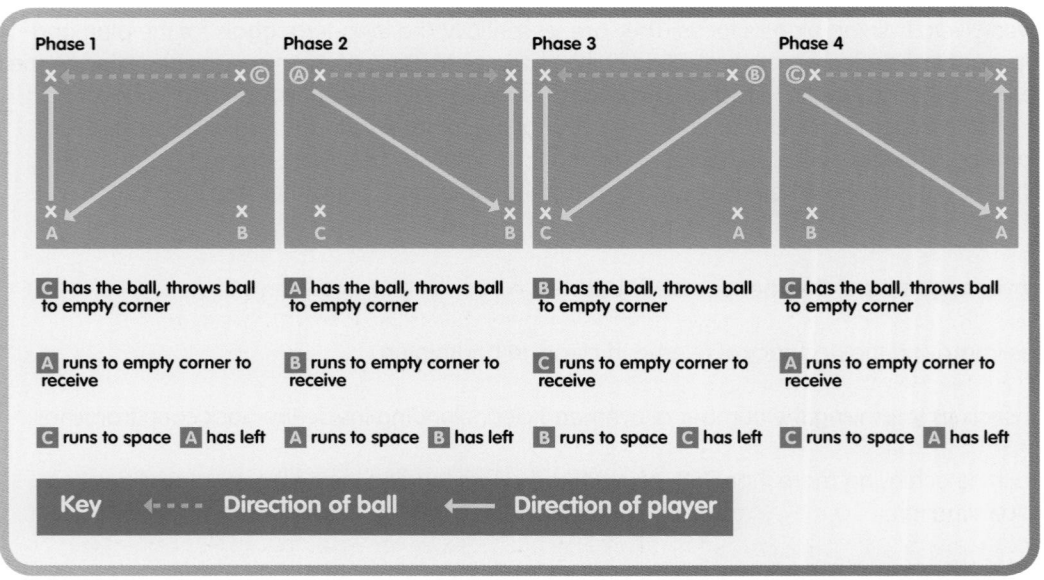

A netball passing drill.

1. Design one training session to tackle a technical weakness that you identified in Activity 2 on page 159 and one training session to tackle a tactical weakness. Don't forget to make sure that your training sessions are:

• planned, by establishing SMART short-term goals for each session
• structured, by containing drills to improve the performer's ability
• safe, by containing both a warm-up and a cool-down.

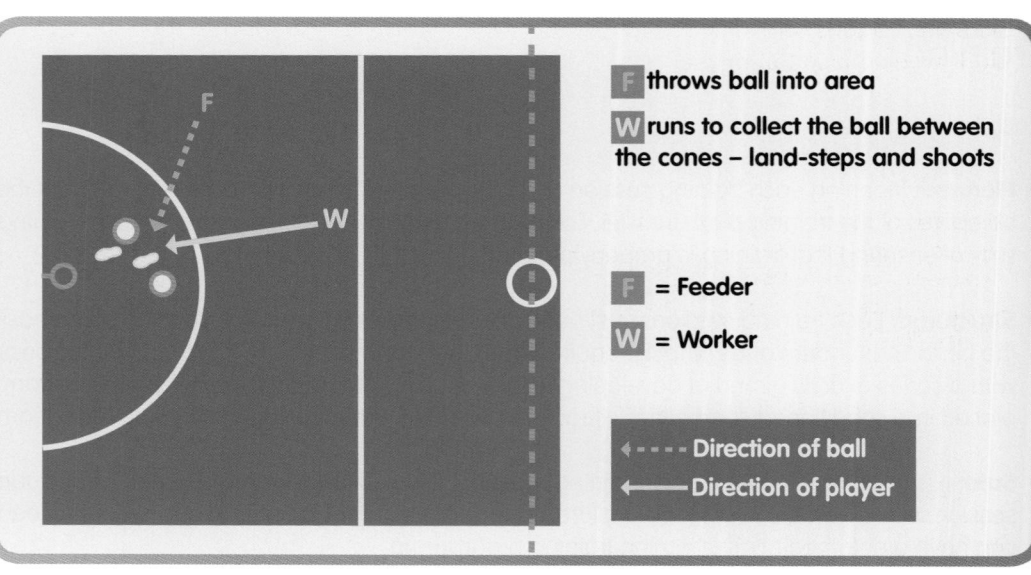

A pressure training drill for a netball shooter.

Keeping a record of a training programme

It is important to keep a record of your training sessions. You could keep a diary, a logbook or a portfolio, a record of witness testimonies, feedback sheets or an observation record, and use audio or video equipment. This allows a meaningful review to take place, by providing evidence that can be analysed to determine the success or failure of the programme. It also allows any problems with a programme to be picked up early, and is a record of reasons for missed training sessions. Without a record of a training programme it is difficult to be objective about it when you come to review it, and this can lead to important changes that need to be made to a programme not being made and unnecessary changes being made.

Reviewing a training programme

When a training plan has been completed, it should be reviewed. Observing, analysing and evaluating the performer's performance at the end of the training programme should identify both the performer's strengths and areas for improvement in relation to the aims and objectives of the training plan, and the strengths and weaknesses of the training plan itself to inform future training plans. It is important to ensure the feedback given to the performer is constructive and positive and, above all, motivates the performer for future training.

One successful model for constructive feedback works like this:

- Ask the performer how well they felt they achieved the aims and objectives of the programme.
- Tell the performer how well you felt they achieved the aims and objectives of the programme.

- Ask the performer what they think they did well.
- Tell the performer what you think they did well, using specific examples from your observation, analysis and evaluation.

- Ask the performer what they think they could do differently or better.
- Tell the performer what you think they could do differently or better, using specific examples from your observation, analysis and evaluation.

- Ask the performer to identify five positive things and five negative things about the training schedule.

- Agree next steps together. These could be short-term or long-term goals and could focus on individual skills, techniques and tactics and/or team tactics. These should form the basis of a new six- to eight-week training plan.

SILVER

2. Research a training session completed by a professional team or player in your chosen sport and analyse the strengths and weaknesses of the training session.

GOLD

3. Suggest improvements that could be made to the training programme that you analysed for Activity 2.

Unit 8 assignment, part two

Background

As a professional sports coach, you are responsible for ensuring that players within your club are suitably prepared for competition, both physically and mentally. You must also ensure that they have the technical skills and tactical awareness to compete successfully.

GRADING CRITERIA TO BE ASSESSED
P4, P5, P6
M4, M5
D2, D3

Task

Design, carry out and review a six-week training programme aimed at developing your technical skills and tactical awareness in your chosen sport. Afterwards, set goals for your future development. You must:

Produce a six-week training programme, with tutor support, to develop your own technical skills and tactical awareness (P4).

Carry out a six-week training programme to develop your own technical skills and tactical awareness (P5).

Review your own development, identifying goals for further technical and tactical development, with tutor support (P6).

Independently produce a six-week training programme to develop your own technical skills and tactical awareness, describing strengths and areas for improvement (M4).

Independently describe your own development, explaining goals for technical and tactical development (M5).

Evaluate the training programme, justifying suggestions made regarding improvement (D2).

Analyse your own goals for technical and tactical development, suggesting how these goals could be achieved (D3).

Tackling the assignment

The obvious way to approach this assignment is to produce, and then follow, six weekly training plans, supported by witness statements from either a teacher or a club coach, and a diary that logs your progress. Remember to include specific practices to develop all the technical skills and tactical awareness required for your sport, and to work on your strengths as well as the areas you have identified for improvement, so that you continue to develop all technical and tactical aspects of your performance.

If you are aiming for a Merit, you must also produce a written description of your own strengths and areas for improvement, and the training plans should show how the areas identified for improvement will improve if the training plans are completed. It would also be useful to consider what factors might prevent you from achieving your goals

and what factors might help you to achieve your goals. If you are aiming for a Distinction, you must ensure that you evaluate the training plan as well as the suggestions you make about your areas for improvement.

After the training plan has been completed, you need to review your development and **identify** (for a Pass), **explain** (for a Merit) or **analyse** (for a Distinction) your goals for further technical and tactical development. The best way to do this is to submit a commentary to accompany your training log, remembering to use the SMART target setting technique to communicate your short- and long-term goals for further development. If you are aiming for a Distinction, remember to consider what factors might prevent you from achieving your goals and what factors might help you to achieve your goals.

Meeting the Pass and Merit criteria

My Rugby Training Programme   **Martin Cooke**

Training session: 1 of 6

Training goal: To develop consistency when kicking in a game situation.

Equipment: Kicking tee and 15–20 rugby balls (or a smaller number and a partner to help retrieve them).

Description:

• Prior to the beginning of my weekly team practice, I will kick 15–20 balls at goal from different positions on the field, focusing on developing rhythm using the techniques described below.

• During breaks in practice I will execute 1–3 kicks per period. This way I will replicate the fatigue I feel during a game situation, which will enable me to develop my skills in a real-life situation.

• I will end the session by taking a further 10–15 kicks to really push myself to kick accurately when tired.

Coaching points:

I have taken these tips from former All Black Grant Fox, in his video on goal kicking:

• **Ball placement and set-up:** Tilt ball forward to expose sweet spot 1/2 to 1/3 of the way up the ball. When setting up, ensure that the non-kicking foot is placed in correct position, a hip's width away from the ball with ankle in line with the seam, and your head is over the ball. Walk back can vary in style, but should be comfortable and, at starting point of the run-up, the kicker should be square on to the ball. Also ensure that contact point is watched at all times whilst walking back.

• **Prior to movement towards the ball:** Establish composure. Fox's method: Imagine successful kick, relax using deep breathing technique, clear head and use key phrases such as 'head down' and 'follow-through'.

• **Approach and foot placement:** At the end of the run-up, the non-kicking side of the body should be turned towards the target and the hips should be open. This is achieved by aiming to land the non-kicking foot a hip's width from the ball, feet pointing directly at the target with ankle in line with the cross-seam.

> Martin's plan gives an impression of what can be expected for each of his first six training sessions, and it would be good to see the details of the other five sessions as well as details of the remainder of his programme. However, the evidence suggests that Martin is well on the way to meeting the criteria for a P4. In fact, he is almost working at Merit level. To meet the criteria for M4, Martin would need to add a description of his strengths and areas for development, as well as make it clear that he has produced his training plan **without tutor support**.

> It is not clear from this whether or not Martin has actually carried out the planned training session, and I would suggest that a witness statement from his team coach and his training log would provide suitable evidence for Martin to achieve P5.

Meeting the Distinction criteria

An evaluation of my training programme

Daisy Bruce

Duration of the programme: 6 weeks (1 hour x 3 sessions per week)

Aim of sessions 1 to 6: To develop my serving skills in badminton

Desired outcomes: An improvement in the low serve, flick serve and high serve

My training programme consisted of six training sessions: one for each of the three types of serve, followed by two sessions aimed at developing disguise in the service, followed by a final session with the sole aim of using the serve in a competitive situation. Each of the sessions was planned from the start but with hindsight it would have been better to have planned session two after session one had been completed, because I learnt things during and after each session which would have changed the way I planned the following sessions.

The training session for developing each serve followed a similar pattern. This made the planning easy and made it simple to follow the routine, but I became bored during the second session and found the third session extremely tedious. This in turn led to a lack of effort on my part, which meant that I didn't make the level of progress I had wanted to. As a result, my low service (session one) developed quite well, whereas my high serve and flick serve did not develop as well. If I were to carry out a similar plan in the future, I would ensure that each session was different so that my interest was maintained at a high level throughout.

My fourth and fifth sessions were good, because I have always had difficulty disguising my service, which means that my opponent is able to predict and respond appropriately. After the two sessions my ability to disguise the service type has been greatly improved, helping to cause confusion and indecision in my opponent. Unfortunately, because the quality of my high service and flick service had not been developed as I had hoped (see above paragraph), I am, as yet, unable to take full advantage of my ability to disguise the service. As stated earlier, next time I would plan the next session only after the previous one had been completed. This would have allowed me to spend session four further developing my high service and flick service, thereby making session five (disguise) more effective.

My final session centred on using the three different service types in a competitive situation. I learnt a lot from this and, as the session progressed, I became more effective when serving against my opponent. Unfortunately, I have subsequently realized that this has only developed my serving tactics against one opponent and next time I would change the six-week plan to incorporate an element of competition in each session. This would allow me to discover which tactics work against several opponents, and which tactics only work against a small number of opponents. It would also allow me to design subsequent sessions based on my evaluation of the previous competitive situation.

In conclusion, I am happy with the developments I have made in the different serving styles but I have learnt several things that would enable me to plan a much more effective training programme in the future.

> Daisy's evaluation is clearly aimed at meeting D2. She makes some important observations about the strengths and weaknesses of her training plan, and makes sensible suggestions as to how she could improve her training plan in the future. Most importantly, she goes on to justify her suggestions by explaining the benefits that would be gained by making these changes. I would be happy to award Daisy D2 for this piece of work if she continues to evaluate the remaining sessions in her training plan in this way.

Unit 9: Psychology for Sports Performance

The psychological demands of sport

Taking part in sporting activities can have a major psychological effect on participants. When placed in a competitive situation, athletes can suffer from sweating heavily, an increased heart rate and extreme nerves. However, some athletes seem to be very good at conquering their nerves and controlling their emotions to achieve success, and it is becoming increasingly apparent that developing our psychological skills is just as important as any physical training we may take part in.

Anxiety

In a sporting context, anxiety is commonly referred to as 'competitive anxiety' and can be subdivided into two main types:

- **Cognitive anxiety:** This type of anxiety affects the mind and thought processes. It can result in worries and negative thoughts or expectations, such as, 'I might not finish the race' or 'We're going to lose this match'.
- **Somatic anxiety:** This type of anxiety has a physical effect on the body and can make the sports performer feel ill. Symptoms of somatic anxiety can include a dry mouth, a faster heart rate, a stomach upset, a tight chest and shaking.

The most effective method of controlling anxiety is to use relaxation techniques, such as breathing techniques and ways to relax the muscle groups. Other techniques include self-hypnosis and meditation.

Self-confidence

In order to perform well at sports, you need to have positive thoughts and self-belief. If you do not have faith in your own abilities, your performance will not be the best it can be. It is also important to have the confidence to take risks, for example, trying a new training technique or switching coaches if you feel that you are not getting anywhere. Someone who has self-confidence will also admit their mistakes and try to resolve them.

The psychological factors that can affect the performance of an athlete

England's Andrew Sheridan and Australia's Matt Dunning fail to control their aggression in quarter-final of the 2007 Rugby World Cup.

Remember:

Each sport makes different psychological demands and our unique personalities mean that we respond differently to those demands.

Aggression

Aggression in sport can be both good and bad. Sports performers need a certain amount of aggression in order to be successful; however, they must channel this aggression in the right way. Some players are purposely aggressive towards other players, and this often results in injury or foul play. This type of aggression is referred to as 'hostile aggression' and is generally unacceptable. In comparison, 'instrumental aggression' usually occurs when a performer is in pursuit of a target or goal, and not because they want to harm or injure their opponent. Instrumental aggression must be controlled but it can help a performer to succeed.

In order to control aggression and aggressive behaviour, sports performers must try to keep calm and not react to sources of irritation around them. Deep breathing and other relaxation techniques can help to keep a bad temper at bay, as can changing the way you are thinking, for example, by focusing on positive thoughts rather than angry ones.

Concentration

It is vital that competitive sports performers have good concentration because most sporting activities require them to remain focused and on task in order to be successful. For example, during a big game or competition where there is a huge crowd watching, competitors must ignore the distractions and concentrate in order to perform to the best of their ability.

Decision making

Sports performers must make a lot of correct decisions in order to be successful. They must make decisions about their training methods, techniques and tactics, or the competitions that they are going to take part in. They must also make decisions during competitive situations, often quickly, under pressure and in response to the action of another participant. For example, in cricket a batsman decides what shot he will play to the ball that has just been bowled. If they are not good at making decisions their progress could be affected.

Snooker players, such as John Higgins, need to try and concentrate throughout the whole match – even when their opponent is at the table.

Problem solving

Often, sport and recreational activities directly require participants to solve problems. For example, outdoor and adventure activities, including orienteering, involve participants working together in order to navigate around the countryside and find solutions to problems. In other sports, participants need to solve problems such as why they can't perform a skill or beat an opponent, for example, by training to improve their technique or by implementing different tactics.

Competitiveness

People who participate in sports are generally competitive and this can often be seen in their everyday lives. They may want to be the best at everything they do, and will be keen to win any game or activity that they take part in. If people who take part in sport are not competitive, they will not have the necessary drive to succeed or reach their targets.

Motivation

In order to be successful in any sport, participants must be motivated to do well. Motivation is the driving force behind all athletes and it is what gives people the desire to take part in sport and be successful. There are two types of motivation. If a performer has 'intrinsic motivation' they have internal reasons for wanting to do well. If they have 'extrinsic motivation' they are spurred on by external factors, such as rewards and prizes.

Whichever type of motivation an athlete best responds to, they should be encouraged by their coach or trainer to do well using motivational techniques, such as target setting and awarding praise.

SILVER

1. Choose three of the psychological factors described on these two pages and explain how they can affect performance in a sport of your choice.

Motivation and its impact on sports performance

Motivation is the need or desire to achieve a goal or certain level of success. A psychology professor called Alan Cox defines motivation as a desire to fulfil a need. Motivation is important to all sports performers because if they lack motivation they will not have the necessary focus and drive to do well.

Influences on motivation

The factors that motivate people to take part in sporting activities generally fall into two categories, intrinsic factors and extrinsic factors:

- **Intrinsic factors** are those that come from within a person. Examples of intrinsic motivation include taking part in a sport because you enjoy being part of a team, because you want to gain experience of competing at a certain level or because you get a sense of self-worth from your achievements.
- **Extrinsic factors** are those that come in the form of external rewards such as praise, encouragement, trophies, rewards or records.

Charlotte Edwards holds aloft the Women's ICC World Twenty20 trophy as the rest of the England team celebrate winning the tournament in June 2009. While the trophy itself may have provided some of the team's motivation, Edwards revealed her inner desire for success ahead of the next tournament in May 2010: "We are number one, we have worked really hard to get there, I want to stay there."

Achievement motivation is another way in which sports performers can remain focused and maintain their desire to be successful. By regularly setting themselves realistic and achievable goals, they can remain motivated to do well because they are always striving to achieve something. Achievement motivation is closely linked with intrinsic motivation because it relies on the performer's need to fulfil an internal desire rather than receiving material rewards.

Attribution theory explains how people interpret events and attribute occurrences to actions. Attribution theory assumes that people try to maintain a positive self-image. This means that if a performer is successful at a particular task, they are likely to want to attribute their success to their own actions, but if they fail, they may try to find someone/something else to take responsibility for that failure. Encouraging this response to events can improve motivation. For example, if a performer does well, then believing it was down to their own ability or hard work might motivate them to continue to train and perform to a high standard. If a performer does not do so well, blaming the poor result on bad luck could imply that the performer will have the opportunity to do better next time if they can perform to a similar standard.

BRONZE

1. Categorize the following statements as examples of either intrinsic motivation or extrinsic motivation:

   a) "I love to win competitions. Winning makes me feel so proud of myself."

   b) "If I score a goal my mum will give me £10."

   c) "I hope I can beat my personal best distance today."

   d) "My coach will be really happy if I get through to the final round."

   e) "I really want to take home the trophy today."

   f) "I want my dad to say 'Well done' to me after the game."

   g) "I don't want to let my teammates down."

SILVER

2a) Think about a time when you felt really motivated, really 'up for it', and remember what happened.

b) Now, write a paragraph about the impact of motivation on sports performance, using your own experience as an example.

Three theories of motivation

There are three theories about how motivation can have an impact on performance. These theories are called:
- the trait-centred view of motivation
- the situation-centred view of motivation
- the interactional view of motivation.

The trait-centred view of motivation
The trait-centred view of motivation is based on the idea that motivation is a result of what an individual considers to be important and states that the goals we have will determine the way that we behave. It suggests that our internal desires to do well are determined by our general personality traits; by what makes us who we are. According to this theory, the basis for motivation is intrinsic.

The situation-centred view of motivation
The situation-centred view of motivation states that a person's level of motivation is dependent on their surroundings or the environment they are in. This includes any other people present in those surroundings. If a certain environment makes a person feel comfortable, they are more likely to be motivated, whereas if they are in a place where they feel uncomfortable, they may not have the same desire, or motivation, to do well.

One view is that Harry's motivation to study is dependent on his surroundings. He finds it easy to study when he is in the classroom, but much more difficult when he is surrounded by his friends. This is the situation-centred view of motivation.

A contrasting view is that Harry has an intrinsic motivation to study that isn't dependent on his surroundings. This is the trait-centred view of motivation.

The interactional view of motivation
The interactional view of motivation states that a person's level of motivation depends on both their personality and the situation that they find themselves in. This theory also states that communication and interaction with other people can play a part in the level of motivation someone experiences. This is important in sport and exercise as an individual is more likely to be successful if they have the right environment, support from others and feel happy within themselves. It is also possible that a person might be highly motivated in a particular environment but surrounded by people they do not feel comfortable with. This would require them to be highly motivated from the outset and driven by the goal they want to achieve. For example, if a person wants to achieve a certain goal but finds that they don't like their coach, they could still be motivated to stay with the coach in order to reach their goal, if their desire to succeed is greater than their dislike of their coach.

SILVER
3. Explain the good and bad points of each of the three theories of motivation when considering sports performance.

GOLD
4. Analyse the three theories of motivation, stating which one you think is the most relevant to sports performers and why.

Strategies that can be used to maintain and increase motivation

The responsibility for motivating a group or individual in a sporting context falls to the coach, manager or teacher. There are many ways to motivate a person, including:

- **Imagery:** This technique involves sports performers picturing themselves in a particular situation, perhaps executing the perfect performance. They can try to implant this image into their subconscious and then recall it when performing.
- **Self-talk:** A performer can increase their motivation and improve their self-confidence by using positive 'self-talk'; an internal running commentary of positive reinforcement. For example, a high jumper may talk themselves through the perfect bar clearance whilst waiting for their turn in a competition.
- **Praise:** If a performer is praised when they do something well they are more likely to be motivated to carry on.
- **Encouragement:** Encouraging a performer, even if they aren't working at their full potential, can help motivate them to do better or strive to be the best they can be.
- **Responsibility:** If a performer is given greater responsibility or a bigger role to play within a group, such as being asked to lead the warm-up activity or captain the team, this can increase their motivation.
- **Rewards:** Sometimes performers respond to material or tangible rewards, such as a trophy, a cash prize or a new record.
- **Goal setting:** Setting goals gives performers something to work towards. One method which gives performers the best chance of reaching their goals is the SMART target-setting technique.

SPECIFIC: Targets should be specific; they should set down precisely what you want to achieve. For example, 'I want to run the 100m in under 15 seconds'.

MEASURABLE: Targets should be measurable so that you can work out if you have achieved them. For example, it is better to say that your target is to run the 100m in under 15 seconds than it is to say that you want to run the 100m faster.

ACHIEVABLE: Goals should be set appropriate to the fitness and skill levels of the performer. They should be close enough for us to see, but not so far away that we can't touch them.

REALISTIC: It is important that we set goals that we have the capacity to achieve. All targets need to be challenging so that you have to work hard to achieve them, but they must also be realistic in order for them to serve their purpose and motivate you.

TIME-BOUND: Targets should have a time limit on them. For example, 'I want to run the 100m in under 15 seconds by the end of August'. If your long-term goals rely on you achieving your short-term goals, then you need to set time limits on your short-term goals in order to reach your long-term goals.

BRONZE SILVER

5. Imagine that you are a Premiership football manager. Your team has lost their last five matches and the players are rapidly losing all motivation. You must come up with a plan to improve your team's motivation if you have any hope of ending your losing streak.

a) Choose and describe three strategies that can be used to maintain and increase motivation.

b) Explain how the three strategies you have chosen might maintain and increase motivation.

GOLD

6. Analyse the plan you have devised for Activity 5 and how effective the suggestions for increasing and maintaining motivation might be.

Personality and its impact on performance

Psychologist Raymond B. Cattel defined personality as 'that which permits a prediction of what a person will do in a given situation'. An individual's personality is unique. It is based on a series of traits or characteristics that are exclusive to that person. There are two main theories of personality: the trait approach and the situational approach.

The trait approach to personality

The trait approach to personality, based on the work of sports psychologist Matt Jarvis, states that personality traits are developed when we are very young and do not change as we grow older. An individual's personality traits make them react in a certain way in any given situation, so factors such as the environment will not affect a person's reaction. For example, if a person is naturally aggressive they will behave aggressively no matter what the circumstances.

This theory also suggests that people can be categorized into two types of personality, 'Type A' or 'Type B'. If a person doesn't fit into either Type A or Type B then they are classed as Type AB.

Introverts and extroverts
Another way of categorizing people into different personality types was developed by Hans Eysenck. He suggested that people are either introverted or extroverted. Introverts are shy people who are happy in their own company. Extroverts are confident and outgoing. They enjoy socializing and are not content to be in their own company. People may be more suited to a particular sport because of their personality. An introverted person, who likes being alone, may choose to participate in individual activities like golf or athletics. An extrovert may choose a team sport, such as wheelchair basketball.

The situational approach to personality

The situational approach to personality is based on the work of Albert Bandura. It is very different from the trait approach because it states that people's personalities cannot be categorized; rather they are influenced by the situations that people find themselves in. This means that how we behave is dependent on our surroundings. For example, a person may be quiet and calm when they are with their family, but they may become aggressive when playing in a competitive situation.

Bandura focused particularly on the concepts of modelling and feedback:
- **Modelling:** This means that people base their actions on the actions of others by observing and copying them. For example, someone who admires David Beckham might watch him play and then try to copy his techniques on the field.
- **Feedback:** When we are given praise or congratulated on our behaviour or performance, we will endeavour to emulate this so that we can receive further positive feedback. Similarly, if we behave badly or our performance is not so good, we will receive negative feedback and will then try to improve so as not to receive such feedback in the future.

Nature versus nurture

The 'nature versus nurture' debate is an ongoing debate that psychologists have about personality. Psychologist Robert Feldman describes the debate as being about 'the degree to which environment and heredity influence behaviour'; that is whether people's personalities are influenced by those around them, especially their parents, or whether people are born with a certain set of characteristics.

When considering this debate in relation to sports performance we might ask ourselves, 'Is he a good tennis player because he was born with a natural ability, or is he good because he has trained and received coaching to improve his performance?' It is true that some people are naturally athletic and can turn their hand to any sports activity with relative ease, but it is also true that others have to work hard in order to be successful. There is no straightforward answer, and psychologists continue to battle over whether 'nature' or 'nurture' is more responsible.

Type A	Type B
Impatient	Patient
Time-conscious	Relaxed
Competitive	Lazy
Outgoing	Tolerant
Aggressive	Easy-going
Driven	Calm
Forceful	Passive
Focused	Stress-free
Rushed	Laid-back

BRONZE

1. Which personality type are you? List eight personality traits that you have and decide whether you are Type A or Type B.

2. Are you an introvert or an extrovert? Write a paragraph describing your personality and decide whether you are an introvert or an extrovert.

3. Who is your role model in sport? Describe the things you like about your favourite sports personality and the effect that they have on you and your performance.

4. Note down the similarities and the differences between the two theories of personality. Explain which you most agree with and why.

Aggression and its impact on performance

Aggressive behaviour is defined as hostile or destructive behaviour. Assertive behaviour is defined as having and showing a confident and forceful personality. When someone displays assertive behaviour, they participate with vigour and intensity, but remain calm, stick to the rules and play fairly. They have discipline and control over their reactions, and do not cause any intentional harm to others around them. In contrast, when someone displays aggressive behaviour they tend to lose control and become angry. There are two types of aggression: hostile aggression and instrumental aggression.

Hostile aggression

Sports performers who display hostile aggression will purposely set out to harm other players, causing physical or psychological harm to their opponents. On 28 June 1997, boxer Mike Tyson attacked his opponent, Evander Holyfield, and bit off part of his ear. This is a classic example of hostile aggression. Tyson clearly intended to harm Holyfield and went against the rules of the competition to do so.

Instrumental aggression

Instrumental aggression lies somewhere between assertive behaviour and hostile aggression. Although a person who displays instrumental aggression is intentionally aggressive, it usually occurs when they are in pursuit of a target or goal, and not because they want to harm or injure their opponent.

Mike Tyson displays hostile aggression as he bites Evander Holyfield's ear in 1997.

Causes of aggression

There are many known causes of aggression, ranging from jealousy to greed. However, in relation to sport, the most likely causes of aggression are as follows:

- **Frustration:** When a performer becomes frustrated in a competitive situation they may react in an aggressive manner. They may be frustrated with themselves for performing badly, or with others for doing well or not sticking to the rules.
- **Lack of self-control:** If an athlete is unable to contain their anger they may lose their self-control and act in an aggressive way towards their opponents, the umpires/referees and, in some cases, even the equipment. John McEnroe often lost his self-control when he played competitive tennis. He would regularly throw his racket down and scream abuse at the umpires when he thought he was right and they were wrong.
- **Learnt behaviour:** According to Albert Bandura, aggression may be learnt from others. For example, if one of your teammates gets into a fight with the opposition you may feel the need to join in. Coaches, parents and teachers may also have an influence on aggression, if the athlete follows their example.
- **Instinct:** Some sports performers have a natural aggressive streak and instinctively react to certain situations in an aggressive manner. This aggression may be one of their underlying personality traits and they would need to work on controlling it if they wanted to become successful in their sport.

Controlling aggressive behaviour

Sports performers must keep calm and try not to react to things that irritate them if they are to control aggression and aggressive behaviour, and improve their chances of success. Some of the methods that may be used to control aggression and manage anger are:

- **Deep breathing and relaxation techniques:** These can help to keep a bad temper at bay because they calm and relax both your mind and your body.
- **Cognitive restructuring:** Changing the way you think can significantly help to control aggressive behaviour by, for example, helping you to focus on positive, constructive thoughts rather than angry, negative ones. Instead of thinking 'That was rubbish, I may as well quit now!', think 'Oh well, that wasn't my best performance but I will aim to do better next time.'
- **Yoga and Pilates:** These help people to achieve a clearer, calmer mind. They also promote sleep and generally help people to become happier.

SILVER

1. You have been feeling under pressure lately when you compete and have begun to lose your patience. You have reacted in an aggressive way on more than one occasion. Choose two methods of controlling this aggressive behaviour. List all of the benefits of these methods and describe how they will have a positive impact on your future performances.

GOLD

2. Imagine that you have regularly practised the two methods you chose for Activity 1. Evaluate their effectiveness, explaining the downsides of using the techniques as well as the benefits.

Developing and reviewing a psychological skills training programme

A psychological skills training programme is very similar to a physical training programme, in that it consists of regular training sessions for the athlete to complete, with set timings and certain techniques to work on. The main difference between the two programmes is that a psychological programme focuses on developing the cognitive aspects of a sports performer, such as their ability to relax and motivate themselves, while a physical training programme focuses on improving physical skills.

There are four stages to developing a psychological training programme.

1. Assessing the performer

The performer's psychological strengths and areas for improvement can be assessed in a number of ways. The performer could carry out a self-assessment or involve people such as their coach. Coaches spend a huge amount of time with their athletes and can effectively judge their athlete's psychological strengths and weaknesses. A training partner or other members of their team may also provide a performer with relevant information about their psychological skills if they work closely with them.

A questionnaire can be used to gather information about a performer. Typical psychological-analysis questions include:

	Always	Sometimes	Never
Do you set goals for yourself?		✔	
Are you determined to succeed?	✔		
Do you perform well under pressure?		✔	

Another method of collecting information about the psychological skills of a performer is called performance profiling. The athlete is asked to rate themselves on a scale of one to ten (one being the lowest and ten being the highest) for a series of up to ten psychological aspects of performance. For example, if they are an extremely anxious person, they may give themselves a nine for anxiety and, if they experience low confidence, they may give themselves a score of three for this aspect. For example:

	1	2	3	4	5	6	7	8	9	10
Motivation						✔				
Anxiety		✔								
Confidence								✔		

2. Planning a training programme

The information gathered using a questionnaire or a performance profile can be used to prepare a psychological training plan which maintains a performer's strengths and develops their weaker areas of performance.

As with any training plan, it is important to be clear about your objectives and set yourself goals using the SMART target-setting technique. The training plan can be short term, medium term or long term, although a medium- to long-term plan is advisable to ensure there is adequate time for improvement to take place.

3. Recording progress

It is just as important to record results while you are completing a psychological training programme as it is to record your results while you are following a physical training programme. It may be useful to keep a diary, logbook or portfolio of the training completed so that you can look back on what has been done. Alternatively, you could video your training sessions, ask your peers or your coach to keep observation records, or collect witness statements.

4. Reviewing a training programme

It is also important that a review is carried out on completion of a psychological training plan. A review will ascertain whether or not the training has had an impact on the athlete and will inform future planning. One way to carry out a review is to assess the performer again, using the same questionnaire or performance profile that was used earlier. You should also analyse whether the objectives and goals set when the plan was created have been met. This will identify any improvements that have been made as a result of the training plan and highlight areas that should be the focus of future training goals.

This is an example of a psychological training plan. You don't have to include timings for the practices, as long as the athlete knows the exercises they must complete during each session.

Week 1: Focus on relaxation techniques to relieve stress and tension

<u>1 hour – Self-hypnosis/meditation</u>

To relax your mind and body, and free you of all negative thoughts.

- Choose a focus. For example, you want to be more positive about your ability or you want to be less anxious when performing.
- Find a quiet place to sit comfortably.
- Allow yourself to think relaxing thoughts. Tell yourself that you ARE relaxed and that you feel warm, comfortable and free from stress.
- Once you are in a completely relaxed state, allow yourself to think positive thoughts about your performance. Tell yourself that you ARE performing at a high level and that you WILL reach the targets you have set for yourself.

<u>1 hour – Progressive muscle relaxation</u>

- Tighten or tense each of your muscles, one by one. Start with your toes and work your way up to your facial muscles.
- Relax each of your muscles, one by one, taking slow, deep breaths in and out as you do so.

Week 2: Focus on motivation for enhancing performance

<u>1 hour – Imagery</u>

- Sit quietly by yourself and relax.
- Imagine that you are about to perform in your chosen sport. Tell yourself that you are feeling good and that you WILL do well in your performance. Picture yourself in slow motion, performing to a very high level, executing the perfect throw or scoring the perfect goal. Feel the positive energy that comes with this brilliant performance. Enjoy the success and believe that it was down to your ability.
- Mentally rewind what you have just seen and play it over again, focusing on your great performance. Tell yourself that now you have seen yourself performing well in your mind, you can repeat the performance physically.

<u>1 hour – Self-talk</u>

Should be completed in a quiet, private place, ideally before and after physical training or competition.

- Tell yourself that you can do it, that you are ready and that you feel positive.
- Tell yourself how you are going to do it. For example, 'I'm going to feel confident and positive when I get to the start line. I will not be nervous. I will be raring to go. When the gun goes off, I will drive myself forward, pumping my arms through the air and clawing the ground with my feet …'.
- When the physical training or competition is over, tell yourself that you knew you could do it and will do even better next time.

<u>1 hour – Goal setting (with coach)</u>

(See page 172)

Week 3: Focus on extending concentration span

<u>1 hour – Focusing/tuning out distractions</u>

Sit in a quiet place and think about what you want to achieve in your sporting career. Think about your short-, medium- and long-term goals, and think methodically about how you are going to achieve them. Also, think of all the distractions that may come your way while you are trying to reach your targets. Consider how you will deal with these distractions and what methods you will put in place to ensure that they do not get in your way. For example, if you are distracted by your most-feared opponent, tune them out of the picture and remain focused on YOUR performance only. What they get up to will not affect you or your performance. Your thoughts must remain fixed on what you want to achieve and you should keep reminding yourself that nothing will get in your way.

<u>1 hour – Imagery</u>

Use the same strategy as described in Week 2, and focus on how you will concentrate fully on your performance and not allow any distractions to affect you.

Week 4: Focus on anger management and controlling aggression

<u>1 hour – Deep breathing</u>

- Sit quietly and focus on your breathing.
- Take slow, deep breaths in and out. Concentrate on your breathing and nothing else. Place your hands on your stomach and watch them move away from you and back towards you as you inhale and exhale deeply.
- Continue to breathe deeply and slowly while you imagine yourself, relaxed, involved in a competitive situation.
- Recall this technique when you are actually taking part in a competition, at a moment when you might be about to get aggressive or angry.

<u>1 hour – Cognitive restructuring</u>

- Find a quiet place where you are alone.
- Consider all the negative things that affect the way you perform. For example, if you get angry and lose your temper quickly when taking part in sport, why is this? What makes you act aggressively towards other players? Does this behaviour actually get you anywhere or does it make things worse?
- Imagine yourself getting upset or annoyed in a series of competitive situations. At the point where you would normally lose your temper, think the word 'STOP'. Say it out loud if you want to.
- Use this technique when you are taking part in sport to prevent yourself from experiencing negative feelings.

Week 5: Focus on developing self-confidence, and dealing with success and failure

<u>1 hour – Imagery</u>

Use the same strategy as described in Week 2, and focus on a situation where you experience failure. Focus on the negative feelings, such as disappointment, that you would normally suffer at this point. Rather than dwelling on the poor performance, try to imagine yourself shrugging your shoulders and walking away from the situation with a smile on your face. Think to yourself that it doesn't matter, that you will do better next time and that you will not give up. Repeat this exercise with a successful situation in mind. Enjoy the feelings of elation and joy when you have performed well.

Controlling anxiety

Recognize the feelings of anxiety as they begin to occur. These may be shortness of breath, or a feeling of fear or panic. When you feel these symptoms, begin your relaxation techniques. These include deep breathing, self-hypnosis and meditation.

BRONZE

1. Create a ten-question psychological-assessment questionnaire for a sport of your choice.

2. Create a performance profile for a sport of your choice.

3. Research one psychological skill, such as relaxation ability, controlling aggression or building motivation, and produce a one-week training plan to develop that skill in a sport of your choice.

Unit 9 assignment, part one

Background

You are a sports psychologist and have been asked to work with the local Sports Development Officer to analyse the psychological demands of sports on a performer. In order to do this, you must interview some performers to find out what it is about their sport that is demanding and how they feel about the pressures they are under when performing.

Task

Having researched the psychological demands that a selected sport has on the performer, you should prepare an informative leaflet suitable for young up-and-coming performers in the sport to inform them of the psychological pressures that they may face. You must make sure that you:

GRADING CRITERIA TO BE ASSESSED
P1
M1

Describe four psychological demands of a selected sport (P1).

Explain four psychological demands of a selected sport (M1).

Tackling the assignment

You should research four psychological factors involved in your chosen sport. Topics such as motivation, anxiety and aggression should be considered. You then need to create a detailed leaflet highlighting the potential demands of these psychological factors and describe the impact they could have on the performer.

For P1, you should **describe** the psychological demands. This involves giving an outline of each factor and highlighting the positive and negative impacts of each on the sports performer.

For M1, you should provide a detailed **explanation** of each demand. This involves describing them in more detail. You should state their causes, the positive and negative impacts they may have on the performer, and explain methods of increasing or controlling these.

Meeting the Pass and Merit criteria

To achieve a Merit, try to refer specifically to the sport that you have chosen. For example, how will anxiety affect a basketball player's dribbling or shooting skills? How will it affect their strategic play?

Psychological demands in basketball

BTEC Level 2 Firsts in Sport

Unit 9 assignment, part one

Sarah Fletcher

Anxiety

During games and training sessions, basketball players can be effected by anxiety. Anxiety can have a physical and psychological effect on performers. They can feel nervous and have self-doubt but they can also suffer physical symptoms such as nausea, stomach cramps and sweating.

In order to control anxiety, relaxation techniques such as breathing techniques and yoga exercises can be used. If a basketball player is suffering from anxiety, they may lose their concentration and their performance may suffer as a result of this.

Motivation

Another factor that can affect the performance of a basketball player is motivation. Players need to be motivated in order to do well in sport. There are generally two types of motivation. These are intrinsic motivation and extrinsic motivation. Intrinsic motivation comes from within the person. For example, they may have a desire to do well and to succeed, or they may get a buzz out of performing. Extrinsic motivation is when people are driven to succeed by external rewards, such as prizes, trophies or praise from others.

If basketball players are not motivated, their performance is likely to suffer.

Well done, Sarah. This is a good start to this assignment. You have identified two of the psychological factors that can affect the performance of basketball players and have given an accurate description of them.

In order to achieve a Pass, you now need to add another two psychological factors that can affect performance.

Unit 9 assignment, part two

Background

You have sustained an injury and cannot play sport for several weeks. In order to remain involved with sport while you are in recovery, your coach has suggested that you assist her with a project that she is undertaking. She has asked you to research and report back to her on the effects that motivation can have on a sports performer, and strategies that can be used to maintain and increase motivation amongst sports participants.

Task

As you will be required to feed back your findings to your coach, prepare a PowerPoint® presentation on the impact of motivation on sports performance, including two strategies that may be used to maintain and increase motivation. You need to:

GRADING CRITERIA TO BE ASSESSED
P2, P3
M2
D1

Describe the impact of motivation on sports performance (P2).

Describe two strategies that can be used to influence motivation (P3).

Explain the impact of motivation on sports performance and two strategies that can be used to maintain and increase motivation (M2).

Analyse the impact of motivation on sports performance and two strategies that can be used to maintain and increase motivation (D1).

Tackling the assignment

In order to achieve the Pass criteria you should research motivation, the different kinds of motivation and how motivation can have an impact on sports performance. You should also provide a detailed description of two strategies that may be implemented to improve motivation.

To achieve the Merit criteria, you need to go a step further, not just describing the impact of motivation on sports performance and two strategies that can be used to influence motivation, but explaining them as well. When you describe something you give a brief outline of the main

components. When you explain something you add more detail to the description, making the topic clear and understandable.

If you want to achieve a Distinction for this assignment, you should include information on the theories of motivation in your analysis. This is because, when you analyse something, you describe it, explain how it works and then talk about the impact that it has. You should justify what you are saying, offer your opinion and provide examples from a sporting situation to back up your analysis.

Unit 9 assignment, part three

Background

There has recently been a spate of poor sportsmanship and aggressive behaviour at the local rugby club. The club manager wants the situation to improve and has asked you to conduct some general research on personality, and also to look into aggressive behaviour and its effect on sports performance. He would also like you to come up with some strategies for dealing with aggressive behaviour so that he can try them out on some of his players.

GRADING CRITERIA TO BE ASSESSED
P4, P5
M3
D2

Task

Design a website about personality, aggression and the effect that these can have on sports performance. You should include a section of 'self-help' techniques on how to control aggression. You must:

Describe personality and how it affects sports performance (P4).

Describe aggression and two strategies that can be used to control it (P5).

Explain two strategies that can be used to control aggressive behaviour (M3).

Evaluate two strategies that can be used to control aggressive behaviour (D2).

Tackling the assignment

To meet the criteria for this part of the assignment, you should produce a visually stimulating website. Remember that you are **describing** to achieve a Pass, **explaining** to achieve a Merit and **evaluating** to achieve a Distinction. As part of the evaluation, you should include details of the different types of aggression and the way this information can be used to help people control their aggression when participating in sport. For example, if a basketball player is displaying hostile aggression towards their opponents, they could be taught methods of relaxation. This might help them to be more calm when in a competitive situation and to channel any aggression they do have into instrumental aggression, which can be used to improve their chances of success rather than producing actions that are harmful to others.

Unit 9 assignment, part four

Background

You have been wondering for some time how you can improve your performance in your chosen sport. You have reached a plateau and now want to improve your performance by pushing yourself further. In order to do this, you have been advised to analyse your psychological skills and identify any areas for improvement.

Task

Using the performance profiling technique, assess your attitudes and psychological skills, and identify your strengths and areas for development. Then, using the findings from your profile, create a six-week psychological training programme which should maintain your strengths and improve your weaknesses. After you have completed your training programme, you need to review your development. You also need to:

GRADING CRITERIA TO BE ASSESSED
P6, P7, P8
M4, M5
D3

Assess your own attitudes and psychological skills in a selected sport, identifying strengths and areas for improvement (P6).

Plan, carry out and record a six-week training programme to improve psychological skills for a selected sport, with tutor support (P7).

Review the psychological skills training programme, identifying strengths and areas for improvement (P8).

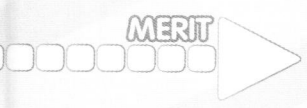

Independently plan, carry out and record a six-week training programme to improve psychological skills for a selected sport (M4).

Review the psychological skills training programme, explaining strengths and areas for improvement (M5).

Review the psychological skills training programme, justifying strengths and areas for improvement (D3).

Tackling the assignment

Once you have assessed your attitudes and psychological skills, and identified your strengths and areas for development, you should plan a training programme which includes a variety of techniques. It could look something like this:

	Week 1	Week 2	Week 3	Week 4	Week 5	Week 6
Monday	Relaxation: yoga, breathing practice	Practise self-confidence techniques		Concentration techniques: practise tuning out distractions		
Tuesday	Goal setting: long-term planning		Improving motivation: imagery, self-talk			

Jennifer has begun to piece together her training programme and has included some relevant psychological training exercises. She must now go into further detail, explaining exactly what she will be doing in each session. Will she be able to complete the sessions alone or will her coach/teacher need to help her?

Unit 10: Nutrition for Sports Performance

The components of a healthy diet

It is vital that all sports performers eat a healthy diet because we need the nutrients to grow strong and to perform to the best of our ability. There are six components of a healthy diet.

Carbohydrates

There are two main types of carbohydrates in food: these are simple carbohydrates and complex carbohydrates.

Simple carbohydrates.

- **Simple carbohydrates** are also referred to as 'simple sugars'. They are found in refined sugar, like the white sugar you might have in tea or coffee or on your cereal for breakfast, and in sweets like lollipops. They can also be found in more nutritious foods, such as fruit and milk. It is more beneficial to get simple carbohydrates from nutritious sources, because foods like milk and fruit also contain vitamins, minerals and fibre, which are all vital to a healthy diet.
- **Complex carbohydrates** are also referred to as 'starches'. They include grains such as wheat – which is used to make most bread and pasta – and rice. As with simple sugars, some foods containing complex carbohydrates are healthier than others. Refined grains, such as white flour and white rice, have been processed, which removes some of the nutrients and fibre. Unrefined grains, however, still contain all their vitamins, minerals and fibre and are therefore better for you. Fibre aids digestion and also makes you feel full for longer so that you are less likely to want more food.

Complex carbohydrates.

Both types of carbohydrates should be eaten in moderation as part of a healthy, balanced diet.

Fat

Cakes contain saturated fats.

Foods contain a combination of three types of fat, which have different effects on the level of cholesterol in our blood. Cholesterol is a substance that is produced by the liver. It is used to make vitamin D in the body, build cell walls, create hormones and create bile salts that are used to help us to digest fat. Although cholesterol has important functions within the body, we should not take too much on board because too much cholesterol can lead to serious illnesses, such as heart disease.

Avocados contain monounsaturated fats

- **Saturated fats** have a negative effect on blood cholesterol and these should be avoided or limited in our everyday diet. They can be found in fatty meats, dairy products, sweets, biscuits and cakes.
- **Polyunsaturated fats:** There are two types of polyunsaturated fat: omega-3 fatty acids and omega-6 fatty acids. Both types are good for you. Omega-3 fatty acids can be found in bread, cereals and fish. They can help to reduce high blood pressure and reduce the risk of blood clots forming. Omega-6 fatty acids are found in brazil nuts, walnuts, sunflower seeds and sunflower oil. They can help to lower cholesterol.
- **Monounsaturated fats** can also help to lower your cholesterol. They can be found in peanuts, seeds and avocados.

Tuna contains omega-3 fatty acids.

Protein

Protein is very important, particularly for a sports performer, because it helps the body with the growth, maintenance and repair of body tissue. Protein cannot be stored inside the body and needs to be replenished every day. Foods that contain a high volume of protein are mainly fleshy foods, such as chicken, fish and turkey. Protein can also be found in eggs, grains and soy products.

Eggs are a good source of protein.

Water

Water makes up around two-thirds of the human body, so it is a vital part of our diet. Water helps to flush out waste products and transport nutrients around the body. It can also help to lubricate joints, assist with breathing and help to regulate body temperature. For example, when we play sport and get hot we sweat out water and other substances, which helps to keep our temperature normal. This means that athletes should drink more water when they are training or performing to prevent them from becoming dehydrated.

Vitamins

Vitamins are an essential part of our diet:
- They help to keep our skin, hair, eyes, bones, teeth, nerves and blood cells in good condition. They help bone and tissue to form.
- Some help our bodies to process carbohydrates, proteins and fats. For example, they help to convert fat and carbohydrates into energy.

Vitamins can be divided into two groups: fat-soluble vitamins (vitamins A, D, E and K) and water-soluble vitamins (vitamins B1, B2, B3, B6, B12, pantothenic acid, folate, biotin and vitamin C).

Vitamins can be found in a variety of foods. A balanced diet of breads, cereals, fruits, vegetables, red meat, fish, poultry, dairy products, legumes, seeds and nuts will ensure that you get a satisfactory amount of the vitamins that your body needs.

Water is an essential part of a healty diet.

Minerals

Minerals provide a range of benefits for our bodies:
- Calcium, which can be found in milk, salmon, sardines, and some cereals and vegetables, helps us to develop strong bones and teeth.
- Zinc, which can be found in meat, seafood, eggs and dairy products, helps to heal wounds.
- Iron is needed to make haemoglobin, which is found in the blood and fights infection. Iron also helps the brain and nervous system to function. Iron can be found in red meat, liver, eggs, seafood, grains and cereals.
- Iodine is used by the thyroid gland to make the thyroid hormone called thyroxine. This is necessary for growth, nervous system development and energy production. It also helps to regulate the speed at which processes within the body work. Iodine can be found in seafood, vegetables, meat, eggs and milk.
- Sodium is involved in many cell processes and can be found in table salt, baking soda and a range of processed food. Too much sodium can lead to some health problems, such as dehydration, high blood pressure and possibly heart disease.

BRONZE

1. Copy and complete the table below, listing as many foods as you can think of for each component of a healthy diet.

Component	Foods
Carbohydrate	
Fat	
Protein	
Water	
Vitamins	
Minerals	

2. Dehydration is a huge problem for athletes, particularly those taking part in aerobic activities in warm weather. Find out:

a) How much water an adult should consume in one day and how much water a child should consume in one day.

b) What can happen to a sports performer if they become dehydrated.

Spinach is a good source of vitamins and minerals. It contains beta-carotene, folate, potassium, iron, vitamin B6, vitamin C, calcium and magnesium.

Eating the right balance for a healthy diet

A healthy diet is not just about eating foods that contain the nutrients that you need to grow. It is also about eating the right balance of those foods; about making sure that you have enough vitamins and minerals, and about limiting treats and serving sizes.

To ensure that you eat a balanced diet you should eat the following quantities of the six components of a healthy diet:

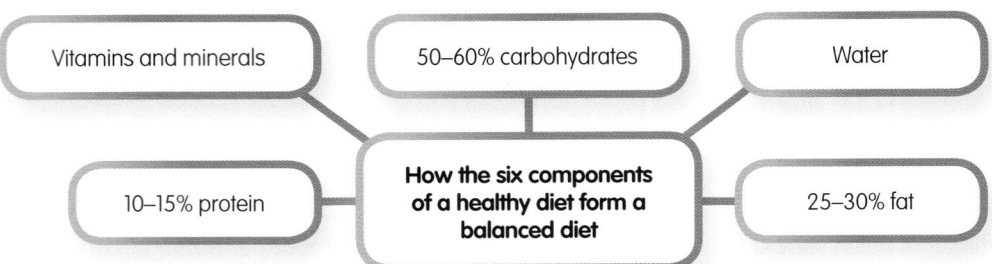

Because each type of food you can eat generally contains more than one of the six components of a balanced diet, it is easier to think about a balanced diet in terms of food groups. The healthy eating pyramid below shows the correct balance of foods you should be eating and drinking if you are to eat a healthy, balanced diet.

Top tips for a healthy, balanced diet

1. A healthy, balanced diet should contain a good variety of nutritious foods because these nutrients give you energy, keep your heart beating, keep your brain active and keep your muscles working.
2. Eating breakfast is an important part of a healthy diet because it kick-starts your metabolism, giving you energy to start the day. Breakfast can also help with concentration and can affect your mood, making you feel happy and positive.
3. Foods that are low in salt and contain small amounts of sugar are better for you. This is because too much salt can cause high blood pressure and dehydration, and too much sugar causes tooth decay and unwanted weight gain.
4. Foods with a high fat content should be avoided, particularly foods containing saturated fat. This is because too much saturated fat can lead to raised cholesterol levels, causing high blood pressure and possible heart problems. So opt for low-fat alternatives, especially when it comes to milk and cheese.
5. Monitoring the total amount of energy-dense or high-calorie foods that you eat is as important as monitoring the total amount of fat in your diet. This is because unused calories are stored as fat. To reduce the energy density of your diet you need to increase the amount of plant foods you eat.
6. Eat more fruit and vegetables. They provide you with essential nutrients and help to make you feel full, so that you don't snack on energy-dense foods or foods that are high in fat.
7. A healthy diet should include only a moderate amount of alcohol. Alcohol is bad for you in many ways, most notably, if drunk to excess it can cause serious damage to your liver. It is also high in calories, which can cause weight gain.
8. Unprocessed foods, foods that are as close to their original state as possible (such as salads, soups, and fresh fruit and vegetables), are better for you than processed foods because they are more easily digested. Salt, sugar and fat are also added to a lot of processed foods, such as ready-meals, cakes and biscuits, during the manufacturing process.
9. Some cooking methods are healthier than others. For example, fried food is immersed in cooking fat or oil, making it an unhealthy option. In contrast, grilled or steamed foods are more beneficial. If meat or fish is grilled any fats will drain away as the food cooks and if vegetables are steamed rather than boiled they retain their minerals and vitamins, which otherwise drain away in the boiling water.

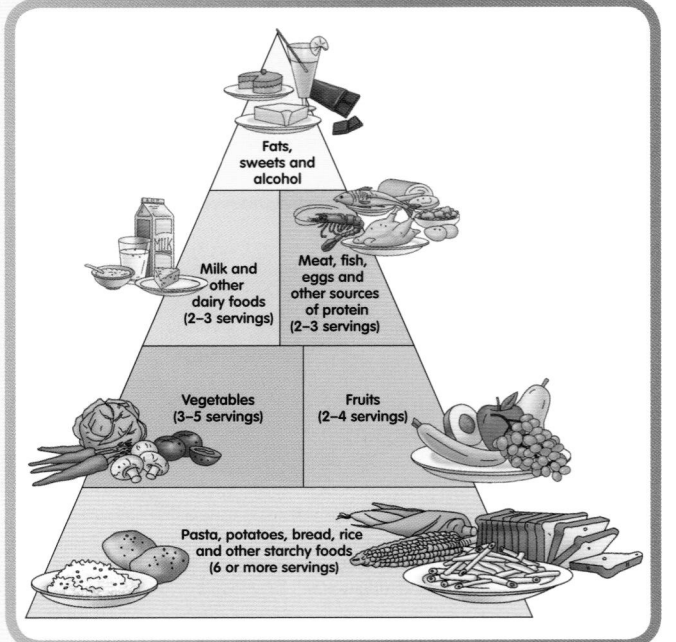

The importance of a healthy, balanced diet

Eating too much or too little of certain foods can lead to health problems. Obesity is fast becoming a problem in the UK, as more and more people consume too much fat and their body weight increases beyond a healthy level. Obesity causes many health problems, including heart disease, diabetes and damage to weight-bearing joints such as your knees. Eating too little can also cause health problems and lead to an illness called anorexia.

A healthy, balanced diet is vital for everyone, particularly sports performers, because a healthy diet helps to keep illnesses at bay and give a person the energy to perform tasks to the best of their ability. In order to maintain a healthy weight for your age and height, a balanced diet and regular exercise is essential.

Measuring your weight

Body Mass Index (BMI) is a way of calculating whether or not your body is of an ideal weight. BMI is a test designed for men and women over the age of 18, and although people under the age of 18 can use it, the results should not be taken to have any significant meaning.

According to NHS Direct (UK):
- If your BMI is less than 18.5 you are underweight for your height.
- If your BMI is 18.5 to 24.9 you are an ideal weight for your height.
- If your BMI is 25 to 29.9 you are over the ideal weight for your height.
- If your BMI is 30 to 39.9 you are obese.
- If your BMI is over 39.9 you are very obese.

To calculate your BMI:
Measure your weight in kilograms.
Measure your height in metres (so 182cm is actually 1.82m)
Calculate your BMI using the following formula:

$$BMI = \frac{weight\ (kg)}{height\ (m) \times height\ (m)}$$

If more than 25 per cent of a boy's weight or more than 32 per cent of a girl's weight is fat then they are classified as obese. Body fat can be measured using special scales available in gyms and health clubs, which measure the percentage of your body that is fat, water and muscle tissue.

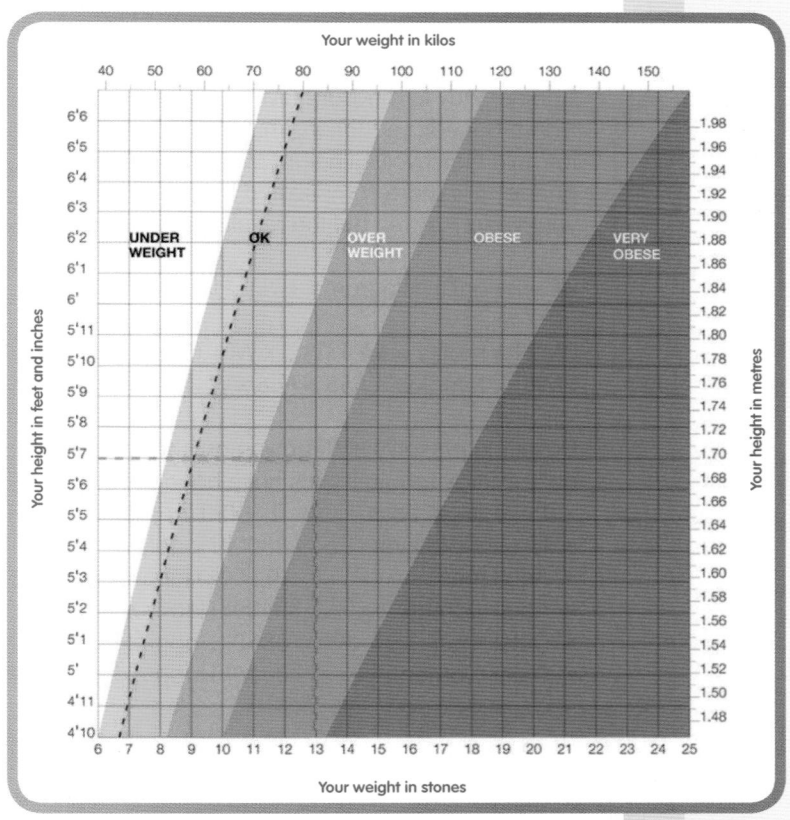

This height–weight chart can also be used as a guide to determine whether a healthy adult is overweight.

Maintaining a healthy weight

The food that we eat provides us with energy and the key to maintaining a healthy weight is ensuring that energy in equals energy out. If your energy intake and energy expenditure is the same, then your weight should be steady. In order to lose weight, the energy intake must be reduced or the energy expenditure increased. To gain weight, energy expenditure should be less than energy intake.

Energy is measured in joules or kilojoules. Food energy can also be measured in terms of the nutritional or 'large' calories it contains. One calorie (Cal) has the same energy value as 4.186 kilojoules (kJ).

How much energy food contains depends on its components. Fats and alcohol are the most energy-dense components. This is why they should only be consumed in moderation, particularly if you are overweight or obese. Below is energy value per gram of some food components:

- fat: 37kJ (9 Cal)
- alcohol: 29kJ (7 Cal)
- carbohydrates: 16kJ (4 Cal)
- protein: 17kJ (4 Cal)
- water: 0kJ (0 Cal).

Basal Metabolic Rate (BMR)

A person's Basal Metabolic Rate, or BMR, is the minimum amount of calories they need in order to function when at rest. If someone takes part in sport they will require more calories than someone who spends their time watching television, in order to provide the energy that they need to perform. There are a variety of factors that can have an effect on your BMR. These are:

- age
- size
- gender
- body composition
- illness
- dieting.

An easy way to calculate BMR is to multiply your weight (in kilograms) by ten. For example, if your weight is 45kg, then your BMR is 450.

Another way to measure BMR is to use the Harris-Benedict equation. This method uses a formula that involves height, weight, age and gender. It is more complicated than multiplying your weight by ten but the results are more accurate.

Energy IN: Food and drinks

Energy OUT: Basal Metabolic Rate (BMR)

Exercise

W = weight in kilograms   H = height in centimetres   A = age in years

BMR for males = 66 + (13.7 × W) + (5 × H) − (6.8 × A)
BMR for females = 655 + (9.6 × W) + (1.8 × H) − (4.7 × A)

Despite a person's BMR having an impact on their individual energy requirements, rough guidelines for the daily energy requirements have been developed:

- 15-year-old boys   11,500kJ (approximately 2700 Cal)
- 15-year-old girls   8800kJ (approximately 2100 Cal)
- Adult men   10,500kJ (approximately 2500 Cal)
- Adult women   8400kJ (approximately 2000 Cal)
- Older men   8800kJ (approximately 2100 Cal)
- Older women   8000kJ (approximately 1900 Cal)

BRONZE

1. Find out your weight and calculate your BMI.

2. Find two food labels, one from something healthy, such as a cereal bar, and one from something unhealthy, such as a packet of crisps. Find out how many calories are in each item and then find out how much exercise is required to burn the calories off.

SILVER

3. Using the same two food labels that you used for Activity 2, compare the nutritional values of each food and explain which is better for you and why.

BRONZE

4. Find out how each of the factors listed above (age, body composition, size, illness, gender and dieting) affects a person's BMR.

5a) Calculate your BMR.

b) Calculate your energy intake on an average day.

c) Calculate the amount of energy you expend on an average day.

d) Using your calculations, decide whether you are taking in enough energy to sustain your daily activities, or if you are eating too little or too much.

Eating for sport

Sports performers must not only eat a healthy and well-balanced diet, they must also ensure that their diet is specifically tailored to their needs as an athlete. It is therefore important that sports performers plan their meals according to their training regimes and competition schedules.

Before training and competition

When preparing for physical activity, athletes must carefully consider what foods they take on board. When preparing for aerobic exercise, such as marathon running or cycling, athletes must load their bodies with energy-providing foods, such as carbohydrates, two to four hours before they begin in order to maximize their stores of glycogen. This process is often referred to as 'carbo-loading'. It is also important to drink plenty of fluids before taking part in sports. This will help a performer to avoid becoming dehydrated.

Different diets for different sports

Not all sports performers follow the same diet plans.

Some performers, such as weightlifters, may follow a high-protein diet. Foods that contain lots of protein are generally low in fat and carbohydrates, which allows athletes to build and repair muscle tissue as well as lose excess fat. Athletes following a high-protein diet should aim to consume around one gram of protein per one pound of body weight.

In contrast, endurance athletes may follow a high-carbohydrate diet. Approximately two to three days before an important race, long-distance runners will carbo-load to ensure that there is a large amount of glycogen in their muscles in order to sustain them during the lengthy period of performance ahead.

During sport

Sports competitors should ensure that they take on board plenty of fluids, in the form of water or a sports drink, when they are performing so that they remain hydrated. If the activity is lengthy, a snack may also be required. Foods that are easy to digest and that contain carbohydrates for energy, such as low-fat cereal bars or bananas, are best. Foods that contain protein may also be eaten because they will help to repair muscle damage.

After sport

Sports drinks are popular amongst athletes, particularly after performing, because they help to rehydrate the body and replace the body's store of energy. They are better for athletes than water because they contain carbohydrates and electrolytes, such as sodium and potassium, which have been lost in sweat and therefore need replenishing. Potassium can also help to speed up the recovery process.

Within one to two hours of completing physical activity carbohydrates may also be eaten to replace energy, as well as protein to help repair muscle tissue.

During rest periods

Athletes often schedule a rest period of two to four weeks per year into their training programmes. During this time, they should try to eat a nutritious, well-balanced diet containing plenty of easily digestible, starchy foods. They should also ensure that they begin each day with a good breakfast to kick-start their metabolism and drink plenty of fluids to remain hydrated.

Supplements

Although we can get most of the energy we require from food, some sports performers supplement their diet with vitamins, minerals, energy bars and protein drinks to enhance their performance or to aid recovery. For example, creatine monohydrate allows an athlete to train harder for longer periods with less recovery time.

Most supplements are legal but some athletes are tempted to take illegal substances, such as anabolic steroids, to improve their performance. If caught using this kind of supplement, sports performers may be banned from taking part in their sport for a period of time and their reputation may never recover from the scandal.

BRONZE

1. Choose one famous sportsperson and find out how their diet supports their training and competition requirements.

GOLD

2. Create a three-day meal plan for an athlete of your choice. The plan should cover the day before the competition, the day of the competition and the day after the competition. It should also include breakfast, lunch and dinner, as well as all drinks and snacks.

187

SPOTLIGHT on a healthy, balanced diet

BRONZE

Completing this activity will help you to achieve a **Pass** in your assignment.

1. Create a 20-question quiz to help a sports performer understand what a healthy, balanced diet is.

GOLD

Completing this activity will help you to achieve a **Distinction** in your assignment.

3. Create a detailed meal plan for a boxer.

SILVER

Completing this activity will help you to achieve a **Merit** in your assignment.

2. Create a poster to explain why each of the six components of a healthy diet is important for sports performers.

Unit 10 assignment, part one

Background

You are a nutritional expert who is visiting local sports clubs in order to offer advice to performers on what they should be eating to support their training regimes. You have been asked to deliver a presentation on the general dietary requirements of athletes, outlining their nutritional requirements and suggesting meal plans.

Task

Create a PowerPoint® presentation that can be delivered to athletes at your local sports club. Your presentation should focus on one particular sport and during your presentation you should:

GRADING CRITERIA TO BE ASSESSED
P1
M1
D1

 **PASS**

Describe the nutritional requirements of a selected sport (P1).

 **MERIT**

Explain the nutritional requirements of a selected sport (M1).

 **DISTINCTION**

Evaluate the nutritional requirements of a selected sport describing suitable meal plans (D1).

Tackling the assignment

In order to meet the Pass criteria for this assignment, you must research the components of a healthy, balanced diet and link these to the nutritional requirements of a performer in your selected sport, describing how their performance will benefit if their nutritional requirements are met.

To meet the Merit criteria, you should go a step further and explain how the performer's nutritional requirements might change before, during and after competition. To meet the Distinction criteria, you should evaluate the performer's

nutritional requirements and provide meal plans for them for before, during and after an event, and also when they are at rest. Remember, explaining something means telling your audience why something is like it is and an explanation often includes the word 'because'. An evaluation goes further and requires you to examine strengths and weaknesses, for example, in this case, commenting on the impact that suggested improvements might have.

Meeting the Pass and Merit criteria

Jessica Slater
Unit 10 assignment, part one
Nutrition for sport

All sports performers should carefully plan what they eat and drink around their training and competitions. Different sports performers have different needs and a long-distance runner needs the right amount of each food type.

As part of their diet, a long-distance runner should have the following components:

- **Carbohydrates:** These are particularly important for an aerobic athlete as they supply the body with energy that can be stored and used when performing. Athletes should try to eat starchy carbohydrates, such as pasta, rather than sugary carbohydrates, which can make you gain weight.
- **Fats:** Long-distance runners need to eat some fats as these will also provide them with the energy that they need. However, they should make sure that they eat unsaturated fats, as saturated fat can result in their cholesterol level becoming too high. 'Good' fats can be found in nuts, olive oil and some oily fish.

Jessica has begun to describe the nutritional requirements for a long-distance runner and, if she continues like this, will meet the criteria for P1. She should make sure that she mentions the importance of fluid intake for a long-distance runner and which supplements might be used to support their diet. She should also include information about the quantities of each component that a long-distance runner requires and make some suggestions as to the way the food is prepared.

To achieve a Merit, Jessica needs to describe how a long-distance runner's nutritional requirements will change to suit their training and performance schedules; how they will change before, during and after a competition.

Meeting the Distinction criteria

This is a great meal plan but, to fully achieve the Distinction criteria, Jessica needs to go further and explain how this meal plan would change according to a marathon runner's training and competition schedule. What should a marathon runner eat before, during and after competition, and what should they eat when they are having a scheduled break from training and competition? Also, are there any supplements that long-distance runners could take when they are training or competing?

A typical meal plan for a marathon runner

Breakfast:
- Porridge with a handful of fruit, such as blueberries
- Two scrambled eggs on wholegrain toast, with mushrooms and tomatoes
- Water

Morning snack:
- A small tin of sardines and a jacket potato
- A handful of dried fruit or fresh fruit, and nuts or seeds
- Water

Lunch:
- Salad with mixed leaves, tomato, red onion, avocado, bean sprouts, carrot, apple, beetroot, cucumber and feta cheese, with an optional olive oil and balsamic vinegar dressing.
- Chicken breast or turkey with rice
- Water

Afternoon snack:
- Chicken breast and a handful of mixed vegetables and rice
- Walnuts, seeds or fruit
- Water

Dinner:
- Lean meat, such as a steak, vegetables and a medium potato
- Water

Evening snack:
- Fruit with yoghurt
- Water

Assessing your diet

As we have seen, a healthy, balanced diet is extremely important for a sports performer. It is therefore important for an athlete to assess their diet on an ongoing basis to determine what food and drink they are consuming, when they are consuming it, and how they feel about their diet and their weight. A good way for a performer to monitor their energy and nutrient consumption is to keep a food diary.

Food diaries

The type of food and drink consumed.

How many kilojoules or calories are contained in the food and drink consumed.

How many grams of protein, carbohydrates and fat are consumed.

Any supplements taken.

A food diary is used to keep a record of what we eat and drink each day, and should include details of ...

The quantity of food and drink consumed.

A daily energy target in kilojoules or calories.

The times that food and drink are consumed.

A comparison between the energy target and the energy consumed.

How you are feeling about your diet. This information can help to inform future meal planning. If, for example, a sports performer is feeling full of energy and positive about their weight after eating a particular way for a week, they can look back on this and use the same foods to create a similar effect in the future.

Here is an example of a food diary:

	7:30am	1 x grapefruit (1g protein, 0% fat, 0% carbohydrates) 1 x glass of water	100 calories
Monday **Target calorie consumption:** 1500 calories **Actual calorie consumption:** 1258 calories	10:00am	1 x cereal bar (6g protein, 0% fat, 21g carbohydrates) 1 x diet cola	110 calories
	1:00pm	1 x jacket potato (180g) (4.2g protein, 0.1g fat, 46g carbohydrates) Tinned tuna fish (200g) (54g protein, 1g fat, 0g carbohydrates) 1 x glass of water	198 calories
	4:00pm	1 x banana (1.3g protein, 0.3g fat, 21g carbohydrates)	100 calories
	7:30pm	Spaghetti bolognaise (240g) (17g protein, 5g fat, 43g carbohydrates) 1 x glass of orange juice (1.7g protein, 0.5g fat, 25g carbohydrates)	750 calories
	Feelings: I was hungry in the morning so had my cereal bar. I felt stuffed after my evening meal. I am wondering if I should eat a larger meal at lunchtime so that I can eat less at dinner and don't feel so full when it is time for bed.		

Analysing your diet

Once you have collected information about your diet, it is time to examine it closely.
You can compare your diet with what you know about the requirements of a healthy, balanced diet and any special requirements you might have when you are training or competing. You can also compare your diet with relevant guidelines, such as the government recommendation that we eat five portions of fruit and vegetables a day, and the recommended daily energy intake.

One way to analyse your diet is to complete a paper-based dietary analysis questionnaire but many fitness centres also have dietary analysis software, which can analyse a client's diet and recommend improvements. The instructor or personal trainer will talk to their client and run tests to find out about things such as their eating habits, their blood cholesterol levels and their Body Mass Index. The instructor can then recommend ways in which the client could change their diet, for example, to lower their cholesterol levels.

Acting on recommendations

When you have collected information about your diet and analysed it using either a questionnaire you have created yourself or dietary analysis software, it is time to use the findings to inform your diet and energy intake in the future.

A dietary analysis will identify strengths in your diet and areas for improvement. For example, it might tell you that you are not drinking enough water when you are training, so you can plan to drink more at these times. It might tell you that the amount of saturated fat in your diet is too high, so you can work to prepare your meals in a different way in order to reduce their saturated fat content. It might tell you that you aren't eating enough protein and carbohydrates after you have exercised, so you can adjust when you eat to ensure your body gets the nutrients it needs when it most needs them. It could also show you that you are eating too many 'ready-meals' or processed foods, and that you should aim to eat more fresh foods, which are rich in vitamins and minerals, instead.

1 medium apple

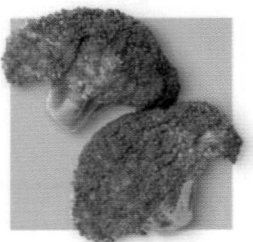

2 broccoli florets

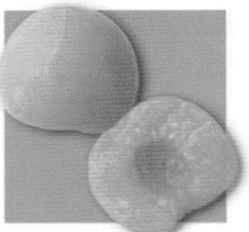

2 halves of canned peaches

1 handful of grapes

1 medium banana

3 heaped tablespoons of peas

1 medium glass of orange juice

7 strawberries

3 whole dried apricots

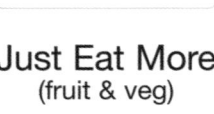

5 A DAY

Just Eat More
(fruit & veg)

www.doh.gov.uk/fiveaday

© Crown copyright 2003

3 heaped tablespoons of cooked kidney beans

16 okra

NHS

Unit 10 assignment, part two

Background

A nutritional analyst is visiting your school or college and has chosen a selection of students to participate in a free health and diet analysis programme. You have been asked to monitor your energy intake over a two-week period, recording everything that you eat and drink. The analyst then wants you to explain your dietary strengths and weaknesses so that they can work with you on making recommendations for improvement.

Task

Collect and record information about your diet over a two-week period. Then use the information you have collected to identify the strengths and weaknesses of your diet and suggest ways in which you could improve it. You must:

GRADING CRITERIA TO BE ASSESSED
P2, P3
M2
D2

PASS

Collect and collate information on your own diet for two weeks (P2).

Describe the strengths of your own diet and identify areas for improvement (P3).

MERIT

Explain the strengths of your own diet and make recommendations as to how it could be improved (M2).

DISTINCTION

Justify the recommendations you made regarding improving your own diet (D2).

Tackling the assignment

The most sensible way to collect and record information about your diet is by keeping a food diary where you note down all the food and drink you consume, when you consumed it, how many calories it contained and its nutritional content. You should also keep a record of how you are feeling generally and, more specifically, how you are feeling about the food and drink that you are consuming.

Using the information that you have collected in your food diary, you need to describe or explain the strengths and weaknesses of your diet (remembering that explanations usually contain the word 'because'). It should then be a relatively easy task to recommend ways to improve your diet if you are aiming for a Merit and also justify your recommendations if you are aiming for a Distinction.

Meeting the Pass, Merit and Distinction criteria

My food diary by Robert Grey

Unit 10 assignment, part two

Monday	Breakfast	Bacon	128 Calories
		Egg	92 Calories
		Beans	197 Calories
		Orange juice	44 Calories
	Lunch	Pepperoni pizza slice	290 Calories
		Sausage roll	240 Calories
		Chocolate cookie	275 Calories
		Can of orangeade	164 Calories
	Dinner	Spaghetti bolognaise	600 Calories
		Garlic bread	100 Calories
		Can of orangeade	164 Calories
Tuesday	Breakfast	Toast	90 Calories
		Cornflakes	140 Calories
		Coffee	16 Calories
	Lunch	Jacket potato	218 Calories
		Cheese	170 Calories
		Beans	197 Calories
		Cola	130 Calories

Robert has clearly collected lots of information about his diet and is well on his way to meeting the criteria for P2, but there are several things he could do to improve his food diary. For example, he doesn't record the amounts of food and drink that he consumes and he doesn't detail absolutely everything he eats. For example, he doesn't mention what he had on his toast; he later talks about butter in his recommendations but it isn't mentioned at all in his food diary. Also, he hasn't noted the timings of his meals, how his food was cooked, or how he felt about the food and drinks he was consuming. Did he feel full after eating? Did he eat each meal at the same time each day and did he have any snacks between meals?

Strengths:
- I have eaten a lot of fruit and drunk fruit juices.
- I have eaten lots of food that is high in protein, such as eggs and fish.
- I have also eaten lots of food that is high in carbohydrates, such as bread, pasta and rice.

Robert has begun to meet the criteria for P3 because he has described the strengths of his diet by listing the things that he ate and drank that are good for him. To meet the criteria for M2 he needs to **explain** why the things he ate and drank are good for him. For example, he could add that the high-protein food that he ate will help his muscle tissue to repair, and that the carbohydrates provided him with the energy his body needed to walk to school and play football with his friends at break time.

Weaknesses:
- The main weaknesses in my diet are fizzy drinks and dairy products. There is a lot of sugar in fizzy drinks, and in the icing on the bun I ate on Wednesday, and this could cause unwanted weight gain and tooth decay. During the early part of the week I had quite a lot of dairy products. Although there is calcium in the cheese and milk that I ate, there is also a high percentage of fat, which again could lead to weight gain.

The information Robert has provided about one weakness of his diet is much more detailed than the information on his strengths. Robert now needs to list (P3) and explain (M2) the remaining weaknesses is his diet.

Recommendations for improvements
I think that my diet could be improved in several ways:
1. I could reduce the amount of fizzy drinks I consume and replace them with natural fruit juice or water instead. This will ensure that I get plenty of vitamins and minerals, and will reduce the amount of sugar in my diet. Some vitamins can help to prevent illness, such as vitamin C, which can be found in oranges and other citrus fruits. This will help me to stay healthy as well as reduce the chances of me putting on weight.

The recommendation Robert has made for improving his diet is excellent. Not only has he explained the recommendation fully (M2), he has also justified his recommendation (D1) by telling us the benefits of the healthier diet he is recommending.

Robert now needs to make further recommendations for improvement.

Implementing and reviewing a personal nutritional strategy

Once you have assessed your diet, it is time to create a nutritional strategy and consider the timings of your food and drink intake. Remember that training and competition put extra demands on your body, which you have to support by ensuring that the food and drink you are consuming before, during and after exercise contains the appropriate nutrients. A nutritional strategy is designed to help a performer get the most out of their diet by eating the correct amount of each nutritional component for their sport.

Help with planning a personal nutritional strategy

Coaches
Although many sports coaches do not have a qualification in giving nutritional advice, they will be able to assist with general queries about food and eating for sport. This is especially true if they are an ex-athlete and have been through the same process themselves.

Nutritionists
Nutritional advisers or counsellors educate people about healthy eating and the benefits of a well-balanced diet. Nutritional counselling may also help people to identify any problems that they have with food and the physical consequences of not eating well, particularly as a sports performer.

People who may be able to help you plan your nutritional strategy

Tutors and teachers
Tutors and teachers may be able to offer advice on nutrition and eating for sport as they will be familiar with the benefits of eating a healthy, balanced diet from their teaching of sports students and delivering sports-related courses in college or school.

Fitness instructors
You might think that someone who works in a gym or a health club deals mainly with exercise and training programmes, but fitness instructors and personal trainers can also give nutritional advice if they have the appropriate qualification or experience.

Reviewing your nutritional strategy

It is important to review a nutritional strategy at regular intervals in order to check that it is suitable and make changes to it if necessary.

If a performer loses too much weight too quickly then their diet may not be providing them with enough energy and their diet plan will need to be supplemented. Similarly, it is important to check regularly that the performer enjoys the food prescribed by their diet plan. Fish is full of protein and many important vitamins and minerals that help growth and repair, but if an athlete doesn't like it then it must be replaced with something that they do like which provides similar nutrients. It is also important to consider the cost and lifestyle implications of a nutritional strategy. If the foods required for the diet plan are too expensive for the athlete, then these should be substituted for cheaper alternatives. Or, if the diet plan requires the performer to eat a hot meal at lunchtime, when they don't have access to facilities to cook or reheat a meal, then it needs to be amended to take this into account.

Lastly, and perhaps most importantly, a nutritional strategy should be reviewed regularly to make sure that it is working as it was intended to. If a performer can show, using their food diary, that they have followed the recommended diet but are not achieving the expected results, then the plan may need to be altered.

Remember:
If a sports performer is going to benefit from a nutritional strategy, they must complete their food diary every day.

BRONZE

1. Find out who can help you to plan a personal nutritional strategy in your local area.

2. Design a nutritional strategy for the friend whose diet you analysed earlier. Don't forget to consider their sporting requirements, their age, their dietary likes and dislikes, their lifestyle and the cost of the strategy you are proposing.

Unit 10 assignment, part three

Background

Having monitored and analysed your diet, the visiting nutritional analyst has advised you to create and implement a personal nutritional strategy so that you can improve your diet. As with all strategies you have agreed to review your progress after two weeks.

GRADING CRITERIA
TO BE ASSESSED

P4, P5, P6
M3, M4

Task

Using the information you gathered for part two of the assignment, create and implement a personal nutritional strategy designed to build on the strengths of your diet and improve your weaknesses. You should also create a two-week meal plan to support your strategy. Then, as you implement your strategy, keep a record of what you are eating and how you are feeling using a food diary. Finally, using your food diary, review the strategy to determine what worked well and how it could be improved.

PASS

Create a personal nutritional strategy, designed and agreed with an adviser (P4).

Implement a personal nutritional strategy (P5).

Describe the strengths of the personal nutritional strategy and identify areas for improvement (P6).

MERIT

Contribute your own ideas to the design of a personal nutritional strategy (M3).

Explain the strengths of the personal nutritional strategy and make recommendations as to how it could be improved (M4).

Tackling the assignment

In order to meet the criteria, you must use all the information you gathered in your food diary for part two of the assignment in order to create a nutritional strategy that is tailored to meet the needs of your chosen sport. Your strategy should include realistic targets to improve your diet. You should also plan meals that are nutritionally balanced and well suited to the demands of your sport, thinking about breakfast, lunch, dinner, drinks and snacks. Remember to be realistic about what you are going to eat. There is no point structuring your meal plan around food that you dislike, although perhaps this is the time to try out something new? Think about how food is cooked too. Can

you still eat your favourite foods, but make them healthier by grilling or steaming them rather than frying or boiling them?

Keep a food diary while you are following your meal plan to record how you are feeling and any points at which you deviate from the plan. Did you feel full after each meal? Did you have plenty of energy? How did you feel generally and about your diet in particular?

Your review of your personal nutritional strategy could be presented as a Word document or as a PowerPoint® presentation.

Meeting the Pass criteria

BTEC Level 2 Firsts in Sport

Unit 10 assignment, part three   *Faye Crowthe*

Personal nutritional strategy

Having reviewed my dietary habits, I am going to plan a nutritional strategy that will aim to improve my diet and better support my training. I have asked my teacher, Miss Greig, to help me to do this.

The main problem with my diet is that I do not eat the appropriate foods for my sport, which is netball. My training sessions are usually about 45 minutes long and a game can last up to 60 minutes. These are quite demanding, so I need to eat more energy-providing food so that I have the stamina to last the training session or game. I therefore need to eat more carbohydrates. I can get these from bread and pasta. It is best if I eat plenty of carbohydrates leading up to a game, as this will give me the energy that I need to perform throughout a whole match.

> For her nutritional strategy to be truly useful, Faye needs to set herself clear targets. She could bullet point each target and describe it in more detail. For example, when she says 'stamina', does she mean cardiovascular endurance? Has she considered muscular endurance?

> Faye states that she will need to eat more carbohydrates and this may be the case pre-competition, but she also needs to identify what percentage of her diet each of all six components of a healthy diet should make up on a day-to-day basis. Her meal plan will help to show if she has understood this but it would also be a good idea for her to include references to these percentages in her description.

Meeting the Merit criteria

BTEC Level 2 Firsts in Sport

Unit 10 assignment, part three   *Stuart Dennison*

Personal nutritional strategy

Boxers need to have muscle and power to execute all of the moves required for a bout, but they must remain lean as there are weight restrictions that they must meet. It is therefore vital that boxers have the correct diet when training and competing.

I have reviewed my diet with my coach and have decided that, based on the weaknesses I have identified and the requirements of my chosen sport, boxing, I will set the following targets:

- To consume the correct amount of carbohydrates, protein and fats.
- To take on board the correct amount of water.
- To avoid eating fatty foods, particularly foods high in saturated fat.
- To reduce the consumption of fizzy, sugary drinks.
- To avoid eating processed food.

As carbohydrates slowly release energy they are ideal for boxers and I will therefore aim for 50 per cent of my dietary intake to be carbohydrates. The best types of carbohydrates to consume are natural ones, such as those in beans and fruit, rather than those in processed foods, such as pasta or ready-meals, because the calorific value of processed foods is too high.

Protein is also extremely important in a boxer's diet because it aids the repair and replacement of damaged muscle tissue.

> Stuart has set some realistic targets for his nutritional strategy and has identified the areas that he would like to improve, explaining why these improvements are important for a boxer. He has stated how much of his diet will be made up from carbohydrates and it would be very good if he could do the same for protein.

> In order to achieve the Merit criteria, Stuart needs to highlight which ideas he has contributed to his personal nutritional strategy. He could do this by adding phrases such as, 'My coach has advised me that I should …', and 'I agree with this, however, I also think that …'.

Unit 11: Development of Personal Fitness

Setting goals for a personal fitness training programme

One of the most important aspects of planning a personal fitness training programme is setting goals. These goals provide the overall aim of the fitness programme and therefore become the foundations of any activity that we take part in.

The importance of goal setting

If they are not being met, goals highlight the need for changes to be made to training programmes.

Goals provide a focus for training programmes, helping to motivate and encourage individuals. They help to keep the performer working hard, giving them a better chance of improving their fitness levels or their individual skills.

The positive effects of goal setting on the performer

Achieving goals demonstrates to the performer that their fitness or skill levels have improved. This motivates the performer to set new goals and continue training.

Goals mentally prepare performers for training or competition.

Long-term goals

Setting your long-term goals is the first step in goal setting. For experienced performers, long-term goals are often based around seasons or competitions. The long-term goals for less-experienced performers may simply be to lose weight or to improve their fitness levels.

Long-term goals can be:
- **Outcome goals:** These are based on performance in competition. For example, a netball team might set themselves the long-term goal of reaching the knock-out stages of a competition.
- **Performance goals:** These are based on previous performances. For example, an 800m runner might set himself the long-term goal of matching or beating his personal best in an upcoming competition.

Team players and coaches need to work together to achieve outcome goals.

Medium-term goals

Long-term goals are broken down into medium-term goals. These normally focus on a period of weeks or months, and concentrate on training. For example, a professional football team might set themselves the medium-term goal of improving their aerobic fitness during the pre-season period, between July and August, in order to be ready for the new season.

Pre-season training often involves a lot of hard work.

Short-term goals

Medium-term goals are broken down into short-term goals, which add detail to training programmes. They are often used as incentives to train hard because they are much shorter in duration. For example, a gymnast may set themselves the short-term goal of completing a floor routine during a training session.

BRONZE

1. Write down a long-term goal for your favourite sporting activity.

2. Break your long-term goal down into medium-term goals.

3. Take your first medium-term goal and break it down into short-term goals.

Elite gymnasts need to show dedication and commitment to their sport in order to reach the world stage. Setting themselves short-term goals gives them the direction they need for each training session.

Gathering information to inform your personal fitness training programme

When you are planning a training programme, it is essential to gather information about the performer in order to make the training programme relevant to that performer. This is because each performer has different goals, fitness levels and a different training history.

Lifestyle: This includes information about how active the performer is in their everyday life and how much time they have to dedicate to a training programme.

Long-term goals

Medical history: It is important to find out if the performer has any medical issues that need to be considered, so performers should always complete a Physical Activity Readiness Questionnaire (PAR-Q) before embarking on an exercise programme. An example of a PAR-Q is provided in Unit 14, on page 263.

Physical activity history: It is helpful to know a performer's previous activity levels so that the personal exercise programme can be planned to suit the performer's individual needs.

Information about the performer

Dietary history and dietary preferences: Diet forms an important part of a fitness training programme. It is therefore important to know about any special dietary requirements a performer might have. For example, are they a vegetarian, a diabetic or allergic to dairy products? It is also important to find out about a performer's dietary preferences, if there are certain foods they don't like and whether or not their diet is generally poor.

Attitudes and motivation: How the performer feels about undertaking an exercise programme will play a large part in how they approach it. Therefore, it is important to understand their levels of commitment and motivation in order to create an appropriate exercise programme.

Supplement use: Sports supplements are substances taken by people involved in physical activity, particularly bodybuilding, to aid the development of muscle mass or to cause fat loss. Sports supplements can also be used to improve sports performance, and recovery from events or training. Any supplements used by a performer should be considered when planning an exercise programme and then monitored throughout, because they might affect the desired outcome. Many supplements available are illegal in professional sports.

Nutritional knowledge: The performer's knowledge and understanding of nutrition, and its effects on the body, should be considered because it is very important that anyone undertaking an exercise programme is aware of how important diet is in fuelling the body effectively.

SILVER

1. Use the information on this page to help you design your own PAR-Q.

2. Conduct a fitness interview with the person sitting next to you, using the PAR-Q you created for Activity 1.

Principles of training

Improving a performer's fitness levels requires training that adheres to the principles of training. The principles of training can be remembered using the acronym 'FITT for SPORT'.

Frequency

Frequency refers to the number of times exercise is undertaken each week.

It is recommended that each of us should take part in a minimum of 30 minutes of physical activity three times each week, to achieve the minimal level of fitness required to live a healthy life. A top-class sportsperson will have to train a lot more than this to achieve success in their chosen sport.

Intensity

Intensity is how hard the exercise is.

While it is important for us to exercise at least three times a week, another important factor is the intensity at which we work. It is recommended that, to stay healthy, we must work in our target zone for at least 20 minutes of our minimum 30-minute sessions. When training for cardiovascular fitness our target zone is between 60 to 80 per cent of our Maximum

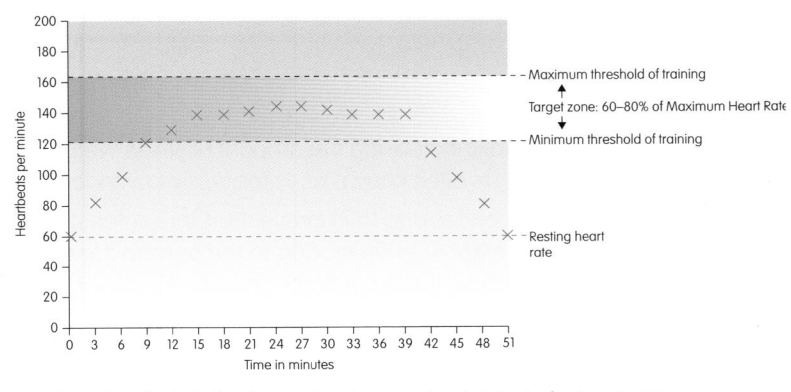

A graph to illustrate the changes in pulse rate when training in the target zone.

Heart Rate and it is important that we train at this intensity because this is where our fitness will increase. When training for strength our target zone is between 60 to 80 per cent of the maximum weight we can lift.

Time

Time refers to how long each exercise session lasts.

It is important that we remain in the target zone for a minimum of 20 minutes to see improvements.

Type

Type refers to the nature of the exercise that the performer completes.

In order to keep training interesting and the performer motivated it is essential that the type of training is varied so that the performer does not complete the same activities every training session. For example, a long-distance runner may train on a track, run up and down hills, or train on the road.

BRONZE

1. List three ways that the intensity of exercise can be increased.

2. Write a paragraph to explain how fitness levels can be improved using FITT.

SILVER

3. Write a one-week training programme for a long-distance runner, using the FITT principles as the basis for your plan.

Both the fun-runner and the elite athlete will have trained hard for the London Marathon, but they will not have had the same training programme.

BRONZE

4. There are potential dangers with regards to overtraining. Write down as many reasons why overtraining can have a negative effect on our fitness as you can think of.

5. Different players in the same team sometimes have different fitness requirements. How many sports, other than football, can you think of where two team members have different training needs? How do their training needs differ and why?

SILVER

6. Develop a training programme for an elite marathon runner and a first-time marathon runner, taking their different training needs into account.

Specificity

Specificity means focusing training on activities relevant to your sport.

To train for a particular sport or event it is important that we apply appropriate training methods because each sport has its own specific requirements. Training programmes should include all the specific actions and skills that are used in the sport or event, and it is important that they are performed at game or event speed during training. Gymnasts and swimmers need to train differently, as do players of the same sport if they play in different positions. For example, a midfielder in a football team may require training that focuses on cardiovascular endurance and speed in order for them to keep going for longer and to increase the speed at which they can move around the pitch. A goalkeeper, on the other hand, would require work that focuses on agility and reaction time.

When we plan a personal exercise programme it is essential that we take the individual needs of the performer into account, so that they are appropriately challenged. A first-time marathon runner would not benefit from using a training plan designed for an elite marathon runner, for example, because their fitness levels would not be high enough. The less experienced runner would find the programme too difficult and would risk injuring themselves.

Progression

Progression means gradually increasing the amount of stress we place on our bodies in order for fitness gains to occur. Progression is often known as 'progressive overload'.

For example, a sportsperson looking to improve their muscular strength would need to gradually increase the amount of weight they lift in order to encourage the muscles to adapt to lifting heavier weights, therefore increasing muscle growth.

Overload

Overload is about training at an appropriate intensity. It means working above our minimum threshold of training (the minimum amount required to make fitness gains) and below our maximum threshold of training, in order to make fitness gains without risking injury. It does not mean training too hard or too much.

Our target zone is between 60 and 80 per cent of our maximum effort, and this can be applied to any type of fitness training. For example, when overload training for muscular strength our target zone is between 60 to 80 per cent of the maximum weight we can lift for six to eight repetitions. When overload training for cardiovascular improvement our target zone is between 60 and 80 per cent of our Maximum Heart Rate for a period of at least 20 minutes.

Reversibility

Our bodies need to be placed under stress in order to improve. If our bodies are not challenged, any strength, tone or skill gains that have previously been made will be reversed.

Our bodies lose any gains made as a result of training three times faster than the gains were made. It really is 'use it or lose it', so it is important not to get injured or become demotivated.

Training too much

Overtraining occurs when the intensity of exercise exceeds the body's ability to recover. A performer who has overtrained will cease to make progress, and can even begin to lose strength and fitness. Overtraining is a common problem in weight training, but it is also experienced by runners and other athletes. It is important to remember that our bodies require time to recover after exercise, so even top-class athletes need to build rest and recovery time into their training programmes.

Warming up and cooling down

All exercise sessions should consist of three distinct parts:
- A warm-up to prepare the body for activity.
- The main activity, which can be a training session, a match or a competition.
- A cool-down to prepare the body for rest and recovery.

Warming up

Warming up properly improves performance because it prepares the mind and body for the main activity.

There are three phases to a warm-up:
1. **Pulse raising:** This aims to gradually raise the heart rate and warm up the largest muscle groups to the working rate. More oxygen is also made available to the working muscles, which will improve performance. Activities often include jogging, sidestepping and skipping.
2. **Stretching:** This aims to lengthen the specific muscles used in the main activity, helping to prevent injury. Most of this should be active stretching, which involves stretching the joints while moving.
3. **Joint mobilization:** This aims to move the joints into positions appropriate to the main activity, again helping to prevent injury. Activities often include rotation exercises, such as shoulder rotation, when the joint is moved carefully through its full range of movement.

Cooling down

Cooling down after a performance is just as important as warming up, although it is often overlooked by amateur performers. It returns the body to its pre-exercise state.

There are three phases to a cool-down:
1. **Pulse lowering:** This is a gentle activity which aims to gradually return the pulse rate to its resting rate. Typical activities include gentle jogging or cycling.
2. **Static stretching:** This aims to remove any lactic acid build-up in the working muscles to prevent stiffness or soreness after exercise.
3. **Developmental stretching:** Developmental stretches encourage the muscles to lengthen, increasing their flexibility. They can be static stretches or PNF stretches (see page 204) and should be held for at least 30 seconds.

A warm-up should take place before any form of physical activity.

BRONZE

1. Devise a warm-up for a sport of your choice. Use the three phases of a warm-up as the basis for your planning: pulse raising, stretching and joint mobilization.

2. Devise a cool-down for a sport of your choice. Use the three phases of a cool-down as the basis for your planning: pulse lowering, static stretching and developmental stretching.

Training methods

There is a wide variety of training methods that can be used to improve each aspect of physical fitness. Which training methods a performer chooses to help them improve their performance will depend on their goals, and the sport or physical activity they are involved in.

Flexibility

Flexibility is the range of movement at a joint. Good flexibility and therefore a good range of movement at the joints can help prevent muscle injury, especially when it comes to activities that require explosive work, so it is important to all athletes but some more than others. There are three training methods that improve flexibility: static stretching, ballistic stretching and PNF stretching.

Static stretching

Static stretching is the name given to the commonly known stretches which are held for between 10 and 15 seconds. It is important that the muscles that will be used most by the performer are stretched. For example, an outfield player in a hockey team might focus their time stretching their hamstrings, quadriceps and gastrocnemii, whereas the goalkeeper in the same team might spend more time stretching their deltoids and each latissimus dorsi. This is because the different positions place demands on different muscles.

A selection of the most commonly performed static stretches.

Ballistic stretching

Ballistic stretching uses the momentum of moving limbs to force muscles beyond their normal range of motion. It should be performed on warm muscles, not cold muscles, to reduce the risk of injury. Martial artists will often perform ballistic stretching because the movements mimic the explosive nature of the sport.

PNF stretching

With PNF (Proprioceptive Neuromuscular Facilitation) stretching a partner pushes the limb to stretch the joint further than the performer can stretch it on their own. It is vital that the partner fully understands what they are doing, otherwise the risk of injury is high.

A coach helping one of her clients with a PNF stretch.

BRONZE

1a) Choose your favourite sport or activity. Fold a piece of A4 paper in half three times to create eight small boxes. In each box draw a diagram of a stretch that is suitable for your chosen sport or activity. Start with the upper body and finish with the lower body.

b) Describe each stretch, making sure that your description includes the name(s) of the muscle(s) being stretched.

SILVER

2. On the reverse of your piece of A4 paper, write a brief explanation as to why you selected the stretches you did for Activity 1.

Strength, muscular endurance and power

Strength is the force being exerted by a muscle or muscle groups against some form of resistance. Muscular endurance is the ability to use muscles repeatedly without them getting tired. Power is the ability to complete movements that require strength at speed. A weightlifter relies on strength, a long-distance runner needs muscular endurance and a 100m sprinter requires power. There are three training methods that can be adapted to improve strength, muscular endurance or power: weight training, circuit training and plyometrics.

Weight training

If you wanted to use weight training to improve strength then you would aim to lift approximately 80 per cent of the maximum weight you can lift for at least three sets of four to eight repetitions each. This type of weight training is useful for sprinters and athletes involved in the throwing events in athletics.

If you wanted to use weight training to improve muscular endurance then you would aim to lift 60–80 per cent of the maximum weight you can lift for at least three sets of 12–20 repetitions each. This type of weight training is useful for middle-distance and long-distance runners.

Improving power using weight training involves performing strength exercises at speed. You would aim to lift approximately 80 per cent of the maximum weight you can lift, performing the lifting phase quickly and the return phase under control. This type of weight training is useful for shot-putters or discus throwers.

Resistance machines can help us to avoid injury by guiding the weight through the correct range of motion.

Weight training can involve resistance machines or free weights:

- **Resistance machines** are the machines usually found in gyms that incorporate a weight stack and a pulley system to provide resistance against a fixed movement. They are excellent for beginners because the range of movement is limited, which helps to prevent injury. They are also effective for use in rehabilitation following injury. When you are using a resistance machine, your movements should be slow and controlled, and the weight should not return to meet the rest of the stack between repetitions. This ensures the tension placed on the muscle is continuous.

- **Free weights** consist of dumbbells and barbells. Performers wanting to develop strength and power usually prefer free weights because they encourage the body to develop its core strength, as the weight load is not as stable or controlled as it is with resistance machines. However, this means good technique is vital, as poor technique often leads to injury. All free-weight exercises should be performed carefully and the body should be worked through a full range of motion in order to develop muscles appropriately. It is often necessary for a 'spotter' to be used in order to ensure that no harm comes to the performer lifting the weight.

Free weights are often preferred to resistance machines when trying to develop strength and power.

It is very important that performers who use weight training rest after each session to give their bodies time to recover. Two days of rest is recommended between sessions in order for the muscles to fully recover, energy reserves to be topped up and muscle tissue to be regenerated.

Circuit training

Circuit training is an excellent way to improve strength, muscular endurance and power as the exercises can be altered to suit the needs of the individual. Sessions are regularly run at local sports centres, often by very experienced personal trainers who can help to motivate people to work hard.

Circuit training involves six to ten different exercises, called stations, which are completed one after another. You perform each exercise for a set period of time before moving on to the next exercise after a brief, timed rest. When you have finished all the exercises you have completed one circuit and there is usually a slightly longer rest period between each circuit. The total number of circuits performed during a training session usually varies from two to six depending on your level of experience and/or your training goals.

Circuit training can be easily adapted to suit the specific requirements of the performer.

Plyometrics

Plyometrics is the name given to a form of exercise training which is designed to produce powerful movements. The strength and elasticity of a muscle is used to quickly flex and contract that muscle, increasing the power of muscular contractions. It is a training method used by performers who want to jump higher, run faster, throw further or hit harder. Plyometric exercises can easily be added to a circuit training session. Stations could include box jumps, skipping and drop jumps.

A basketball player can use plyometric exercises, such as box jumps, to increase the height of his/her jump. The performer jumps up onto a box from the floor, completing three sets of 10–15 repetitions.

BRONZE

3. List as many sporting situations as you can think of that require:

a) strength
b) muscular endurance
c) power.

4a) Use your knowledge of weight training to construct a weight training plan that you could use to improve strength, muscular endurance or power. The plan should include at least six exercises, and should mention the number of repetitions and sets the performer should complete.

b) Create a work card, containing diagrams and instructions, for each exercise you have included in your plan.

5a) Design a circuit training session to improve strength, muscular endurance and power. The circuit should consist of eight stations.

b) Create a work card, containing diagrams and instructions, for each station.

Aerobic endurance

Aerobic endurance is the ability to exercise the body for long periods of time. During aerobic exercise, the body's demands for oxygen are met by the body's intake of oxygen. There are three training methods that improve aerobic endurance: continuous training, fartlek training and interval training.

Continuous training

Continuous training requires the performer to work within their target zone for a minimum of 20 minutes to have a positive effect on the cardiovascular system. It is known as continuous training because there are no rest periods scheduled into the session. Running, cycling, swimming, rowing and step aerobics are all suitable for continuous training.

Continuous training is one of the most appropriate methods of training for somebody who has not exercised for a while and wants to improve their general fitness. They could start with a brisk walk for 20 minutes and, over time, increase this to a slow, steady jog.

Interval training

Interval training mixes fixed periods of work with fixed periods of recovery. The recovery phases are built into the training session so that the performer can recover from the preceding work period and therefore work at a higher level of intensity during the next work period.

Because of the recovery periods, interval training is considered a high-intensity workout and is often used by top-class performers, although it can be adapted to suit almost any performer by altering the duration of the workout, the intensity of the workout, the length of the work and recovery periods, and the number of sets. For example, a beginner looking to improve their aerobic capacity may mix steady jogging for their work periods with brisk walking for their recovery periods.

Fartlek training

Fartlek training is a form of interval training. It makes use of the natural terrain to combine periods of fast and slow running. Rather than changing pace at regulated intervals, fartlek training requires the performer to choose (for themselves) when to increase their pace for a short period and when to slow down in order to recover before performing another sprint. A performer might decide to run off-road or through local woodland, and use hills and trees as markers for the start and end of their sprint periods.

Fartlek training originated in Sweden and the word means 'speed play' in Swedish.

Speed training

Speed describes the quickness with which an individual is able to perform a movement, such as throw a javelin, or cover a distance, such as run 100m. Speed is an integral part of almost every sport and is often the key ingredient to success. Speed training is about training your body to move faster. There are two training methods that improve speed: interval training and fartlek training.

Interval training

By increasing the intensity and number of sprints in an interval training session a performer will improve their speed. For example, a 400m runner might perform three sets of six repetitions of a 200m sprint followed by a 200m brisk walk in order to generate recovery.

Fartlek training

In order to improve their speed using fartlek training, the performer would undertake a series of high-intensity sprints followed by short periods of recovery.

Usain Bolt is currently the world's fastest man, running the 100m in 9.58 seconds to win gold at the World Championships in 2009.

BRONZE

6. Design a simple interval training session for a sport of your choice.

BRONZE

7. Design a speed training session for a games player who is looking to improve their speed.

Exercise adherence factors

Adherence factors are the things which keep people committed to a course of action; in this case, exercise. The most important adherence factor is overcoming all the barriers that stop people taking part in sport and exercise. When people have managed to do this and find an activity they enjoy taking part in, they are more likely to stick with it.

What do you like doing?

Motivation: Our level of personal motivation will have the biggest influence on our ability to remain dedicated to our fitness training. To some people, fitness is a part of their life and they are highly motivated to participate; they find the money, make the time and make sure they get access to appropriate facilities. Other people find it hard to motivate themselves to exercise and make excuses not to train.

Access to facilities plays a large role in our ability to participate. If you live in a town or city that has gyms, swimming pools and leisure centres within easy reach, then it is fairly easy for you to join up and take part. However, if you live in an area where these facilities aren't readily available then it becomes much more difficult for you to participate. People who live in rural areas often face a 60-minute drive to get to the local swimming pool, for example.

Barriers to adherence

Time: It is difficult to find time in our increasingly busy lives to spend a few hours a week working on our fitness, because people often put their fitness as a lower priority behind school, college, work and family responsibilities.

Cost: The cost of joining a health club, gym or sports team can be expensive. Gym memberships cost an average of £35 a month, with some health clubs charging a lot more to use their facilities. Sports teams often charge more than £200 for a year's subscription. This can lead to people not being able to participate due to the large financial commitment of joining such clubs. Because the cost can be high, many people cannot afford to get fit or think it is an unnecessary expense.

Taking part in enjoyable activities

If you participate in activities that you enjoy, then you will be more likely to continue with your training. When you are working out in the gym, for example, there are going to be activities that you don't enjoy so much. However, thoughtful planning can allow you to hide the least pleasurable activities amongst the ones you do like to help you stay committed to your fitness programme.

BRONZE

1. List all the barriers to taking part in a personal fitness training programme that you face.

SILVER

2. Choose two of the barriers to adherence that you listed for Activity 1 and explain in detail how you could overcome these problems.

Remember:

Staying fit does not have to cost the earth. Careful planning, shopping around and making use of the great outdoors can often save far more than a few pennies.

Exercise adherence strategies

There are a number of strategies that can be used to strengthen a person's adherence to exercise once they have overcome the initial barriers to participation. The most effective way for a performer to stay motivated is to set themselves targets to help them improve their performance or fitness enough to meet their short-, medium- and long-term goals. Receiving support from people around them and rewards for meeting targets also help people to stay focused and maintain their enthusiasm for the duration of their exercise programme.

Setting SMART targets

Effective target setting must follow the SMART principle. SMART targets are:

Specific
Targets should be specific. You might aim to get fitter but this isn't a specific objective. Instead you need to break your broad aim down into specific objectives, or targets, which are related to the aspect of fitness that you want to improve. For example, if you previously achieved Level 6.3 on the multistage fitness test, your specific target might be to achieve Level 7. It is a good idea to conduct fitness tests before setting specific targets.

Measurable
Targets need to be measurable so that you know if you have achieved them or not. You can also use measurable targets to help you analyse your performance against recognized norms. If your goals are measurable then they automatically become specific.

Achievable
Targets should be appropriate to the fitness and skill levels of the performer. They should be close enough for us to see but not so far away that we can't touch them.

Realistic
It is important that we set targets that we have the capacity to achieve. All targets need to be challenging so that you have to work hard to achieve them, but they must also be realistic in order for them to serve their purpose and motivate you.

Time-bound
Targets need to be linked to a point in time when they should be achieved by or it becomes too easy to put them off. By setting a date for re-testing there is a clear end to the phase of training and this can act as motivation to stay focused. Elite athletes often have a big event as their focus.

The benefits of a personal fitness training programme

There are a number of benefits to having a personal fitness training programme, all of which aid adherence:
- It provides a focus for training, encouraging motivation.
- It sets out what to do in each training session, making it harder to find excuses not to do what should be done.
- It sets out a clear pathway for achieving personal training goals.

Support and reinforcement

Support and reinforcement can motivate people to achieve their goals. Often people will receive support from friends and family when attempting to achieve their lifelong goals, such as running the London Marathon. People can also receive support from the personal trainer at their local gym, or the coach/manager at their local club. Such people can provide valuable and knowledgeable support for performers, helping them to change their training to achieve a different result or explaining how to perform new exercises that challenge the performer.

Rewards for achieving goals

It is important to reward yourself when you achieve a goal that you have set yourself. When elite athletes meet their goals they are often selected to represent their country or rewarded with medals, cups, trophies and even cash prizes. People can also reward themselves for doing well, sticking to a training programme, and achieving weight loss or strength goals.

BRONZE
1. Set your own SMART targets to help you achieve the short-term goals you set out for Activity 3 on page 199.

SILVER
2. Explain why each SMART target you set for Activity 1 will help you to meet your long-term goals.

GOLD
3. Evaluate why each SMART target you set for Activity 1 will help you meet your long-term goals.

Implementing a personal fitness training programme

A personal fitness training programme is a training plan designed to improve a person's health, fitness and performance. It should be designed around a performer's goals, to suit their individual needs. A personal fitness training programme should be completed over a period of six weeks, with a series of fitness tests carried out at the beginning and end of the programme. Thorough planning and careful discussion between a performer and their coach will lead to its effective implementation. There are also a number of other factors to consider when implementing a personal training programme.

Take part in planned sessions: Taking part in a training session that has been planned is more useful for a performer than taking part in one that hasn't. When entering a gym it is important for the performer to know what they are going to do, when they are going to do it and how long they are going to do it for. Without direction, training sessions can become meaningless. Circuit training and fitness classes, where qualified instructors provide you with an intensive session, are run by local leisure centres. These classes are often well attended because people enjoy having someone there to manage their training and provide feedback on their performance.

Importance of commitment: Commitment is considered to be one of the main qualities needed for success in most sports and this desire to succeed has to come from within the performer. It is important that the performer commits to the training programme in order to achieve their goals.

Gain agreement for any missed sessions: If it is necessary to miss a training session then it is important to get permission from your manager or coach. Remember, if you are cancelling a session with a personal trainer it is important to give them plenty of notice so that you can rebook your training session close to your original appointment and they can fill your slot with another booking.

Factors to consider when implementing a personal training programme

Perform to the best of your ability: To get the most out of a training session and to feel a sense of satisfaction when it is finished, the performer must work to the best of their ability throughout.

BRONZE

1. Find planned training sessions that you could take part in and which could form part of a personal fitness training programme that would help you to meet your targets.

2a) Thinking about the type of personal fitness training programme that you will complete, write a training diary entry for one session. Remember to include all the information that a training diary should record.

b) After each entry in your training diary, explain why you have included the information that you have noted down. It may be beneficial to use a different coloured pen.

Training diary

A training diary can record an enormous amount of information about a training programme, including the date of each session, the type of training completed and details such as how far or fast you have run, or how much weight you have lifted. It should also include details of any modifications that are made to the programme in order for you to meet your targets or to maintain your motivation for training. This information can be used to inform future planning and provide the basis for future training programmes.

Hull City FC show their commitment to improving their performance by staying on the pitch at half-time to think about how to improve in the second half.

Keeping a record of each training session means that you can track your progress, helping you to determine when you have achieved milestones in your training.

Keeping a record of how you felt about each training session, how motivated you were and how well you think it went will help you to understand how your attitude towards training affects how you train. It can also help you to see any positive or negative trends in your week, which can help inform you for future planning.

Unit 11 assignment, part one

Background

As a personal trainer you are responsible for creating personal fitness training programmes for your clients. You meet with your clients and find as much information as possible about them, their goals and the factors that might prevent them from completing their programme. You then use this information to develop a six-week personal fitness training programme which helps them to meet their targets.

Task

Design and complete a six-week personal fitness training programme with the support of a personal trainer, coach, or your teacher or tutor. Maintain a training diary throughout the programme, remembering to consider your personal exercise adherence factors and strategies both during the planning stages and once you have started the programme. You will need to:

GRADING CRITERIA
TO BE ASSESSED

P1, P2, P3
M1, M2
D1

PASS

Plan, design and agree a six-week personal fitness training programme with a coach (P1).

Describe your personal exercise adherence factors and strategies (P2).

Implement a six-week personal fitness training programme, maintaining a training diary (P3).

MERIT

Contribute your own ideas to the design of a six-week personal training programme (M1).

Explain your personal exercise adherence factors and strategies (M2).

DISTINCTION

Evaluate your personal exercise adherence strategies for overcoming barriers to exercise (D1).

Tackling the assignment

Think about this assignment in two phases: planning your personal fitness training programme and implementing your personal fitness training programme.

The first phase involves setting your goals and using them to set your SMART targets, completing a PAR-Q, identifying the training methods that most support your targets and applying the principles of training to your six-week exercise programme. At this point, it would also be a good idea to consider your personal adherence factors and the strategies you will use to overcome any barriers to participation that you might face.

The second phase involves completing the training sessions you have set for yourself and keeping your training diary throughout the six-week programme. Remember to record how well your exercise adherence strategies are working in your training diary and also anything else of note about your personal adherence factors.

Make sure that your personal fitness training programme is relevant and interesting to you, including any sport-specific training requirements that you have. It is also important to be realistic about the amount of exercise that you intend to complete.

Meeting the Pass criteria

BTEC Level 2 Firsts in Sport

Unit 11 assignment, part one   **By Rashid Khan**

The personal exercise adherence factors that I have are:

Time
I play football a lot, and have school work and chores to do at home, so I don't have lots of free time.

Cost
I do not have a lot of money so I can't afford to join a gym.

Implementing enjoyable activities
I like sport so it will be easy for me to complete my training programme.

> Rashid has set his work out well and has begun to describe how each exercise adherence factor affects his ability to commit to an exercise programme. However, Rashid's work is a little vague and very brief. He needs to include a lot more detail about the barriers that affect his participation in exercise. He also needs to explain what strategies he is planning to use to overcome these barriers. If he does this, he will achieve P2.

Meeting the Merit and Distinction criteria

> Here, Nicole has explained – gone into detail about – two personal exercise adherence factors and the strategies she is planning to use to overcome them, meeting the criteria for M2.

BTEC Level 2 Firsts in Sport
Unit 11 assignment, part one
By Nicole Kirkby

My personal exercise adherence factors are:

Cost
I am currently only 15 years old and, therefore, I don't have a job. As a consequence I am unable to pay the high fees charged by my local gym to use their facilities, so I will find it difficult to complete any weight training as there are no other gyms nearby. The local swimming pools are fairly reasonable though, providing a good possibility for training sessions. School facilities are also free during lunch and after school, so long as there isn't a club on.

> Nicole has evaluated the strategy she has put in place to ensure that she remains motivated and therefore committed to her personal exercise programme throughout the six weeks. She has broken the strategy down into its component parts and assessed why each part will help her to remain motivated. Therefore, Nicole has met the criteria for D1.

Motivation
Motivation is a major factor for some people when it comes to achieving their fitness goals, as work and family commitments can often get in the way of fitness training. In order to ensure that I remain motivated to achieve my goals I have set myself SMART targets. They are specific to me and the reasons I am doing my personal fitness training programme. I have made them measurable by using my body weight and the time in which I aim to run a set distance. I have kept my targets achievable and realistic, to provide me with the motivation to remain committed to my programme. My training programme is six weeks long, so I aim to achieve my targets over this time period. I have ensured that I am not training too often, as I have a lot of other things in my life that require my time and effort.

Reviewing a personal fitness training programme

A fitness training programme should be reviewed at regular intervals to help the performer remain motivated and to find out how well it is going, so that any issues can be resolved quickly. The most important review comes at the end, however, when the six-week programme has been completed. This final review should consider what the client has done and how they feel about their performance, as well as evaluating the progress made and the effectiveness of the programme. All this information is important for preparing future fitness training programmes.

Modifying a personal fitness training programme to achieve planned targets

It may be necessary to modify a training programme part-way through. For example, if you get injured or miss a couple of training sessions because of other commitments, then it may be necessary to alter the training plan so that you can still reach the targets you have set for yourself by the end of the programme. Changes to facilities or equipment available may also require modifications to be made to your training programme.

Focus on strengths

It is important for the personal trainer or fitness coach responsible for working with a performer to pay specific attention to the targets they have successfully achieved. These successes are the reason the performer has been taking part in the training programme and can therefore be used to motivate the performer to continue with their fitness training.

Focus on areas for improvement

Areas in which the performer has not achieved their planned targets need to be given some careful thought. It is important that the reasons for any lack of success are addressed and that these targets are turned into new challenges for future fitness training programmes.

An end-of-programme evaluation should include:

- An overall assessment of the programme: How did it go?
- Fitness testing, to establish the performer's fitness levels after the programme (for comparison with their fitness levels before the programme).
- Evaluation: Were the intended targets achieved? Why? Why not?
- Planning the next personal fitness training programme: What will the next programme be like?

BRONZE

. Write a questionnaire that could be used by a personal trainer after a personal fitness training programme has been completed to help them review t. Think about including questions that cover all aspects of the completed training programme and that focus on setting targets for the next training programme.

Unit 11 assignment, part two

Background

As a personal trainer another important part of your job is to review clients' personal fitness training programmes to see how they went. These reviews should focus on the targets set down at the beginning of the training programme, highlighting targets that have been met and identifying areas for improvement in the future.

GRADING CRITERIA TO BE ASSESSED
P4
M3
D2

Task

Complete a review of the personal fitness training programme you have undertaken, using this and your training diary to:

 **PASS**

Describe the strengths of the personal fitness training programme and identify areas for improvement (P4).

 **MERIT**

Explain the strengths of the personal fitness training programme and make suggestions for improvement (M3).

 **DISTINCTION**

Justify your suggestions related to the identified areas for improvement in the personal fitness training programme (D2).

Tackling the assignment

Break this part of the assignment down into two phases. First, carry out an end-of-programme review of your personal fitness training programme. Then, stand back and consider the strengths and weaknesses of the original programme. If you were completing the programme again, what would you do again in exactly the same way and what would you attempt to improve?

Meeting the Pass criteria

BTEC Level 2 Firsts in Sport

Unit 11 assignment, part two   **By Samuel Yates**

After completing my six-week personal fitness training programme I feel that it went quite well.

The strengths of my personal fitness training programme

- The use of activities that are relevant to my sport: I included activities that are specific to my needs as a hockey player, so that the training programme would help me develop my ability to perform.
- Variety of activities: I used a variety of activities, including running, swimming, cross-training and circuit training, to ensure that I remained interested in my training programme.

The areas of my personal fitness training programme that could be improved

- The intensity at which I performed some of the cardiovascular exercises.
- How often I trained.
- The inclusion of more sport-specific skills work.

> Samuel has clearly taken a logical approach to the task and has met the criteria for P4 because he has described the strengths of his programme and has identified some areas for improvement. In order to meet the criteria for M3, Samuel needs to explain the strengths and areas for improvement in more detail.

Meeting the Merit and Distinction criteria

BTEC Level 2 Firsts in Sport

Unit 11 assignment, part two   **By Patrice Traore**

The strengths of my training programme

Specificity: My training programme was specific to my individual needs, which helped me to improve in my sport.

Progression: At the start of the training programme I found it difficult to run continuously for more than 15 minutes. However, by the end of the six weeks I was able to run for 25 minutes without stopping or slowing to a walk.

Overload: By using a heart rate monitor I was able to ensure that I was working in the target zone for the duration of my sessions.

Suggestions to improve my training programme

Tedium: I did a lot of running outdoors in my training programme and by the end of the six weeks I really did not feel like running anymore, even though I did. Next time I will try to use a variety of different cardiovascular fitness machines in order to change the type of training I do, because this will help me to maintain enthusiasm for my training and therefore delay the onset of boredom.

Intensity: Again, I performed a lot of continuous running and although I found it hard, I feel I would have benefitted from working at a higher intensity for shorter periods of time. For example, in the future I think interval training would be a more appropriate way for me to meet my targets and increase my fitness to a higher level.

> Patrice has used the principles of training to explain the strengths of his training programme and how it could be improved. This is a very good idea as it makes his work very clear. It has enabled him to achieve the criteria for M3.

> Patrice has achieved the criteria for M3 here because he has explained his suggestions for improvements. Don't forget that to achieve a Merit you must explain the strengths and suggested improvements, and not just describe them. When you describe something you give an account of it and when you explain something you need to give details of the reasons why it is as it is.

> Patrice has achieved the criteria for D2 as he has justified his suggestions for improvement; he has told us why he thinks the improvements are necessary and how he thinks they will lead to an improvement in his personal fitness training programme.

Unit 12: Lifestyle and the Sports Performer

Managing time

Very few sportsmen and women are fortunate enough to be professional athletes and, even for those who are, there is a fine line between success and failure. Not only do sportsmen and women have to train hard, eat correctly and recover well, they must also manage the pressures and commitments of everyday life. A large proportion of daily life is taken up with basic activities such as sleeping, eating and washing. This vastly reduces the number of hours available for training and competing, and all the other commitments a person has. This makes managing your time effectively a very important skill for athletes.

Work commitments

The vast majority of sports performers are amateurs. This means that they are not paid to train and compete, and have to fit their sporting activities into a busy life that is largely taken up with work commitments. This includes the time that is spent at work, as well as the time that is spent working at home, and commuting to and from a place of work. Work takes precedence over training for most amateurs because it pays the bills, and time for training and competition is often limited as a result.

A key problem for amateur athletes is being able to prioritize their time so that their training can be effective. Often, at the end of a long day at work, motivating oneself to train can be incredibly difficult. The most successful amateur athletes are often flexible in their approach to working and training. For example, they might choose to start work earlier than their colleagues so that they can finish earlier and have time to train after work. Or, they might train early in the morning before they go to work. It is important to remember, however, that a performer must agree flexible working hours with their employer in advance. This requires an athlete to confidently discuss their needs with their employer in order to come to a compromise that enables the athlete to do their job well and have time for training. Many employers may be worried that both an athlete's work and their relationships with their colleagues will suffer if they receive special treatment, and will need to be convinced that a workable compromise is possible. Offering to test the new arrangement over a trial period might encourage an employer to take the risk, and give the athlete the opportunity to prove that it is possible to succeed at work and in their chosen sport.

Another key problem for athletes needing to balance work and training commitments is the availability of training resources close to their place of work. Some modern office buildings incorporate a fitness centre, making it easier for employees to train before or after work and even at lunchtimes. However, at the other end of the scale, a climber who is employed in a city-centre office may well have to travel for more than two hours after work to find a suitable training environment.

Many sports players not only have to hold down a steady day job, they also have an evening job or study at night school to gain further qualifications. This further reduces the amount of time available for training and competing, and increases the level of daily fatigue the performer has to endure.

As a result of work commitments, many amateur sports players are only able to commit to competition and are often unable to train on a regular basis. The likelihood of this occurring tends to increase with age, as the level of responsibility at work increases. It tends to have a negative effect on their performance in the long term because a player can only compete successfully, at any level, if they are able to train regularly to maintain peak fitness levels.

Leisure time

Leisure time can be defined as the time left over after work commitments and essential life activities, such as sleeping, eating and washing, have been accounted for. For most people this tends to be a short period of time in the early evening on weekdays, and large chunks of time at the weekend. Many people refer to the things they do in their leisure time as their social life. For an athlete, leisure activities can be classified as either appropriate or inappropriate:

* Appropriate social activities, such as playing golf, camping and going to the cinema, enable an athlete to relax and to think about something other than work and sport. However, they also allow the body to rest and recover from training or a competition, and therefore support a training programme.
* Many inappropriate activities may well be socially acceptable but they are inappropriate for sports performers because of the detrimental effect they might have on health and performance. For example, consuming alcohol in small quantities is not considered inappropriate by many people but it is high in calories, which can cause weight gain, and also causes dehydration. Smoking, which is becoming more and more socially unacceptable, is also inappropriate for athletes in training because it reduces the oxygen-carrying capacity of haemoglobin in the bloodstream and therefore reduces the athlete's ability to compete aerobically. There are also leisure activities, such as taking drugs, which are not only socially unacceptable and inappropriate for an athlete, but which are also illegal.

It is important for an athlete to make time for leisure activities in their busy schedule. However, the key is to make the right choices about how best to use that time, opting for appropriate activities that promote rest and recovery and avoiding inappropriate activities that can have a harmful effect on performance.

Living away from home

Many athletes choose to live away from home, so that they can be nearer to specialist training facilities. This allows the athlete to train using the appropriate equipment in the appropriate environment, which in turn leads to improved performance. However, choosing to live away from home is not a decision that should be taken lightly because the athlete has to cope with other factors that may distract them from training. For example, they may become homesick or miss the access to support from family and friends. There are also financial implications of living away from home.

Planning your time

A diary, either paper or electronic, can help an athlete to manage their time effectively. Managers and coaches can also help athletes to prioritize their commitments, and elite sportsmen and women might also have a personal assistant to help them keep on top of all their commitments and make sure they have enough time to train.

BRONZE

1. Copy and complete the table below to analyse how you have spent your time over the last three days.

	Essential activities	Work/study commitments	Leisure activities
Day 1			
Day 2			
Day 3			

2. Using the completed table from Activity 1, produce a time management plan for the next seven days that allows you to increase the amount of time you spend training for, and competing in, your favourite sport.

SILVER

3. Explain why you have organized your time in the way you have for Activity 2.

Managing pressure

All athletes are under pressure to succeed, but only those who are able to cope with pressure enjoy sporting success. Pressure comes in many different forms and from many different sources, including people pressures, lifestyle pressures and the pressure an athlete puts on themselves to perform well in training and competition.

People and lifestyle pressures

Everyone in an athlete's life puts pressure on them from time to time. These pressures can support an athlete to succeed. For example, a coach might emphasize the vital importance of the next competition if the athlete wants to achieve their long-term goals, and this pressure might motivate the athlete. However, these pressures can also have a negative effect on an athlete's performance. Although they might be made in passing, comments from friends about never seeing an athlete might make them want to miss training sessions to spend time with those friends. People close to an athlete can also make much more deliberate attempts to put pressure on them to miss training, for example, by openly making them feel guilty about spending so much time training and competing.

Pressure can come from any or all of the following:

- peers
- family
- coaching staff
- teammates
- teachers
- partners.

It is important to remember that the role that each of these people has will change from time to time, and that one individual can both support and put pressure on an athlete depending on the circumstances.

Performance pressures

The most successful athletes thrive on the pressure of competition, while others struggle to handle the level of expectation that competition brings. Sometimes the pressure from competition is made worse by friends, family, teammates and the media but, most often, the main pressure to succeed comes from the performer themselves.

Competition is the culmination of weeks, months and sometimes years of training, and the possibility of failing at the final hurdle leads some performers to choke under the spotlight. Conversely, the pressure of performance targets can help some performers, because it provides them with short-term goals and tangible targets, which help to keep motivation levels high. It is therefore important for athletes to make sure that the pressure they place upon themselves is appropriate, because if they push themselves too hard in an effort to succeed, they might suffer an injury, which could set back their training by many months.

Spending time with your friends is good for your emotional well-being, but the differences between their own lifestyle and the lifestyle of their friends can put pressure on an athlete.

Dealing with pressure

Coping with pressure is the key to ensuring success in training and competition. While there is no set routine or magic wand for doing this, there are some important strategies that athletes can adopt.

Time planning
It is important to plan time effectively to make the most of the hours in the day, and to find time for training, working, socializing, sleeping and all the other daily tasks that need to be carried out. Keeping your fingers crossed and hoping that you will be able to fit everything in doesn't work!

Media training
Many professional athletes are unfazed by competition but dread the media spotlight that is placed on them during the preparation for, and in the aftermath of, competition. For team sport players, this is often managed by avoiding the media and allowing other teammates and the manager to be interviewed on behalf of the team. For individual athletes, avoiding the media is much more difficult and taking a course in media training is one of the best ways to help to relieve the anxiety of performing in front of the camera.

Strategies for dealing with pressure

Lifestyle changes
There are many things in a performer's lifestyle that can add to the pressure they are under. Lack of sleep, poor nutrition and too much responsibility at work will all have a detrimental effect on performance. While some things are easy to change, such as going to bed an hour earlier, others are much more difficult to alter, such as relinquishing some responsibility at work or moving home to be nearer to a training venue. However, making the change is vital if the performer wants to succeed in their sport.

Support network
A support network is a group of people that a performer can rely on to help them when things get difficult. Support can be practical, for example, the parents of a young athlete might drive them to training and to competitions. Support can also be emotional. Speaking about anxieties with other people can often help to relieve the symptoms of pressure and stress. This can be done in a group situation, for example, talking about fears with teammates before a competition, or on a one-to-one basis, such as speaking to a friend, colleague, coach or doctor.

Colin Montgomery does not tend to respond too well to pressure, whereas Phil 'The Power' Taylor thrives on pressure situations.

BRONZE

1. Note down three examples of people or lifestyle pressures that you have experienced.

2. Choose two elite athletes, one team player and one individual athlete, and make a list of the pressures that they face.

3. Describe the ways in which the athletes you chose for Activity 2 could manage the pressures you listed.

SILVER

4. Compare and contrast the pressures faced by an amateur athlete and the pressures faced by an elite athlete.

Unit 12 assignment, part one

Background

As an aspiring Olympic athlete, you understand that there is a fine line between success and failure. Success is dependent upon excellent time management skills, the ability to cope with pressure, and the ability to set realistic goals and targets. In addition, you have to be able to cope with the financial burden of training, the media spotlight and the responsibility of being a role model to younger athletes.

GRADING CRITERIA TO BE ASSESSED
P1, P2, P3 M1, M2

Task

Produce a two-part presentation that can be delivered to aspiring young athletes. The first part of the presentation should show them how you have planned your work commitments and leisure time to allow yourself the opportunity to train and compete. The second part of the presentation should identify and explain the pressures faced by elite athletes, and suggest ways in which they can cope with these pressures. You must:

Produce a realistic plan for work commitments and leisure time, for one month (P1).

Describe three different pressures on elite athletes (P2).

Identify strategies that can be used to deal with pressures on elite athletes (P3).

Explain the way work commitments and leisure activities have been planned (M1).

Explain three different pressures on elite athletes and suitable strategies that can be used to deal with these pressures (M2).

Tackling the assignment

The first step is to produce a time management plan. Commitments for each day need to be planned accurately for one month, so that a sensible amount of time is available for training, work and school or college commitments, as well as leisure time. A simple visual plan will be appropriate if you are aiming for a Pass level. However, if you are aiming for a Merit then the plan should be accompanied by an explanation of how it has been designed and why certain decisions have been made.

Having completed the time management plan, the next step is to describe (for a Pass) or explain (for a Merit) three different pressures faced by elite athletes and identify (for a Pass) or explain (for a Merit) a series of strategies that can be used to cope with these pressures.

Meeting the Pass and Merit criteria

Mark Wilson		Time management plan			February 2010	
Mon	Tue	Wed	Thu	Fri	Sat	Sun
1 0800–1700 / 1700–1930 / 2000–2130	*2* 0800–1700 / 1700–1930 / 2000–2130	*3* 0800–1700 / 1700–1930 / Rest	*4* 0800–1700 / 1700–1930 / 2000–2130	*5* 0800–1700 / 1700–1930 / 2000–2130	*6* 0600–0830 / 0830–1930 / 2000–2130	*7* 0600–2300
8 0800–1700 / 1700–1930 / 2000–2130	*9* 0800–1700 / 1700–1930 / 2000–2130	*10* 0800–1700 / 1700–1930 / Rest	*11* 0800–1700 / 1700–1930 / 2000–2130	*12* 0800–1700 / 1700–1930 / 2000–2130	*13* 0600–0830 / 0830–1930 / 2000–2130	*14* 0600–2300
15 0800–1700 / 1700–1930 / 2000–2130	*16* 0800–1700 / 1700–1930 / 2000–2130	*17* 0800–1700 / 1700–1930 / Rest	*18* 0800–1700 / 1700–1930 / 2000–2130	*19* 0800–1700 / 1700–1930 / 2000–2130	*20* 0600–0830 / 0830–1930 / 2000–2130	*21* 0600–2300
22 0800–1700 / 1700–1930 / 2000–2130	*23* 0800–1700 / 1700–1930 / 2000–2130	*24* 0800–1700 / 1700–1930 / Rest	*25* 0800–1700 / 1700–1930 / 2000–2130	*26* 0800–1700 / 1700–1930 / 2000–2130	*27* 0600–0830 / 0830–1930 / 2000–2130	*28* 0600–2300

Work
Family/Leisure
Training

My plan sets out my commitments for the month of February 2010. I am conscious that my training needs to be regular, both in terms of the days that I train and the times that I train, if it is to be effective. I have therefore planned to train at the same time each day during the week and at the same times on a Saturday. I plan to have a rest from training on a Wednesday.

The first stage in setting out my plan was to note down the things that can't be adjusted, most obviously my work commitments. Because I work in an office I have regular hours, leaving home at 8:00am and returning at 5:00pm each weekday and not working at weekends.

The second stage in planning was the most crucial: finding a way to balance my training with my family and leisure commitments. I have two young children who go to bed at 7:00pm every night, so I did not want to train straight after work as this would mean not seeing my children during the week as they would have been in bed when I got home. For this reason, I chose to spend time with my family before the children's bedtime and to train once they were asleep. Returning home at 9:30pm still leaves me time to spend with my wife each evening. I also chose not to train early in the morning, because this time is spent getting myself ready for work and my two children ready for school.

Weekends have been planned so that I can put in extra training on a Saturday morning, because during the summer months this is the time when I am usually competing. Keeping to this schedule will prepare me better for the competition season. Sundays are a day of rest from training and for spending leisure time with my family.

Mark has used a very simple strategy to plan his training schedule and it makes a clear visual impact. It is easy to see at a glance when Mark will be at work, when he will be training and when he will have leisure time. My only concern is that each day is very rigid. Doesn't Mark have any other commitments that he should be taking account of, such as birthdays, hospital appointments and parent's evenings? It may be that, in February, Mark doesn't have anything like this in his diary but it is a point that should be considered. I would be happy to award P1 for this piece of work, providing that Mark is able to confirm that he doesn't have any other commitments that should have been included in the plan.

Mark's explanation of his plan is very clear and concise. He has considered his work and family responsibilities, but has also ensured that he has time to train effectively. His decision to train on a Saturday morning at the time he would normally compete is very sensible. His reasoning for not training each weekday morning and his explanation for not training on Sundays are well thought out. I would be happy to award the marks for M1 for this piece of work.

To achieve a Pass for this assignment, Mark now needs to go on to describe three different pressures that elite athletes face and to identify strategies that can be used to deal with these pressures. To achieve a Merit, Mark must explain the three different pressures and the strategies that can be used to tackle them.

Appropriate behaviour for an elite athlete

Behaving appropriately, both on and off the playing field, is of paramount importance for sports performers because sporting success brings media attention and public expectation. Sports players who are caught cheating, being drunk and disorderly, or committing a crime are rarely able to keep the details out of the newspapers. Meanwhile, the public expects elite athletes to behave impeccably and set a good example to impressionable young people who see them as role models. Sportsmen and women who are caught behaving inappropriately often find that it becomes a barrier to success. For example, sponsors may no longer wish to be associated with them and, without financial backing, many find it difficult to continue to compete at the highest level.

Adherence to rules

Elite athletes bend the rules regularly and, although it is often against the spirit of the game, it is usually looked upon as a necessary evil in the search for success. However, blatant cheating is usually publicly condemned. In recent years there have been several scandals involving elite athletes breaking the rules, including Indian cricketer Sachin Tendulkar fiddling with the ball and 'bloodgate', where Tom Williams of Harlequins used a fake-blood capsule to simulate an injury during a rugby match. Both of these incidents were caught on camera and the players, teams and coaches involved were widely condemned both within their own sports and throughout the media. Despite otherwise impeccable reputations, these sportsmen will always be remembered for these scandals by many people.

When Williams joined the game between Leinster and Harlequins in the 69th minute on 12 April 2009 he was carrying a fake-blood capsule, allegedly in his sock. He burst it in his mouth in the 75th minute, allowing Harlequins' goal-kicker Nick Evans to return to the game. Despite this, Leinster beat Harlequins 6–5.

Images picked up by television cameras during the second test match between India and South Africa in 2001 suggested that Tendulkar might have cleaned the seam of the cricket ball. The match referee, Mike Denness, found him guilty of ball tampering and handed him a one-match ban. After a thorough investigation, the International Cricket Council made it clear that Tendulkar had not been found guilty of ball tampering, but had received the punishment for removing grass from the ball without informing the umpires.

Respect for others

As role models, professional sports players are expected to show respect to their teammates, the opposition and, more importantly, the match officials at all times. Nowhere is this more prevalent than in football's Premier League. In 2008, the FA introduced the 'Respect' campaign, aimed at improving the treatment of players, referees and other match officials within the sport. According to the FA: 'On average, thousands of referees quit football every year because of the abuse they receive from players and from the sidelines. Lots of children also pack it in because of the attitude and actions of over-enthusiastic and pushy parents.' The campaign sets out what is acceptable and what is not, providing clubs, officials and players with advice on how to deal with a lack of respect.

Essentially, there are four key elements to achieving respect in any sport:

- acceptable behaviour from spectators
- codes of conduct
- taking responsibility for oneself, which is ideally enforced by club captains
- allowing officials to take control of a situation.

Clothing, conduct and manners

Clothing, conduct and manners may seem like trivial things, but getting them right makes a huge difference to the way an individual or a team is perceived by the public. Almost all professional rugby teams travel to away games and arrive at home games wearing a suit and tie. This creates the impression that the players are professional and are going to behave appropriately on and off the pitch.

The most respected professional athletes, such as Kelly Holmes, are surrounded by stories of how well they speak to other people, from their manager right down to the tea lady! In fact, when Fabio Capello took over as manager of the England football team, he introduced a strict code of conduct for meal times, stating that all players must show respect to the staff and that mobile phones are not allowed at the table. The aim was to establish increased team discipline and create an air of professionalism, in recognition of the important responsibility the players have as role models.

Professional athletes and sports players are on show 24 hours a day, 7 days a week and have to be on their best behaviour in all areas of their life, regardless of whether they are at home, out socializing with friends, or training and competing. For example, John Terry lost his role as captain of the England football squad in January 2010 when it was revealed that he had had a relationship with the girlfriend of fellow England teammate Wayne Bridge.

BRONZE

1. Choose one elite athlete who is seen as a good role model and one elite athlete who is seen as a poor role model. Note down five reasons why you think each athlete is either a good or poor role model.

SILVER

2. Choose two sports performers who have been caught cheating and explain how their misdemeanours have affected their public reputation.

GOLD

3. Evaluate how David Beckham's public profile changed after his sending off in the 1998 FIFA World Cup™.

Unit 12 assignment, part two

Background

As an aspiring Olympic athlete, you understand that there is a fine line between success and failure. Success is dependent upon excellent time management skills, the ability to cope with pressure, and the ability to set realistic goals and targets. In addition, you have to be able to cope with the financial burden of training, the media spotlight and the responsibility of being a role model to younger athletes.

GRADING CRITERIA TO BE ASSESSED
P4
M3
D1

Task

Produce a leaflet which describes acceptable and unacceptable behaviour for an elite athlete, supporting your written arguments with examples from professional sport. Your leaflet should:

 **PASS**

Describe appropriate behaviour for elite athletes in three different situations (P4).

 **MERIT**

Explain appropriate behaviour for elite athletes in three different situations (M3).

 **DISTINCTION**

Evaluate the effects and consequences of the behaviour of elite athletes (D1).

Tackling the assignment

This assignment is very straightforward, and the assignment task makes it clear that you must produce a leaflet to showcase your work.

There are many different situations that elite athletes find themselves in and which you could explore for this assignment, including:
- taking part in pre- and post-match interviews
- attending award ceremonies
- relaxing during leisure time, for example, shopping, eating out and so on
- travelling to and from competitions
- signing autographs
- appearing on television, as a panellist on Question of Sport or on Match of the Day, for example.

If you are aiming for a Pass or a Merit, a three-page leaflet, with one page for each of the three situations you are covering, will be fine. However, if you are aiming for a Distinction, you will need to add an extra couple of pages to your leaflet to cover the effects and consequences of the behaviour of elite athletes.

Meeting the Pass and Merit criteria

Steven's introductory information and the paragraph under the heading 'When performing' both describe appropriate behaviour for athletes. He does not offer any real explanation as to why athletes should behave in the way he describes. Simply saying that they are role models isn't a thorough explanation. This means that Steven is meeting the criteria for P4 here.

BTEC Level 2 Firsts in Sport

Unit 12 assignment, part two

The Behaviour of Elite Athletes   **Steven Ireland**

Elite athletes have to consider how they will behave in a number of situations. As role models for a younger generation they are constantly being watched and analysed by the media, and are therefore on show 24 hours a day. For this reason they have to behave appropriately when:

- performing
- being interviewed
- socializing
- attending award ceremonies
- meeting fans.

I have chosen to consider the first three of these situations.

When performing

It is necessary for athletes to follow the rules of their sport at all times. This means accepting the decisions of referees and not trying to cheat opponents. Professional sports players should always show respect to the referee, and should never swear at or verbally abuse match officials. Elite athletes should always wear appropriate clothing and should never wear offensive logos on their shorts or shirts. It is important to remember that elite athletes are important role models.

Being interviewed

For many athletes, the most common form of interview takes place immediately after a match or event has finished, and it usually involves being stopped when leaving the field of play, having a camera and a microphone thrust in front you and being asked a question about the game by a reporter. This is often the time when athletes' behaviour is at its worst. Tensions are running high, a player may be feeling dejected at having lost the match, or may disagree with some of the decisions made by match officials. Even so, athletes should always try to keep their tempers in check, because reporters will seize upon comments made in anger. The following list suggests a set of rules that should be followed in the post-match interview:

- Refuse politely to answer questions if you are not in the right frame of mind. (It is better to answer questions later when you've had time to calm down.)
- Always pay tribute to your opponents. (This shows good sportsmanship and an appreciation of other athletes – remember you are a role model.)
- Never criticize match officials. (You may not agree with their decisions but at this stage you won't have had a chance to see video replays of key incidents. When you watch them again you may well decide that the officials made the correct decisions.)
- Never gloat when you have won. (As the old saying goes, 'What goes around comes around' and next time you might be on the losing side.)
- Dress appropriately. (If the interview takes place immediately after the game then sports kit is appropriate. However, if you are stopped when leaving the stadium an hour later, you should be showered, changed and preferably wearing a shirt and tie.)

Steven has developed his answer more thoroughly here. His bullet points alone (for example, 'Never criticize match officials.') are only descriptions, but the information in brackets explains each bullet point by answering the question, 'Why is this appropriate behaviour for elite athletes?' This means that, in this part of his leaflet, Steven is meeting the criteria for M3.

Overall, Steven can only be awarded a Pass for this piece of work. Even if the third situation he covers is explained in detail, the fact that he has only described the first situation means that he cannot meet the criteria for a Merit.

Meeting the Distinction criteria

BTEC Level 2 Firsts in Sport
Unit 12 assignment, part two

The consequences of an athlete's behaviour   Louisa Turner

The behaviour of elite athletes is the subject of much controversy in the modern media. Far too often stories of elite athletes' poor behaviour is spread across newspapers and television. Instances of good behaviour are rarely reported, not because they don't happen but because it is difficult to sensationalize them in a newspaper.

Examples of poor behaviour

In 2010, John Terry was accused of having an affair with the ex-girlfriend of his England teammate Wayne Bridge. Initially, Terry had sought a court order to prevent the story from being reported and this attempt at secrecy only made the story more sensational when it was finally printed. The public response was to criticize Terry's behaviour and this led to calls for him to be sacked as England captain on the grounds that someone who was a much better role model for younger players should hold the position. Fervent football supporters also argued that if the manager didn't punish Terry it could lead to a rift between players in the dressing room. It was thought that swift action by the manager could deal with the situation before it became too serious. Eventually John Terry was stripped of the captaincy by the manager, Fabio Capello, as a result of his actions. It has been estimated that Terry could lose up to £10 million in sponsorship deals tied to his role as England captain.

A further consequence of the incident was that Wayne Bridge subsequently withdrew from playing international football, stating that he didn't want the other players in the dressing room to have to take sides. However, every cloud has a silver lining and Rio Ferdinand was awarded the captaincy as Terry's replacement.

Such controversies can also be found in other sports. In 2009, Tiger Woods (the number one golfer in the world at the time) admitted to having several extra-marital affairs. He took an indefinite break from the sport and lost some of his biggest sponsorship deals, because the large sports companies only wanted to associate themselves with clean-living sports stars. Again, although Woods suffered as a consequence of his actions, others benefited because it gave them a greater chance of winning the major tournaments in his absence.

Examples of good behaviour

David Beckham is no stranger to controversy. In 1998, he was sent off during a World Cup match that England went on to lose. Many blamed Beckham for the loss and, for a while, he was public enemy number one. However, Beckham learnt from his mistake and became a much better role model, both on and off the pitch, after the incident. He let his football do the talking until the public perception of him began to change. He became England captain in 2000.

One defining moment in his career occurred in February 2000. He missed a Manchester United training session and was unceremoniously dropped for the next match by his manager, Sir Alex Ferguson. It later transpired that Beckham had missed training because his son was ill. This led to a huge public debate, with headlines such as 'Should Beckham put family before football?' Many in the media argued that Beckham had been right to put his family first and that it showed he was not simply a wealthy footballer who craved media attention. Others suggested that it was this incident that made it acceptable for fathers to take time off work to look after their sick children: if it was ok for the England captain, it was ok for everyone else.

A decade after the incident, it is certainly no longer expected that it should always be women who take time off work when their children are poorly. Whether this is a direct result of the Beckham incident is a question that will never really be answered though. However, football insiders have suggested that the incident signalled the beginning of the end for Beckham at Manchester United, with comments such as, 'No player is bigger than the club' and 'The manager has to show his authority' doing the rounds afterwards. Beckham was sold by United to Real Madrid in 2003 and it seems that what is seen as good behaviour by some may be construed as poor behaviour by others.

Louisa has taken a sensible approach to this assignment, by selecting elite athletes and analysing their behaviour in specific incidents rather than making sweeping statements such as 'David Beckham is a superb role model'. I particularly like the way she has used two examples from the same sport to support examples of each type of behaviour, especially as this is backed up by a third example from a different sport.

Louisa has offered suggestions as to the effects and consequences of the athletes' behaviour, both on the performers themselves and on their teammates or opponents. I particularly like the way she has analysed the public perception of the players involved, and her comments about loss of earnings show that she understands the full effects and consequences of the incidents. This is further supported by her final comment, 'what is seen as good behaviour by some may be construed as poor behaviour by others'. This indicates that Louisa has analysed the behaviour from several angles, not simply from the most common media perspective.

I would be happy to award Louisa the marks for D1 for this piece of work.

Career planning

It may appear to most sports fans that success 'just happens' for some athletes or that some performers are just lucky. The reality could not be more different. A successful sports career is usually the result of years of hard work and dedication, coupled with a plan made up of short-, medium- and long-term goals. Rebecca Adlington did not win two gold medals at the Beijing 2008 Olympic Games because she was in the right place at the right time; winning was the culmination of over six years' hard work and planning!

Goal setting

An athlete's goals can be short term, medium term or long term, and all three play an important role in achieving success. Typical examples of three types of goals for an Olympic athlete are as follows:

- **Short-term goals:** These are usually set over a period of 6–12 weeks and focus on minor changes to techniques or tactics. For example, an Olympic javelin thrower might have a short-term goal to improve the speed of their approach run. After this has been achieved, they will set themselves a new short-term goal. A series of short-term goals provide the focus for achieving the medium-term goal.
- **Medium-term goals:** These are set over a period of six months to two years. For example, a triple-jump athlete may set themselves a medium-term goal of qualifying for the triple-jump final at the next Commonwealth Games. Medium-term goals are seen as stepping stones along the journey to achieve the long-term goal.
- **Long-term goals:** These are ultimately aspirational and will, for an Olympic athlete, focus on the Olympic and Paralympic Games, which take place every four years. A typical example would be to achieve a medal in an Olympic final or, for those who have already achieved this, to strive for a gold medal.

Planning an athletic career

When planning for a career in sport, an athlete has to consider many factors, even though some of these may be outside their direct control.

Current expectations as an elite athlete

A sports performer must take stock of their current performance and use this information to set realistic short-term, medium-term and long-term goals. All sportsmen and women start out with the intention of becoming the best but only a very small minority ever achieve this. By setting realistic goals a performer is able to stay motivated, which in turn helps to improve performance.

Key review dates

Although an athlete, together with their coach, is continually reviewing their performance, it is important that a series of key review dates are planned into a training schedule. These usually coincide with a review of short-term goals every six to eight weeks. A key review should focus everyone's attention on whether the training schedule is working, because there is no point continuing if it isn't.

Changing club or coach

Sometimes, changing coach is unavoidable because the coach becomes ill, is injured or retires, but when this is not the case, the decision to change the people supporting an athlete should not be taken lightly. Andy Murray decided to sack his coach, Mark Petchey, over a 'difference of opinion' early in his professional career. In the long term this has worked in Murray's favour, and his career has gone from strength to strength. However, there are several examples of players parting company with their coaches or managers with a less favourable outcome. For example, under Sven-Goran Eriksson the England football team had reached the quarter-final stage of the previous three major tournaments but following the appointment of Steve McClaren as his replacement they failed to even qualify for the 2008 European Championships.

Similarly, changing clubs is not a decision to be taken lightly and the pros and cons of the move should be carefully considered. For example, a young athlete who shows promise may decide to move to a new club, which they hope will provide them with greater opportunities for success, with better facilities and better coaching. However, they may find that they have to travel so far to get to the new club that their training suffers as a result or they may discover that they miss the support network that they relied on at their old club. Sometimes, athletes themselves are not responsible for initiating a change in clubs. This is particularly the case in football, for example, if a player is surplus to the manager's requirements and can be sold for a suitable price.

Illness, accident or injury

Suffering from an illness or an injury is every sports performer's worst nightmare. Missed training leads to a loss of fitness and, for players in team sports, it can often cost them their place in the first team. However, having a contingency plan that can swing into action as soon as an illness or injury occurs can minimize its effects. For example, if a physiotherapist is already working with a performer they will be able to respond immediately to any injury and will provide a better chance of restricting the damage. The psychological effects of illness or injury can also be significantly reduced if training schedules are altered and goals are reassessed straight away. Serious injury may well jeopardize a performer's long-term goals but even minor injuries often mean that the short-term goals have to be re-evaluated.

Second career

Very few sports players are able to compete at the highest level for more than a decade or so, and even those that are, such as golfers, often find that they move further and further away from the top-ranked players as they get older. Many professional athletes therefore find that their sporting career is over by the time they reach their mid-thirties, and they have to look towards finding a second career. For some this means continuing to work within their own sport, as a coach, a manager or a media pundit, while for others it means working in a related field, such as teaching, physiotherapy or sports development.

The vast majority of second career options require external qualifications to support experience. For this reason, elite athletes need to have a long-term plan for their second careers and many begin studying while still competing at the highest level. Those elite athletes who choose sports medicine, for example, will usually find they need a post-graduate qualification, which can take up to five years to achieve.

British decathlete Dean Macey suffered a series of injuries throughout 2007 and 2008, most notably an elbow injury that required reconstructive surgery. He was forced to miss competitions and failed to record enough points to make a place in the British team for the Beijing 2008 Olympics, where he was aiming for a medal after finishing fourth in 2000 (Sydney) and 2004 (Athens). He subsequently retired after it became clear that he wouldn't be competing at another Olympic Games.

Steve Parry, former British swimming captain and Athens bronze medallist, set up 'Pools 4 SchoolsTM' when he retired from competitive swimming.

Financial management

The amount of money an athlete can earn varies considerably from sport to sport and from player to player. Most Premier League footballers earn in excess of £10,000 per week, whereas competitors in less popular sports, such as badminton and bobsleigh, may well earn little more than this in a whole year and will have to work to ensure they can cover their expenses.

Sports performers have to make sure they have enough money to cover daily living expenses – including rent or mortgage payments, utility bills, council tax, food and drink, clothing, money for social activities, and saving for a rainy day – in the same way that a plumber, teacher or solicitor has to. They also need to make sure they have enough money to pay for the equipment that they need to compete, and some athletes will also have to account for their travel expenses and accommodation when competing.

Other areas of financial management that must be considered are:

- **Investments:** Some elite athletes will receive significant sums of money in the form of prizes, appearance fees and from sponsorship. Once daily living expenses have been taken care of, a performer should consider investing the remaining money to ensure that they have a nest egg when they retire. Investing in the stock market or in property can be risky, but the return on the initial investment could be much greater than it would have been had the money been put into a normal savings account.
- **Taxation:** Everyone who earns an income over a set amount has to pay income tax. If you work for a company this tax is usually deducted before you receive your wages. However, tax is not deducted at source from prize money and lump sums received from sponsors, so sports performers who receive such windfalls must arrange to pay the necessary tax to HM Revenue and Customs.
- **Pensions:** All sports performers have to consider what they will do when they are no longer able to compete or when they retire from their second career. Usually this means setting aside an amount of money each month, which is paid into a pension fund.
- **Sponsorship:** Sponsorship is the lifeblood of many sporting careers because it enables some athletes to compete professionally without the need for another job. Sponsorship is easy to come by for sportsmen and women who play for well-known clubs because most of the agreements are made on their behalf by their club. However, for less well-known athletes and for those who compete in individual sports it can be a time-consuming exercise, which adds yet more pressure to an already busy schedule. Gaining a sponsor requires persistence and patience because few companies are willing to throw money at athletes without first being convinced that they will see a return on their investment.
- **Insurance:** Sports performers need to make sure that they have appropriate insurance. Health insurance is particularly important, because it is vital that athletes receive prompt care if they become ill or are injured. They also need to insure themselves against loss of future earnings including loss of sponsorship, not being able to complete contracts with their clubs or sponsors, and death and dismemberment if they take part in high-risk sports. They should also consider insuring any equipment that they use which is expensive to replace.
- **Legal and contractual arrangements:** Sports performers must also consider the financial implications of any contractual arrangements they enter into. Does their contract with their coach or agent state that they have to pay them a percentage of their winnings, for example?

Elite athletes at large clubs will often have the support of a financial adviser to help them make the right financial decision. However, most athletes will have to find their own financial adviser to help them or manage their own finances.

BRONZE

1. Research an up-and-coming athlete, perhaps someone who has recently been successful in junior competitions, and set realistic short-, medium- and long-term goals for them.

2. List five reasons why a competitor might seek funding from a sponsor.

SILVER

3. Explain the goals you have suggested in Activity 1.

4. Explain four potential second career choices for an athlete of your choice.

GOLD

5. Justify the selection of two of the second career choices that you explained in Activity 4.

Unit 12 assignment, part three

Background

As an aspiring Olympic athlete, you understand that there is a fine line between success and failure. Success is dependent upon excellent time management skills, the ability to cope with pressure, and the ability to set realistic goals and targets. In addition, you have to be able to cope with the financial burden of training, the media spotlight and the responsibility of being a role model to younger athletes.

GRADING CRITERIA TO BE ASSESSED
P5, P6
M4
D2

Task

Consider your own recent performances in your chosen sport and set yourself short-, medium- and long-term goals. You should also think about the financial implications of your plan. You must:

Describe realistic goals in a personal athletic career plan, including second career choices (P5).

Describe three financial issues elite athletes need to consider (P6).

Explain goals in a personal athletic career plan, and second career choices (M4).

Justify goals in a personal athletic career plan, and second career choices (D2).

Tackling the assignment

This assignment can be approached in a number of ways, including a video blog or a PowerPoint® presentation, but the most obvious choice is to produce an essay-style piece of writing.

The key to creating a personal athletic career plan is to use the SMART target-setting technique to set down your short-, medium- and long-term goals, before going on to explain these goals if you are aiming for a Merit and justifying these goals if you are aiming for a Distinction. More information on how to set SMART targets can be found on page 209. You also need to decide on a suitable second career choice and

then explain (Merit) and justify (Distinction) the reasons behind this choice. Remember, a second career can mean either:
- a career that runs alongside competition (for example, working as both a part-time footballer **and** a part-time teacher)

or
- a career change that takes place once professional competition has ended (for example, becoming a football manager at the end of a playing career).

Lastly, you need to include simple, direct descriptions of the financial pressures that athletes face.

Meeting the Pass and Merit criteria

Personal goals for my decathlon event, by Tim Stewart

As a decathlete, I have to compete in ten separate track and field events, which means that my training sessions are extremely varied. It also means that weaknesses in my performance are easy to spot and I have realized that the long jump tends to be my weakest event. An observation and analysis session with my coach suggested that I lack speed in my approach run, which leads to a poor take-off at the board. I have therefore set the following medium-term goals to ensure improvement:

Specific	Develop acceleration over the first 10m of the run-up.
Measurable	Reduce the total approach time, the time from the start point to the take-off board.
Achievable	Reduce total approach time by 0.3 seconds.
Realistic	More than 0.3 seconds would be almost impossible to achieve at this stage.
Time-bound	Achieve the time reduction stated by the end of pre-season training, in 12 weeks.

My goal is very sport **specific** and also very technique specific. I know from my times in the 100m and the points gained in competition in this event that my top sprinting speed is very good, so the weakness in my long jump approach run has to be due to poor acceleration at the start. My goal is therefore very specific to the acceleration part of my approach run.

My target is also **measurable**. I will begin by measuring the speed of my approach run five times, making sure that I rest between each attempt, to establish an average speed. Throughout the 12-week training period I will repeat this process three times – at four weeks, eight weeks and 12 weeks – to find out if I am making progress. By making my goals time specific, I will easily be able to measure my progress and see the improvements that I make.

Tim has adopted a sensible approach to this part of the assignment. He gives a simple account of his own performance as an athlete and a simple explanation as to why he has chosen the medium-term goal of improving his long jump technique. Breaking this goal down into SMART targets is also a sensible thing to do. If Tim continues in this manner, describing his short-term goals and his long-term goals in this way, and goes on to describe his second career choices and three financial issues that elite athletes need to consider, he will meet the criteria for a Pass.

Tim has begun to explain each part of his SMART targets, which showcases the reasoning behind his choices. His explanations are simple to understand and provide an excellent example of how to meet the criteria for M4. Assuming that Tim continues to develop his answer to include the other three targets (achievable, realistic and time-bound) and then does the same for his short- and long-term goals, before explaining his second career choices, I would be happy to award Tim a Merit.

Meeting the Distinction criteria

As a swimmer, I have a goal of competing in the 2016 Olympic Games. This already has implications for my training and means that I am beginning to think about alternative career choices. I am fully aware that only a handful of young athletes are fortunate enough to achieve their life-long ambition of competing in an Olympic Games, so I have to be prepared for the worst, in case injury or lack of ability prevents me from making my dream a reality.

I have considered several alternative careers, all of which revolve around sport, including physiotherapist, sports scientist, sports dietician, coach and so on. This is because I have always had an interest in sport and I play other sports, including squash and tennis. I also watch sport on television all the time and would hate to think that my daily life did not revolve around sport. In addition, I am used to being active and I don't think I would enjoy sitting behind a desk all day.

My most likely second career choice is sports physiotherapy. Although this is a popular choice for many aspiring athletes, access to courses at university to gain the necessary degree qualification are quite limited and the entry requirements tend to be strict. However, my grades have always been very high (straight As and A*s) so I am confident I will be able to get onto the course of my choice. Loughborough University is seen by many as the best place to study for a degree in physiotherapy, and it is also the home of the ASA (Amateur Swimming Association), so I would be studying alongside other aspiring Olympic athletes.

In addition, my choice is led by my desire to be at an Olympic Games. If I cannot make it as a competitor, then my next best chance is to be there as part of the team supporting the athletes who are competing. However, even if none of this becomes a reality, a career in sports physiotherapy would allow me to work with professional athletes in other sports, such as football and rugby. It is for all of these reasons that I have chosen sports physiotherapy for my second career choice.

Nicola is clearly able to justify her choice of a second career and puts forward a number of compelling reasons why it is the best option for her. However, the criteria for D2 – as well as P5 and M4 – clearly state that second career choices, not simply a single career choice, need to be justified. So, although Nicola gives an excellent justification for her choice of becoming a sports physiotherapist, she also needs to justify her reasons behind at least one more possible career choice if she is to achieve a Distinction for this piece of work. She also needs to justify her goals too.

Coping with the media spotlight

Some people were born to be in front of a camera, while others were born to play sport. Rarely is someone confident in both situations but as an elite athlete it is impossible to avoid the media spotlight. Consequently, most professional athletes are given advice and guidance on how to deal with the press and, over time, many learn to cope with the additional pressure that media attention can bring.

Different forms of media

Television: Television engages the audience with visual images, so the pictures are as important, if not more important, than any text on screen or voices describing the action.

Radio: Radio engages its audience aurally and, in the context of sport, this is usually through the spoken word. It is therefore vitally important that information is presented clearly and logically if it is to be broadcast on the radio.

Newspapers, magazines and the Internet: These are collectively known as print media and their online counterparts. They communicate through the written word and photographs. Print media comes in various formats, and each format is usually targeted at a specific group of people. For example, it is generally accepted that broadsheet newspapers, such as *The Independent* and *The Times*, are aimed at more intelligent readers so the descriptions tend to be detailed and analytical. In contrast, tabloid newspapers, such as *The Sun* and *The Mirror*, tend to use snappy headlines full of puns and alliteration to attract the reader. Print media can also be aimed at a local, national or international audience. This means that local sporting heroes are just as likely to be interviewed by the media as elite sports stars.

Communication skills

Communication is one of the most important skills required for dealing with the media. There are two main forms of communication:

1. **Verbal communication:** This is the communication that takes place when people speak to each other. When a performer is interviewed by the media, they should speak clearly and accurately. They should be precise, keeping the information simple and not using too many words or technical terms. This avoids confusion or ambiguity, which could lead to the interviewee being misquoted or made to look foolish.
2. **Non-verbal communication:** This is all the communication that takes place without using words and includes hand gestures, body language, tone of voice and facial expressions. Non-verbal communication can be very effective when performing but in a media interview even the smallest hand gesture can be misinterpreted. Many sportsmen and women deal with this by keeping their hands flat on the table or holding a piece of sports equipment while they are being interviewed, and by employing active listening skills when the interviewer is talking.

Active listening shows the person who is talking to you that you really are listening and involves maintaining eye contact, stopping what you are doing and giving the person who is talking to you your full attention. This can be reinforced by nodding or agreeing from time to time, and by asking questions to check your own understanding. The important thing is not to get distracted by things going on around you or fiddle with any sports equipment you are holding.

Communicating effectively with the media is a skill that develops with experience. To begin with it is sensible for athletes to take part only in formal, planned interviews, and to be supported by a teammate or a coach, until they develop the necessary skills and confidence to be interviewed on their own.

Communication skills also extend to written material. It is essential that an elite athlete is able to extract important information from documents, including training plans, travel arrangements and even newspaper articles. It is also important that they can write clearly, to express their own plans and ideas, and ask questions in a form that others can easily understand. This ensures that there are no crossed wires, and that the athlete can focus on training and competition.

Working with others

Elite athletes are surrounded by other people that they have to work with day in, day out, including coaches, managers, teammates and event organizers. Very often, they would not choose to socialize with these people but they must create a positive working relationship with them if they are to succeed. Good communication skills are a fundamental part of this process. The vast majority of athletes accept this, and as a result many attribute their success to the hard work and dedication of others as much as themselves. In professional tennis, many top players train together, and therefore have to be able to develop a relationship that allows them to train together one day and compete against each other the next. Sportsmen and women who are unable to form such working relationships rarely make it to the top of their sport, and those that do rarely compete at an elite level for very long. However, even those who work well with others need to review their working relationships from time to time and try hard to make improvements where necessary.

Preparing for an interview

The key message for any athlete taking part in an interview is 'be prepared'. Approaching an interview unprepared can lead to disaster, because journalists are trained to probe for answers to questions that may be controversial. When preparing for an interview, consider the following points:

- **Consider the purpose of the interview:** Why the journalist wants to conduct an interview should be considered from the outset. Is it to show the public the human side of an athlete or is it to try to find out about a potential controversy, such as a rift between the performer and his coach or manager? The benefits to the performer should also be considered. Is the interview a chance for them to increase their profile and raise sponsorship funding, or is it a chance to put the record straight over an issue that has previously been misreported?
- **Anticipate likely questions:** What questions is the journalist likely to ask? How would they best be answered?
- **Prepare prompt sheets:** It is perfectly acceptable for an athlete to take a prompt sheet into an interview, to help them remember the key points that they wish to cover regardless of the questions they are asked.
- **Rehearse:** Taking part in a mock interview before meeting the journalist is one way of learning how to deal with difficult questions. Mistakes can be made in a safe and supportive environment, without worrying that slip-ups will be reported to the public.
- **Consider your appearance:** The way an athlete presents themselves to the media can have an effect on the style of interview conducted by a journalist. Wearing casual clothes, such as jeans and a T-shirt, can encourage journalists to conduct a more relaxed interview, where they could lull the performer into a false sense of security before asking a really controversial question. Arriving in sports attire gives the impression that the performer wants to concentrate on sporting issues, while wearing a suit and tie signals that the interview is going to be more formal or will be limited to a prepared statement.

- **Consider how to tackle sensitive issues carefully:** When communicating with the media about sensitive issues, a performer should try to present a formal statement rather than inviting probing questions. Where this is not possible, a performer has to choose between answering questions truthfully or avoiding questions altogether by refusing to answer.
- **Where to go for help and advice:** There are many specialist media agencies that offer support and advice to those taking part in interviews. If such advice is not available or is too costly, performers are well-advised to take part in group interviews rather than one-on-one interviews.

Taking part in an interview

The aim of any interview is to engage the audience. This means that the way the information is delivered is of paramount importance. The interviewer should ask precise questions and the responses given by the interviewee should be equally clear. A good interviewer will pace the interview with questions to keep it flowing but, at times, will allow an extended pause after a difficult question to pressure the interviewee into filling the silence. A well-prepared interviewee will be expecting this and should be able to refrain from talking unnecessarily.

People watching an interview will study the body language of the interviewee to try and work out if they are confident about the answers they are giving. If the interview is live on television, a producer will often encourage the interviewer to ask more probing questions if they read the body language of the performer and think that he or she is hiding something.

The pitch, tempo, volume and intonation of a performer's voice can also communicate how they are really feeling, and a good interviewee will be able to control their voice to project a confident image. 'Pitch' describes how high or low a voice is, 'tempo' describes how fast or slow someone is speaking and 'intonation' describes the rise and fall of a person's pitch when they are talking.

BRONZE

1. Choose a sporting news story that has been covered by three different forms of media and list the key points of the story that have been provided by each one.

2. Write ten probing questions that you would like to ask your favourite sports star.

SILVER

3. Compare and contrast the different reporting styles in the forms of media you explored for Activity 1.

GOLD

4. Observe a television interview with one of your favourite sports stars and critically analyse the responses that are given.

WBA world heavyweight champion David Haye is always well-spoken and commands attention when he meets the media, yet he also uses the media to his own advantage to wind up his opponents and build the hype before a fight.

Unit 12 assignment, part four

Background

As an aspiring Olympic athlete, you understand that there is a fine line between success and failure. Success is dependent upon excellent time management skills, the ability to cope with pressure, and the ability to set realistic goals and targets. In addition, you have to be able to cope with the financial burden of training, the media spotlight and the responsibility of being a role model to younger athletes.

ING CRITERIA
ASSESSED

6

Task

Produce a poster or a PowerPoint® presentation giving advice on using communication effectively in a sporting environment. Then, use your ideas to prepare for, and take part in, a media interview. You should:

PASS

Describe the skills needed to communicate and work effectively with others (P7).

Prepare, and be the subject of, a media interview, describing your own strengths and areas for improvement (P8).

MERIT

Explain the skills needed to communicate and work effectively with others (M5).

Explain your own strengths and areas for improvement when participating in a media interview (M6).

DISTINCTION

Present recommendations on how to improve your own media interview skills (D3).

Tackling the assignment

Begin by producing a visual display, in the form of a poster or a PowerPoint® presentation, describing (if you are aiming for a Pass) and explaining (if you are aiming for a Merit) the communication skills that are used in effective communication. Remember to consider both verbal and non-verbal communication skills.

Next, you should prepare for and then take part in a media interview. You could video your interview to provide you with the evidence you need, or your teacher or tutor could provide you with a witness statement. However, a video recording – or even a sound recording – will be a great help when you are preparing the final section of this assignment.

You then need to describe (if you are aiming for a Pass) and explain (if you are aiming for a Merit) your own strengths and areas for improvement when taking part in a media interview. Because you will not really know what your strengths and weaknesses are until you have completed your interview, you must carry out you interview before you tackle this section of the assignment.

Finally, if you are aiming for a Distinction, you need to present recommendations on how to improve your media interview skills. Here, you should suggest how you can make the improvements that you have identified, such as going on a course, observing others or learning new techniques to cope with nerves.

Meeting the Pass criteria

BTEC Level 2 Firsts in Sport

Unit 12 assignment, part four   Charles Day

Communication

- **7% WORDS:** Words are only labels and the listeners put their own interpretation on speakers' words.
- **38% PARALINGUISTIC:** The way in which something is said – the accent, tone and voice modulation – is important to the listener.
- **55% BODY LANGUAGE:** What a speaker looks like while delivering a message affects the listener's understanding most.

Types of body language

Remember that you are dealing with 'PEOPLE'.

- **(P)OSTURE AND GESTURES:** Use hand gestures and stand up straight. Don't slouch.
- **(E)YE CONTACT:** Look at the person you are talking to. Look them in the eye.
- **(O)RIENTATION:** Sit or stand to face the person you are talking to. Don't sit or stand sideways-on.
- **(P)RESENTATION:** Dress appropriately to get other people's attention.
- **(L)OOKS:** Is your appearance appropriate for the situation?
- **(E)XPRESSION OF EMOTION:** Use facial expressions to express emotion: smile, laugh or be stern.

Charles makes some interesting points in his presentation. He has clearly researched the issues, as shown by his first slide describing how information is absorbed by listeners. I particularly like his second slide, which describes an easy way to remember the main points to consider when presenting to an audience.

My concern with Charles' piece of work is that he does not give any description of the skills associated with verbal communication. Although he has shown that words only account for seven per cent of communication, he has also stated that a further 38 per cent of the communication is paralinguistic and this is a form of verbal communication. Charles' work therefore fails to describe almost half of the skills associated with communication. For this reason, Charles' work does not yet meet the required standard to meet the criteria for P7.

Meeting the Merit criteria

Review of performance

Laura James

Having taken part in a media-style interview, I have watched my performance on a video recording. The table below lists my strengths and areas for development.

Strengths	Areas for improvement
Well planned	Too quiet
Accurate information given	Negative body language
Polite and well mannered	Lack of eye contact

Areas for improvement

My areas for improvement are all very similar, and revolve around the way in which I relate to my audience and the interviewer. Of my three areas for improvement, my negative body language is the most important. Having looked at the video in detail, I appear to have a very closed body shape. The video shows that I am sat with my legs crossed and my shoulders turned away from the interviewer. I think this is because I lack confidence in the situation. However, although I know it is caused by a lack of confidence, the audience might assume it was because I wasn't interested in the interview and wanted to get it over with quickly. This would mean that I was unsuccessful in getting my message across to the audience, making my interview, in essence, a failure.

By using a table Laura makes it immediately clear that she has reviewed her performance in a media interview, and that she is fully aware of her strengths and areas for improvement. Her explanation of negative body language shows that she understands the effects this can have on an audience and she has been able to explain the consequences of her actions.

Laura has made a good start with her first slide, but she needs to do more work. As it stands her presentation lacks the depth required to meet the criteria for M6. She has made no attempt to explain her strengths and she has not explained the other areas for improvement that she has listed in her table.

Meeting the Distinction criteria

Improving my media skills

Before taking part in a future media interview, I would try to improve the skills that I have demonstrated in my first attempt. I would be sure to ask myself the following questions:

What do the media want?

Do they want good quotes, a fresh angle on a story, pictures, a talented sportsperson with a clear speaking voice or something new?

Why am I speaking to the media?

Do I want access to my audience in order to develop my credibility and believability, or an opportunity to state my case?

If I am unable to answer these questions effectively then I would choose not to take part in the interview. However, if I can answer the questions then taking part in the interview will become less daunting.

Media training

Many companies offer media training. Two examples are given below:

Associated Media Training Ltd.
45 Southfield Road, Highgate, London, N6 4LR
For bookings and general enquiries, contact Paula on 020 7561 4267.
To discuss course options, contact Tony on 020 7561 4268.
Email: info@associatedmediatraining.co.uk
www.associatedmediatraining.co.uk

Jonas Burch
Telephone: 0845 7491567
Email: info@jonasburch.co.uk
Post: Jonas Burch, 42 Bishopgate Street, Leeds, LS1 5TF

Both companies offer media training sessions, ranging from a one-day course priced at around £350 to a course tailored to the individual starting at around £750. However, for the purpose of improving my own media skills, the use of a specialist company would be too expensive.

Sophie has targeted this piece of work at D3 but as yet the content does not meet the criteria. Sophie has attempted to suggest how she could develop her media skills but has only succeeded in providing more questions than answers.

Sophie's second slide is good, because it makes it clear that one way to improve media interview skills is to take part in some form of media training. However, she needs to develop this slide to include examples of the work that would be undertaken on such a course.

Developing my media skills I

My media interview was not particularly good, largely because I did not do enough research beforehand. In future, I would write a list of questions and ensure that I knew the answers to them **before** the interview took place. I would ask questions, such as:

1. What is my aim?
What do I want to happen as a result of the interview?
What do I want people to think or do?

2. Who is the target audience?
Who do I want to influence?
Who is most affected?
Who am I speaking to?

3. Message
What do I need to say to motivate my audience?
What are the right words and images that I need to use?

Sophie Martin

Sophie needs to develop her final slide by suggesting exemplar answers to the questions she has posed. For example, Sophie could easily have chosen a specific event that she needs to publicize, such as a fund-raising day, and use this as a basis to answer each question. Doing this would have proved that Sophie understands how asking herself these questions would help to improve her media interview skills.

Unit 13: Work Experience in the Sports Industry

Organizations in the sports industry

The sports industry offers a wide range of opportunities for people who want to work in an ever changing, exciting and challenging environment. The sports industry is made up of a mix of voluntary, public and private sector organizations. There are also some joint and dual use providers.

Voluntary sector providers

The voluntary sector plays a vital role in providing sporting opportunities for all age groups in a variety of sports. The types of organization found within the voluntary sector include:

- sports clubs, including football, rugby, swimming, tennis and athletics clubs
- charities that employ volunteers to run projects designed to engage disaffected individuals and communities through sport.

Because they are 'not for profit' organizations, paid work is limited – but not unheard of – in the voluntary sector. However, it might be the ideal environment in which to gain experience, especially since there is a fair chance that you are a member, or have been a member, of a voluntary sports club and already have an appreciation of the type of work experience opportunities that exist within the sector.

You may want to spend your work experience helping out at a voluntary sports club in your area.

Public sector providers

Public sector organizations are funded by local authorities or central government.

In larger urban areas, facilities will include indoor swimming pools, sports centres, outdoor tennis courts and athletics tracks. Even the smallest villages are likely to have somewhere, such as a playing field, where sport can be played. At a national level there are four large national sports centres that are managed by Sport England. They provide a range of high-quality international standard training and competition facilities for a range of sport governing bodies.

The public sector has a well-established track record for offering structured and varied work experience placements in sport. Next time you visit a public sector facility, have a look at the type of placement that you could apply for.

There may also be a dual use or a joint use facility in your area that could provide an interesting opportunity for a work experience placement. Dual or joint use facilities are often based on educational sites, so a school can use them during the day and they are open to the public in the evening, at weekends and during the school holidays.

Could there be a potential work experience opportunity for you in the public sector?

Private sector providers

The private sector continues to grow as the nation becomes more aware of the importance of following a healthy lifestyle. The facilities provided by private sector organizations are often state of the art and include high quality health clubs and fitness centres, and private golf, tennis and squash clubs.

Because the private sector is driven by profit, the cost of using private sector facilities is often too high for many members of the community. However, although the membership fees may be too expensive for you at the moment, there is no reason why you shouldn't consider a period of work experience at one of the private sector organizations in your area.

Opportunities for work experience placements also exist within the private sector.

Similarities between the sectors

Despite their differences, all organizations in the sport industry share some features:

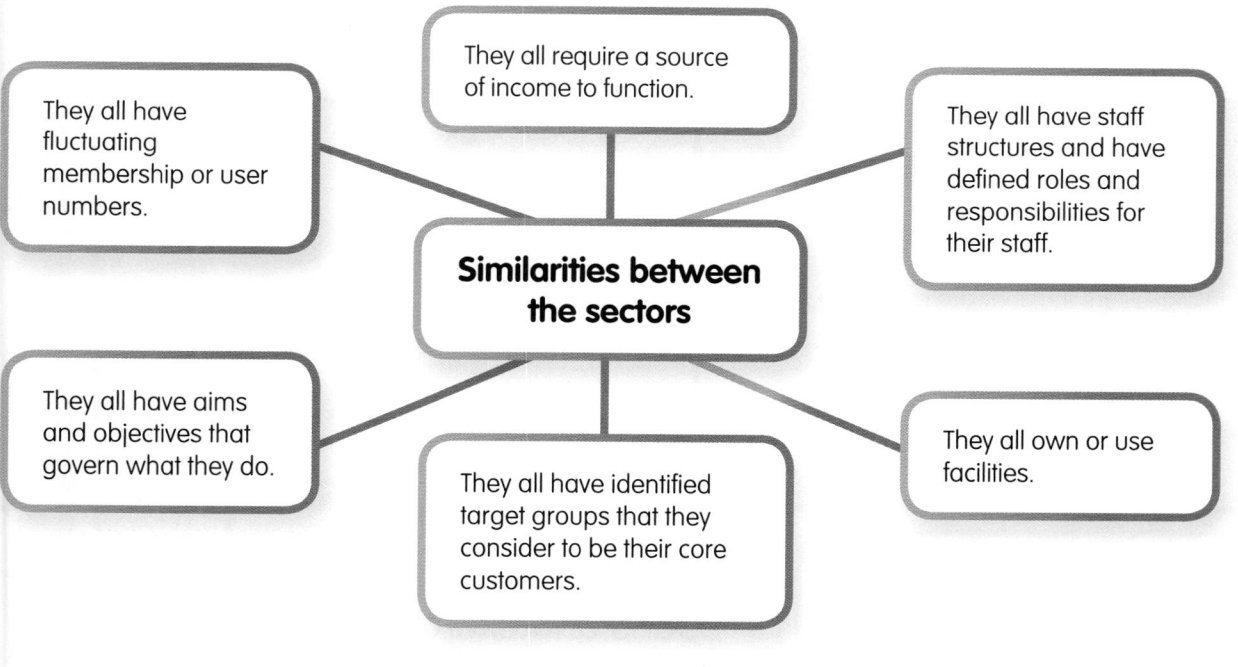

They all require a source of income to function.

They all have fluctuating membership or user numbers.

They all have staff structures and have defined roles and responsibilities for their staff.

Similarities between the sectors

They all have aims and objectives that govern what they do.

They all have identified target groups that they consider to be their core customers.

They all own or use facilities.

BRONZE

1. Choose one organization from each sector in your local area and find out about it. Try to answer the following questions:

- What is the organization's name?
- Where is the organization located?
- What facilities does the organization own or use?
- What are the aims and objectives of the organization?
- How many volunteers and staff does the organization employ?
- Where does the organization's income come from?
- Who are the organization's target groups?
- What else have you discovered about the organization?

Occupations in the sports industry

There are so many potential occupations in the sports industry that it would be impossible to look at them all. However, we will be investigating the responsibilities of some in detail and exploring the skills required to carry them out.

Sports assistant

A sports assistant is someone who helps out more senior staff. Their responsibilities could include:

- observing activities and the way in which equipment is used to ensure the safety of clients and staff
- maintaining the cleanliness of facilities
- setting up, checking, taking down and storing equipment
- dealing with customer enquiries and first aid incidents
- assisting in the organization of sport events.

Fitness instructor

There are many fitness instructors working in both the public and private sectors, and many who are self-employed and work at a variety of locations. Their responsibilities include:

- carrying out fitness assessments, consultations and inductions with new clients
- showing clients how to use resistance machines and free weights properly
- supervising clients to make sure that they are exercising safely and effectively
- leading group exercise classes such as circuit training, aerobics or spinning
- giving advice on healthy eating and personal exercise programmes.

Physiotherapist

Coach

Coaches work in all three sectors of the sports industry. Their responsibilities include:

- demonstrating an activity
- communicating instructions clearly
- encouraging participants to gain and develop new skills and techniques
- evaluating performance, assessing the strengths and weaknesses of a participant's performance, and providing feedback
- enthusing participants to continue and progress in sport
- developing their own knowledge and understanding of fitness, injury, nutrition and sports science.

Sports and exercise scientist

Sports and exercise scientists work with clubs and/or individual performers to maximize performance. Their responsibilities include:

- working alongside sport coaches to monitor athletes and teams, helping to improve their performance
- preventing illness and improving the health of performers
- working with performers and other medical staff on rehabilitation programmes.

Sports and exercise scientists may also be involved in supporting the development and manufacture of sport-related equipment and advances in sport technology.

PE teacher

Sports development officer

Outdoor education instructor

Professional performer

Sport retailer

Sport administrator

Skills

Many of the skills and qualities required to perform jobs in the sports industry also apply to occupations in other industries. Some of the most important ones are:

- **Good communication skills:** People working in the sports industry come into regular contact with members of the public and therefore need to be able to communicate with them, as well as other agencies and colleagues, effectively. Verbal and non-verbal communication skills are equally important.
- **Reliability and consistency:** It is important for people working in sport to be reliable and keep to the commitments they make. It's no good agreeing to take a coaching session and then not turning up! It is also important, especially when working with members of the public, to be consistent. You need to have a smile on your face even when you don't feel like it. Problems should be left at home and should not affect your day-to-day performance at work.
- **Effective team working skills.**
- **The ability to work well under pressure:** There are times in any job when tight deadlines have to be met but high standards have to be maintained. For example, a funding bid needs to reach Sport England before the closing date or the changing rooms need to be cleaned before the next set of customers use them.
- **Enthusiasm and dedication:** Many people working in the sports industry are responsible for trying to improve someone's performance, help them get fit or help them enjoy the activity they are taking part in. Being enthusiastic and dedicated, making sure your own enjoyment and love of sport comes across to the people you are working with, is vital if you are going to do this successfully.
- **The ability to use your initiative when required.**
- **Punctuality and good time management.**

As well as these general skills and qualities, many occupations in the sports industry also require specialist skills and knowledge. For example, a coach needs a thorough understanding of the skills, techniques and tactics of the sport they are coaching, while a fitness instructor needs to know all about anatomy and physiology and the effect of exercise on the body.

BRONZE

1. What ten jobs would you most like to do in the sports industry? Don't forget to be realistic. Manager of the England Football Team is probably a bit too ambitious!

2. Choose three occupations that haven't been described in detail and identify five responsibilities for each one.

BRONZE SILVER

3. Which three skills are most important for the occupation you would most like to do during your work experience? For each skill:

- describe what the skill is
- explain why the skill is needed, giving examples.

Identifying work and work experience opportunities

No-one is going to walk up to you in the street and offer you the work placement or job you want. You are going to have to find it yourself, so it is important to be aware of how to find out about the opportunities out there.

Websites for sport-related organizations

For example:
- ISPAL (the Institute for Sport, Parks and Leisure): www.ispal.org.uk
- ISRM (the Institute of Sport and Recreation Management): www.isrm.co.uk
- SkillsActive (the Sector Skills Council for Active Leisure and Learning): www.skillsactive.com

Sport periodicals

For example:
- *Leisure Opportunities*
- *Sports Management*
- *Opportunities*

How do I find out about available opportunities?

Local newspapers

Recruitment agencies

For example:
- www.sportsrecruitment.com
- www.industryrecruit.co.uk/Sports
- www.flowsports.co.uk

Remember:

Jobs can be full-time, part-time or casual, which means you work when you are needed, so your work experience placement could take any of these forms. For example, you might complete your placement in one block like a full-time job or over a period of time like a part-time or casual job. Remember that you might need to be flexible!

An example of a website offering job opportunities in the leisure industry.

BRONZE

1. Use as many sources as possible to find as many sports-related job adverts as you can. While you are doing this, note down anything you don't understand about the adverts and then see if you can find the answers to your questions.

SILVER

2. Look at the job adverts that you collected for Activity 1. Can you identify appropriate work experience opportunities in any of them?

Unit 13 assignment, part one

Background

As part of your course you have the opportunity to take part in a period of work experience. Your teacher always enrols the help of Connexions to make sure everyone is offered positive placement opportunities and is well prepared for their interview and their placement.

Task

The Connexions adviser is conducting an initial interview with all students before offering them a placement and insists that everyone is well prepared for this meeting. Prepare for your meeting. You will be expected to:

> GRADING CRITERIA
> TO BE ASSESSED
> P1, P2, P3
> M1, M2

Describe three different types of organization within the sports industry, giving examples (P1).

Describe three different occupations within the sports industry and the skills that each requires (P2).

Locate three advertisements for jobs from different sources available within the sports industry (P3).

Explain the skills required for three different occupations within the sports industry (M1).

Use advertisements for jobs available in sport to identify appropriate work experience in the sports industry (M2).

Tackling the assignment

This task is all about preparation, making sure you are prepared for the meeting by carrying out plenty of research beforehand.

You will be presenting your research verbally, during the meeting, but you should prepare some information sheets to take in with you. You can use them to remind you of everything you want to say and they can always be given to the adviser as evidence of your research if you get a bit tongue-tied!

Make sure that you research three **different** types of organization and three **different** types of occupation. You won't meet the criteria if you look at three sports centres

and three different sports coaches, for example. A good approach would be to look at one organization from each of the three sectors (the voluntary, public and private sectors) and occupations associated with them, such as a sports coach, a sports assistant and an administrative occupation.

Finally, you need to show that you have found three advertisements for jobs in the sports industry, each from a different source. If you are aiming for a Merit, you must then use them to identify appropriate work experience opportunities for you. Note that the key word here is 'appropriate'. It would be unrealistic to expect that you would be able to find a work experience placement as a sports centre manager, for example.

Meeting the Pass criteria

BTEC Level 2 Firsts in Sport

Unit 13 assignment, part one
Balraj Bahaat

The first organization I am going to look at is Alvastree Hockey Club.

The club is a **voluntary club** that coaches young people between the ages of 11 and 16. It doesn't have its own facilities but trains and plays its matches on the pitches at the Racecourse Recreation Ground.

It has six boys' teams and one girls' team. Each team has a manager and an assistant manager, who coach for about three hours a week. The club also has a chairperson, fixtures secretary and a treasurer who looks after the money.

The aims of the club are to provide sporting opportunities for young people and to develop their understanding of health and fitness issues, which they can use in other aspects of their life.

The club gets its funding from the membership fees and weekly training subscriptions paid by club members. It also has a local sponsor who contributes approximately £600 per year, which the club uses to pay for the cost of hiring facilities.

This is an encouraging start by Balraj, who is painting a very clear picture of the organization. If he continues with this approach for two further organizations, perhaps an example of a public sector sports centre and a private health club, he will meet the criteria for P1.

To fully meet the criteria for a Pass, Balraj now needs to describe three different occupations within the sports industry and the skills that each requires (P2) and locate three advertisements for jobs from different sources available within the sports industry (P3).

Meeting the Merit criteria

Bradley Thomas
Skills required for a coach

A coach needs to have good communication skills because:

• They will have to give clear instructions to a range of performers, some of whom may be young and inexperienced. They will need things explaining clearly and with demonstrations.
• They may also need to communicate complicated tactics at an advanced level to individuals or teams.
• A coach may also be required to communicate with parents to give reasons why their son or daughter has not been selected for the team. This would need the coach to be sensitive, which is another important skill.

Bradley has given three clear reasons **why** a coach needs good communication skills. If he goes into a similar level of detail for the other skills a coach needs, and explains the skills required by two other people who work in the sports industry, he has every chance of achieving M2.

Applying for a job or work experience placement

Before you are offered a job or a work experience placement you still have two important stages to go through: applying for a position and being interviewed. Your application must look professional and present your skills and qualities in a positive light. If you don't get the application right, then securing an interview can be very difficult. There are three main ways to apply for a job: completing an application form, writing a letter of application or providing a CV.

Application form

An application form is provided by the organization advertising the job, and it clearly identifies the information they need from you. You may get the opportunity to expand on some areas, such as your suitability for the job, but the format is very structured.

Many organizations now ask applicants to apply online or download an application form from their website.

Remember:

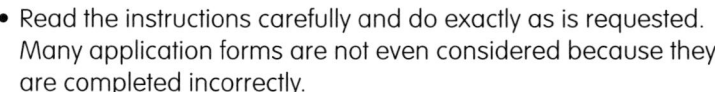

Whichever way you apply for a job or a work experience placement you must make sure you:

- Read the instructions carefully and do exactly as is requested. Many application forms are not even considered because they are completed incorrectly.
- Provide all the information requested.
- Make sure the information you present is legible. Word processed applications are far easier to read and you can use the spell checker to make sure there are no spelling mistakes!

Please complete this form legibly and return it on or before the closing date specified in the advertisement. Late applications will not be considered. ONLY INFORMATION PROVIDED ON THIS APPLICATION FORM WILL BE CONSIDERED BY THE PANEL. Curriculum vitae will not be accepted. Candidates will outline clearly how their qualifications and experience meet both the essential and preferred requirements. All information given will be treated with the strictest confidence. Continuation sheets may be added if necessary.

1. POSITION APPLIED FOR: _____

2. PERSONAL DETAILS

Surname:	Telephone number (Home):
Forenames:	Telephone number (Mobile):
Dr/Mr/Mrs/Ms:	Telephone number (Work):
Address:	
Postcode:	

Do you have a clean, current driving licence?	Yes	No
Have you a car/access to a car for business use?	Yes	No

3. EDUCATION

From	To	Name of School	Examinations Taken and Qualifications Gained (Specify Grades)

4. FURTHER/HIGHER EDUCATION

From	To	Name of Institution (state if Full– or Part-Time)	Subjects Taken and Qualifications Gained (Specify Grades or Degree Class Obtained)

5. MEMBERSHIP OF PROFESSIONAL ORGANIZATIONS

Date Joined	Institute/Organization	Grade of Membership (Where Appropriate)

6. EMPLOYMENT RECORD or work experience (Please list chronologically, starting with current or last employer)

Name and Address of Employer and Nature of Business:	From: To:	Job Title: Job Function/ Responsibilities:	Final Salary and Reason for Leaving

7. TRAINING

Details of training courses attended and awards achieved, including dates, if appropriate

8. SUITABILITY FOR THIS POSITION

Please detail your suitability for this position under the relevant headings below. What skills, qualities and experience do you have?

9. REFEREES

Please give the details of two work-related referees, including your current or most recent post. Referees will **not** be contacted without your prior approval.

Name:	Name:
Position:	Position:
Company:	Company:
Address:	Address:
Telephone Number:	Telephone Number:
Nature of Relationship:	Nature of Relationship:

10. VERIFICATION OF INFORMATION

I certify that all information that I have provided is correct. I understand that any false information given may result in a job offer being withdrawn.
Signature: Date:

BRONZE

1. Look at the adverts for jobs in the sports industry that you have collected and note down the different ways in which the applicants are asked to apply. Are there any trends? For example, do more senior positions require applicants to complete an application form or supply a CV, while more junior positions only require the applicant to apply in writing?

An example of an application form for a sport-related position.

Letter of application

A letter of application can take two forms:

- You may be asked to apply for a job in writing.
- You may send a speculative letter, enquiring if there are any vacancies and, if there are, asking if they would consider you. Don't underestimate the power of a speculative letter. They can get you an interview, immediately or after some time if your details are kept on file for future reference.

The format and content of a letter of application is very much up to you. Here is an example of a speculative letter of application:

> Use the person's name if possible. You may have to telephone the organization to find out their name if you don't know it already. If you can't find it out you should address the letter to 'Dear Sir/Madam'.

> A letter of application must contain information about your education and your work experience to date. Including all this would make your letter very long, so it is a good idea to summarize the key points in your letter and send a CV, containing all the detail, with it.

> These are excellent examples because they are very relevant to the post being applied for.

> It is a really good idea to mention some of the generic skills that you possess and that make you suitable for the position you are applying for.

> This is a really positive and polite way to finish the letter.

Abigail Fyfe
9 Juniper Close, Worksop
Nottinghamshire, S81 7RJ

Paul Woodman
Duty Manager
Worksop Leisure Centre, Jubilee Road, Worksop
Nottinghamshire, S81 9LP

31 March 2010

Dear Mr Woodman

Work experience application for the position of Sports Assistant

I am writing to apply for the position of Sports Assistant as part of the work experience unit of my BTEC Level 2 Firsts in Sport course.

I have attached a copy of my CV for your information, which includes my educational qualifications and work experience to date.

In support of my CV I would like to add that I am currently helping out with coaching duties at the swimming club where I train, working with the junior development squad. I really enjoy the work and gain a great deal of satisfaction seeing the younger swimmers improve and enjoy their training.

I have also helped the teachers at my old primary school run their sports day for year 5 and 6 students. I was asked to run some training sessions before the sports day and then on the actual day I was responsible for making sure the children were at the start line and ready for their event in plenty of time.

I would also like to add that I am a hard-working person who can be relied on to work well as part of a team or on my own if necessary. I am also very enthusiastic about sport and during my voluntary work with the swimming club have never missed a session. The club have told me that they will pay for me to take the Swimming Level 1 Coaches Award when I am old enough, so that I can get more involved in coaching.

Thank you for considering me for the position. I very much hope that I can expand on my application at an interview.

Yours sincerely

Abigail Fyfe
Abigail Fyfe

> How you sign off your letter depends on how you have addressed it. If you have used the person's name you need to use 'Yours sincerely'. If you have addressed your letter to 'Dear Sir/Madam', then you need to use 'Yours faithfully'.

> If you have word processed your letter you need to sign your name above your typed name. If it is a handwritten letter then your signature is enough, although if it is difficult to make out your name it is always a good idea to print it as well!

A Curriculum Vitae (or CV for short)

A CV is a brief summary of your educational achievements, your employment history to date, your pastimes and the contact details for two referees. Sometimes a CV on its own is sufficient when applying for a job, while on other occasions you may be requested to provide a CV in addition to a covering letter or application form.

Abigail Fyfe
9 Juniper Close, Worksop, Nottinghamshire, S81 7RJ
Tel: 07777 888999 Email: abigail1984@coolmail.com

Educational achievements

ASDAN Citizenship Award (2008)

Currently taking:
- BTEC Level 2 Firsts in Sport (anticipated grade Merit or 4 x GCSE at grade B)
- GCSE Maths (anticipated grade A)
- GCSE English (anticipated grade B)
- GCSE Science (anticipated grade B)

Work experience

Worksop Whales Swimming Club

I am currently helping out with coaching duties at the swimming club where I train, working with the junior development squad. I really enjoy the work and gain a great deal of satisfaction seeing the younger swimmers improve and enjoy their training. I have to:
- organize the equipment for the lanes I help to coach
- ensure health and safety in the lanes
- advise swimmers how to improve their techniques
- perform timekeeping duties.

Brookside Primary School

I have helped the teachers at my old primary school run their sports day for year 5 and 6 students. I was asked to:
- run some training sessions before the sports day
- be responsible on the actual day for making sure the children were at the start line and ready for their event in plenty of time
- help record results.

Interests and hobbies

I really enjoy sport, especially swimming, and have been competing in regional and national events for five years. I have now started coaching and would like to progress in this area.

When not playing sport I enjoy reading, especially crime novels. I also like fashion and have started to buy and sell jewellery on eBay.

I have recently been abroad for the first time, to Spain, and would like to travel throughout Europe when I have a job.

References

Suzanne Smith
Head of PE
Worksop Community Sports College
Eckington Road, Worksop
Nottinghamshire, S81 7XN

Karl Constantine
Head Coach, Worksop Whales Swimming Club
c/o Central Baths
Mansfield Street, Worksop
Nottinghamshire, S81 7RB

The organization needs to know who you are and how to get in touch with you, so that they can – hopefully – invite you to an interview.

The advert may state that you need certain qualifications, such as GCSE Maths and English, so you need to mention the qualifications you have already achieved **or** those you are studying towards.

You can use this section to showcase your skills and experience, making specific reference to the skills and qualities that are required for the job you are applying for. This is a very important part of the CV.

Let the person reading your CV know about your pastimes or hobbies. It is good for them to see what you are like outside of the work or school/college environment.

The organization will need to check your suitability with someone who knows you well, so provide contact details of people who know you in an educational or a work setting. But make sure you ask the people you are naming as referees before you send out your CV. It might be a shock for them if a request for a reference arrives without any prior warning!

BRONZE

2a) Complete an application form to apply for a job in the sports industry that you would like to do on your work experience placement. Ask your teacher for an application form.

b) Choose a different job in the sports industry and produce a letter of application and a CV to apply for it.

SILVER

3. Imagine you have secured an interview for one of the positions you applied for in Activity 2. You know the interviewer is bound to ask you to **explain** your personal skills and qualities in relation to those required for the job, so you have decided to make some notes to help you answer these questions well during the interview.

GOLD

4. Ask a friend or family member if they can help you role play the interview you prepared for in Activity 3. They should play the part of the prospective employer and you should play yourself. Use the opportunity to practise **evaluating** your skills and qualities in relation to the job you are applying for. Think carefully about your strengths and explain how the job will help you develop gaps in your skills or knowledge.

The interview

The interview is often seen as the most nerve-racking part of applying for a job or work experience placement, but it can be painless – and even quite enjoyable – if you approach it in the right manner.

The interview process can be split into two phases: preparing for the interview and the actual interview itself.

Preparing for the interview

As with most aspects of work life, time spent on the planning phase is crucial to a successful interview. Here are the key things you need to plan:

The interview procedure

- Do you have to take anything, such as certificates, with you?
- What will you be expected to do during the interview? If you have to deliver a presentation, have you prepared for it?
- What sort of questions do you think you will be asked? Check over the job description and see if you can prepare some answers.
- Do you know a bit about the organization?
- Have you planned some questions to ask the interviewer?

Confirming your attendance

- Do you need to confirm your attendance at the interview? If so, by when and who to?

Travelling to the interview

- Where is the interview to take place?
- Do you know how to get there?
- How long will it take you to get there? If you need to travel during rush hour, will the journey take longer?

Your appearance and attitude

- What will you wear? Are your clothes ready or do they need washing and ironing?
- Do you need a haircut?
- Are you in the right frame of mind? Think positively and see the interview as a great opportunity to show the interviewer that you are the right person for the job.

The interview

These two young people certainly look the part and will create a really positive first impression at their interviews. They are smart, well groomed, seem relaxed and appear confident.

BRONZE

1. What questions do you think you would be asked in an interview? What answers would you give to those questions?

The interview itself

When you get to the interview, well presented and well prepared, you must use the opportunity to sell yourself as effectively as you can. It is inevitable that you will be nervous – most people are at interviews – but whoever is interviewing you will take this into account. However, there are certain things you can do to help you perform well at interview:

Make sure your body language is positive. Smile, look as if you are pleased to be at the interview and maintain eye contact with the interviewer or interviewers throughout.

Get there with plenty of time to spare so that you can relax a little and think about the interview, and not worry about being late or rushing to get there on time! If you are running late, telephone the interviewer, apologize and give them your estimated time of arrival.

Listen carefully to the questions you are asked and seek clarification if you don't understand any of them. Reply clearly, giving the fullest answer you can.

Ask questions of your own at the end of the interview, such as 'When will I hear if I've been successful?'

Take the opportunity to thank the interviewer for interviewing you. A firm and confident handshake before you depart will also leave a lasting positive impression.

BRONZE

2. Find someone – a parent, carer, teacher or friend – to carry out a mock interview with you. Take this opportunity to practise your interview skills seriously, preparing fully and even dressing the part. Encourage the person who is interviewing you to give you constructive feedback: what did you do well? What could you do better next time? Then use their feedback to help you prepare better for your next interview.

Unit 13 assignment, part two

Background

As part of your course you have the opportunity to take part in a period of work experience. Your teacher always enrols the help of Connexions to make sure everyone is offered positive placement opportunities and is well prepared for their interview and their placement.

GRADING CRITERIA TO BE ASSESSED
P4, P5, P6
M3
D1

Task

The Connexions adviser has identified a possible placement for you and has suggested you draft an application so that they can check it over before you send it off. They have also agreed to run through a mock interview with you so that, if you do get an interview, you will be properly prepared to present yourself effectively. You will need to:

PASS

Produce an application for work experience in sport (P4).

Prepare for an interview for work experience in sport (P5).

Undertake an interview for work experience in sport (P6).

MERIT

Explain your own personal skills and qualities in relation to those required for an occupation in sport (M3).

DISTINCTION

Evaluate your own personal skills and qualities in relation to those required for an occupation in sport (D1).

Tackling the assignment

As with a real job application, the secret to success is preparation. Spend time on your letter of application and accompanying CV, which should both be produced using ICT. Make sure that you include all the information that is required and double check it for spelling mistakes.

You need to explain to the person reading your application why your own personal skills and qualities make you an ideal candidate for the job, so remember to go into detail and give them reasons. Use the word 'because' to help you do this. When it comes to evaluating your personal skills and qualities you need to go a step further. You need to place emphasis on **how** your strengths will help you carry out the roles and responsibilities associated with the job

and explain how the placement or job will help you to address some of the areas you feel need improving.

When you are preparing for your mock interview, remember to find out about the interview procedure and where the interview will take place, consider your appearance and think about how you will make sure you arrive on time. It is also a good idea to note down all the skills and qualities you have that will help you if you get the job. Focus on your strengths, but also give some thought to your weaknesses and how the work experience placement will help you address them. You won't be able to take notes into the interview, so you need to commit them to memory. A dress rehearsal wouldn't go amiss!

Your work-based project

Having secured your work experience placement, you want to do everything you can to make the most of the opportunity. You will have to carry out many routine tasks associated with the job, but you also have to complete a project during your work experience placement.

Themes

You could think about ideas for your project before the placement starts. You could even present them at your interview if you want to make a really positive impression! However, it is far more likely that a suitable project will emerge once your work experience starts. Here are some themes you may want to consider:

Marketing
You could look at helping the organization market a new service or conduct some market research to find out what new services customers want.

Staff training
You could develop an induction procedure if the organization doesn't have one, or improve the one they do have.

Recruitment
You could help the organization recruit new volunteers to help them expand the number of teams they run.

Themes for a work-based project

Participation rates
You could help to monitor participation rates, finding out what time of day or year numbers drop and thinking about ways to overcome these dips.

Customer service
You could conduct a customer satisfaction survey to see how happy customers are with the level of service at the organization.

Health and safety
There are lots of things you could do here. For example, you could help complete a risk assessment or review existing risk assessments.

Remember:

Your project will need to be fully approved by your supervisor or line manager at the organization where you are working, so they need to be involved in the planning process. They may even have some ideas for you to consider, so use their expertise!

Could you help your organization achieve Clubmark or Quest status as part of your project?

BRONZE

1. Thinking about your work experience placement, identify at least two possible projects for each of the themes identified above. Try to come up with projects that will benefit the organization you are working for and will develop your own skills and experience.

Planning your project

Whatever theme you decide for your project, you must plan your project carefully if it is to be a success. Your planning needs to consider:

Remember:

Your project, and your placement as a whole, provides you with an excellent opportunity to develop many personal skills, including practical skills, technical skills and people-related skills.

BRONZE

2. Imagine that your work experience placement is at your local leisure centre and you have decided to focus your project on the theme of marketing. You have discussed your ideas with your supervisor and have agreed that you will carry out some market research to find out what new services clients would like the leisure centre to offer. Create a plan for your project.

- **The aims and objectives of the project:** Your aims (what you want to achieve overall) and objectives (the steps you will take to get there) should be specific to the organization you are working for and personal to you. An example could be 'I aim to improve my customer care skills' with the objectives of 'working with different customer groups, watching experienced staff in action and dealing with challenging situations when they arise'.
- **The expected outcomes:** These are the things that you hope to achieve by the end of the project. An organizational outcome might be that, by the end of the project, you will have produced an induction booklet that can be issued to new volunteers at the sports club where you are conducting your placement.

A personal outcome could be that you will be able to import graphics into a document and use them to enhance your message.

- **Your targets:** Your aims and objectives should be expressed as SMART targets. More information about SMART targets can be found on page 209.
- **Do you need to make any arrangements?:** Do you need to arrange transport for people to attend a fixture? Do you need to arrange for a parking space or accommodation for a guest speaker visiting the organization?
- **Do you have any other requirements?:** Do you need any training before you can complete your project? Is there any special equipment or clothing required? Will you need access to the organization's database of customers?

Legislation

At every stage of your project, throughout the planning and during the placement, you must make sure you are working within the law and conforming to relevant regulations. Your work experience provider should shoulder much of the responsibility for making sure this happens, but you need to be aware of your responsibilities. If you have any concerns about your health and safety during your placement you should raise them with your placement supervisor, or your teacher if you feel more confident talking to them.

Has a risk assessment been carried out so that I can do what I have been asked to do safely? (Management of Health and Safety at Work (Amendment) Regulations 1999)

Have I been provided with the correct protective equipment or clothing to do this job? (Personal Protective Equipment Regulations 1992)

I wonder if some of the potential tasks on my work programme will be removed due to my inexperience in the role? (Health and Safety (Young Persons) Regulations 1997)

I wonder where I will leave my clothes when I change into my work clothing … and where will I be able to sit down and eat my sandwiches at lunchtime? (Offices, Shops and Railway Premises Act 1963)

Does the organization I will be working for have the necessary insurance to offer work experience placements? (The Employers' Liability (Compulsory Insurance) Regulations 1998)

Have I received Criminal Records Bureau (CRB) clearance or have I been cleared under the vetting and barring scheme, because I am going to be working with children or vulnerable adults? (The Protection of Children Act 1999 and The Care Standards Act 2000)

Carrying out your project

To help maximize your chances of completing your project successfully you need to make sure you:

- manage your time effectively
- keep records of what you are doing as the project progresses, which you can use during your presentation to review the project and your performance
- carry out formative reviews of your progress with your supervisor or line manager at regular intervals, recording feedback in an effective way so that it can be used during your presentation to review the project and your performance
- identify any problems you are encountering and get support to overcome them as soon as possible
- put maximum effort and energy into your work. Always do the best that you can!

Collecting information

Here are some of the methods you can use to collect information while you are carrying out your project. You will need to use this information during your presentation, to review your project. Each method has advantages and disadvantages and some of these are described below.

Method	Advantages	Disadvantages
Interviews	• Questions can be asked to seek clarification. • Additional information can be provided on request.	• Can be time consuming to arrange and conduct. • Dominated by the person answering the questions, as opposed to a discussion where everyone's views are given equal attention.
Task sheets	• Easy and quick to complete.	• Need to be designed carefully to ensure all the relevant information is collected.
Witness testimony	• There is time to explore things in detail. • Ensures you have the views of an expert.	• May not focus on the specific skills or knowledge under review. • May be completed by someone who hasn't been fully involved in the project or placement.
Video	• Provides a very accurate account of what happened. • Can make a presentation very visual and eye-catching.	• Someone is needed to set up and look after the video camera during filming. • Will almost certainly need editing.
Audio	• Provides an accurate account of what actually took place. • Can make a presentation more interesting.	• Someone is needed to set up and look after the equipment during recording. • Will almost certainly need editing.

Filming your formative reviews with your supervisor or line manager would provide you with some very eye-catching footage for your presentation, but your supervisor might be so distracted by the camera that they might not pick up on small problems with the progress of your project that you could easily correct if they had brought them to your attention.

BRONZE

3. What information do you need to collect about your project as you complete it and how are you going to record it? Note down your ideas, thinking through the advantages and disadvantages of each method of collecting information that you have chosen. If you don't know what your project is going to be yet, use the one that you planned for Activity 2.

Presenting your project

Having completed your project and collected a considerable amount of information about how it went, you now need to present it. Your presentation should include a description of what you did and a summative review.

A summative review

A summative review is a review that takes place at the end of a project and that gives you the opportunity to identify strengths and areas for improvement from four key perspectives:

- from the perspective of the aims, objectives, expected outcomes and targets that you set out to achieve
- from the perspective of the organization that provided you with your work placement
- from your own perspective
- from the perspective of your school or college.

A SWOT analysis

A SWOT analysis is an effective way of organizing all the information you have into a manageable format. For example:

STRENGTHS	**W**EAKNESSES

Look at the good things to emerge from your project and detail its benefits to the organization you worked for, yourself and your school or college.	Look at the things that didn't go to plan and detail the drawbacks to the organization you worked for, yourself and your school or college.
OPPORTUNITIES	**T**HREATS

Detail the opportunities that exist for the organization you worked for, yourself and your school or college to build on the strengths and address the weaknesses you have identified.	Detail the barriers there are to the organization you worked for, you or your school or college grasping the opportunities you have identified.

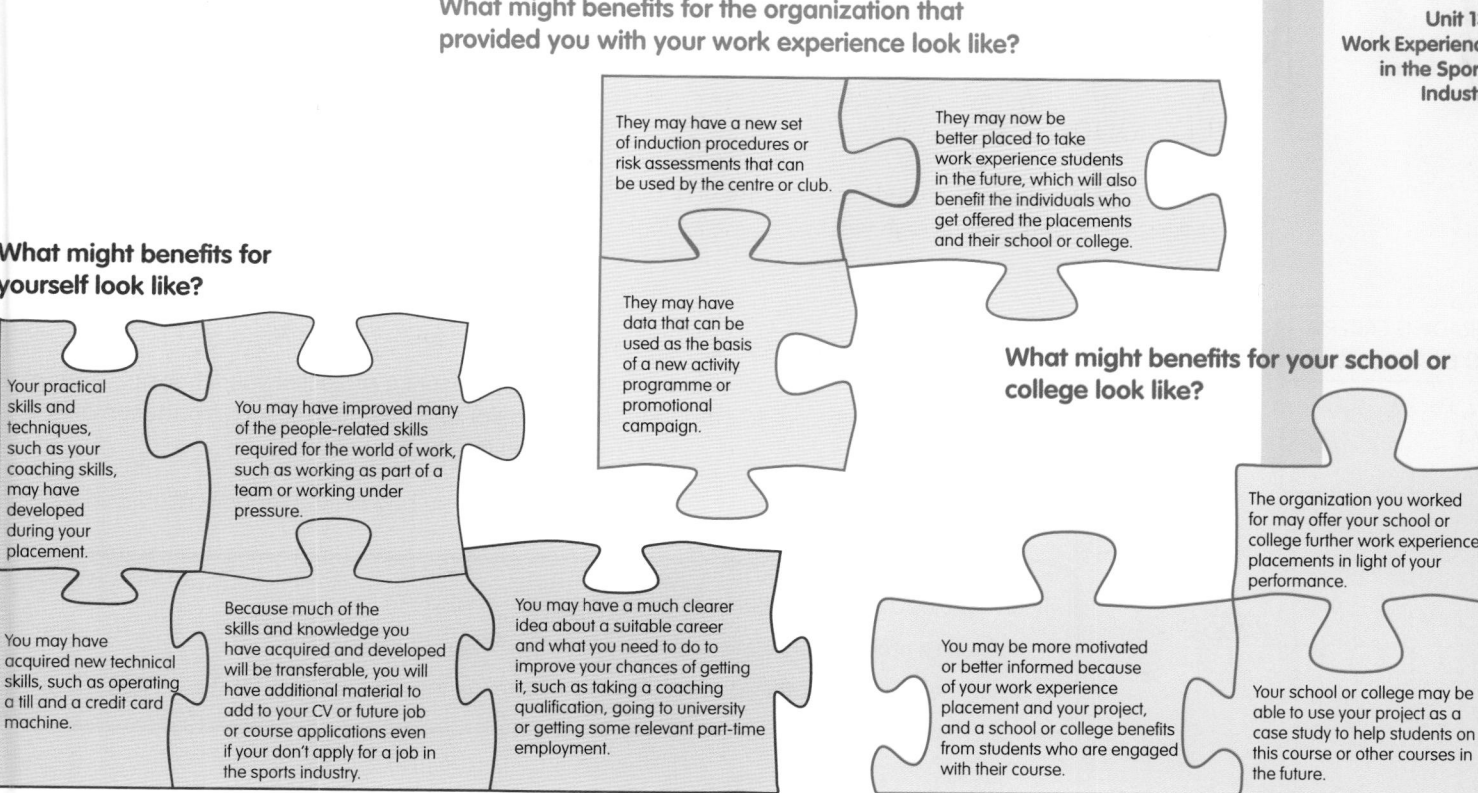

What might benefits for the organization that provided you with your work experience look like?

They may have a new set of induction procedures or risk assessments that can be used by the centre or club.

They may now be better placed to take work experience students in the future, which will also benefit the individuals who get offered the placements and their school or college.

They may have data that can be used as the basis of a new activity programme or promotional campaign.

What might benefits for yourself look like?

Your practical skills and techniques, such as your coaching skills, may have developed during your placement.

You may have improved many of the people-related skills required for the world of work, such as working as part of a team or working under pressure.

You may have acquired new technical skills, such as operating a till and a credit card machine.

Because much of the skills and knowledge you have acquired and developed will be transferable, you will have additional material to add to your CV or future job or course applications even if your don't apply for a job in the sports industry.

You may have a much clearer idea about a suitable career and what you need to do to improve your chances of getting it, such as taking a coaching qualification, going to university or getting some relevant part-time employment.

What might benefits for your school or college look like?

The organization you worked for may offer your school or college further work experience placements in light of your performance.

You may be more motivated or better informed because of your work experience placement and your project, and a school or college benefits from students who are engaged with their course.

Your school or college may be able to use your project as a case study to help students on this course or other courses in the future.

Recommendations for improvement

It's no good conducting a thorough review and then doing nothing with your findings. By completing a SWOT analysis and identifying the opportunities for addressing the weaknesses you have noted, you have identified areas that require improvement. Now you need to make recommendations as to how these weaknesses can be addressed, taking any barriers you have identified in your SWOT analysis into consideration.

For example, you may have identified the length of your placement as a weakness, because you didn't have enough time to complete your project fully, and you would like to recommend that the length of the placement is extended by one week. You acknowledge that it might be difficult for the organization you worked for to extend the length of the placement and for your school or college to allow you to spend longer away from the classroom, but you think that a longer placement would really benefit you and the organization. If the placement had been longer you would have completed your project and improved your communication skills as a result.

BRONZE

4. How are you going to present your project? Note down all the different ways in which you could present your project, giving examples of when each method would be most useful.

5. Imagine that you have completed your work experience with the local Sports Development Team, helping them to run a health and fitness awareness scheme with 15 local primary schools. Identify the benefits of your project for the Sports Development Team, for yourself and for your school or college. Use this information to complete a SWOT analysis for the project.

SILVER

6. Imagine that you identified dealing with angry customers as a personal weakness and developing your customer service skills as a personal opportunity when you completed your SWOT analysis. Make a recommendation for improvement based on this analysis.

GOLD

7. Justify the recommendation for improvement that you made in Activity 6. Remember, when you are justifying something you need to put forward strong reasons why it is needed or necessary.

Unit 13 assignment, part three

Background

You have secured your work experience placement and have settled in well. After being introduced to your colleagues and having a thorough induction it is time to get to work.

GRADING CRITERIA TO BE ASSESSED
P7, P8, P9
M4
D2

Task

During your work experience placement you must plan, carry out and present a project of your choosing. Your plan must be developed in consultation with your line manager or supervisor and you must collect information about your progress and your performance as your project progresses. You must:

 **PASS**

Plan a project, related to a theme, for work experience in sport (P7).

Undertake a project in work-based experience in sport (P8).

Present the project, describing the benefits and identifying areas for improvement (P9).

 **MERIT**

Present the project, explaining the benefits and making recommendations for improvement (M4).

 **DISTINCTION**

Present the project, evaluating the benefits and justifying recommendations relating to identified areas for improvement (D2).

Tackling the assignment

You need to be well organized to achieve all the criteria for this assignment. The first thing you need to do is plan your project, taking into account such things as:

- your aims, objectives and expected outcomes
- your targets, including any timescales you have set or been set
- any specific requirements or arrangements you may need to make.

It is a good idea to think about the methods you intend to use to collect the information about your project before you begin, and to think about how you will present your project when it is finished as you are working on it. This will help you organize all the information you collect **and** give you more time to plan an effective presentation when you have finished your project.

Most importantly of all, though, enjoy the project. It's what this unit is all about!

Meeting the Pass criteria

Project Theme

I am going to be planning and then helping to run a five-a-side tournament for the football club where I am spending my work experience. The event takes place every year and is a way for the club to raise funds. This year they hope to get more teams interested. Last year there were 12 teams and they want 16 this year.

AIMS AND TARGETS

- To raise £200 for the club.
- To get 16 teams involved.
- For everyone to have a good time.

PERSONAL TARGETS

- To increase my understanding of promoting an event.
- To develop my ability to manage an event as I will be in charge on the day (although the club coach will be there to help).

PRESENTATION IDEAS

I will have lots of information to use to present my project, including copies of marketing materials, fixture lists, results, tables and match reports. I also intend to write up a short report on my work at the end, which will help tie everything together.

REVIEW

The head coach has given me a review timetable. I will have a meeting with him every three days during my 12-day placement. I have produced a witness statement form that the coach has agreed to complete at each review meeting. I also intend to use a questionnaire with some of the teams to get their views on how I organized and ran the tournament.

This is a good project and it is very clear what Alfie's theme is.

It is good to see that Alfie is setting himself targets, but the personal targets are not easy to measure. It would be better if they were expressed as SMART targets.

Alfie has started to look ahead and think about how to present his project, building in some clear methods for collecting formative feedback. This organized approach will certainly help him when he comes to present his project.

Alfie has made a very promising start. Once he has outlined his timescales and the type of resources he needs he will have a comprehensive plan in place and will achieve the criteria for P7.

Meeting the Merit and Distinction criteria

Benefits to the work experience provider

I helped the assistant Sports Development Officer produce an induction programme for future work experience placements. This is a major benefit because:

- they didn't have one before, which meant a few placements did not work out too well
- I could give my point of view because it affected me
- the Sports Development Department is now better placed to offer work experience placements, including to students from universities.

Ralph has focused on three benefits his project provided but he needs to go into more depth to achieve M4. He needs to explain **why** the benefits he has identified are actually benefits to the work experience provider.

The benefits I got from the placement

One of the major benefits I got from the placement was improving my understanding of the health and safety requirements that are relevant to the Sports Development Unit. This is important for me because I would like to work in this area after completing my studies and will always need to be aware of safe working practices, especially as I would like to work with children.

Ralph has clearly explained one of the benefits he got from the placement and therefore is on his way to achieving M4. He needs to continue with this approach for other benefits and also make some recommendations as to ways in which he could improve in areas where he may not have performed so well.

Areas for improvement

Although I developed my understanding of health and safety issues I found it difficult to summarize the information in a format that could easily be understood by someone on a work placement.

This is important because anyone reading the information needs to understand it and apply it in the work environment.

The Senior Sports Development Officer suggested I practise summarizing information I was more comfortable with, such as the rules of rugby or the fundamentals of running an activity session. She also suggested I should look at other induction packs the council has produced to see how they presented health and safety information. I did this and found it useful. It also gave me some ideas I could use in the future.

Ralph has justified (or shown the effectiveness of) the recommendation made by the SDO as to how to improve his ability to summarize information. If he continues with this level of detail, he will achieve the criteria for D2.

Unit 14: Exercise and Fitness Instruction

Health and safety considerations

When designing a fitness programme for a client, a trainer needs to take a multitude of different factors into account to ensure success. Not only must the programme follow the principles of training, but it must also be designed to ensure the health and safety of the **individual client**. This means considering many things, including the client's current fitness levels, their medical history, their prior experience of fitness training and making sure that you follow the exercise and fitness 'Code of Ethical Practice'.

Ethics and fitness training

All fitness trainers and sports professionals are required to follow the 'Code of Ethical Practice' for exercise and fitness. This is a set of guidelines which is designed to protect the trainer, the client and the trainer's employer from injury, harm or litigation. It governs the relationship between the trainer and the client, with a code of conduct for the trainer and details of the responsibilities of the client. For example, the trainer is responsible for ensuring that the training programme is suitable for the client's current level of fitness, and that the client understands how and why they are to use any equipment safely, while the client is responsible for being open and honest with the trainer about their previous experience and medical history.

Informed consent

Before designing a programme for a client and before a client uses any item of equipment, a trainer should ensure that the client has given their informed consent. Basically, this means that the client should complete a form stating their name and address, and giving details of their medical history, their current injuries, their previous experience of exercise and their expectations from the training programme. The client must also sign the form as proof that they have given the trainer permission to work with them on improving their levels of fitness. An example of one of these Physical Activity Readiness Questionnaires (a PAR-Q) can be found on page 263.

Induction

The induction process requires the trainer to make the client aware of the health and safety regulations for the venue (such as the fire and other emergency procedures), the guidelines for ensuring consideration of other clients (such as wiping down resistance machines after use) and where to seek help if a problem arises.

Most importantly, the trainer must explain how to use the equipment in a safe and sensible manner. This will include showing the client how to check the safety of each piece of equipment before using it, how to adjust the resistance on certain machines, the purpose of using each machine and the correct techniques to be followed. The trainer should also explain how the stability and correct alignment of the joints will improve the effectiveness of the training and reduce the likelihood of injury occurring, the importance of maintaining momentum when cycling, running or rowing as a stuttering technique can also lead to injuries occurring, and the correct clothing and footwear to be worn when training.

BRONZE

1. Design a code of ethical practice that you and your peers could use when leading fitness sessions. Remember to include the obligations for both the trainer and the client.

SILVER

2. Comment on the potential problems that a trainer in a local fitness centre may have when applying the code of ethical practice you have designed.

Warming up and cooling down

The two most important parts of any training session are the warm-up and cool-down. The middle part of the session, the main activity, will only be effective if the warm-up and cool-down are carried out safely and effectively.

Warming up

Before taking part in the main activity of an exercise session, the body needs to be prepared. This process is called 'warming up' and it has three main functions:

- Raising the temperature of the blood and working muscles to enable them to stretch further without becoming injured.
- Enabling the enzymes within the muscles to become more active, making energy more readily available.
- Opening the blood vessels wider to allow more blood to reach the working muscles, so that more oxygen can be delivered and the waste products (carbon dioxide and lactic acid) can be taken away more quickly.

An effective warm-up consists of three parts: pulse raising, stretching and joint mobilization.

- **Pulse raising:** The aim here is to gradually raise the heart rate to the level at which the main activity will take place. This is usually between 60 and 80 per cent of the Maximum Heart Rate (MHR).
- **Stretching:** Most of the stretching should be active stretching, which involves stretching the joints while moving. Examples of active stretches include heel-toe walks and lunge walks. Static or ballistic stretching can lead to injury when the muscles are cold.
- **Joint mobilization:** The aim here is to warm up and move the connective tissues around the joint, such as the tendons and the ligaments. This is done by rotating the joints, for example, when performing hip circles or a bowling action.

England fast bowler James Anderson mobilizes his shoulder joint as part of a warm-up.

A full and effective warm-up should take around 20 minutes, and the performer should only move on to the main part of the session once it has been completed.

Cooling down

The aim of the cool-down is to return the body to its pre-exercise state. In practice this means lowering the heart rate back to resting level and lowering the body temperature to normal. In addition, the cool-down is used to prevent future injury by stretching the muscles so that they become more elastic in the long term.

The cool-down is completed in three phases:

- **Pulse lowering:** The aim here is to gradually reduce the level of demand which is placed on the heart and the cardiovascular system. This is achieved by steadily decreasing the intensity of the workout, most often by starting with a slow jog that gradually reduces to a walking pace. By lowering the pulse rate slowly the heart is kept working for a while, which allows waste products, such as lactic acid and carbon dioxide, to be flushed away from the muscles and replaced with fresh blood, rich in oxygen. If an athlete stops exercising too quickly and doesn't lower their pulse rate gradually, blood pooling is likely to occur. This is when all the waste products and a large amount of the body's total blood volume are left in the working muscles, which can cause cramp, dizziness and fainting.
- **Static stretching:** The aim here is to perform stretches, which are held for 10–16 seconds, of each of the muscles that have been working. This reduces the risk of injury from a torn muscle in the next activity. It can also help to reduce DOMS (Delayed Onset Muscle Soreness), which is the pain felt in muscles 24–48 hours after a strenuous workout.
- **Developmental stretching:** At the very end of the cool-down, while the muscles are still warm but also fairly relaxed, top athletes will complete a series of developmental stretches. Often, these are passive stretches, where a partner slowly forces the muscle past the point of comfort. Over time this leads to the muscle becoming more elastic, like a rubber band, which helps to reduce the likelihood of injury when competing.

BRONZE

1. Design a warm-up and cool-down routine that could be used by a professional athlete in a sport of your choice.

2. Suggest ways in which your warm-up and cool-down routine could be adjusted to meet the needs of professional athletes in other sports.

Principles of fitness training

The principles of fitness training are rules or guidelines that should be followed by anyone taking part in a training programme. The rules are there to make sure that training is effective and worthwhile, and failure to follow these guidelines could result in a lot of wasted effort and little or no gain in physical fitness.

FITT for SPORT

'FITT for SPORT' is a way of remembering the principles of training.
It stands for:

F	–	Frequency	for	**S**	–	Specificity
I	–	Intensity		**P**	–	Progression
T	–	Time		**O**	–	Overload
T	–	Type		**R**	–	Reversibility
				T	–	Training too much (overtraining)

Specificity

All training should be specific to the activity or sport you are taking part in, the type of fitness required for that sport (aerobic or anaerobic) and to the particular muscle groups that sport uses most.

Progression

Training should get harder as the weeks go by and as the body adapts. If an athlete sticks to the same training plan for a long period of time their level of fitness will plateau and no further improvements will occur.

Frequency
You can overload by training more often but be careful not to overtrain.

Intensity
You can overload by training harder each session, by working at a higher heart rate or by increasing the level of resistance.

Time
You can overload by training for longer during each session or, for example, by spending longer on a muscle group.

Type
You can overload by changing the type of training for example, by running up hills rather than on a running track.

Overload

Reversibility

Training too much (overtraining)

...body and the ...ing muscles have to ...posed to a level of ... that is more difficult ...hey are used to. By ...oading the muscles ...earn to adapt by ...ing stronger, so ...hey can cope with ...ased demands in ...ture.

'Use it or lose it' is the key phrase here. If a player stops training, either through injury or boredom, fitness levels will begin to decrease. Fitness declines almost three times as fast as it improves!

Each training session should be followed by a period of 24 hours rest for the muscle groups involved, otherwise muscle fibres can become damaged and injuries can occur.

Planning an exercise programme

Now you understand the basics of a fitness session, the next step is to design an exercise programme for an individual or group. There are many factors to consider here, including the reasons for exercising, the age of the participant(s), the sport that they play and their current level of fitness.

The plan

Every fitness programme needs to start with a long-term goal. The two most common long-term goals are to increase muscle strength or size, and to reduce body fat percentage (to lose excess weight). Other goals might be to increase speed or reduce the time taken to cover a set distance, such as a half-marathon.

Whatever the long-term goal is, it needs to be SMART:

Specific	⟶	such as reducing body fat
Measurable	⟶	such as reducing body fat by a fixed percentage
Achievable	⟶	such as reducing body fat percentage by 4 per cent
Realistic	⟶	such as reducing body fat percentage by 4 per cent (and NOT by 14 per cent)
Time-bound	⟶	such as reducing body fat percentage by 4 per cent (and NOT by 14 per cent) over three months

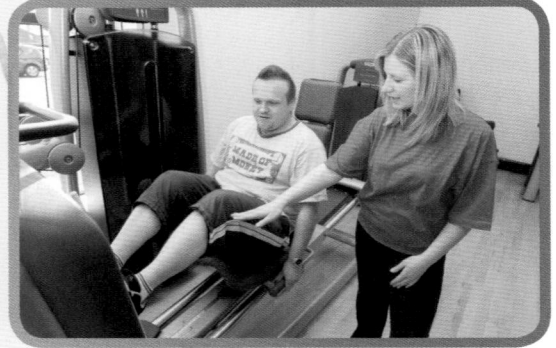

Once the long-term goal has been established, the next step is to decide how it will be achieved and to put in place some medium-term objectives. For example:

Long-term goal (Six months)	Medium-term objective (Three months)
To compete in a 10km road race and to complete the event in under 75 minutes, without stopping or walking.	• Increase cardiovascular endurance • Increase muscular endurance • Increase speed

Close attention should be paid to the principles of training (FITT for SPORT) throughout this process.

Working with the client

Throughout the planning process the most important thing to do is to work with the client. It is no use setting up a programme if it does not suit the needs of the client on a practical day-to-day level. Working with a client is a three-step process:

Step 1: Assess the client's current level of activity and consider their lifestyle.
Step 2: Decide which areas of fitness need to be developed.
Step 3: Set the short-term targets, which will need to be met in order for the client to meet their medium-term objectives and their long-term goals.

Step 1: Assess the client's current level of activity and consider their lifestyle

The most common and effective way of assessing the client's current level of activity and considering their lifestyle is to use a standard screening questionnaire, sometimes called a Physical Activity Readiness Questionnaire or PAR-Q (see page 263). Collecting this information enables the trainer to tailor the programme to the needs of the individual in a safe and effective manner. Just because someone looks fit and healthy does not mean that they are ready to take part in an intensive exercise programme.

Step 2: Decide which areas of fitness need to be developed

Next, determine which components of fitness (see Unit 1: Fitness Testing and Training, pages 4–6) need to be developed to ensure that the client becomes, or remains, fit and healthy. This is likely to include a reduction in the client's body fat content, because this is the most common reason for someone joining a gym. However, for an elite-level athlete it may be much more specific, such as building strength in the abdominal muscles for an international rower or increasing muscular endurance for a professional cyclist. The key is to ensure that any decisions made at this stage are taken in full consultation with the client.

Step 3: Set the short-term targets

The short-term targets will be determined by considering the results of the screening questionnaire, any fitness-test results and, crucially, the long-term goals of the client. For example, if the client's long-term goal is to run a 10km race, then the short-term targets should include something like increasing the duration of the training sessions and decreasing the time taken to run a kilometre.

The client

Clients broadly fall into one of three categories: professional athletes, amateur athletes and non-sports players. However, it is important to remember that each client should be treated as an individual, considering different lifestyles and cultural requirements, levels of fitness, experience and long-term goals. Sometimes it may be appropriate to design an exercise programme for a group of people, such as a football team, but this should only be a starting point. Once the exercise programme has begun, it will need to develop at a rate appropriate to each individual.

Activity selection

The activities built into an exercise programme need to suit the requirements of the individual. Using the FITT for SPORT model will help, because it should ensure that the trainer adheres to the needs of the individual. Other factors must also be taken into account, such as the client's lifestyle, daily routine, likes and dislikes, the availability of equipment, and the money they have available to spend on training. Some activities, such as walking to work, could fit easily into a client's routine. Other activities, such as hill cycling for an elite cyclist, may be more difficult to include because of the potential cost and time involved in travelling to a suitable place to train.

Physical Activity Readiness Questionnaire

Please take a few minutes to answer the following questions.

Name: _____ DOB: __/__/__ Age: _____ Sex: M/F

Occupation: _____ Have you used a gym before? Y/N

Emergency contact: _____

Relationship: _____ Telephone number: _____

....

Part A: Medical considerations

It is our professional duty to ask all participants, no matter what age, to complete the following questions. Please tick all those that apply.

- ❏ Has a family member, under 60, suffered from heart disease, a stroke, raised cholesterol or sudden death?
- ❏ Are you a male over 35 or female over 45 and NOT used to regular vigorous exercise?
- ❏ Are you on any prescribed medication?
- ❏ Have you been hospitalized recently?
- ❏ Are you pregnant?
- ❏ Have you given birth in the last six weeks?
- ❏ Do you have any infections or infectious diseases?

Do you have or have you ever had:

- ❏ Gout ❏ Glandular fever ❏ Heart condition ❏ Stroke
- ❏ Rheumatic fever ❏ Heart murmur ❏ Diabetes
- ❏ Dizziness or fainting ❏ High blood pressure (over 140/90)
- ❏ Epilepsy ❏ Stomach/duodenal ulcer
- ❏ Palpitations or pains in the chest ❏ Hernia
- ❏ Liver or kidney condition ❏ Raised cholesterol/triglycerides
- ❏ Asthma ❏ Arthritis ❏ Muscular pain ❏ Cramps

Do you have any pain or major injuries in the following areas:

- ❏ Neck ❏ Knees ❏ Back ❏ Ankles

Please give details of any conditions:

_____

_____

_____

If you have ticked any of the above, you need a signed medical clearance from your doctor before starting exercise.

Doctor's signature: _____ Date: __/__/__

I warrant that I am physically and mentally well enough to proceed with usage of the facility.

Client's signature: _____ Date: __/__/__

Part B: Lifestyle and current exercise habits

Are you currently exercising regularly? Yes ❏ No ❏

If yes, please give details below:

● Type of exercise: _____

● Frequency of exercise (times per week): 1 ❏ 2–3 ❏ 3–4 ❏ 5+ ❏

Do you currently drink more than the average amount of alcohol per week (21 units for men and 14 units for women (1 unit = ½ pint of beer/cider/lager or 1 small glass of wine)) Yes ❏ No ❏

Do you currently smoke? Yes ❏ No ❏

Are you or is there any possibility that you might be pregnant? Yes ❏ No ❏

Do you know of any other reason why you should not participate in a programme of physical activity? Yes ❏ No ❏

BRONZE

1. Design a set of SMART targets for yourself. They should focus on the first steps you would need to take to achieve excellence in your chosen sport.

2. Design a set of SMART targets for a member of your group. This is even more effective if you choose a partner with whom you rarely work. Remember to use the Physical Activity Readiness Questionnaire.

SILVER

3. Using a combination of SMART targets and your knowledge of the principles of training (FITT for SPORT), design a training programme for your tutor or teacher.

GOLD

4. Suggest ways in which the training programme you designed for Activity 3 could be adapted to suit a professional athlete in the same sport. Justify your decisions.

Unit 14 assignment, part one

Background

As part of the interview process for the job of personal trainer at your local fitness centre, you have been asked to demonstrate:
a) Your knowledge of the principles of training.
b) Your awareness of health and safety issues.
c) Your ability to design training programmes for a variety of clients.

If successful in the first phase of the interview, you will then be asked to lead and review an exercise session for a small group of clients.

GRADING CRITERIA
TO BE ASSESSED

P1, P2, P3
M1, M2
D1, D2

Task

Design a ten-minute presentation or short speech that can be delivered to a panel of three people at the first stage of your interview. You should provide handouts where appropriate and make sure you:

Describe the principles of fitness training (P1).

Describe the health and safety issues an exercise instructor needs to consider for their clients (P2).

Produce exercise programmes for three different types of client (P3).

Explain the principles of fitness training (M1).

Produce detailed exercise programmes for three different types of client (M2).

Relate the principles of fitness training to a range of clients with different needs (D1).

Produce exercise programmes, justifying the range of activities suggested, for three different types of client (D2).

Tackling the assignment

As is often the case in interviews, the easiest way to tackle this assignment is to use a PowerPoint® presentation. However, to be successful in an interview, it is important to stand out from the rest of the applicants. The use of diagrams, photos and video footage in your presentation will help you to achieve this. However, the most important thing is to make sure you meet the objectives that have been set – namely to showcase your knowledge of the principles of fitness training and health and safety issues,

and your ability to design a safe and effective training programme.

If you are aiming for a Merit or a Distinction, then M2 and D2 are best achieved by producing a plan for an amateur, a regional/national competitor and a professional athlete. This will give you the opportunity to produce handouts that showcase your ability to manipulate a training programme in order to suit clients of differing abilities.

Meeting the Pass criteria

Unit 14 assignment, part one

Health and safety, and the principles of training

By Hakan Sur

- Specificity: make the training match the sport.
- Progression: make the training get more difficult over time.
- Overload: the body should be worked harder than normal each session (see FITT).
- Reversibility: use it or lose it.
- Training too much: allow time for rest and recovery or you will get injured.

By using PowerPoint® slides, Hakan's presentation has a visual impact but it would have been better if the information had been supported with drawings or photographs.

Overload (FITT)

The best way to overload the body is to use the FITT principles:

- **F**requency: train more often to increase fitness.
- **I**ntensity: increase the weight/resistance/distance.
- **T**ime: increase the duration of the session.
- **T**ype: change the activity to make it more difficult and to keep it interesting.

The keyword in the Pass criteria is 'describe' but, unfortunately, Hakan has failed to do this in enough detail, and has therefore failed to meet P1 and P2. His work clearly covers the relevant points (the principles of training, and the health and safety issues an exercise instructor needs to consider), but he has done little more than 'state' each one. He needs to look again at his presentation and support his knowledge with examples to prove his understanding.

Hakan would also need to go on to include exercise programmes for three different types of client in order to meet P3.

Health and safety

A trainer should always make sure that their clients are safe when training and are protected from injury. This means that they should get the client to fill in an 'informed consent' form and also consider:

- current fitness levels
- medical history
- previous training experience.

Meeting the Merit and Distinction criteria

Alexandra has shown that she is able to apply the principles of training to a programme and has demonstrated the adjustments that can be made to ensure the training programme is suitable for different clients. I particularly like the way she has used a table format. This shows that she is beginning to work towards the criteria for D1 (Relate the principles of fitness training to a range of clients with different needs), although she needs to explain each of the components in detail to achieve M1 (Explain the principles of fitness training) and then justify her plans in order to achieve D1.

This piece of work has met the criteria for M2 (Produce detailed exercise programmes for three different types of client) at this stage.

BTEC Level 2 Firsts in Sport
Unit 14 assignment, part one
Alexandra Hanover

Training programme for a sprinter

The key components of fitness for a sprinter are power, speed and strength. These enable the athlete to produce acceleration at the start of the race and maintain the speed throughout. As such, any training programme for a sprinter should concentrate on strength training and on sprinting.

Who is this programme suitable for?
The training programme described below is suitable for a range of sprinters, because the FITT principles are variable and can be adjusted to suit all individuals.

Principle		Amateur	Regional	National
Specificity		Strength training for increased power	Strength training for increased power	Strength training for increased power
Progression		Increase the training each month	Increase the training each month	Increase the training each month
Overload	Frequency	2 x per week	3 x per week	4 x per week
	Intensity	85% max lift	90% max lift	95% max lift
	Time/number	6 reps x 3 sets 2 x repeat	6 reps x 5 sets 4 x repeat	8 reps x 7 sets 5 x repeat
	Type	Quads press Calf press Shoulder press Deltoid extension	Quads press Calf press Shoulder press Deltoid extension	Quads press Calf press Shoulder press Deltoid extension Biceps curl Triceps curl
Reversibility		Keep to the schedule	Keep to the schedule	Keep to the schedule
Training too much		Allow rest days	Allow rest days each week	Allow rest days each week

Alexandra does need to make sure that she includes a description of the principles of fitness, and health and safety issues that a fitness instructor needs to consider, in order to meet the criteria for P1 and P2.

Leading an exercise session

One of the most daunting parts of becoming a fitness instructor is leading your first training session; even experienced trainers get nervous and make mistakes. However, the quality of a session and the response of the client can be maximized by following the simple guidelines below. Also, don't forget the golden rule: every client, regardless of their experience, should always complete a screening questionnaire and induction (led by a fully qualified fitness instructor) before taking part in a training programme.

Starting the session

Before the client uses any item of equipment, it must be checked by the trainer first. In practice, this usually involves checking the equipment is safe and working properly before the client arrives.

The trainer should welcome the client and remind them of any emergency procedures before encouraging them to take part in a thorough warm-up. Next, the trainer should explain and demonstrate the correct technique for using each item of equipment to the client. Clients should then be monitored throughout the session to ensure they are exercising safely and effectively.

Lastly, and perhaps most importantly, a trainer needs to motivate their client at this point. This can be achieved by a few carefully chosen words of encouragement, or a discussion about previous training sessions and their successes. Getting the client motivated at the start of the session will increase their chances of successfully achieving their long-term goal.

During the session

Throughout the session, the main role of the trainer is to ensure that all clients are actively engaged, working safely and making progress. To do this, the trainer should be moving around the training area – not sitting at a desk! The trainer needs to make sure that all of the clients are applying the correct techniques for the equipment they are using, while at the same time making regular visual checks of the equipment to make sure it is safe.

Remember: A fitness sesssion is only as good as the trainer leading it!

One of the best things a trainer can do is to appear to be everywhere at all times. This is physically impossible but a good trainer will create the impression of being everywhere by, for example, projecting their voice across a room and shouting words of encouragement to a client at the opposite end of the training area. Another way of creating a presence is to continually talk to clients about what they are doing and adapting their exercises, using the FITT for SPORT model, where necessary. Looking for signs of confusion in clients and then acting before you are asked a question also helps to maintain the illusion of omnipresence. A good trainer can predict problems and act before they become a reality.

Ending the session

At the end of the session, the trainer should always ensure that clients complete a suitable cool-down. Some clients will have completed a strenuous workout while others will have undertaken a gentle training session, so it would be inappropriate for them to complete an identical cool-down. Some clients will be happy to do one on their own but others will need to be led through a suitable routine. Again, this is about knowing the client, their ability and their experience.

During the cool-down, or immediately after it, clients should be given feedback on their training session. This should be specific to individuals and related to what they have – or have not – done. A 'one size fits all' comment, such as "Well done everybody", has little or no value for most clients.

Finally, before the clients leave it is important to allow them an opportunity to ask questions or make comments on the session. If a client feels fully engaged in their training, they are more likely to continue with it.

The last phase of the training session takes place after the clients have left. This involves checking the equipment for damage or wear and tear, and putting it away safely, if necessary, ready to be used next time.

After a training session, a trainer should check all the equipment that has been used.

Reviewing an exercise programme

A good trainer will make sure they get regular feedback about training sessions from their client, because it is just as important for the trainer to listen to the client as it is for the client to follow the trainer's instructions. The client might not be enjoying the training any more or they may be finding it too easy/hard. Their long-term goals might have changed – maybe the event they were training for has been cancelled or the date has changed. All of these things should trigger a trainer into changing an exercise programme.

A key part of the review is to check the clients' views on the trainer's performance, and on health and safety issues. Clients will sometimes make comments about safety issues but they often need to be prompted to comment on a trainer's performance. Trainers should not be afraid to ask clients to give feedback on how the session was managed and controlled. It is only by receiving honest and accurate feedback that a trainer can improve their performance in the future.

Another important part of a review is to re-test the client's fitness levels. This will show whether the clients' fitness levels have increased, stayed the same or, in rare cases, even declined. Whatever the outcome, the exercise programme should be adjusted based on the results of the fitness tests and in consultation with the client.

Modifying an exercise programme

It has been noted several times throughout this unit that the FITT for SPORT principles of training are key when designing an exercise programme. They are also vital when modifying a programme. For example, fitness tests after six weeks may show a huge increase in fitness levels, but there may be little or no change between weeks six and twelve. If this is the case, the training session should be modified, by increasing either the frequency of the training, the intensity of the sessions or the time (duration) of each session. In some cases, it also may be necessary to alter the type of activities taking place – nothing leads to a lack of effort faster than boredom! It is important to remember that the most common reason for the failure of an exercise programme is a lack of adherence by the client; the client doesn't follow the routine correctly all the time.

Developing the skills of the trainer

Just as clients can become bored with the same exercise programme, trainers can become bored with doing and saying the same thing day after day. Trainers also need to keep their skills up to date to enable them to cope with future client needs. The best trainers avoid boredom by continually refining their technique and researching alternative training methods. This is generally done in two ways: by watching more experienced colleagues and by attending training courses. However they choose to do this, the trainer needs to take responsibility for their own personal development and set themselves SMART targets to ensure they meet their professional goals.

BRONZE

1. Get into groups of five and take it in turns to perform the role of the trainer while the remaining four group members act as clients. You should each try to lead an induction session and at least one of three types of training session: a cardiovascular training session, a resistance training session or a circuit training session.

2. Write a short review of your own performance, listing at least three strengths and three areas for development. Then repeat this process for one of the other members of your group.

SILVER

3. Having completed Activity 2, rank your areas for development, placing the things that you need to change most urgently at the top of the list and the things that you need to change least urgently at the bottom. Then, use the Internet to research possible development opportunities for each of your areas for improvement.

Unit 14 assignment, part two

Background

As part of the interview process for the job of personal trainer at your local fitness centre, you have been asked to demonstrate:
a) Your knowledge of the principles of training.
b) Your awareness of health and safety issues.
c) Your ability to design training programmes for a variety of clients.

If successful in the first phase of the interview, you will then be asked to lead and review an exercise session for a small group of clients.

Task

Lead an induction session, a resistance training session, a cardiovascular training session and a circuit training session for a small group of 'clients'. The group should consist of people other than your peer group. Afterwards, you will need to review three of the four sessions, identifying strengths and weaknesses, and establishing a plan for your personal development. You need to:

GRADING CRITERIA TO BE ASSESSED
P4, P5
M3, M4
D3

Assist in instructing induction, resistance training, cardiovascular training and circuit training sessions for selected clients (P4).

Review three different exercise sessions identifying strengths, areas for improvement and personal development needs (P5).

Demonstrate effective communication with selected clients (M3).

Justify identified personal development needs (M4).

Demonstrate competence in monitoring and adapting exercises to suit different client ability levels (D3).

Tackling the assignment

The only way to tackle this assignment is by leading an induction session, a resistance training session, a cardiovascular training session and a circuit training session.

While it is possible to do this in a sports hall, it works best in a properly equipped fitness centre.

Unit 15: Sport and Leisure Facility Operations

Organizational structures and staff responsibilities

In the UK today we have a great range of sport and leisure facilities to choose from and they all need to be carefully managed and well staffed to ensure they operate smoothly.

Facilities

The main aim of most sport and leisure facilities is to encourage people to stay fit and exercise by taking part in competitions or recreational classes, or just working out. There are a range of facilities offering these opportunities:

Leisure centres

Health clubs

Swimming pools

Sports clubs

Gyms

BRONZE

1. Identify a local example of each of the five types of sport and leisure facility.

Organizational structures

All sport and leisure organizations create an organizational structure to show:
- roles (what jobs staff do)
- hierarchy (who is in charge of whom)
- the way in which communication is expected to flow.

The type of organizational structure a sport and leisure facility has depends on the kind of facility it is and the sport and leisure activities it delivers. For example, an outdoor centre does not have the same set-up, people or purpose that a swimming pool has.

Duty manager (weekday)
Responsible for the day-to-day running of the centre during the week, for marketing and managing the gym.

Centre manager
Ensures the centre runs efficiently and meets its targets, and that staff work effectively.

Duty manager (weekend)
Responsible for the day-to-day running of the centre at weekends, for organizing classes and coaches, and ensuring health and safety.

Secretary or administrator
Supports the centre manager and duty managers, facilitating good communication.

Receptionist
Takes bookings and responds to customer queries.

Fitness instructors
Design personal fitness training programmes for clients and advise clients using the gym.

Recreation assistants
Set up and maintain equipment, and ensure the centre is clean.

Coaches
Lead classes and activity sessions.

This is an example of a typical organizational structure for a leisure centre, showing common roles for the staff shown.

Using the structure as a guideline, the managers can establish responsibilities for each role and set up procedures to be followed. For example, they might decide that the receptionist is responsible for all court bookings and set down procedures for what the recreation assistants have to do when setting up the badminton courts.

The organizational structure, and the roles, responsibilities and procedures that it covers, help when recruiting and training new staff. The information can be used to decide on the person specification for a job, which sets out what sort of person is best for a job and the qualifications they need, and what responsibilities will be outlined in the job advertisement. Someone's position in the hierarchy will also determine their opportunities for promotion, their pay scale and who they report to.

BRONZE

2. Create an organizational structure for a swimming pool which has a small gym attached, and identify the roles and responsibilities each person will have.

3. Find out, perhaps by visiting a local sport and leisure facility, if there are any other staff responsibilities or personal skills that could be added to this page.

4. Look at each of the personal skills described above and rate your ability in this area on a scale of one to five, with one being a skill you need to work very hard at developing and five being a skill that you are confident you have mastered.

SILVER

5. Create a person specification for the job of centre manager at a leisure centre which has indoor facilities for a range of sports, and then list the responsibilities this employee would have.

GOLD

6. Design a job advertisement for a recreation assistant at a large multi-activity centre such as Doncaster Dome or Guildford Spectrum. It should outline the responsibilities of the role, the requirements of the candidate, information on who the successful applicant will report to, the hours they will work and their pay scale.

Staff teams

All sport and leisure facilities are run by teams of staff. Each team has a different role to play, but they all work together to give customers a good experience so that they return and help the facility grow its customer numbers. Here are details of the typical responsibilities which different staff teams have:

Staff team	Typical responsibilities
Management	Day-to-day control of operations
Maintenance	Upkeep of machinery, equipment and buildings
Instructors	Coaching, training and assisting customers/participants
Lifeguards	Lifesaving and pool cleaning
Reception	Telephone enquiries, taking bookings and general administration
Grounds staff	Upkeep of gardens and playing surfaces, including keeping them free of litter
Security	Patrolling key areas, monitoring CCTV and responding to problems
Cleaning	Cleaning toilets, changing rooms and foyers

Personal skills

Most sport and leisure facilities will expect staff to be flexible in the way that they work and employ a series of personal skills, regardless of the staff team they belong to.

Timekeeping: Arriving at work on time, perhaps a little early if time is needed to change into work clothes, and not leaving early or exceeding allocated break times.

Professionalism: Doing your work competently. This means being qualified to do your work and carrying it out effectively and efficiently.

Accountability: Taking responsibility for the things you do, when they turn out well **and** when they don't turn out so well.

Reporting to line management: Reporting issues at work, both good and bad, to your line manager (also known as your boss or your supervisor).

Personal presentation: Wearing clothes suitable for the work to be done, or a uniform if it is required, and always looking tidy.

Financial duties: Receiving and handling cash from customers and keeping records in line with procedures, as well as ensuring that cash is kept securely. It is also important to keep within your budget if you are authorized to purchase supplies.

Communication skills: Demonstrating good verbal and written communication skills and good body language with customers, colleagues and managers.

Key holder duties: Taking responsibility for opening and closing the facility if this is part of your job role or if you are asked to do so in special circumstances.

Attitude: Being pleasant to colleagues and visitors; being motivated to carry out routine tasks and maybe even willing to do that bit extra when called on.

Record keeping: Keeping good records so that accurate information about customers, yourself or your work is kept for future reference. This includes accident reports, certificates achieved, courses attended and lesson plans if you are a coach or instructor.

Continuing Professional Development (CPD): Updating your skills on a continuous basis so that you have all the necessary skills and qualifications to work in IT or to work with people with disabilities for example.

Tidying: Keeping an eye open for things that may have been left out by colleagues or customers and which need tidying away, such as bats and balls, towels, noticeboards, files and litter.

Unit 15 assignment, part one

Background

Imagine you have just been promoted to the role of duty manager in a large leisure centre in your area. The centre manager is also new to his job and has asked you to brief him on his staff and their roles and responsibilities.

Your leisure centre has a sports hall and a small hall which is used as a flexible play area, two squash courts, a spinning room and a gym, as well as a meeting room, changing rooms and a reception area in a small foyer which also contains three vending machines. Outside there is a car park and a single multi-play area. There are four main staff teams:

- Three duty managers who work shifts and normally appoint new staff in conjunction with the centre manager.
- Three receptionists who work part-time taking bookings. They also carry out all other administration tasks, including organizing job advertisements.
- Four fitness instructors for the gym, with two on duty at any one time.
- Eight recreation assistants who also carry out the cleaning and perform basic coaching and maintenance tasks.

Task

Prepare a chart to show the organizational structure of the leisure centre and annotate it to show the responsibilities of the four staff teams. The briefing should:

GRADING CRITERIA TO BE ASSESSED
P1, P2
M1
D1

PASS

Describe the organizational structure of a selected sport and leisure facility (P1).

Describe the responsibilities of four different staff teams from a selected sport and leisure facility (P2).

MERIT

Explain the responsibilities of four different staff teams in a selected sport and leisure facility (M1).

DISTINCTION

Evaluate the responsibilities of four different staff teams in a selected sport and leisure facility (D1).

Tackling the assignment

One straightforward way to tackle this assignment would be to use a page from a large flip chart to mark out the organizational structure in the centre of the page, with boxes for each job role and lines to show who manages whom. You could then add smaller boxes describing, explaining and evaluating the responsibilities of the staff teams. However, if your IT skills are good, you might decide to create your organizational structure in PowerPoint® and add hyperlinks to take you to the information about the staff teams.

Remember, you don't have to base your briefing on the scenario described above. You could base it on a sport and leisure facility in your local area.

Meeting the Pass criteria

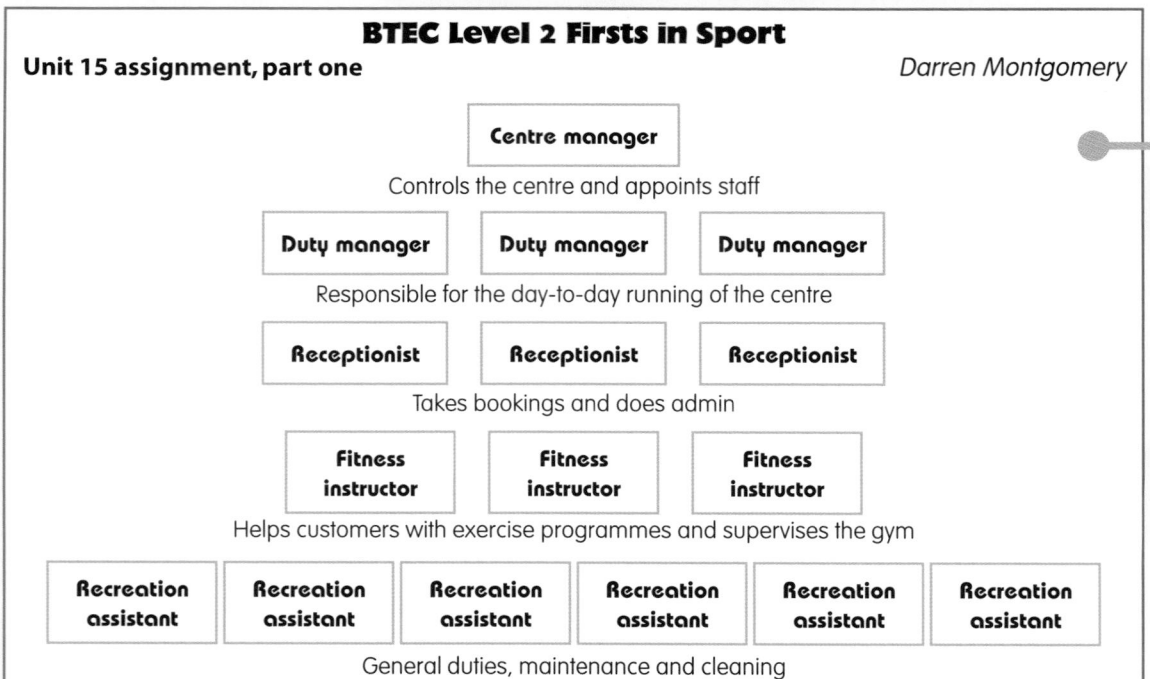

BTEC Level 2 Firsts in Sport

Unit 15 assignment, part one *Darren Montgomery*

Centre manager
Controls the centre and appoints staff

Duty manager | **Duty manager** | **Duty manager**
Responsible for the day-to-day running of the centre

Receptionist | **Receptionist** | **Receptionist**
Takes bookings and does admin

Fitness instructor | **Fitness instructor** | **Fitness instructor**
Helps customers with exercise programmes and supervises the gym

Recreation assistant | **Recreation assistant** | **Recreation assistant** | **Recreation assistant** | **Recreation assistant** | **Recreation assistant**
General duties, maintenance and cleaning

> Darren has quite a lot more work to do before he meets the criteria for a Pass. He needs to add a paragraph describing what his organizational structure represents, and add the lines of responsibility connecting the different staff teams and describing who reports to whom.

Meeting the Merit and Distinction criteria

BTEC Level 2 Firsts in Sport

Unit 15 assignment, part one
Eva Bronlinski

Duty manager: As the head of the organization when on duty, the duty manager is responsible for all staff and customers. He or she will have a set of procedures to follow for most situations, including finance, staffing, customer relations and running activities. Any operational issues will be reported up to the duty manager by other staff through the chain of command. Leisure centres usually employ more than one duty manager and sometimes as many as three working in shifts. For example, one duty manager could be responsible for the day, one for the evening and one for weekends.

Receptionist: The receptionist holds a key communications role in the organization, reporting up to the duty manager, down to the recreation assistants and out to customers. Each receptionist seems to work for one duty manager which means that they will have a close relationship, but if there were changes to the rotas it might take people time to adjust to the working style of their new colleague. The receptionists need to be able to multi-task and have good customer service and IT skills. They need to follow booking procedures carefully to avoid double-bookings.

> Eva has evaluated the responsibility of two staff teams by assessing the importance of the roles in the context of the smooth running of the whole centre and has therefore begun to meet the criteria for D1. To fully meet the criteria she must do the same for two more staff teams.

> Eva has explained – provided detailed descriptions of – two staff teams but, to fully meet the criteria for M1, she needs to do the same for two more staff teams.

Providing a safe and secure environment

It is a requirement under the law for every organization to care for the people on its premises. This is called a 'duty of care'. So it is vitally important that all sport and leisure facilities have procedures in place to provide a safe and secure environment for their staff and visitors.

Checking facilities

As part of their responsibilities staff will normally be required to check the facilities. They are looking for hazards, such as wet and slippery floors and broken equipment. Think of the injury a broken cable on a resistance machine or a faulty electrical switch could cause. If a member of staff spots a problem, it is their responsibility to report it to their line manager so that the problem can be fixed immediately or warning signs can be put up and repair scheduled.

Some checks, especially in high-risk areas such as around a swimming pool, will be frequent. Other checks, such as checking the toilets and changing rooms, may take place every two hours, while a number of checks, such as equipment checks, might be carried out once a day. Checking that the alarms are on and the doors are locked will probably be the final check of the day.

Risk assessment

Checking and spotting hazards is part of the risk assessment process, which all organizations are required by law to carry out.

6. Review your decisions regularly and make changes if necessary

1. Identify the risk (for example, a wet and slippery floor in the changing room)

2. Decide who might be harmed and how (for example, children in the changing room are at risk of slips and falls)

5. Record your findings and implement them

4. Decide how to prevent or reduce the level of risk, implementing control measures (for example, place warning signs in the affected area immediately and mop the affected area regularly)

3. Identify the level of risk (for example, the level of risk is high because it is very likely that the hazard will cause harm)

BRONZE

1. Complete a risk assessment for an activity area within a sport and leisure facility that you know well. An example of a completed risk assessment form which you could use to help you can be found in Unit 5, on page 112.

Legislation and regulations

UK Acts of Parliament and EU regulations exist to make sure that a number of aspects of operations in all facilities are safe. Here are the most common ones that apply to sports centres:

Health and safety at work
The Health and Safety at Work etc. Act 1974 is just one of the pieces of legislation that protects the health and safety of staff, visitors and suppliers. It covers virtually all workplaces, including offices, halls, pools, gyms and clubs. It states that reasonable protective measures must be in place to make sure that everyone is safe and not in danger while they are on the premises. The rules apply to employers and employees who have a responsibility to look after their own health and safety.

Reporting diseases
The Reporting of Incidents and Disease and Dangerous Occurrences Regulations 1995 state that things like outbreaks of food poisoning or swine flu have to be reported so that measures can be put in place to make the facility more hygienic or prevent the disease spreading.

Reporting dangerous occurrences
The Reporting of Incidents and Disease and Dangerous Occurrences Regulations 1995 require a manager to report dangerous situations which occur, such as scaffolding collapsing while repairs are being carried out to the sports hall roof.

First aid
The Health and Safety (First-Aid) Regulations 1981 state that trained first-aid staff must be on duty all the time a sport and leisure facility is open. Fixed and mobile first-aid boxes must also be on display and easily accessible. They should also be checked after they are used, to make sure they are fully stocked. Most leisure centres will have a first-aid room too.

Manual handling
The Manual Handling Operations Regulations 1992 govern what staff can lift and carry, how they lift and carry and how best to avoid back injuries and other accidents. It is particularly relevant in sports centres where members of staff regularly move equipment around.

Working hours
The Working Time Regulations 1998 cover the hours that staff are allowed to work. They apply to full-time and part-time jobs and detail the hours under-18s can work.

BRONZE

2. Copy the plan of the layout of a small private sports club and position the following security devices in the most appropriate place on the plan, then explain what each device is designed to prevent:

- Three CCTV cameras
- Sensors for the windows
- Two pressure pads
- One laser
- Two panic alarms
- Two swipe card entry systems
- One voice-activated entry system
- Five fire exit signs.

3. Describe five security situations which might occur at a swimming pool.

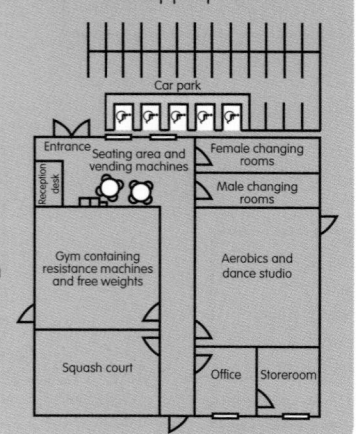

Security

In operational terms, a sport and leisure facility should have procedures and mechanisms in place to provide a secure environment for staff and visitors and to prevent the following anti-social behaviour:

- **Violence:** This can be verbal abuse and threats from rude customers or physical assaults.
- **Theft:** This includes stealing by staff and visitors, and stealing from the leisure centre or stealing from people at the leisure centre.
- **Fraud:** Fraud takes place when a person or thing pretends to be something it is not. Sometimes people sell fake tickets or use a membership card that doesn't belong to them, and this is fraud.
- **Vandalism:** Graffiti or breaking into vending machines are the most common forms of vandalism at a leisure centre.

Procedures

Staff and, in certain circumstances, customers need procedures to follow to ensure a safe and secure environment and in case an incident happens. A good operational plan will have tried and tested procedures in place to cover all eventualities.

Here are some of the most important procedures:

Fire
How to locate, choose and use a fire extinguisher; using fire doors; what the alarm sounds like and where to assemble.

Safety signage
What the colour coding means; which signs to follow when evacuating.

Security
Personal security: what to do if threatened; how to report problems.
Facility security: how to open and close the building and activate and deactivate alarms; how to check all rooms; how to report problems.

Money
Taking and securing cash; giving receipts; dealing with credit card transactions and refunds.

First aid
Checking and refilling first-aid boxes; reporting and recording incidents and accidents.

Property
How to deal with lost property; how to check inventory or stock.

Surveillance
Closed-Circuit Television (CCTV): checking cameras are operational; noting problematic activities.

Staff identification
ID cards or signing in; use of keys; wearing of uniforms for identity.

Emergencies
Evacuation procedures; marshalling duties for guiding customers safely off the premises.

Maintenance
Routine and non-routine tasks for equipment, buildings (including equipment that monitors the atmosphere such as air conditioning, extractor fans and vents) and playing surfaces; environmental systems.

BRONZE

1. Choose one of the procedures outlined above and describe in detail what it is and how real organizations put it into practice.

2. Carry out some research on the location of safety equipment and then add the following to the plan of the sports centre you drew for Activity 2 on the previous page: fire extinguishers, fire assembly point(s), fire alarms, emergency lighting, first-aid boxes, lockers and a safe.

SILVER

3. Choose two parts of a sport and leisure facility and explain how procedures help to ensure safety and security there.

The busiest parts of a sports and leisure facility need special attention to ensure that operations there run smoothly. The hotspots and the procedures needed are:

Car park   Spaces for disabled visitors and parents with young children near the door; surveillance; clear access for emergency vehicles.

Reception   Queuing procedures; keeping information up to date; staffing.

Changing rooms   Cleaning; checking for lost property; checking for damage.

Main areas of activity   These can be wet or dry and include a pool, a sports hall, a gym and an outdoor pitch: checking they are clear; checking they are litter free; checking equipment is ready and safe to use; cleaning.

Unit 15 assignment, part two

Background

Continuing in your role as a newly-promoted duty manager for a sport and leisure centre, you have been asked to create an induction document for a team of temporary staff which the centre employs over the summer holidays. Most of the temporary staff will be students who have basic coaching and leadership awards and some experience of working with children.

GRADING CRITERIA TO BE ASSESSED
P3, P4
M2

Task

Create a booklet or presentation to outline the most important aspects of safe and secure facility operations. It should contain:

 **PASS**

A description of why it is important to provide a safe and secure environment (P3).

A description of the procedures used to ensure a safe and secure environment in areas within a selected sport and leisure facility (P4).

 **MERIT**

An explanation of how procedures help to provide safe and secure sport and leisure facilities (M2).

Tackling the assignment

Regardless of whether you choose to produce a booklet or a presentation, it is important to be creative in the way that you present the material to keep your audience interested. You also need to pay attention to details to cover all the points required, make sure your descriptions and explanations are very clear, and include examples of best practice.

You might be able to base your booklet or presentation on a local leisure centre or the sports centre at your school or college. You could interview someone who works there or arrange a visit so that you can have a look around behind the scenes. You may also be able to find some useful information to help you on the Internet.

In this context, a description is a clear outline of what you know. An explanation requires you to explain why your description is as it is.

Meeting the Pass criteria

BTEC Level 2 Firsts in Sport

Unit 15 assignment, part two   Mohammed Al-Jerez

Why it is important to provide a safe and secure environment?

Sports organizations and leisure centres have to make sure that their customers and staff are safe while they are playing and changing. They must also make sure that property and possessions don't go missing, for example, by having lockers. It is also important to make sure fitness equipment is not broken. The chlorine level in swimming pools needs to be correct and the pool must be cleaned to kill germs.

Procedure for taking and securing money

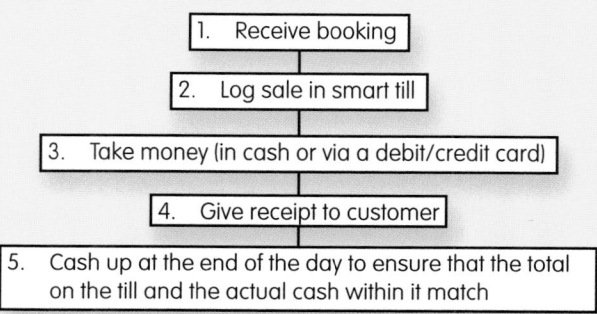

1. Receive booking
2. Log sale in smart till
3. Take money (in cash or via a debit/credit card)
4. Give receipt to customer
5. Cash up at the end of the day to ensure that the total on the till and the actual cash within it match

> Mohammed has described what a safe and secure environment looks like but he hasn't described **why** it is important to provide one. To meet the criteria for P3, he needs to describe what might happen if a safe and secure environment wasn't provided for customers and staff. For example, if there are no procedures in place for taking and securing money, staff will be more likely to be falsely accused of taking it.

> Mohammed has provided a detailed description of the procedure for taking and securing money. To fully meet the criteria for P4 he needs to describe the other procedures used to provide a safe and secure environment in areas of a selected sport and leisure facility. He also needs to clearly note which areas of the sport and leisure facility the procedures apply to.

Meeting the Merit criteria

BTEC Level 2 Firsts in Sport
Unit 15 assignment, part two
David Verras

The procedure	How the procedure helps to provide safe and secure sport and leisure facility
Following directions for safe moving and lifting of equipment.	Reduces accidents and injuries to staff because it ensures that everyone knows how to lift and move the equipment safely.
In the event of a fire the alarm should be sounded and the building evacuated via the fire exits.	Prevents deaths because it ensures that the building can be evacuated quickly and safely.
Providing lockers and notices to remind visitors about security	Keeps possessions safe because the centre may get a bad reputation and customers may stop using it if possessions aren't secure. Regular thefts will also generate a lot of extra work and may increase the cost of insurance.

> Explanations often include the word 'because', so it is clear that David has explained how the procedures ensure the safety and security of sport and leisure facilities. However, to fully meet the criteria for M2, David's explanations would benefit from a bit more detail in places. What are the implications of lifting and moving equipment safely, for example?

Customer service

The concept of customer service can be defined as an organization's ability to meet the needs and wants of its customers in a positive manner, thereby creating a satisfying experience for the customer. Good customer service, it might be argued, is the most important thing that staff can provide on behalf of the organization they work for, because it makes it more likely that customers will come back.

The importance of good customer service

Giving satisfaction is the primary reason for offering good customer service, but it brings other benefits which make it important:

Increased sales
Satisfied customers buy more goods and services.

Increased profits
The purchase of more goods and services means more income for a facility and, hopefully, more profits.

Better image
The image of the facility can be enhanced by satisfied customers recommending it to their friends.

Better reputation
A good reputation means top-quality staff want to work at a facility. It might attract new business too.

Competitive edge
All of these factors help make a facility more popular and give it a competitive edge over others in the area.

Methods used to maintain business

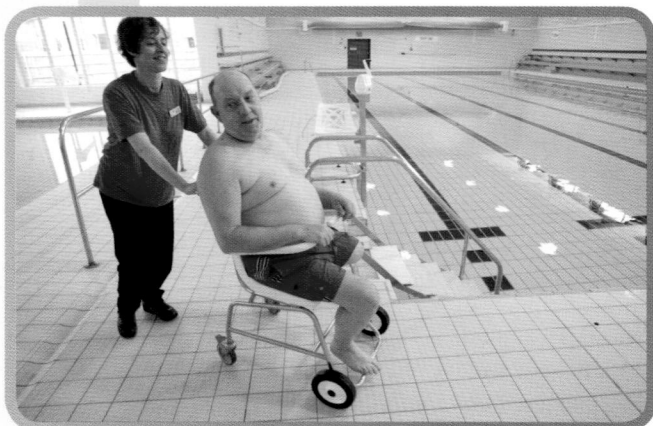

Providing services for customers with specific needs will help to maintain good customer relations.

There are other business practices, which complement good customer service, that help a business grow and flourish:

- **Creating good customer relations:** This includes giving discounts to loyal customers who use the facilities regularly, sending customers promotional mailshots about offers or events you know they will like, and asking for and acting on customers' suggestions for improvements.
- **Maintaining positive relationships with customers:** Welcoming regular customers by name, asking how they are in passing, always being courteous and saying 'see you again' when they leave all help to maintain a positive relationship with customers.

Customers

Segmenting customers, dividing them up into types, and making sure the needs of each type are fully met, is another way of 'getting it right' with customers.

Groups
For example, teams needing a practice session, clubs wanting to play matches and school groups.

Individuals
For example, overweight ladies, people on GP referral schemes and male bodybuilders.

People of different age groups
For example, children under 12, teenagers, 20–40-year-old males and the over-60s.

Types of customers

People with specific needs
For example, people with disabilities, pregnant women and parents with babies.

People of different cultures
For example, Muslim women and Chinese visitors.

The needs of many types of customers can be anticipated. For example, all customers might need:

- Information about activities, events, opening and closing times and prices.
- Assistance with finding their way around.
- Advice about buying products such as sports kit.
- Advice about purchasing services such as coaching sessions.

Procedures

Once customers have been segmented and their needs identified, procedures can be put in place so that all their needs are fully met. Remember, though, that it is almost impossible to identify all the needs of all customers, and responding positively to needs you have never come across before and don't have a procedure for is all part of good customer service.

It is also important to have procedures in place to cover more awkward situations with customers, especially when they complain. Staff should be able to use their common sense to deal with minor complaints. For example, if a customer complains about the pools of water in the changing rooms, an apology can be offered and the water can be quickly mopped up. However, for more serious complaints, about the theft of money or belongings for example, the manager will usually have to be called and a formal report completed.

The way in which a member of staff responds to a customer who is complaining is very important. If the staff member is polite, has a positive attitude, acknowledges the customer's complaint and tries to seek a solution, then the customer is more likely to leave the leisure centre feeling satisfied. On the other hand, if the member of staff is sullen, unhelpful and isn't interested in resolving the customer's complaint, then the customer is more likely to get angry. A complaining customer will make a very quick judgement about whether a member of staff is going to help them, so first impressions are very important. Smartly dressed staff, who have good personal hygiene, are going to make a much better impression on customers.

The way in which members of staff respond to each other is also very important, particularly in front of customers, and organizations also need to have procedures to deal with disagreements between staff.

BRONZE

1. For each of the types of customer listed, describe what you think their main needs will be when visiting a fitness suite for the first time, to ensure they leave happy and plan to return.

2. What procedures would you put in place to ensure that staff know how to deal with the following situations appropriately?
a) A person in a wheelchair comes into the leisure centre where you work and asks about using the gym.
b) A group of Muslim women want to book the dance studio for a practice. It is available on Saturday and Sunday, but the centre is hosting a men's five-a-side football tournament on the same weekend.

3. Look at the two cartoons below. They both show a customer complaining. Role play both scenarios with a partner twice, showing bad customer service first and then good customer service. Make sure you both take on the role of the customer.

These boys are making much too much noise!

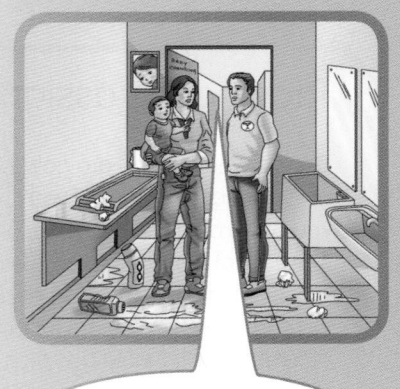

This changing room is filthy!

Unit 15 assignment, part three

Background

In your role as a duty manager for a sport and leisure centre, the centre manager was so pleased with your materials on safety and security that he has asked you to do the same for customer service training: create an induction document for a team of temporary staff which the centre employs over the summer holidays. Most of the temporary staff will be students who have basic coaching and leadership awards and some experience of working with children.

GRADING CRITERIA TO BE ASSESSED
P5, P6 M3

Task

Create a booklet or presentation to outline the procedures at the centre for ensuring good customer service and why it is so important. You should:

Identify procedures used to provide effective customer service in a selected sport and leisure facility (P5).

Describe the importance of providing effective customer service in a selected sport and leisure facility (P6).

Explain the importance of effective customer service, and procedures used to achieve it, in a selected sport and leisure facility (M3).

Tackling the assignment

Decide whether you are going to create a booklet or a presentation. Perhaps, if you chose the booklet route last time, you could opt for a presentation this time. The task specifies that you take all your examples from one sport and leisure facility, so you also need to decide if you are going to choose the same one as you did for part two of the assignment or a different one. It would be helpful if you visited the facility you select to assess good practices in action.

The section where you identify, and possibly also explain, the procedures used to provide effective customer service should cover different customer types, what staff must do to deal with incidents and complaints and the professionalism of staff. The section where you describe, and possibly also explain, the importance of providing effective customer service needs to cover the benefits customers, staff and the organization might gain from great customer care.

Meeting the Pass criteria

The procedures Emily has identified so far are very good but, unless the leisure centre that Emily has chosen to base her assignment on only has a swimming pool, she has more work to do to meet the criteria for a Pass. She needs to describe the customer service procedures that take place in other parts of the facility. She should, for example, describe the complaints procedure in detail because it is one of the most important customer service procedures.

Procedures for staff to follow when working with customers at the swimming pool

- Booking customers in for a lesson: Make sure that you collect all their details and fees for lessons, and that they know when the lessons start and finish.
- Giving new customers a tour of the facility: Tours should be carried out with groups of visitors to save time. Make sure everyone in the group can hear your explanations, ask for questions at each stopping point and return to reception at the end of the tour.
- Advising a disabled swimmer: Make sure they are comfortable talking to you about their needs, use a sheet of paper to note down specific needs and consult with other staff on when they can swim.
- Dealing with a complaint: All complaints should be dealt with following the leisure centre's complaints procedure.

The importance of following procedures when working at the swimming pool

1. Following procedures makes staff more effective.
2. Customers are more easily satisfied if staff are efficient.
3. Customers will return if they are satisfied. This will increase sales and hopefully profit.
4. The reputation and image of the leisure centre is enhanced if customers are happy.

The information Emily has provided about the importance of providing effective customer service is useful, but there are lots more advantages to good customer service for her to add before she achieves the criteria for a Pass. It might help her to break these advantages down into three groups: advantages to the customers, advantages to staff and advantages to the organization.

It is great to see Emily thinking about different customer types and providing information about the procedures for dealing with disabled swimmers. I would like to see her go a step further though and think about other customer types. Does the facility she is examining have special procedures in place if children want to go swimming?

Meeting the Merit criteria

Good customer service

Good customer service has many dimensions to it and provides many benefits:

1. Giving customer **satisfaction** is the main aim of good customer service and this has to be done consistently. My visit to a local sports centre showed that consistently good customer service was needed in order for the centre to achieve its Quest award. I visited the centre on three different occasions, like a mystery visitor, to see if they were always good at customer service and I made sure I talked to different staff every time. They were always very helpful.
2. Good customer service can mean **increased sales**. If staff leading sessions are caring and motivating, participants are more likely to want to come back for more.
3. Customer service techniques can be used to **maintain business**.
4. Good customer service is important for the success and **profitability** of the centre. More happy people returning means more income.
5. The **image and reputation** of a centre can be greatly improved amongst customers if they receive good service because they will recommend the place. If they do not have a good experience they may well gossip about how bad it is and put other people off going. On my visits to a local sports centre, I never heard anyone say anything bad about the centre.
6. If there is a lot of competition between sport and leisure facilities in an area, the one with the best customer service might have a **competitive edge** over the others.

It is good to see Joe mentioning the local sports centre he visited because the criteria ask for the information about customer service to be described or explained with reference to a selected sport and leisure facility.

Joe has made a good start. For each point he has made, he has explained why effective customer service is so important, rather than just stating – or describing – why it is important. The only exception to this is point three, where he needs to explain how customer service techniques can be used to maintain business and why this could be important for a sport and leisure facility.

To fully meet the criteria for M3, Joe needs to finish explaining why effective customer service is important to customers and the business. He should also explain why it is important for staff. He then needs to go on to explain the procedures that can be used to achieve good customer service, and this is where the research he carried out at his local sports centre will come in really useful.

Setting up, checking, taking down and storing equipment used for sports activities

Some of the most important procedures in a sports and leisure facility involve the setting up, checking, taking down and storage of equipment.

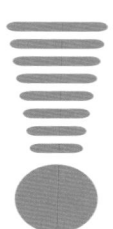

Remember:

It is important to get help setting up larger pieces of equipment, such as trampolines, so that you do not hurt yourself and someone else can check the settings.

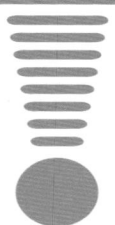

Remember:

Keep an inventory of all equipment removed from the store and check it back in again.

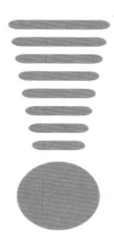

Remember:

It is good to anticipate what might be difficult or go wrong so that you can brief anyone who is helping you accordingly.

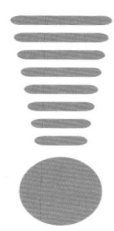

Remember:

It is good practice to have a storage plan on the wall close to the light switch to help staff find and return equipment quickly and safely.

Set up

Manufacturers will have recommended ways of setting up their equipment and it is important to follow their instructions. If necessary, managers can put on training sessions so that new staff can learn and practise what to do.

Following correct procedures will save time and reduce accidents. The consequences can be quite severe if equipment is not set up properly and it collapses and causes injury: staff or managers can be sued if it is found that they have been negligent (have acted carelessly), press coverage of accidents can damage a facility's image and insurance costs will go up.

Check

Equipment should be checked before it is used, while it is in use and again before it is put away:

Staff should check all parts are there and in working order as the equipment is assembled.  Once assembled, another check should be performed quickly just before use. → One further check whilst the equipment is in use is advisable, in case anything has worked loose, so that any alterations can take place. → While the equipment is in use staff should observe that participants are using it safely, that spectators are at a suitable distance, and organizers are ensuring the health and safety of participants. → A final check should be made before the equipment is put away, and any damaged equipment should be removed or repaired. Make sure that participants pay for any damages.

Take down

After all participants, spectators and organizers are clear of the equipment, take down can begin. Staff need to ensure they have assistance when appropriate and that they can manoeuvre the equipment back into storage safely. Again, it is vitally important to follow correct procedures. Improvisation or short cuts usually leads to disaster!

Store

You will, no doubt, have seen an untidy sports storeroom at some time, with kit, balls and general clutter all over the floor so that it is difficult to see what is what. This is why it is important to have an effective storage system with:
- Clear labelling so that you can find items quickly.
- Suitable containers, nets and shelves to hold the equipment so that it isn't all over the place.
- Clear access so that you can get in and out of the store and use it properly.
- Maximum use made of the space, without over-packing, so that you can fit as much as possible in.
- Secure locks to deter thieves.
- Heavy items stored on the floor for safety. Lifting heavy items off a high shelf can be very dangerous if they are dropped.
- Good lighting so that you can see what you want and don't hurt yourself getting it or putting it away.

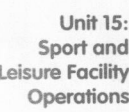

Badminton practice sessions: nets, rackets and shuttles.

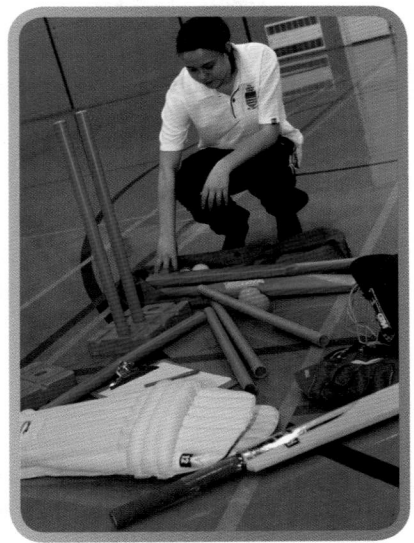

Quick cricket indoors: several bats of different weights and sizes, indoor-cricket balls, pads, wickets, gloves, helmets (if players are novices or fearful) and a scorebook or scoreboard.

Review

Reviewing equipment set up, take down and storage can benefit a leisure centre and its staff, by helping to create quicker, safer and easier procedures. The review can be done individually or as a team.

Two types of review are common:

- A **formative review** takes place during training sessions or training as staff familiarize themselves with what is required. Formative feedback helps to shape and improve the way that individuals work and the way that teams work together.
- A **summative review** usually takes place after an event and assesses a team or an individual member of staff's achievements in relation to the tasks set.

Feedback

For a review to effectively cover all procedures, feedback needs to be gathered from a variety of sources, including:

- participants
- colleagues who helped or who have done set up, take down and storage before
- observers, such as a supervisor.

Feedback should always be given sensitively and should always be constructive.

Recommendations

Once feedback has been gathered, it can be used by supervisors and individual members of staff to identify their strengths and areas for development. Supervisors can make recommendations to their staff on things they need to improve and these recommendations can be built into future training sessions and staff appraisal and development schemes. Usually, if there are few areas for improvement, an action plan with SMART targets is devised to give structure to the recommendations.

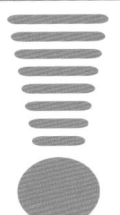

Remember:

SMART targets are Specific, Measurable, Achievable, Realistic and Time-bound.

Action points for some members of staff might focus on personal development, building their inter-personal skills and developing their confidence for example. Others might need to identify where they can get the specialist support they need, to develop their technical capabilities or lifting techniques for example.

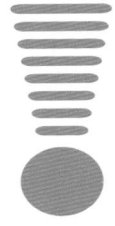

Remember:

Improving your skills and capabilities might mean a pay rise, promotion or more recognition and responsibilities.

BRONZE

1. Create a procedure to help someone set up, check, take down and store the equipment needed for a trampolining club or a table tennis club.

2. Review the procedure your partner created for Activity 1. Remember to make sure that your feedback is sensitive and constructive.

SILVER

3a) Create a checklist that you can use to assess a person setting up, checking, taking down and storing a range of sports equipment.

b) Observe someone setting up, checking, taking down and storing sports equipment and review their performance using your checklist to gather feedback for them.

c) Give the person you observed your feedback and recommend ways in which they can improve.

Unit 15 assignment, part four

Background

You have got a new job as a recreation assistant at your local sport and leisure centre. You are responsible for setting up, checking, taking down and storing all the equipment that customers want to use while they are at the centre.

GRADING CRITERIA TO BE ASSESSED
P7, P8
M4, M5
D2

Task

As part of your training, you are required to demonstrate to your supervisor that you are able to set up, check, take down and store a range of different equipment. Your supervisor would also like you to review your performance, so that she is confident that you will be able to train the next recreation assistant that is appointed. You are required to:

Set up, check, take down and store equipment for three different sports activities with tutor support (P7).

Review your own performance in the setting up, checking, taking down and storage of equipment for three different sports activities (P8).

Independently set up, check, take down and store equipment for three different sports activities (M4).

Review your own performance in the setting up, checking, taking down and storage of equipment for three different sports activities, making suggestions for your own development (M5).

Review your own performance in the setting up, checking, taking down and storage of equipment for three different sports activities, justifying suggestions relating to your own development (D2).

Tackling the assignment

The first part of this assignment is practical. Your teacher or tutor can help you if you are aiming for a Pass, but if you are aiming for a Merit it is important that you complete the set up, check, take down and storage of the equipment by yourself. It would help you prepare for the assignment if you compiled a checklist of everything that needs to be done, so you can tick each task off as you complete it. You can also make notes on your checklist straight after the practical, to help remind you of your strengths and areas for improvement when you come to review your performance.

Meeting the Pass criteria

BTEC Level 2 Firsts in Sport

Unit 15 assignment, part four Lois Turnbull

Sport one: Trampolining

Setting up

Based on formative feedback from other students who were learning how to set up the trampoline, I didn't move it into a safe position with good height clearance. That meant that I hadn't really followed the correct procedure. I got it right on my second attempt.

Checking

Other students had to remind me to check that it was locked in a safe position the first time, and I noted this down for next time. I did remember to check around the trampoline between performers and to adjust the safety mat too, which is good practice, and the participants thanked me for doing it.

Taking down

I completed the take down perfectly. I didn't make any mistakes and my tutor complemented me as he was watching.

Storing

I did require help from other people to move the trampoline, but I think that was good because it is large and heavy.

> Lois has structured the review correctly and has noted both her good summative performance and her not-so-good formative performance. She has also mentioned feedback from several different sources. To fully achieve the criteria for P7, she could add a summary of her overall performance and needs to complete the process for two other sports activities.

Meeting the Merit and Distinction criteria

BTEC Level 2 Firsts in Sport
Unit 15 assignment, part four
Philip Bradshaw

Sport two: Basketball

Set up: In the formative stages I was slower than my colleagues at swinging the backboards out from the wall. I was trying to do it perfectly, so took my time. I took care to check that the retaining wires were firmly anchored to the wall fitting. To improve my performance I should try to speed-up the process, but not at the cost of damaging the equipment. I could also use a pole to help with the pushing.

Checks: Once in place the backboards need to be checked. My colleagues watched me demonstrate because our tutor said that I was meticulous and they could learn from me. I checked the anchor point, nets and the position of the boards over the playing area. I suppose I could have also suggested that the retaining bolts were checked as well. And it would be worth checking everything again at half-time to ensure that it was still secure after the impacts during play.

> Philip has made suggestions for his development but he could go further and establish an action plan in order to fully meet the criteria for M5. The action plan could contain SMART targets focusing, for example, on how he plans to tackle speeding-up his performance.

> To meet the criteria for D2, Philip needs to justify the suggestions he makes for his development. He could do this by referring to feedback from his tutor, participants and fellow students to explain why he thinks it is important to improve in the way he has outlined. For example, he might justify the need to speed-up his performance by explaining that participants waiting to begin a game of basketball began to get restless while they waited for him to set up the backboards.

> Obviously this is just part of Philip's work, so he needs to complete it to fully meet the criteria. He needs to review his performance taking down and storing the basketball equipment and he needs to review his performance setting up, checking, taking down and storing the equipment for two other sports activities.

Unit 16: Leading Outdoor and Adventurous Activities

Types of outdoor and adventurous activities

Outdoor and adventurous activities, usually referred to as OAA, are sporting activities that take place in an outdoor environment and which involve an element of danger or risk. Usually, the aim is to conquer the environment, for example, climbing a rock face or skiing down a mountain, although there are competitions in most OAA sports, such as downhill ski racing.

Orienteering

Rock climbing

Mountain biking

Sailing

Caving

BRONZE

1. The photographs on this page show a few of the outdoor and adventurous activities (OAA) that you can take part in. What other land-based activities can you think of? What other water-based activities can you think of?

Skills associated with good outdoor and adventurous activity leadership

Leaders play an important role in outdoor and adventurous activities, so it is vital that they have the necessary skills to organize and run training sessions and activities successfully.

Communication

Communication is one of the most important skills required for leading outdoor and adventurous activities. There are two main ways in which an OAA leader communicates:

1. **Verbal communication:** This is done by speaking to people. A leader should be clear and precise in what they are saying. They should keep the information simple and not use too many words so there is no confusion and the group remains focused throughout.
2. **Non-verbal communication:** This is done using lots of different methods, including hand gestures, body language, tone of voice and facial expressions – anything except speaking to people. Non-verbal communication can be very effective when leading a group, particularly if the area they are working in is noisy. Some learners also respond better to non-verbal communication, having a skill demonstrated to them for example, than they do to verbal communication.

A leader using a demonstration to instruct a group.

A successful leader also has the ability to listen to their group and deal with any issues or concerns about the event or session that is taking place. It is important that the leader is understanding and that members of the group feel that their leader is approachable.

Use of language

The way in which a leader speaks to their group can have an effect on the group's behaviour and their performance. For example, when leading young children, basic, exaggerated instructions with lots of demonstrations will make the leader more easily understood; but, where teenagers and adults are concerned, the information can be more detailed and the terminology more specific.

Organization of equipment

Organization is another key skill when planning an outdoor or adventurous activity. Leaders should be aware of both the facilities and the equipment available, and ensure that they have everything in place prior to the session. They should consider the following:

- **Size of the group:** How many are attending the session? Is more space or equipment needed because the group is large?
- **Condition of the equipment:** Is the equipment safe to use? Has it been maintained to a good standard?
- **Selection of equipment:** Is there something for people of all abilities? Different equipment may be required for people who are disabled or have special educational needs. Equipment of different sizes will also be needed, such as climbing harnesses or walking boots.
- **Return of equipment:** It is important that borrowed equipment is returned in the same condition it was in when it was taken. This will ensure a positive relationship between the lender and the borrower is maintained and that future hire of equipment is possible.
- **Use of equipment:** It is essential that outdoor equipment is used correctly by **all** participants. Misuse of items can render them dangerous, and in extreme cases this can lead to serious injury or even loss of life.

BRONZE

1. Decide which of the following are examples of verbal communication and which are examples of non-verbal communication:

- Telling someone to sit down.
- Demonstrating a paddle stroke in canoeing.
- Putting your finger on your lips to quieten the group.
- Asking someone what their targets are.
- Pointing to the clock to show them the time.
- Saying 'Well done'.

2. Try these games. What do they teach you about communication skills?

a) Sit back to back with a partner. One of you must describe an object without saying what it is, while the other draws the object being described. Then name the object and see how accurate the drawing is.

b) Stand back to back with a partner. Recite a nursery rhyme, taking it in turns to say a line. While reciting the rhyme, walk away from each other.

3. You are running a session for a group of 15 11-year-old boys. You want to teach them simple navigation skills using a map and compass.

- How many compasses do you need?
- What other equipment will you use?
- How much space will you need?
- Will your session run indoors or outdoors?
- What else do you need to consider?

Knowledge

Most importantly, OAA leaders should have an in-depth knowledge of the skills, techniques, rules and regulations of the activity they are delivering to ensure that they give out accurate information and that participants are safe. For example, they need to know about different canoe strokes if they are leading a canoeing session or about different knots if they are leading an abseiling session. In addition, they should usually hold a coaching qualification in the activity being taught, such as a Mountain Leader Award for coaching hill walking.

A leader should also possess detailed information about the people in their group to ensure that they know about medical issues or other special requirements. For example, knowing the age of participants means the leader can make sure that parental consent is obtained for all children under 16 to take part. This information can be obtained by asking participants to fill in a questionnaire or by talking directly to individuals.

Leaders must also be aware of the health and safety implications of the session taking place, and should have completed or viewed a risk assessment prior to the session. They should also have a basic understanding of first aid and be aware of the emergency procedures and appropriate rescue techniques.

UIMLA provides the opportunity to gain internationally recognized qualifications such as the 'International Mountain Leader' award.

Supervision and support

An OAA leader must know when to supervise an individual or group and when to support them. Supervising a group means observing them without interfering. Supporting a group means asking probing questions to check the participants' understanding or demonstrating techniques to them.

Outdoor activities are exciting because of the sense of adventure and danger. If the leader offers too much support, the element of danger is removed and the activity becomes less interesting. However, a leader has to step in if the level of risk is too high. This is a delicate balancing act, and a good leader is adept at exposing participants to an element of risk and danger in a safe environment.

Decision making and improvisation

A good OAA leader must make the right decision at the right time. For example, they may have to decide between continuing an expedition in poor but not life-threatening weather and cutting it short because the weather is going to get worse. Whilst good decision making relies on knowledge of an activity, it is something which only really comes with experience. In rare instances the wrong decision will be made and, although this isn't ideal, the situation can be rectified if the leader is able to improvise. This can mean anything from camping in an alternative location to using an unusual knot in a climbing rescue situation. Again, improvisation requires a high level of knowledge, but it is a skill that is developed and honed through experience.

BRONZE

4. Design a questionnaire to obtain information about the participants in your activity session. You need to know how old each participant is, if they have any medical conditions and any other important facts that might have an impact on how you lead the session.

5. Find an example of a real-life OAA leader for each of the skills associated with good outdoor and adventurous leadership.

SILVER

6. Choose two OAA leaders and list all the skills associated with leadership that each of them has. Then compare the two lists and explain the differences and the similarities between the two leaders.

GOLD

7. Look at your answer to Activity 6. Based on their skills, which, in your opinion, is the best OAA leader and why?

Qualities associated with good outdoor and adventurous activity leadership

In addition to all the necessary skills, a good outdoor and adventurous activity leader should also possess a range of qualities that makes them well suited to working with others in a leadership capacity.

Leadership style

There are many different leadership styles that sports leaders can use with their groups, but the three main ones are:

- **Autocratic (Command):** This is a straightforward leadership style where the leader gives out instructions that the group follow. It can be effective when dealing with large numbers of people because there is less chance of the instructions being misinterpreted.
- **Democratic:** This leadership style is more laid back and, unlike the autocratic approach, the leader involves the group in the decision making. This approach is effective with smaller groups and, as the group members are asked for their opinion, it gives them a sense of responsibility for the session or event.
- **Laissez-faire:** This is a very relaxed leadership style in which the responsibility for decision making is largely given to the group.

Autocratic leadership is often the most appropriate style to use when an individual or group is in danger.

Democratic leadership is a great style of leadership to use when leading an expedition, because it allows participants to see the consequences of their decisions in a safe environment where the leader can still take responsibility if necessary.

BRONZE

1. Which of the following statements show an autocratic leadership style, which show a democratic leadership style and which show a laissez-faire leadership style?

a) 'Are you happy with your bivouac now? Would you be happy to sleep in it?'

b) 'Place your foot on the ledge and reach for the next hold.'

c) 'Would you like to take a rest now?'

d) 'OK, what would you like to do in today's climbing session? What about some gentle bouldering to start off with?'

e) 'You must use the correct technique when capsizing if you wish to pass the course.'

2. For each style of leadership, identify an OAA leader who mainly employs this style.

Laissez-faire leadership can only really be effective if the group members are responsible and experienced, because incorrect decisions could cause problems.

Leadership qualities

Leaders all have their own individual personalities. However, they must possess certain qualities in order to communicate well with the members of their group.

Have authority
An OAA leader must have authority over their group and be able to discipline participants, but they should also be aware of when and where it is appropriate. The most obvious time to show authority is when a group or individual is in danger, or is likely to put themselves in danger, through poor decision making.

Be confident
An OAA leader should be confident in his or her own abilities.

Have a sense of humour
At times outdoor and adventurous activities can be physically and mentally demanding. They can also become dangerous at times. A good OAA leader will use humour to raise the morale of a group or to release tension when a group becomes wary or scared. Whilst humour is an important tool in a leader's armoury, knowing when to use it is even more important. There are times, during a mountain rescue for example, when humour should be used very sparingly.

Leaders should...

Be organized
A good OAA leader is responsible for organizing their group throughout an activity, not just during the preparation stage. This includes all the obvious things, such as transport and equipment, but also includes things such as organizing the group during an overnight stay or during a hazardous activity. As with all aspects of OAA leadership, the higher the quality of the leader, the more trust he or she will place in the group to organize themselves while at the same time making sure that nothing has been missed or badly organized.

Demonstrate initiative
A good OAA leader will use his or her initiative to adapt to a situation and to improvise. Initiative is all about making the right decision at the right time and about seeing the best solution to a problem, not just the most obvious solution.

Being part of a group led by a cheerful, enthusiastic and motivated leader goes a long way to ensuring that participants in OAAs have a great time. An unconfident leader or a leader who is too serious can limit the enjoyment for participants.

BRONZE

3. Why is it important for an OAA leader to be confident? What effect does a confident OAA leader have on a participant? When might participants most need a confident OAA leader?

4. Find an example of a real-life OAA leader for each of the qualities associated with good leadership.

SILVER

5. Choose two OAA leaders and list all the qualities associated with good leadership that each of them has. Then compare the two lists and explain the differences and the similarities.

GOLD

6. Look at your answer to Activity 5. Based on their qualities, which, in your opinion, is the best OAA leader and why?

Responsibilities associated with good outdoor and adventurous activity leadership

When running an outdoor and adventurous activity, leaders are responsible for all the people involved, as well as the equipment and the venue or location being used.

Professional conduct: Leaders must behave professionally and responsibly at all times. Young children often look up to their leader and view them as a role model, in which case their actions and behaviour must be impeccable in order to have a positive impact on the members of their group.

Health and safety: It is the leader's responsibility to make sure that their group is safe and well while participating in outdoor and adventurous activities. This involves duties such as checking that there is a current risk assessment in place for the activity taking place and checking that the equipment is in full working order. Leaders should also ensure that individuals and groups behave safely and obey the rules they have been given during activities to minimize the risk of injury. The leader should also be first aid trained, and know where to get help quickly if it is needed in an emergency.

Transport arrangements: OAA leaders are responsible for ensuring that the travel arrangements for any activity or expedition are in place, and that the transport used is suitable for the activity. For example, if the expedition involves using mountainous roads in winter, then the leader should make sure that they have a set of snow chains and spare blankets in case it snows and the vehicle gets stuck or breaks down.

Equipment: It is the duty of the leader to ensure that all equipment used is fit for purpose and in good working order. This includes checking items before they are used, checking them after they have been used and storing them correctly. It is also the leader's responsibility to ensure equipment that is used off-site is transported safely and securely.

Contingency plans: OAA leaders should always have a back-up plan in case something goes wrong. In the case of an expedition, this is usually a series of escape routes that can be used to remove the group from danger safely. In the case of canoeing, it may be to carry an extra length of rope that can be used to lash all the canoes together in poor weather. Contingency plans should be designed in advance, though minor adjustments may have to be made once the full circumstances of the emergency become apparent.

Nutrition and hydration: When taking part in an outdoor and adventurous activity, it is important for participants to take in enough calories to provide them with the energy they will need to expend and enough water to ensure they remain hydrated. How much energy and water is needed can sometimes be difficult to estimate because the weather conditions can have a huge effect on a participant's nutrition and hydration needs. For example, trekking in the Peak District in warm, dry spring weather requires significantly less energy but more water than the same trek in cold, wet conditions. The weather can also change very quickly and unexpectedly in remote areas. It is therefore the responsibility of an OAA leader to make sure that group members set off with adequate food and water and consume it at appropriate moments throughout the day.

Protection of the environment: At the end of any activity or expedition, the leader should ensure that all traces of the activity are removed. This involves a range of things, from simply collecting and removing litter, to repairing fences and scattering any rocks that have been used to make a hearth for a fire. The key is to plan to cause as little damage as possible, as this is much easier than repairing the environment once the damage has been done.

Dehydrated food weighs less so is easier to carry.

Pasta is high in carbohydrates so provides lots of energy without being too heavy to carry.

BRONZE

1. Taking your own experience and qualifications as a starting point, find out about the next leadership qualification that you could take for an outdoor and adventurous activity of your choice.

SILVER

2. Explain the following responsibilities of being an OAA leader, giving examples to support your answer:

- An OAA leader should ensure that all participants are safe, all of the time.
- It is the responsibility of the OAA leader to ensure that activities cause little or no lasting environmental impact.

Unit 16 assignment, part one

Background

You have been successful in gaining a work placement at a local OAA centre. While on placement, the manager has asked you to assist him in leading a training weekend for prospective instructors. This will involve giving a presentation on leadership, before leading and reviewing two different activities.

GRADING CRITERIA TO BE ASSESSED
P1
M1

Task

Create a presentation that can be delivered to a small group of trainee OAA instructors. Your presentation should:

Outline the skills, qualities and responsibilities associated with successful leadership of three different outdoor and adventurous activities (P1).

Explain the skills, qualities and responsibilities associated with successful leadership of three different outdoor and adventurous activities (M1).

Tackling the assignment

The easiest way to approach this assignment is to create a PowerPoint® presentation. This will help to ensure that you stay focused on the task in hand, and don't go off on a tangent. However, try not to stun your audience with 'death by PowerPoint®'. Don't put everything you are going to say on your slides; use them as a prompt. You want your audience to concentrate on what you are saying, not on reading the slide over your shoulder.

Alternatively you could approach this assignment by making your presentation interactive and ask for audience participation. This style of presentation is much more engaging and enjoyable for both the presenter and the audience, although you may have to work hard to get your audience involved to begin with.

Meeting the Pass criteria

Canoe leadership
Tom Townroe

There are three key areas that a leader should be aware of when delivering a canoeing session. These are:
1. Skills   2. Qualities   3. Responsibilities.

A working knowledge of all three is essential for a successful leader.

Leadership skills in canoeing

Communication: verbal and non-verbal
1. Wait until everyone is listening.
2. Use the correct hand signals for canoeing in open water.
3. Use the following ways to get attention in open water: whistle, shout, banging the paddle against the canoe.

Organization of equipment
1. Size and type of canoe and paddle.
2. Condition of equipment: is it safe or is the canoe damaged?
3. Are you using the correct type of buoyancy aid?

Knowledge
1. Techniques of canoeing: paddling, capsizing and launching.
2. Participants: medical history, canoeing experience and likely behaviour.
3. Location: swimming pool or open water? Are you familiar with the facilities?

> Tom has made a promising start to this assignment. He has clearly separated his presentation into skills, qualities and responsibilities and related it to one OAA. Tom's second slide is well planned and presented, and showcases his knowledge of the skills associated with canoeing. He has applied his knowledge well, using examples that are specific to the sport (for example 'banging the paddle against the canoe') rather than generic to all OAAs.

> Tom still has a lot of work to do, though. He needs to continue his presentation, working through the qualities and responsibilities associated with canoe leadership, before developing slides related to two further OAAs.

Meeting the Merit criteria

> The handout that Martin has produced is to be used in conjunction with his presentation. As such, it focuses on a specific area, namely health and safety. By approaching the task in this way, Martin has been able to show that many aspects of health and safety are common to all mountain environments.

Leadership responsibilities in outdoor and adventurous activities

Martin Parker   **Unit 16 assignment, part one**

Outdoor and adventurous activities leaders have a huge responsibility for the safety and enjoyment of the participants, and for the protection of the environment.

The responsibilities of a leader in OAA sessions are similar across all activities and can be categorized as follows:
1. Health and safety.   2. Planning.
3. Equipment.   4. Protection of the environment.

Health and safety

> Martin has developed his points throughout the leaflet. He not only **states** his ideas, he also **explains** them. For example, he makes the point that by doing pre-expedition checks, a leader is able to 'minimize risk and avoid placing themselves and their participants in danger'. By doing this, Martin is working at Merit level, although more work needs to be done before he fully meets the criteria for M1.

When leading a snow-based activity, the leader is responsible for their own health and safety, and for that of all participants in their care. This means that they have to check the safety of the environment in advance of the session to make sure they know which slopes and lifts are open, and what the avalanche risk rating is. They should also check what the weather is likely to be like. Similar checks should be made by a mountain leader before embarking on a mountain walk, and by a climbing leader before embarking on a climbing expedition. By doing these checks, leaders can minimize risk and avoid placing themselves and their participants in danger.

Before setting out on any of the activities above, a leader should know the ability and experience of all participants, and should also have a list of emergency contacts for each person in case of injury. The leader should also know where the nearest hospital is and have planned a safe escape route from the mountain or rock face, in case something does go wrong. They should also be trained in emergency first aid, because it may take some time for the emergency services to reach the scene of an accident in poor weather.

Another responsibility of the leader is to check the state and suitability of any equipment being used such as skis, boots and clothing (skiing); climbing belts, boots, clips and ropes (climbing); and stoves, clothing, boots, tents and food (mountain trekking).

Presentation handout for participants   Page 1 of 5

Planning and leading outdoor and adventurous activities

Leading outdoor and adventurous activities is a daunting task. The level of risk is significantly higher than in most other sports and, in order to reduce the level of risk, the leader needs to spend a significant amount of time and energy planning to ensure that all aspects of safety have been considered. In fact, it is not uncommon to spend more time planning than actually leading an activity.

Plan

Outdoor and adventurous activities come in many guises, from straightforward learn to ski courses on dry slopes, to trekking across the Himalayas. In order to plan and lead an OAA successfully, the following factors should be considered:

Participants:
- How many people are taking part? How will you split the group up?
- How old are the people taking part?
- Are the people taking part male or female, or will there be a mix of male and female participants? Does your activity require children to work in single-sex groups?
- What ability are the people taking part? Are they all beginners or will you have a mixture of experienced and inexperienced participants?
- Do any of the participants have medical or other specific needs? How will you ensure that these are met? Will you need to differentiate the activities?

The structure of the activity:
- What will you cover in the session? Do you need to include a warm-up and a cool-down?

Resources:
- What equipment will you need? Can you access all the equipment you need when you need it? Is it fit for purpose and in good working order? For example, do you have up-to-date copies of the maps and/or guides you are using and do you have waterproof protection for them?
- Are you fully aware of how to prepare, use, pack, store and carry the equipment you are using?
- Do you have an appropriate venue or location for the session? Will the venue or location be accessible to you before and after the session so that you can set up and pack away the equipment?
- How long is your session? Have you allocated timings to the different parts of your session? Can the planned activities be completed within the time allowed for the session?

Locations and environment:
- Have you completed a preliminary visit to the area you will be using?

- Have you scoped out potential hazards and completed a risk assessment?
- Have you considered how your activity will affect the environment and have you thought about ways to minimize these effects?

Transport arrangements:
- Do you have travel plans for all parts of the activity or expedition in place?
- Is the transport suitable for the activity? Is it affordable, convenient and, if you are using public transport, does the timetable fit with the timings you have allocated to each part of your session?
- Have you planned your route in advance?
- If appropriate, have you prepared copies of the route with details of times and locations to give to participants before the activity begins?

Contingency plans:
- What are your contingency plans?
- If you are leading an expedition, where are your escape routes from the planned routes?
- If you are in a remote area, how will you make contact with the emergency services? Will you have mobile phone reception or will you need a satellite phone?

Conduct:
- What rules of conduct will you set down for the participants?
- Does your planned activity meet the safety guidelines set down by the outdoor centre you are visiting?
- Does your planned activity meet the safety guidelines set down by the Adventurous Activities Licensing Authority (AALA)?
- Does your planned activity meet the guidelines set down by the activity's governing body?

Lead

It is important to keep a record of any outdoor and adventurous activity that you lead. You could keep a diary, a logbook or a portfolio; record witness testimony; keep feedback sheets or an observation record; and use audio or video equipment. Whichever method you choose, you must ensure that you get information from at least two sources, one of which should be your own evaluation of your performance.

Review

It is important for OAA leaders to evaluate the activities that they run to provide them with feedback on their performance. If an activity is unsuccessful for any reason, the leader can work on improving things for subsequent sessions. Equally, if something worked really well, this method can be used again in the future.

When evaluating leadership it is important to gather information from everyone involved, including the participants, other leaders and any volunteers, to build an accurate picture of how it went. You might want to ask people about:

- **Planning:** How well was the activity planned? Did the leader stick to the plan, or did they have to improvise?
- **Content:** How suitable was the content of the activity for the participants? Was there enough/too much going on?
- **Organization:** How organized was the leader before the activity and on the day? Did they remain calm?

- **Health and safety:** Were the participants safe? Were there any incidents? If anyone was injured or ill, were they treated efficiently? Did the leader follow activity guidelines set down by the governing body of the activity?
- **Personal qualities of the organizers:** How appropriate was the leadership style employed? How confident was the leader? How fun and friendly were they? How good were they at communicating?
- **Strengths and areas for development:** What went well? What could have been done better? What should the leader do next time to make sure the activity runs more smoothly?

Reviewing an event is easiest if everyone involved is asked the same questions, in the same format. The most common way of doing this is to use a questionnaire, which should include a series of simple open-ended questions that allow participants to express their opinions effectively.

Setting targets for improvement and development

After you have reviewed your activity, you should set yourself targets for improvement and development. These should be SMART targets:

*S*PECIFIC: Targets should be specific; they should set down precisely what you want to achieve. For example, 'I want to run the 100m in under 15 seconds.'

*M*EASURABLE: Targets should be measurable so that you can work out if you have achieved them. For example, it is better to say that your target is to run the 100m in under 15 seconds than it is to say that you want to run the 100m faster.

*A*CHIEVABLE: Goals should be set appropriate to the fitness and skill levels of the performer. They should be close enough for us to see, but not so far away that we can't touch them.

*R*EALISTIC: It is important that we set goals that we have the capacity to achieve. All targets need to be challenging so that you have to work hard to achieve them, but they must also be realistic in order for them to serve their purpose and motivate you.

*T*IME-BOUND: Targets should have a time limit on them. For example, 'I want to run the 100m in under 15 seconds by the end of the summer.' If your long-term goals rely on you achieving your short-term goals, then you need to set time limits on your short-term goals in order to reach your long-term goals.

Having decided on your targets you can create a development plan, summarizing both your short-term and long-term goals and ways in which you can achieve them. For example, you might mention training courses that you would like to attend, or mentoring or coaching opportunities you would like to experience.

Unit 16 assignment, part two

Background

You have been successful in gaining a work placement at a local OAA centre. While on placement, the manager has asked you to assist him in leading a training weekend for prospective instructors. This will involve giving a presentation on leadership, before leading and reviewing two different activities.

GRADING CRITERIA TO BE ASSESSED
P2, P3, P4
M2, M3
D1

Task

Plan, lead and review sessions for two different outdoor and adventurous activities. You should:

 **PASS**

Produce a plan for leading two different outdoor and adventurous activities, with tutor support (P2).

Lead, with tutor support and under supervision, two different outdoor and adventurous activities (P3).

Review your own performance in planning and leading outdoor and adventurous activities, identifying strengths and areas for improvement (P4).

 **MERIT**

Independently produce a plan for leading, and lead under supervision, two different outdoor and adventurous activities (M2).

Explain your own strengths and areas for improvement in leading outdoor and adventurous activities, making suggestions relating to improvement (M3).

 **DISTINCTION**

Evaluate your own performance in leading outdoor and adventurous activities, commenting on your own leadership effectiveness, strengths and areas for improvement and development (D1).

Tackling the assignment

Planning and leading the session is best done in a style you are comfortable with. It is no use trying to be a very outgoing person if you are usually quite quiet. As such, plan to your strengths and your session is likely to be successful.

It is acceptable to plan your own session and discuss it with your tutor before leading the activity, and still achieve M2. However, if your tutor makes huge changes to your plan, this would be classed as planning **with tutor support** and you would achieve P2.

There are two ways to approach a review of your session so that you have evidence for an examiner: to write an essay or to produce a film. The advantage of making a film is that your tutor or a fellow student can prompt you by asking you questions, but this approach can be time consuming. You can also amend an essay as many times as you like, so it is probably a better approach if your written communication skills are good.

Meeting the Pass and Merit criteria

Unit 16 assignment, part two   **James White**

I was pleased with the orienteering and canoeing sessions that I led. The two activities were quite different and I had to change my leadership style.

When orienteering, it was easy to talk to the group in the classroom, but it was difficult to control them when they were out searching for control points. This meant that I had to stay in one place so that everyone knew where I was, so I wasn't able to see them while they were running around. Next time I would ask them to come back to a central point after each control point, so that I could check they were doing things right. In contrast, I was with the group all the time in the canoeing activity, but because of the echo in the swimming pool I found it hard to make everyone hear me. Next time I would use a whistle or a clap to get everyone's attention, and wait until they were listening before speaking.

My organization of equipment for orienteering was good, and I had enough compasses and maps for everyone to use. I got these ready before I started so that it didn't waste time. However, the canoes were too hard to lift on my own, so I had to ask the group to get these ready at the start of my session. This took a lot longer than I thought it would and so I didn't have time to teach everything I had planned to teach.

Overall my planning for both activities was OK, but I should have put more detail into my plans. I spent too much time trying to remember what I was going to ask students to do, and this meant that the behaviour of the group wasn't very good because they were bored. Next time I would plan in more detail, and make sure I knew exactly what I was going to do throughout. This would help to keep things moving faster and keep everyone involved.

Strengths	Areas for development
• Timekeeping	• Timekeeping of sections within each session
• Organization of equipment for orienteering	• Organization of equipment for canoeing
• Control of the group in the classroom	• More detailed planning
• Range of activities planned	• Communication in the swimming pool
• Health and safety	

> James' review of his sessions is quite basic and he only mentions three or four things. I would like to have heard more about health and safety, because he lists it as one of his strengths but has not developed this within his review.

> James is clear on the areas he needs to develop but makes no suggestions as to how he will work on these areas to improve them. Perhaps he could have listed some training courses, or suggested an example of a good leader that he could observe in future. Because of this, I would be happy to award James P4, but he is a long way from meeting the Merit criteria.

Meeting the Distinction criteria

Unit 16 assignment, part two   **Zoe Whittaker**

I led two very different sessions, a rock climbing activity on an indoor climbing wall at school and a slalom ski session while on a school ski trip in France. The latter session was completed under the supervision of a qualified instructor, but I am pleased to say that he did not intervene and afterwards told me he was impressed with my session.

I planned my sessions independently, although I checked the rock climbing session with my teacher and the skiing session with the instructor before I led the sessions. Although this was not actually necessary, I was conscious of the dangers involved in both activities and wanted to be sure that I was not going to put anyone at risk of injury. Thankfully both plans were met with approval from the staff.

Throughout the two sessions I made sure that everyone was safe, but in doing this I took away some of the risk elements involved. For example, I asked students to ski one at a time rather than setting a second skier off when the first person was at the halfway point. I also spent too much time speaking to individuals after each ski run, and did not allow the next person to start while I was doing this. Afterwards I realized that it would have been better to give feedback to an individual while the next person was active. In order to develop this skill, I spent a couple of hours the next day watching the instructor working with another group, and I realized that he did not look at the person he was speaking to because he was watching the next person ski at the same time as giving feedback. By doing this, people were skiing more often and did not become bored. In contrast, while I was leading, one or two students became a little bored and started to mess around. This could have been dangerous and at the time I thought it was because they were being naughty, but in hindsight I am able to see that it was because they were bored.

Having observed the instructor, I changed my approach when leading the climbing session. I allowed two people to climb at a time, and I gave feedback to one person while the next person was on the wall. This meant that more people were involved (one receiving feedback, two climbing, two belaying and two backing up), and so people were less likely to become bored. Whilst this was an effective way of keeping people involved, I felt that the quality of feedback I gave suffered because I was too distracted by watching the people on the wall and the people belaying. I think this is a skill that I will develop as I gain more experience.

Throughout the two sessions I was pleased with my communication skills. People listened to me and in general did what I asked them to do. However, I struggled to communicate with people higher up the climbing wall. I think this is because I am a quiet person and I find it difficult to shout so people were having difficulty hearing me.

> Throughout the third and fourth paragraphs, Zoe clearly evaluates her performance, because she not only explains her strengths and weaknesses but also evaluates them by describing the effects her performance had on others. She also shows that she found a way to develop her skills and then put her new abilities into practice. Throughout these two paragraphs Zoe is working at Distinction level, and is meeting the criteria for D1.

> In the last paragraph, Zoe explains what the difficulty was (that she is a quiet person), but she does not develop this idea any further and cannot be said to be evaluating her performance. For example, did Zoe's voice sound panicked when she shouted, and did this upset the people at the top of the wall? And how will Zoe develop her skills in this area? If she continues in this style Zoe will only achieve the criteria for a Merit.

Unit 17: Expedition Experience

Safety considerations

Taking part in a multi-day expedition gives participants a chance to live without modern conveniences, television, shopping, the Internet and the car for a few days. In essence, it means going back in time a couple of hundred years, although there are some modern items of equipment, such as a tent and a stove, that are useful to take along! However, before undertaking any expedition, and certainly a multi-day expedition, it is necessary to carry out a risk assessment, have a series of escape routes in mind and have a working knowledge of emergency procedures.

An injured hiker is carried on a stretcher by a mountain rescue team in the Lake District.

Risk assessment

The *Oxford English Dictionary* defines risk as 'the possibility that something unpleasant or unwelcome will happen'. If we apply this to the context of an expedition, we could say that risk is 'the possibility that an injury to one or more participants will happen'. Most people would agree that preventing an injury occurring makes more sense than dealing with it once it has happened, and this is where risk assessment comes in. By assessing the dangers that could occur, participants and leaders can take steps to remove some of the hazards. A risk assessment is a careful examination of what, in your activity, could cause harm to the participants.

The six-step process
There are six steps to producing a formal risk assessment document. Failure to complete any of the six steps could lead to someone being seriously injured.

6. Review your decisions regularly and make changes if necessary: Hazards change on a regular basis, so the risk assessment must be reviewed to keep it up to date. This is even more important for OAAs due to changes in the environment, such as the weather, so risk assessments must be dynamic.

5. Record your findings and implement them: By law, the risk assessment findings must be written down. It is also important to put in place the control measures you have decided on. For example, making someone responsible for checking all equipment on a weekly basis.

4. Decide how to prevent or reduce the level of risk: Practical solutions to reduce the level of risk, called 'control measures', must be found. For example, checking all equipment once a week to make sure it is not broken and therefore dangerous, and making a commitment to remove or repair damaged items.

1. Identify the hazards: Have a good look around at all equipment, the venue and the participants and decide what could cause harm, no matter how minor. For example, a broken piece of equipment would be a hazard.

2. Decide who might be harmed and how: Decide whether it is the participants, the leader or the general public who might be harmed. Then decide what may happen to them. What injuries will they receive? Might they even die? For example, climbing on an eroding cliff face could lead to a fall.

3. Identify the level of risk: Decide how likely it is that the potential accidents you have identified will occur. For example, damaged climbing equipment would represent a high level of risk.

BRONZE

1a) Consider a remote location that you have visited or seen on television. What could cause problems for, or injure, participants? Make a list of at least five potential hazards.

b) Now suggest ways that the level of risk could be reduced.

Emergency procedures

Emergency procedures should be followed if someone gets into difficulty during an expedition. Emergency situations can include a participant going missing, suffering from hypothermia or breaking a leg. Before setting out on an expedition, you must have made arrangements for dealing with emergencies.

Rescue: contacting the emergency services

The first thing to do in an emergency is dial 999 or 112, the international emergency number. You will be put through to the call centre for the emergency services, and should ask for the police, ambulance service, fire service or the mountain rescue service (which deals with casualties in remote mountain areas). You will then be asked to give exactly the same information as you would if you were calling from home:

- The name and age of the casualty, and their date of birth if you know it.
- A description of the injuries they have sustained or a description of the problem.
- The time and nature of the accident.
- The exact location of the incident, giving map or GPS coordinates if possible.
- Details of any hazards present.

You may well be asked further questions about the weather, the number of people in your party, the amount of time you have been on the mountain and whether or not a first-aider is present. Answer all questions calmly; panicking at this stage will not help anyone. When the emergency services do arrive, continue to remain calm and follow the instructions you are given precisely.

Rescue: distress signals

A distress signal is a way of attracting attention when you are in trouble. There are two ways to attract attention, using visual signals that people will see or audible signals that people will hear. A combination of the two is usually most effective, but in certain situations one type of signal – for example, using light to attract attention at night or sound to attract attention in dense woodland during the day – will be better than the other.

An SOS signal can be broadcast using light or sound. It consists of three short blasts of sound or flashes of light, followed by three long blasts of sound or flashes of light, followed by three more short blasts or flashes. You should then pause for five seconds and repeat the process. SOS stands for 'Save Our Souls' and the arrangement of beeps or flashes is derived from the Morse code signal for 'SOS'.

Consider the following ways to attract attention:

- Using a light (your torch or perhaps even your mobile phone) to broadcast an SOS signal.
- Using a whistle to broadcast an SOS signal.
- Using a mirror (or any reflective surface) to reflect light to broadcast an SOS signal or attract the attention of a passing aircraft, such as an air ambulance.
- Lighting a fire or using a fire to create a smoke signal. Three fires, especially in a triangle, are a recognized distress signal.

Survival

If you are stranded or you are waiting to be rescued, it is important to be able to look after yourself and others in your party. By knowing some basic survival techniques, you can greatly increase the amount of time you are able to survive before being rescued. The following procedures should be followed in a survival situation:

- Contact the emergency services. If you have no signal on your mobile phone, use a satellite phone or send at least two people to the nearest landline or to high ground to find phone reception. You must send at least two people in case one of them gets injured or lost on the way.
- If possible, move the casualty to a sheltered place, away from the wind, rain or direct sunlight (consider sunburn or sunstroke). If this is not possible, because the casualty has a serious injury and cannot be moved, build a shelter around yourself and the casualty. Use anything available, including sticks, rucksacks, stones and sleeping bags.
- Raise the casualty off the ground if at all possible. The cold ground will sap warmth and strength from his or her body very quickly.
- Put extra dry clothing on yourself and the casualty and huddle together for warmth. You get cold faster when you are still. Use a survival bag if you have one.

Escape routes

Escape routes are easy ways to exit an expedition. They are rarely used, but must be planned in detail as they are vital to keeping everyone safe in an emergency. When trekking in a remote area it is not uncommon for the weather to change from warm sun to heavy rain or snow in minutes and, when this happens, it might be sensible to abandon the expedition. Escape routes are also useful if someone injures themselves. Escape routes, one for every two hours walking in remote or mountainous regions, should be identified at the planning stage.

Equipment

You must consider not only the equipment you are going to take with you, and therefore what you are going to leave behind, but also how that equipment is to be transported. Equipment should be shared amongst the group in such a way that the strongest members of the group carry the heaviest kit and the smallest members of the group carry the lightest loads. This might seem unfair but remember, a group is only as fast as its slowest member.

Following the correct procedure while waiting for someone to be rescued can be crucial if they are to survive.

First-aid kit: The first-aid kit should always be carried by the first-aider in the group. However, with larger groups, it may be necessary to carry more than one first-aid kit in case the group gets separated.

Shelter: This will usually be a tent although it could also be a bivouac sheet. You should also consider carrying a survival bag in case of emergencies. Each member of the group should carry their own sleeping bag or bivouac sheet, which should be wrapped in polythene to keep them dry, whereas a tent should be divided into poles, pegs and inner/outer tent and then shared amongst those who will be sleeping in it.

Essential expedition equipment

Food and drink: Food should be lightweight and dehydrated where possible. It should also be high in carbohydrates to provide energy. Dried soups and pasta are good examples. Food should be shared amongst the group or carried by a few individuals on behalf of everyone. Each member of the group should carry their own high-energy snacks, such as chocolate bars or nuts, and their own water.

Flammable or combustible items: These include gas canisters and methylated spirits containers, both of which are used in camping stoves. These should be stored in airtight canisters, and should be kept away from all sources of ignition. In practice this means at the very least carrying fuel and lighters or matches in separate compartments of a rucksack, but ideally they should be carried by separate members of the group.

Participants in expeditions should make sure that they have the correct equipment and clothing for all conditions that they are likely to face.

Safety guidelines

Advice on safety in remote areas can be found from a variety of sources. Governing bodies for activities, such as the Ramblers or the British Mountaineering Council, can offer advice to individuals considering taking part in an expedition in mountainous areas, and can often give advice based on a specific location.

The Adventure Activities Licensing Authority (AALA), which is part of the Health and Safety Executive (HSE), sets out the legislation that governs what schools and colleges can do with regard to outdoor and adventurous activities including expeditions. It has the power to stop groups travelling into remote areas if they are not satisfied with the plans that are put in place. In practice, this role is delegated to Local Authorities, and any school or college wishing to take students on an expedition must first gain approval from their Local Authority.

Anyone trekking in remote areas should also seek advice from the local centre for the region. Most areas that are popular for trekking are home to either private or council-owned centres and best practice dictates that schools and colleges use these centres wherever possible, because of the local knowledge and experience their employees have. This also means that schools and colleges have to follow the specific safety advice and guidelines set down by an individual centre.

Whilst all of this advice, guidance and legislation may seem over the top, it is in place to ensure that everyone can use the countryside safely, minimizing the pressure on the emergency services.

BRONZE

2. You are on a three-day expedition on Dartmoor with three friends. One of your friends slips and hurts himself. He doesn't think he has broken his leg, but it is too painful to walk. It is getting dark and beginning to rain, and you don't have any mobile phone reception or a satellite phone. However, you were well equipped for the expedition and have a first-aid kit, a survival bag, sleeping bags and a tent in your rucksacks, as well as food, clean and dry clothes, and a stove. What do you do?

3. Identify a route for an imaginary expedition on an OS map. Your route should pass through a remote area of mountains or woodland. Now plan three escape routes from your route.

Environmental considerations

Expeditions, particularly multi-day expeditions where you stay overnight, can easily have a detrimental effect on wildlife, and can cause pollution and erosion. So everyone who uses the countryside should be concerned about looking after it and preserving it for others to enjoy. We call this conservation.

Both plants (flora) and animals (fauna) can be protected by following a few very simple rules:

- Guard against all risks of fire and, when you light a fire, do so in a suitable area and make sure that it is fully extinguished before you leave.
- Leave all gates exactly as you find them. Close them if they are closed and leave them open if they are already open.
- Avoid contact with animals whenever possible.
- Do not remove anything, including plants, rocks and shells, from their natural habitat.
- Keep to footpaths. This limits erosion and damage to wildlife habitats (the homes of plants and animals).
- Use gates and stiles to cross fences and walls, rather than climbing over them.
- Do not make any unnecessary noise.
- Take all your litter home with you. It spoils the countryside for others and can cause injury to wild animals and pollute fresh stream water.
- If you need to go to the toilet, bury your waste well away from sources of fresh water.

Natural England (www.naturalengland.org.uk), the organization that is responsible for advising the government about the natural environment in England and Wales, publishes the Countryside Code on its website. This is a common-sense code which sets out the responsibilities of both the public and landowners for looking after the countryside.

The litter spoiling this beautiful view of Lake Debar in Macedonia highlights the impact of pollution.

Classification of land

All land in the UK is classified. Some belongs to private landowners and some has been protected by law for us all to appreciate. Different rules apply to different types of land and it is important to know which type of land you are using so that you can follow the guidelines set down by the landowners or organization responsible for that land.

Areas of Outstanding Natural Beauty (AONBs)

The National Association for Areas of Outstanding Natural Beauty describes AONBs as 'a precious landscape whose distinctive character and natural beauty are so outstanding that it is in the nation's interest to safeguard them'. There are 47 AONBs in the UK, and they are cared for by local authorities and volunteers.

Rights of way

Rights of way are public highways across the countryside. They often cross private land and can be used by anyone at any time on foot. Some of them can also be used by people riding horses, cyclists and people driving vehicles.

Sites of Special Scientific Interest (SSSIs)

SSSIs are sites around the UK that contain flora, fauna and geology which is of special interest. There are over 4000 SSSIs in the UK, which are legally protected in order to preserve them. According to Natural England, which is responsible for working with landowners to protect SSSIs, they 'include some of our most spectacular and beautiful habitats: large wetlands teeming with waders and waterfowl, winding chalk rivers, gorse and heather-clad heathlands, flower-rich meadows, windswept shingle beaches and remote uplands, moorland and peat bog'.

Durdle Door is just one of the highlights of the Dorset AONB.

Open access land

Open access land is all land that has been mapped as open country or is registered as common land. Open country is land that is predominantly mountain, moor, heath or down and which is largely free of buildings. Land is classified as common land if it has been given this status by the Land Registry. There are approximately 865,000 hectares of open access land in England and the Countryside and Rights of Way Act 2000 grants the public the right to access it on foot and move about freely without keeping to footpaths. Activities such as camping are not permitted on open access land by the Countryside and Rights of Way Act 2000 but they may be permitted locally, and this is something you should check as part of your planning.

National Parks

There are 14 National Parks in the UK, incorporating beautiful areas of mountains, meadows, moorlands, woods and wetlands. The National Parks are areas of protected countryside that everyone can visit, and where people live, work and shape the landscape. Each one has an organization that looks after the landscape and wildlife and helps people enjoy and learn about the area. Access to all 14 National Parks is free, and outdoor and adventurous activities are very popular within the parks.

BRONZE

1. Find the Countryside Code on Natural England's website (www.naturalengland.org.uk) and summarize it in poster format, to remind people of the dos and don'ts of the countryside.

2. Choose two areas where you could go on your expedition and find out how the land there is classified.

SILVER

3. Choose one section of the Countryside Code and explain how the advice given helps protect the environment.

4. Explain what effect the land classification for the areas you chose for Activity 2 would have on your expedition.

The skills and techniques required for a multi-day expedition

A multi-day expedition is not something which should be entered into lightly. It requires detailed planning, permission to access the land and the right equipment. But above all, an expedition requires a special set of skills and inexperienced participants can find themselves in serious danger if they lack the skills and techniques that are required.

Navigation

Navigation is the process of plotting a route on a map and following it on the ground. It encompasses a wide range of skills, including reading a map and using a compass. Poor navigation can lead to walkers becoming lost or disorientated in a remote area.

Map reading

The Ordnance Survey is responsible for mapping the UK and anyone travelling on a multi-day expedition must carry an up-to-date OS map with them. OS maps come in different scales. For an expedition it is usual to use a 1:25,000 scale map in the OS's Explorer series and an example from one of these maps can be seen below.

Contours

Contour lines – the brown lines on an OS map – are used to show the height of the land above sea level. A contour line joins together all the points of equal height.

The spacing of the contours shows how steep the land is; what the gradient of the land is. Closely placed contours show us that the land increases in height over a short distance, so it is steep. It has a steep gradient. Widely placed contours show us that the land increases in height over a longer distance, so it is gently sloping. It has a gentle gradient. The pattern of the contour lines shows the shape of the land so being able to recognize gradients, both on a map and out in the countryside, can be a useful tool in helping you work out where you are.

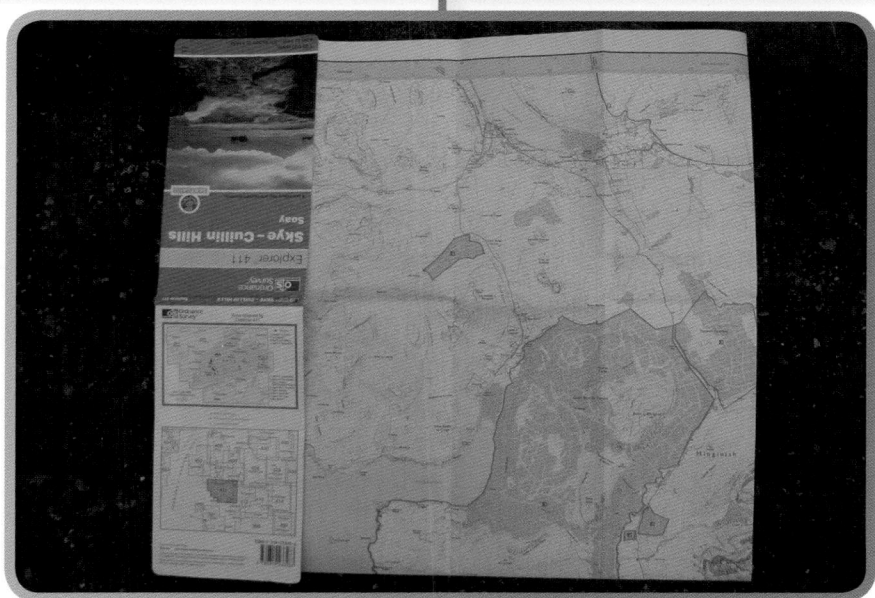

Grid referencing

Grid lines divide maps into squares. Each line is numbered and these numbers are used to give a grid reference. If you tell someone the grid reference they will be able to work out exactly where you are if they have the same map. We can give a four figure grid reference for a whole square or a six figure grid reference for a specific point within a square.

Features

Symbols are used on maps to help us identify features. The symbols used are shown in the map key and can help us work out where we are. Examples include buildings, paths and electricity pylons.

BRONZE

1a) Find a map of your local area, and label ten points of interest that aren't already on the map. For example, you could mark on your house, your friend's house, your favourite shops or the local bowling alley. Remember to use an existing symbol from the map's key to mark your points of interest, or create a new symbol and add it to the key.

b) Write out a six figure grid reference for each of your chosen places of interest. Then swap your grid references with a partner and try to find each other's places of interest.

2a) Draw a map of your school or college, and mark all the major features on it. Make sure that your map is to scale.

b) Choose two features on your map and take a compass bearing from one to the other. Then go outside and, starting at the first feature, try and follow your compass bearing to the second feature. How accurate was the bearing? If it is inaccurate, is it a problem with your map or a problem with your compass skills?

SILVER

3. Explain how contour lines help you to navigate.

Compass readings

Using a compass and map you can navigate your way across the countryside.

1) Place the long side of the compass on the map between where you are and where you want to go, making sure that the arrows on the baseplate of the compass point in the direction you want to go.

2) Turn the round bevel on the compass until the North-South lines are parallel to the grid lines on the map and the 'N' on the bevel points in the same direction as the 'N' on the map.

3) Hold the compass horizontally in front of you and turn your body until the needle points to the 'N' on the bevel. The directional arrow on the baseplate indicates the direction you want to go.

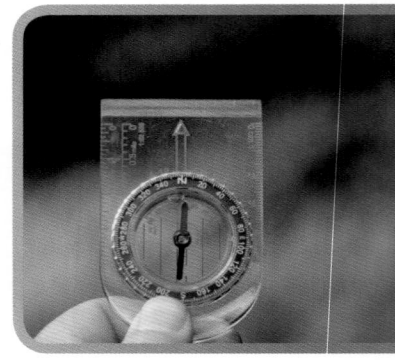

Compass bearings should be checked regularly, as walking on the wrong bearing for even a few hundred metres can have serious consequences, so you should carry your compass so that it is accessible at all times; on a loop around the neck is the most common way.

Direction finding

It is sometimes necessary to be able to find the right direction without using a compass, because it is lost or broken or you don't know where you are on the map. The easiest way to do this is to find three or four features that you can see, such as a hill, a valley or electricity pylons, and locate these features on the map. Then, remembering that the map is really just an aerial photograph, turn the map so that it lines up with the features you have selected. You can now use the map to locate North and to find the direction you need to travel.

Walking at night or in limited visibility

Navigating at night or when visibility is poor, for example when it is foggy, takes effort and concentration. The first thing to remember is to avoid using a torch except when it is absolutely vital, for looking at the map for example. Your eyes will adjust to the light level, and you will be surprised how well you are able to see without artificial light. The next thing is to set the map, set the compass, and then follow them closely, checking every 30 seconds or so. This will slow down the speed at which you are able to travel, but it is better to arrive in the right place a little late, than to arrive in the wrong place on time!

Route plans

Route plans are instruction cards that you fill in before you set off on an expedition. They detail each part of the journey, usually in 50m to 500m sections, containing information about direction of travel, compass bearing, gradient, distance and estimated time. Each section (or leg) should also contain information about the type of ground you are likely to be walking on, such as fields, open countryside or roads and so on. Route plan cards are an important part of route planning, because they focus attention on small stages of the route rather than longer distances. They also enable the route to be planned in greater detail, therefore reducing the likelihood of getting lost when walking in remote areas.

ROUTE PLAN (use one per day) OS Map Explorer OL 24 The Peak District White Peak Area 1:25,000				NAMES OF GROUP MEMBERS						NAME OF GROUP OR UNIT	
Day of the week: Monday		Date: 30/4/07	Date of venture: 30/4/07– 2/5/07								
Leg	PLACE WITH GRID REF.	General direction or bearing	Distance (km)	Height climbed (m)	Time allowed for leg	Time for stops for meals	Total time for leg	Estimated time of arrival (ETA)	Setting out time: 1100		
									Details of route to be followed		
SP	Haddon Hall CP GR 234661										
1	TO Track Jct GR 217654	SW	1.5	70	35 mins	10 mins	45 mins	1145	Up over main feature to track junction		
2	TO Rd/ Track Jct GR 213657	NW	0.7	5	20 mins	5 mins	25 mins	1210	Across open ground low ground to left towards metalled road		

GOLD

4. Get into two teams and hold a debate, one team arguing for the statement below and one team arguing against the statement below. Remember to make sure that any point you make, for or against the statement, is fully justified:

'Producing route plans is time consuming and unnecessary. They are not an important part of planning an expedition.'

Camping

While it is possible to stay in a youth hostel or a camping barn, these facilities are limited in many areas, and you are most likely to spend the nights during your expedition in a tent. Campsites are usually chosen in advance, as part of your planning, but it is sometimes necessary to change the plan due to unforeseen circumstances, such as bad weather, illness or injury.

Choosing a campsite

Commercial campsites are often the best option for novice hillwalkers because they provide fresh water and cooking and washing facilities. But for more experienced people, and those who want an authentic multi-day expedition, the choice of where to camp is determined by the type of land and the likely location at the end of the day's walking. Wherever possible, you should choose to camp in a location that is:

- sheltered
- dry (short springy grass is a sign of dry ground)
- flat (avoid sleeping on a slope but if you have to, sleep with your head up-slope)
- close to water (for cooking, washing and keeping food cold)
- not privately owned (unless you seek permission first).

A well set up campsite helps to make camping fun.

Setting up camp

Camping is great fun if it is done well. Badly planned campsites can lead to an awful night's sleep, and poorly stored equipment can make the onward journey a terrible experience. Follow these simple rules and you should have a pleasant experience:

- Begin to set up camp well before nightfall. It is not easy setting up a tent in the dark.
- Pitch your tent so that the 'door' is away from the wind. This will help to keep you warm, and will reduce the likelihood of rain getting inside.
- If possible, choose a tent that has a porch area and use this to store your walking boots, rucksacks and any items that do not need to be in your sleeping area. Make sure everything is kept well away from the sides of the porch though, or they might get wet if it rains during the night.
- Never go inside the sleeping area in wet clothes or boots. Sleeping in a wet tent is uncomfortable and cold.
- Any spare clothes can be stored in a polythene bag. If you put a towel over the top of the bag, it makes a useful pillow and saves you carrying a normal pillow in your rucksack.
- Wash your body and clean your teeth as normal. If you feel sweaty and dirty, then you probably are sweaty and dirty; clothes rubbing against sweaty, dirty skin can cause sores. You'll also sleep better if you feel clean.
- Choose an area well away from your tent for a toilet. This not only helps with hygiene by preventing germs spreading, it also ensures more privacy. Bury any waste, do not leave toilet paper lying around and wash your hands thoroughly afterwards.
- Store perishable food in a sealed plastic bag in a cold place, such as a hole in the ground or in running water.
- Wash pans and dishes immediately after you have used them. They will clean better when they are warm, and leftover food will attract insects (and sheep!).

Transport

The obvious way to travel on a multi-day expedition is to walk, and it is unlikely that you will take part in an expedition that doesn't involve walking at some point. However, you can also cycle, take public transport, including trains, buses and ferries, travel by canoe or kayak and ski or snowboard. However, whichever option you choose, you need to plan carefully in advance. You don't want to arrive for a ferry, only to find you've missed the last one of the day – or even the week!

BRONZE

5. Walk around your school or college site, and make a list of five good places to pitch a tent. Suggest three reasons why each place is suitable.

6. Pitch a tent on one of the five sites you chose for Activity 6. Practise until you can pitch it in under ten minutes (this will be important if it is raining on your expedition).

7. Cook a simple meal on a lightweight camping stove.

8. Pack a rucksack with items that you think are essential and then compare what you have packed with what other people in the group have packed.

9. Create a route plan for a simple route in an environment you are unfamiliar with, with help from your teacher or tutor. Use an Ordnance Survey map and make sure your route plan includes compass bearings and information about the direction of travel, gradients, type of ground you will be walking on, distance and estimated time each leg will take to complete.

SILVER

10. Create a route plan for a simple route in an environment you are unfamiliar with, without help from your teacher or tutor. Use an Ordnance Survey map and make sure your route plan includes compass bearings and information about the direction of travel, gradients, type of ground you will be walking on, distance and estimated time each leg will take to complete.

Unit 17 assignment, part one

Background

As part of your training for your Duke of Edinburgh's Award Bronze programme, you must plan, take part in and review a multi-day expedition. You must also be able to assess the impact your expedition will have on the environment, and demonstrate your knowledge of the skills, techniques and equipment involved in undertaking an expedition safely.

GRADING CRITERIA TO BE ASSESSED
P1, P2, P3 M1, M2 D1

Task

Produce a short lecture about multi-day expeditions which can be delivered to a group of your peers. You should include information on safety and the environmental impact of expeditions, as well as demonstrating your knowledge of the equipment, skills and techniques that are needed for a successful trip. You should use visual aids where appropriate. During your lecture, you should:

PASS

Describe the safety and environmental considerations for a multi-day expedition (P1).

Demonstrate the skills and techniques required for a multi-day expedition (P2).

Describe the equipment required for a multi-day expedition (P3).

MERIT

Explain safety and environmental considerations for a multi-day expedition (M1).

Explain the skills and techniques required for a multi-day expedition (M2).

DISTINCTION

Justify use of skills and techniques in the undertaking of a multi-day expedition (D1).

Tackling the assignment

A lecture can take many forms, including a PowerPoint® presentation, a demonstration, a film or a speech. You can even produce handouts to support your spoken words. Any of these options are valid, although a speech or a demonstration would need to be filmed or supported by a witness statement to provide the necessary evidence.

The key to this assignment is to tackle it in stages, because it is easy to miss some of the criteria. The first stage is to produce a section of your presentation on the safety and environmental considerations of a multi-day expedition. This can take the form of a simple description if you are

aiming for a Pass or a more detailed explanation, discussing why the safety and environmental considerations you have described are important, if you are aiming for a Merit.

Next you should describe the equipment required for a multi-day expedition (P3). Although this means skipping over P2, M2 and D1 for the moment, approaching the assignment in this way means that when you come to demonstrate the skills and techniques required for a multi-day expedition, in the last section of your lecture, you will be using the equipment you have already described.

Meeting the Pass and Merit criteria

Unit 17 assignment, part one

JOEL TAYLOR

SAFETY

- **Check equipment**
- **Consider where you will spend the night**
- **Consider escape routes**
- **Check the weather forecast**
- **Complete a risk assessment**
- **Have a contingency plan**

ENVIRONMENTAL CONSIDERATIONS

- **Guard against fires**
- **Leave no trace**
- **Avoid contact with animals**
- **Keep to footpaths**
- **Take litter home**
- **Keep the noise down**
- **Avoid damage to plants**

Things to consider for safety

Everyone should enjoy an expedition but they must also return home safe and sound. Safety on an expedition is the responsibility of everyone involved, although the expedition leader is in charge. In many cases, injuries occur because of freak accidents but it is possible to remove a large proportion of the risk if some basic rules are followed before and during the expedition. It is important to check your equipment before you set off on an expedition. Is your equipment up to the task ahead? Will everything fit properly into your rucksack? Packing a rucksack so that it is bursting at the seams is asking for trouble. It is also important to plan where you are going to stay for the night. Will you stay in camping barns or do you need to take tents with you? Camping barns may be warmer and may save you carrying a tent, but where will you stay if you can't reach your overnight stop because the weather turns bad or someone injuries themselves?

Of the two considerations that we can see, Joel has described the importance of checking your equipment before you leave, thereby meeting the criteria for a Pass. However, he not only describes the importance of choosing appropriate accommodation, he also goes on to explain why it is important and notes the consequences of making a poor decision. This paragraph therefore meets the criteria for a Merit.

Joel has approached this assignment in a sensible way. The handout could be used to support a verbal presentation and would ensure that his audience were able to take the most important information away with them.

The bullet point lists on the left-hand side suggest that Joel has considered a range of safety and environmental considerations, and the main body of the text shows that he is going to talk about each of the considerations in more detail. We can only see two of the considerations here, so Joel will need to continue with his handout, describing or explaining the other safety and environmental considerations for a multi-day expedition and completing the other sections of the lecture, to fully meet the criteria for this part of the assignment.

Meeting the Distinction criteria

When taking part in a multi-day expedition, the skills and techniques required can be classified under three headings: navigation, preparing meals and shelter.

When navigating, there are three main options: map, map and compass, or GPS (Global Positioning System). The choice of which to use has to be based on the knowledge, skills and experience of those taking part in the expedition.

GPS equipment is very expensive and although some mobile phones now incorporate this technology, they are rarely accurate enough to be used in remote areas. Moreover, GPS systems can only give a person's current location; they cannot plan the route for you. As such, I would always avoid relying on GPS technology when trekking as part of a group, although I might use it to check my location in conjunction with a map and compass.

Using a compass is great if you know how to do it properly but it is easy to make silly mistakes. Transferring a compass bearing onto a map can lead you way off your target destination if a mistake of as little as one degree is made. Also, magnets such as those found in watches or mobile phones can affect the accuracy of compasses. Complex calculations also need to be made to transfer a compass bearing (aimed at magnetic north) to a bearing on a map (aimed at true north). A compass therefore provides a useful backup, much like a GPS device.

My preferred choice would be to use only a map if at all possible. Careful map reading combined with careful analysis of features on the ground is usually sufficient for navigation purposes in the UK. It is possible to orientate a map without a compass, simply by spotting three features that you can see on both the ground and on the map. As long as the map is checked every few minutes, or more often in areas such as dense woodland, it is difficult to take the wrong route.

Emma has sensibly grouped the skills and techniques under three main headings. Her discussion regarding navigation techniques is concise and well ordered, and works through the choices available in a logical order. She has justified her preferred choice by analysing the strengths and weaknesses of each option before making a clear decision as to which is the most appropriate. Assuming that the rest of Emma's presentation is of an equal standard, she will meet the criteria for D1.

Planning a multi-day expedition

Successful multi-day expeditions are the result of meticulous planning and a thorough understanding of the equipment you are taking with you.

The equipment

Before embarking on any expedition, you must practise using all the equipment you plan to take with you. Arriving on site and not knowing how to pitch the tent you are carrying, or discovering that the stove you have brought with you doesn't work, will inevitably lead to an unsuccessful expedition. It also needs to be fit for purpose. There is no point taking a six-man tent with you if there are only four people going on the expedition, for example. The extra weight will not seem like a good idea after you have been walking for five hours!

Shelter and rotection
Essentially this means sleeping bags and tents.

- You need to ensure that your tent is lightweight, waterproof and big enough for the number of people who need to sleep in it.

Tents with solid poles tend to be heavier, so you should choose a tent with fibreglass poles if possible. You should also try to choose a tent with a porch area, as this provides valuable storage space overnight.

- You should choose a sleeping bag with an appropriate season rating for the conditions you are likely to be trekking in. Taking a winter sleeping bag on a summer expedition, for example, will mean you are too hot at night. Your sleeping bag also needs to be lightweight and to pack into as small a bag as possible.

Clothing and footwear
It is better to wear lots of thin layers of clothing than one or two thick layers. Air is trapped between thin layers, helping to keep you warm. Layers can also be added or removed in stages to regulate your body temperature. Outer layers should be waterproof and lightweight, and you should always carry a pair of waterproof overtrousers just in case.

Never attempt an expedition without walking boots. They are waterproof, sturdy and provide protection in case of slips and trips. You must look after them to ensure that they are in tip-top condition when you need to use them, waterproofing them regularly. They must also be kept dry and clean when not in use.

Stoves and food storage
You have a choice between open fires, gas stoves, paraffin stoves and methylated spirit stoves. Which to use comes down to personal preference. The advantage of a liquid fuel stove is that they tend to stay lit better in windy conditions, but the advantage of a gas stove is that it is easier to carry because there is no liquid to spill and refill cartridges tend to be more readily available. As all camping stoves are different, it is important to always follow the manufacturer's instructions. Open fires are much more difficult to control, and are also more of an environmental hazard due to the damage to vegetation and the possibility of them burning out of control.

When carrying food on an expedition, it is always best to carry dehydrated food because this simply has to be stored in a cool, dry place. Any fresh food should be wrapped in an airtight container (or bag) and stored in cold water to keep it cool. Alternatively, it should be kept in a sealed plastic container and stored in a small hole in the ground, but if using this method, you must be sure to replace any loose earth when you have finished.

Expedition equipment

Rucksacks
Try to choose a rucksack that you can carry comfortably, and one which allows you to pack the heaviest items at the top because carrying weight high up on your shoulders rather than low down on your back reduces the level of effort needed. Choosing a rucksack with plenty of pockets is also a good idea. It enables you to pack items such as stove fuel and matches well away from each other, and a rucksack with both top and bottom access to the main compartment allows you to get at most of the contents without having to remove everything.

The plan

When you are planning an expedition, it helps to work through a checklist. This ensures that nothing is missed out, reducing the likelihood of complications once you are in the wilderness. It is best to work through the checklist below in order, from top to bottom, but personal preference may dictate that some sections are completed in a different order.

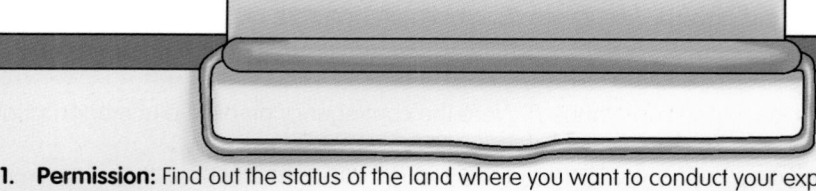

1. **Permission:** Find out the status of the land where you want to conduct your expedition. Do you need to plan a route that avoids privately-owned land with minimal footpaths or do you need to get permission to camp where you would like to? There is no point wasting time planning a route in detail until you are certain that you have permission to use the land in question.

2. **Accommodation:** If you intend to use camping barns, youth hostels or commercial campsites, check that these are open and have availability on the dates you intend to use them, then book places. If you cannot, you will have to change your choice of accommodation or the dates of your expedition. If you intend to camp, check that there is a suitable site for pitching a tent in the area you have chosen to walk.

3. **Route plan:** Plan your route around the first two items on this checklist, because you need to ensure that you can get from one overnight stop to the next in a day, without trespassing. Spend plenty of time planning your route and creating accurate route cards. Think carefully about how long it will take you to cover distances. The average walking speed is 5km per hour, but this slows considerably if you are walking up a steep gradient, over difficult terrain or are carrying a heavy rucksack. Don't forget to include escape routes. And remember the old saying, 'Fail to prepare, and prepare to fail'.

4. **Transport:** If your route involves using public transport, be sure to check that it is running and, if necessary, pre-book tickets. If you need to use private transport, getting a lift in a car or a minibus, check that your intended driver is available on the dates and at the times you need them.

5. **Equipment:** Source all the equipment you are going to need. You may find that you have to order some items, such as stoves and rucksacks, so you need to start organizing your equipment well in advance of the date you need it. Remember that you will have to carry everything you are taking with you, so limit yourself to essentials only.

6. **Food:** Try to plan a menu that meets the requirements of the expedition. The food should be lightweight (preferably dehydrated), easy to cook on a camping stove, meet any dietary requirements of the group (is anyone vegetarian or vegan for example?) and contain little or no packaging (because you'll have to carry the litter with you after you've eaten the food). Most importantly, it should be full of energy (preferably carbohydrates).

7. **Risk assessments:** These should be completed for all sections of the plan, particularly for the transport, accommodation and likely route. Remember to include any contingency plans.

8. **Emergency contacts:** Before setting off on your expedition, leave a list of emergency contact details with someone who is going to be available during your trip. If you run into difficulties, you then only have to telephone one person who will contact everyone else. This is obviously a very responsible task so the emergency contact person needs to be someone very reliable. You should also leave full details of your expedition with this person, including your route plan and details of any accommodation you are using.

9. **Check the weather forecast:** This is the last thing to do before setting out because you don't want any nasty surprises once you are out in the wilderness. These days, the Internet is the best source of information about the weather, but try to use trusted websites like the BBC weather pages or the Met Office. If you are in any doubt about the likelihood of severe weather, it is wise to postpone or cancel the expedition.

BRONZE

1. Create a poster that gives advice on the equipment that should be taken on a multi-day expedition.

2. Prepare five meal plans suitable for a backpacking expedition. Remember to consider different dietary requirements and to include breakfast, lunch, dinner and snacks.

Reviewing an expedition

It is important to evaluate the expedition to provide feedback on how successful it was. If an expedition is unsuccessful for any reason, you can work on improving things for your next trip. Equally, if something worked really well, you will want to remember this for the future.

When evaluating an expedition it is important to gather information from everyone involved, including the participants, the supervisor and anyone else involved, to build an accurate picture of how it went. You might want to ask people about:

- **Planning:** How well was the expedition planned? Were the contingency plans in place appropriate? Was the route plan accurate?
- **Equipment:** How suitable was the equipment you chose to carry? Did you take too little or too much?
- **Organization:** Did you organize other people, such as drivers, effectively? Did they respond to changes from the original plan calmly and efficiently?
- **Health and safety:** Were the participants safe? Were there any incidents? If anyone was injured or ill, were they treated efficiently?
- **Areas for improvement and recommendations for future events:** What could have been done better? What should you do next time to make the expedition run more smoothly?

Reviewing an expedition is easiest if everyone involved is asked the same questions, in the same format. The most common way of doing this is to use a questionnaire or comment cards, which should include a series of simple questions such as those above. It is important to ask open-ended questions, because this allows people to express their opinions more effectively.

BRONZE

1. Create a questionnaire or comment card that can be given to participants to review a multi-day expedition they have participated in.

SILVER

2. Design a set of SMART targets to improve something you perceive as a weakness in your expedition experience.

GOLD

3. Justify the targets you wrote for Activity 2, giving reasons why you chose those strategies for improving your performance.

Setting targets for improvement and development

After you have reviewed your expedition, you should set yourself targets for improvement and development. These should be SMART targets:

SPECIFIC: Targets should be specific; they should set down precisely what you want to achieve. For example, 'I want to improve the accuracy of my compass bearings when planning a route'.

MEASURABLE: Targets should be measurable so that you can work out if you have achieved them. For example, it is better to say that your target is 'to develop meal plans to include vegetarian, vegan and halal options', than to say you want to 'broaden the range of meal options available on the expedition'.

ACHIEVABLE: Targets should be set appropriate to the fitness and skill levels of the performer. They should be close enough for us to see but not so far away that we can't touch them. For example, 'I want to improve my understanding of contour lines before the next expedition'.

REALISTIC: It is important that we set targets that we have the capacity to achieve. All targets need to be challenging so that you have to work hard to achieve them, but they must also be realistic in order for them to serve their purpose and motivate you. For example, 'I want to learn to navigate effectively in open countryside by the end of the summer'.

TIME-BOUND: Targets should have a time limit on them. For example, 'I want to develop meal plans to include vegetarian, vegan and halal options before my next expedition in six weeks'.

Having decided on your targets you can create a development plan, summarizing both your short-term and long-term goals and ways in which you can achieve them. For example, you might mention training courses that you would like to attend, or mentoring or coaching opportunities you would like to experience.

Unit 17 assignment, part two

Background

As part of your training for your Duke of Edinburgh's Award Bronze programme, you must plan, take part in and review a multi-day expedition.

Task

Plan, take part in and review a multi-day expedition. You must also assess the impact your expedition will have on the environment, and demonstrate your knowledge of the skills, techniques and equipment involved in undertaking an expedition safely. You should:

> GRADING CRITERIA
> TO BE ASSESSED
>
> P4, P5, P6
> M3, M4, M5
> D2, D3

 **PASS**

Produce a plan, with tutor support, for a multi-day expedition (P4).

Carry out, with tutor support, a multi-day expedition, demonstrating the use of relevant skills and required equipment (P5).

Review own performance in the planning and undertaking of a multi-day expedition, identifying strengths and areas for improvement (P6).

 **MERIT**

Independently produce a plan for a multi-day expedition (M3).

Independently undertake a multi-day expedition, demonstrating the use of relevant skills and required equipment (M4).

Explain identified strengths and areas for improvement, suggesting strategies to improve future performance (M5).

 **DISTINCTION**

Justify decisions made in the planning of a multi-day expedition (D2).

Evaluate performance in the planning and undertaking of a multi-day expedition, suggesting strategies to improve future performance and justifying suggestions (D3).

Tackling the assignment

There are three distinct sections to this part of the assignment. Firstly, you must produce a plan for your expedition. The plan must contain a risk assessment, a route plan and an outline of times and locations. Other points to consider are: meals, transport and equipment. This section of the assignment is assessed by P4 and M3, and must be completed before other parts of the assignment are attempted. If you draw up your plan with minimal support from your tutor or teacher then you will be working towards a Merit, but if you require help from your tutor or teacher on a regular basis then you will be working towards a Pass. If you are aiming for a Distinction you must also justify the decisions you made during the planning process (D2).

Secondly, you must carry out the expedition. If you are aiming for a Pass (P5) it is expected that your tutor or teacher will have significant input into the organization and delivery of the expedition. If you are aiming for a Merit (M4), you should take

responsibility for your own expedition, including deciding when and where to stop for a rest, camp and food. Remember, though, that even if you are aiming for a Merit your tutor or teacher will be present throughout the expedition and will take charge in an emergency situation.

The third and final section of the assignment requires you to identify (P6) or explain (M5) your strengths and areas for improvement on the expedition. If you are aiming for a Merit, you also need to suggest strategies that could be used to improve your performance in the future (M5). And, if you are aiming for a Distinction, you need to provide more detail in order to evaluate your performance, both during the planning process and during the expedition itself, and you need to justify the strategies you have suggested for improving your performance (D3). This section of the assignment is best approached by providing a written summary as evidence.

Meeting the Pass and Merit criteria

BTEC Level 2 Firsts in Sport

James White

Unit 17 expedition: planning

Equipment

Participants to provide:

- Toiletries and towel
- Plastic mug, plate, knife, fork and spoon
- Torch with spare batteries
- Notebook and pencil
- Personal first-aid kit
- Watch
- Money (no more than £10)
- Nightwear
- Walking shoes that support the ankle
- Trainers for in and around camp
- Underwear, socks and T-shirts for two days
- Loose-fitting trousers, such as tracksuit bottoms or cargo pants
- Pullover, sweatshirt or fleece
- Hat and gloves

- Waterproof jacket/cagoule
- An empty, one-litre plastic bottle for water
- Two strong bin liners
- Food for breakfast, lunch, dinner and snacks

To be borrowed from college:

- Tents
- Rucksacks
- Cooking stoves
- Roll mats
- Compasses
- Sleeping bags
- First-aid kit

Outline plan

We will be picked up by a minibus at the college reception at approximately 14:45 on 1 May 2010 and will be driven, by Mr Jones, to Haddon campsite where we will camp overnight. The following day we will walk eight miles to our first overnight stop at Watton campsite. On the third day we will walk five miles to meet the minibus at Crinks Junction, for the return journey. We will be dropped off at the college reception at approximately 20:00 on 3 May 2010.

James has clearly thought about all the equipment he needs for his expedition and where he is going to get it from. He has considered transport arrangements and his outline plan suggests that he has thought about the need to set up camp before darkness falls on the first night. However, James' planning is not yet complete. He needs to provide more detail about the food and drink he is planning to take with him, and it would be helpful to see a full menu plan for the expedition. He also needs to provide a route card for each day of the expedition and my main concern is that James' plan shows no evidence of a risk assessment. Without this vital piece of planning the expedition cannot go ahead. James' work therefore falls short of the requirements for P4 (if he had significant input from his tutor or teacher) and M3 (if he had little or no input from his tutor or teacher) at the moment.

**BTEC Level 2 Firsts in Sport
Unit 17 assignment, part two**

A review of my multi-day expedition planning   **Thomas Bird**

I approached the planning process in stages, which began by choosing an appropriate area for the expedition. Nottinghamshire Local Authority states that Duke of Edinburgh Bronze expeditions 'should take place within the county boundary'. This narrowed down the choice of areas, so I chose Clumber Park as my base station. This is because it is close to school, making transport arrangements fairly easy, but quite rural, so I would be walking in a remote area. In addition, there is a campsite at Clumber Park that I have stayed at in the past and this made the risk assessment part of the plan easier to complete.

Having decided on a location, the next stage was to decide on a suitable date for the expedition. I checked the school calendar to see if there were any suitable dates available. Health and safety rules state that expeditions should not take place between October and the end of March, except in exceptional circumstances. As this was a simple Duke of Edinburgh Bronze expedition, exceptional circumstances did not apply. Another consideration was to avoid all examination periods. This meant that the expedition had to take place before the second week in May because this week marks the start of GCSE examinations. This allowed a six-week window of opportunity, from the start of April to the second week in May. There were some other commitments already in the school diary and my tutor was not available for two of the weekends. Eventually, the third week in April was chosen, with the first weekend in May pencilled in as a back-up if poor weather meant that the first date had to be cancelled.

The next stage was to compile a list of the camping equipment held at school and decide what I needed to provide myself.

Planning decisions have to be justified in order to meet the criteria for D2 and Thomas has done this throughout his review. At each stage of the planning process he has explained why he made the decisions he did. He has outlined the things which limited his decisions, presented the options and then explained why he made his final choices. For example, he has explained that his choice of date for the expedition was limited by health and safety considerations, the school calendar and the availability of his tutor. He looks at the alternatives and then makes a choice which takes everything into account. If Thomas continues with his step-by-step approach to this section of the assignment, I am confident that he will also achieve the criteria for D3.

Unit 18: Effects of Exercise on the Body Systems

The short-term effects of exercise

Whenever we take part in any form of physical activity, be it walking the dog or running the London Marathon, our body systems undergo a series of changes. These are necessary for our bodies to work effectively and they happen automatically. The changes that happen each and every time we exercise are known as 'short-term responses'; this is because they are reversed once we stop exercising. Many of these short-term changes are really obvious – you can tell if someone has been running because they will be breathing a little faster than normal – but some are more subtle, such as the redirection of blood flow around the body.

Investigating the short-term effects of exercise

Participating in practical activities
One way to understand the short-term effects of exercise is to take part in some form of physical activity, such as playing football or volleyball, or going for a run. The increase in your level of activity places extra demands on your body, over and above the normal daily requirements. These demands include an increased need for oxygen in the blood and an increased need for energy in the muscles. In turn, this creates an increased amount of waste products in the blood and muscles, which have to be removed. The body responds to these demands by changing the way it works. To fully appreciate these changes, you need to feel them happening. Try completing Activity 1.

Taking physiological measurements
Another way to investigate the short-term effects of exercise is to take a series of physiological measurements before and after exercise, including:
- pulse rate, preferably with a heart rate monitor
- blood pressure
- flexibility, using the sit and reach test (see Unit 1, page 23)
- ventilatory function, particularly the volume of air inspired and expired by the lungs in one minute, using a device called a spirometer.

Try Activity 2.

Comparing data sets
The final way of investigating the short-term responses to exercise is to compare sets of data. This is extremely important, because it enables us to identify those responses which happen each and every time we exercise, as opposed to those that occur as a one-off. By recording data before and after exercise (as you did for Activity 2) on a regular basis, we can make comparisons that are meaningful. For example, an increase in blood pressure due to exercise can only be described as a true short-term response if it happens on a regular basis. The only way to prove or disprove whether this is the case is to investigate what happens to blood pressure after exercise on several different occasions. Try Activity 3.

A spirometer in use.

The short-term physiological responses to exercise

For decades sports scientists have been investigating the responses of the human body to physical activity. While some of these investigations have required the use of highly specialized equipment, some of them have mirrored those that you have undertaken in Activities 1, 2 and 3 (albeit on a much larger scale, involving tens of thousands of participants). The key findings can be separated into changes to the musculoskeletal system, the cardiovascular system and the respiratory system.

Musculoskeletal responses

- **Increased range of joint mobility:** As the body temperature increases, the muscles and connective tissues (the ligaments and tendons) get warmer, and this makes them more elastic, like a rubber band. The warmer they become, the further they are able to stretch without tearing and this allows the joint to move more freely.

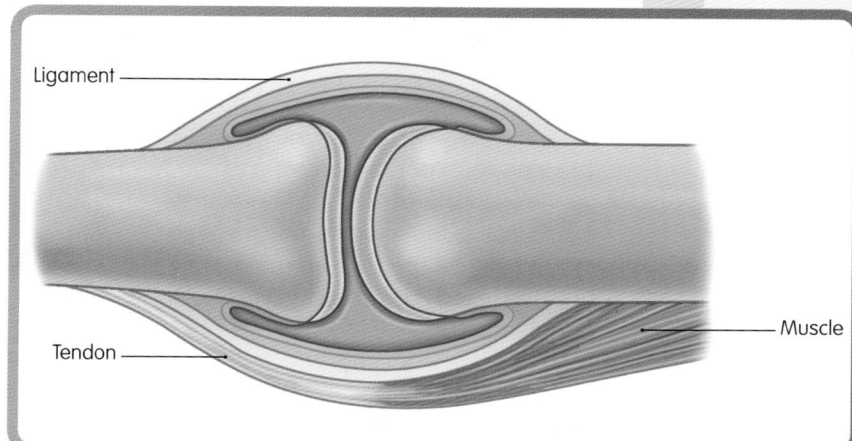

- **Micro tears in muscle fibres:** Each muscle is made up of thousands of individual fibres and, as the muscle works, some of the fibres tear. In the short term this is a potential problem because if too many fibres tear at the same time, this can lead to serious injury. However, in the long term, tears to a small number of muscle fibres are a good thing (see long-term effects of exercise on page 318).

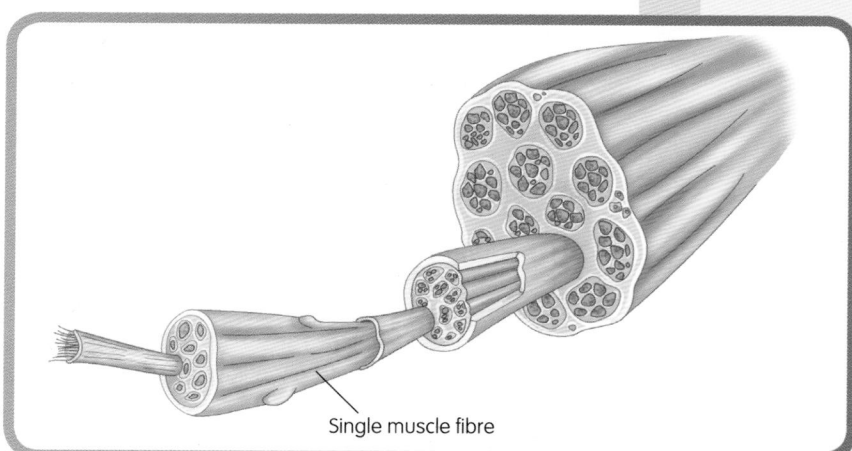

Single muscle fibre

Cardiovascular responses

As the body undergoes physical activity, the amount of oxygen needed by the working muscles increases. To supply the necessary oxygen, more blood is required and this causes:

- **Increased heart rate:** The heart rate is the number of times the heart contracts (or beats) per minute. The faster the heart contracts, the more blood is circulated around the body and to the working muscles.
- **Increased blood pressure:** The amount of blood ejected with each contraction of the heart, which is called the stroke volume, increases. When the stroke volume increases, thus increasing the amount of blood that passes through a blood vessel, extra pressure is put on the walls of the blood vessels, which can be measured as an increase in blood pressure.

Respiratory responses

The following are the body's respiratory responses to the need for more oxygen:

- **Increased breathing rate:** In order to supply the extra oxygen needed by the blood to fuel the working muscles, the respiratory system has to work harder. One way to increase the amount of oxygen taken in is to breathe faster. This is known as an increased breathing rate.
- **Increased tidal volume:** Breathing faster is usually coupled with an increase in the amount of air taken in with each breath, known as the tidal volume.

SILVER

4. Take a look through the short-term responses to exercise you discovered by completing Activities 1, 2 and 3. Create a flow chart showing which physiological responses to exercise happen first and which are secondary responses.

The long-term effects of exercise

If the body is subjected to physical activity on a regular basis, it **adapts** over time. The musculoskeletal, cardiovascular and respiratory systems undergo a series of changes which help them to cope with the short-term effects of exercise on the body. These changes are called **adaptations** and they are semi-permanent, which means that they are permanent as long as training continues, but that they will be reversed if training stops for any length of time.

Adaptations of the body systems

The long-term adaptations of each body system relate directly to the short-term responses of that system. This means that, over time, the short-term responses become less evident because the body has adapted to cope with them.

While you may well be out of breath after swimming six lengths of the swimming pool, the same level of exercise would have much less of an effect on 800m Olympic gold medallist, Rebecca Adlington!

Musculoskeletal adaptations

- **Hypertrophy:** Muscles adapt to training by increasing in size. This is called hypertrophy and it occurs because the muscle fibres grow back thicker when the small tears, which happen as a short-term response to exercise, repair.
- **Increased tendon strength:** The tendons, the fibres which attach muscles to bones, become stretched as a short-term response to exercise. They adapt by growing thicker and stronger, which helps to prevent them from tearing during activity.
- **Increased bone density:** The bones of the body are put under stress during activity, and so they adapt by becoming thicker and heavier (more dense), which helps to prevent fractures occurring.
- **Increased thickness of hyaline cartilage:** The ends of long bones are covered in a layer of hyaline cartilage. It acts as a shock absorber, helping to prevent the bones being damaged during physical activity and the ends of the bones wearing away. Over time, the body adapts by increasing the thickness of the hyaline cartilage to increase the protection for the bones.

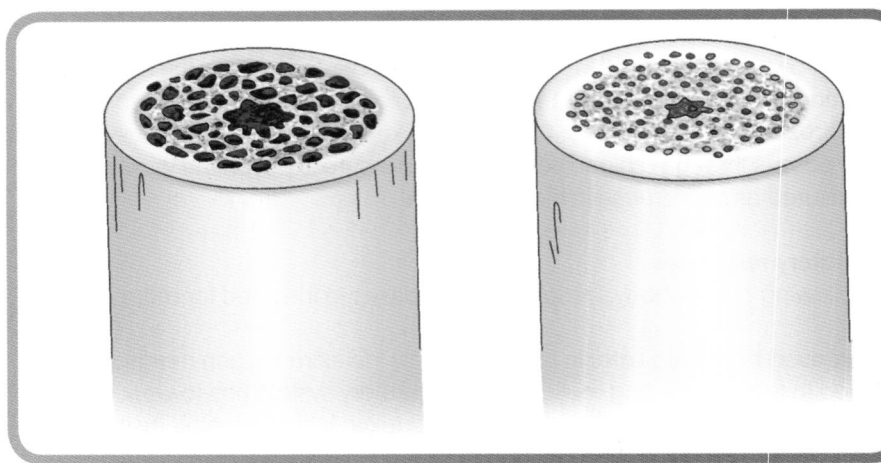

The increased density of the bone on the right, compared with that of the normal bone on the left, helps to prevent fractures occurring.

- **Increased production of synovial fluid:** All the freely moveable joints in the body are lubricated by an oily liquid called synovial fluid. This acts like the oil in a car engine in that it prevents wear and tear on the moving parts – in this case, the bones, cartilage and ligaments. The body adapts to training by increasing the amount of synovial fluid that is present in each joint, thereby reducing the risk of damage to the cartilage, bones and ligaments.

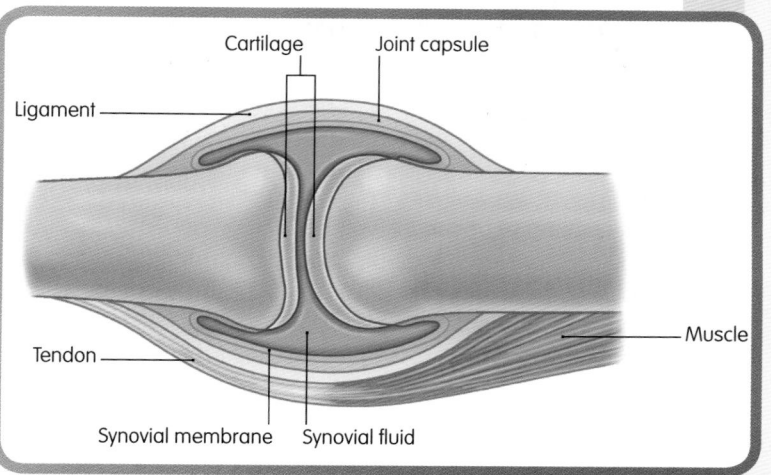

Training can lead to an increase in the amount of synovial fluid in a joint, which reduces the risk of certain injuries.

Cardiovascular adaptations

- **Increased heart size:** The heart has to adapt to cope with the extra demands that are placed on it by regular exercise. The most common adaptation is cardiac hypertrophy, an increase in the size of the heart. In endurance athletes this is typified by an increase in the volume of the left ventricle, the chamber that pumps oxygenated blood to the muscles; whereas power athletes tend to exhibit an increased thickness in the muscular wall of the left ventricle.
- **Increased stroke volume:** Cardiac hypertrophy enables the heart to eject more blood with each contraction, which is known as an increase in stroke volume. In endurance athletes this is because the left ventricle can hold, and therefore eject, a greater amount of blood. In power athletes the increased stroke volume occurs because the thicker muscular wall of the left ventricle enables every last drop of blood to be forced out of the heart and into the aorta.
- **Decreased resting heart rate:** When stroke volume increases, the resting heart rate decreases. This is because the body requires a set amount of blood when resting, typically around five litres per minute. When more blood is being ejected from the heart with each contraction (because of an increase in stroke volume), the heart has to contract less often to pump the required amount of blood around the body and, hence, the resting heart rate slows. This is shown by the equation:

Cardiac output = heart rate x stroke volume

Respiratory adaptations

- **Increased vital capacity:** The volume of air which can be exhaled in one breath, the vital capacity, increases with training. This is because the muscles surrounding the ribs undergo hypertrophy, which makes them more powerful. As a result, they are able to lift the ribcage upwards and outwards further than before, allowing the lungs to expand further and thus increasing the volume of air they can hold.
- **Increased surface area of the alveoli:** Oxygen passes into the blood stream via a process called gaseous exchange, which takes place at the alveoli in the lungs (see Unit 4, page 83). Training encourages the alveoli to adapt by growing bigger, which means that there is more surface area for gaseous exchange to take place and therefore more oxygen can pass into the blood stream.

BRONZE   SILVER

1. Create a table, flow chart or diagram showing how the body's short-term responses to exercise, which you identified in Activity 4 on page 317, lead to adaptations in the long term.

Unit 18 assignment, part one

Background

As a fitness consultant, you have been asked by the local hospital to produce a series of leaflets, which can be given away in the outpatient department, showing the benefits of regular exercise and the importance of maintaining the effectiveness of all three energy systems. You have also been asked to give a lecture to point out the potentially harmful effects of taking shortcuts to improve fitness through the use of performance-enhancing drugs. You have been asked to consider all participants, regardless of the sports they take part in.

GRADING CRITERIA TO BE ASSESSED
P1, P2, P3, P4
M1, M2, M3
D1

Task

Design a leaflet which informs the reader of both the short-term and long-term effects of exercise. You should include pictures, diagrams and/or photographs to show patients how they can investigate the changes for themselves. Your leaflet should:

PASS

Describe the short-term effects of exercise on the musculoskeletal, cardiovascular and respiratory systems (P1).

Investigate the short-term effects of exercise on the musculoskeletal, cardiovascular and respiratory systems, with tutor support (P2).

Describe the long-term effects of exercise on the musculoskeletal system (P3).

Describe the long-term effects of exercise on the cardiorespiratory system (P4).

MERIT

Explain the short-term effects of exercise on the musculoskeletal, cardiovascular and respiratory systems (M1).

Investigate the short-term effects of exercise on the musculoskeletal, cardiovascular and respiratory systems, independently (M2).

Explain the long-term effects of exercise on the musculoskeletal, cardiovascular and respiratory systems (M3).

DISTINCTION

Analyse the short- and long-term effects of exercise on the musculoskeletal, cardiovascular and respiratory systems (D1).

Tackling the assignment

Leaflets always look more professional if they have been produced using a computer rather than being handwritten. The leaflet needs to be eye-catching as well as informative, so try and use a mixture of text, tables, graphs, drawings and photographs.

It may be necessary to create a small booklet rather than a single page leaflet if you are aiming for a Merit or a Distinction, otherwise you risk not including enough information to show that you are able to describe, explain and analyse the effects of exercise.

Vyktoria has made a really good start to this assignment but there is still a lot of work to do. The leaflet contains lots of relevant information but I'm not sure about the way it is presented. I think there is too much writing to make a real visual impact. How many people would pick it up and read it if it was on display?

The effects of exercise on the cardiovascular system by Vyktoria Stone

The effects of exercise can be separated into short-term changes (which happen each and every training session) and long-term changes (which happen over a period of weeks or months).

Short-term effects

Physical exercise (or training) causes the body to change the way in which it works. The various body systems all respond to exercise to make sure that the body can cope with the demands being placed upon it.

Cardiovascular system (heart and blood vessels)

Exercise

Increased heart rate
(more beats per minute)

Increased stroke volume
(more blood pumped out per beat)

Increased cardiac output
(more blood pumped out per minute)

More oxygen available for the working muscles per minute.

The table below shows how the body changes and responds to exercise in the short term

Cause	Response	Effect
Increase in carbon dioxide	Increased heart rate and stroke volume, which leads to an overall increase in cardiac output	Increased blood flow through the heart to flush out waste products
Increased body temperature	Vascular shunting – blood is redirected so that it travels closer to the skin	Heat is passed out through conduction, helping to cool the body
Increased blood pressure due to increased blood flow	Blood vessels widen to allow more blood to flow through them	Blood pressure is reduced

The short-term effects of exercise

As the body begins to exercise, it has to change the way in which it works to cope with the physical demands being placed upon it. The first thing that happens is that the muscles begin to produce more carbon dioxide, increasing the acidity of the blood. If this continues for too long, the body stops working efficiently and the performer has to slow down or stop. To enable the performer to continue working, the cardiovascular system responds by increasing the cardiac output (heart rate x stroke volume). This pushes more blood around the body, which delivers more oxygen to the muscles and, crucially, removes more of the acidic carbon dioxide.

At the same time as this is happening, the body temperature begins to increase (because the chemical reactions that produce energy also produce heat). Again, if left unchecked, this heat increase can cause the performer to slow down or stop. To combat this, blood is redirected so that it travels nearer to the skin, where heat can be lost through conduction. The redirection of blood occurs because the brain sends a message to the arteries to get wider where more blood is needed and narrower where less blood is needed. This is called 'vascular shunting' and involves vasoconstriction (narrowing) and vasodilation (widening) of blood vessels.

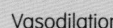

Vasoconstriction   Normal   Vasodilation

In terms of the content, Vyktoria has clearly described and explained the effects of exercise on the cardiovascular system, but she needs to develop this to include the musculoskeletal system and the respiratory system. She has also included some analysis of the short-term effects of exercise on the cardiovascular system, but she needs to include the other two systems and consider the long-term effects if she is to achieve D1. At present, I would not say that Vyktoria has fully met any of the Pass, Merit or Distinction criteria.

Energy systems

Humans take part in countless different physical activities, ranging from the 100m sprint to the Tour de France, and from archery to gymnastics. All activities have one thing in common: they require energy! The human body creates energy in two main ways, either aerobically (with oxygen) or anaerobically (without oxygen), and the energy system used depends on the demands of the physical activity.

Anaerobic energy production

Although the term 'anaerobic' means 'without oxygen', it does not mean that you should hold your breath while taking part in an activity. It simply means that at the point in time when the energy you are using is created there is not enough oxygen present, and this is usually because the short duration of the activity does not allow the body to create enough oxygen. Anaerobic energy production is used during events that last less than one minute.

There are two parts to the anaerobic energy system: the alactic/phosphocreatine energy system and the lactic acid energy system.

The alactic/phosphocreatine energy system ⟶ The 'first ten seconds' energy system

The anaerobic alactic energy system is referred to as the stored or start-up energy system. It provides the majority of the energy athletes use when they perform bursts of high speed or high resistance movements lasting up to ten seconds.

The stores of energy in the muscles, which are used up during the intense burst of activity, return to normal levels after two to three minutes of rest.

The lactic acid energy system ⟶ The 'ten seconds to one minute' energy system

The lactic acid energy system is capable of high levels of intensity but this prevents waste products being removed from the body. The lactic acid energy system operates without oxygen, so there is not enough oxygen available to facilitate the removal of waste products from the body. As a result, lactic acid accumulates in muscle cells and blood cells. This is a major cause of fatigue, which eventually slows the athlete down. The more intense the exercise, the faster the rate at which lactic acid builds up to a level that causes high fatigue. For example, a 400m sprinter will accumulate high levels of lactic acid after 35–40 seconds. An 800m runner runs more slowly and accumulates lactic acid at a slower rate, resulting in high levels of lactic acid after about 70–85 seconds.

Getting rid of lactic acid after physical activity is a much slower process than replacing the energy stores in the alactic energy system. It may take more than one hour for lactic acid levels to return to their pre-exercise level. Light activity, such as walking or jogging, following intense efforts speeds up the removal of lactic acid. The first ten minutes of active recovery produces the greatest reduction in lactic acid levels.

Aerobic energy system ⟶ The endurance energy system

The aerobic energy system requires oxygen. It is used in lower-intensity exercise and provides the energy for most human activity during our lives. It is also important in the recovery from exercise of all intensities.

The aerobic energy system is very efficient and resists fatigue because there is enough oxygen to allow the waste products to be removed from the body. This means that the heart and the lungs, which help to move oxygen around the body, are very important in aerobic activity. It takes longer to overload the aerobic energy system than it does to overload both the anaerobic energy systems, so an aerobic training session must last a minimum of 20 minutes.

Sporting application of the energy systems

Energy systems

Alactic energy system
Sports that use this energy system include:
- 100m sprint
- weightlifting
- gymnastics (vault).

Competitors in the long jump use the alactic energy system.

Lactic acid energy system
Sports that use this energy system include:
- 200m sprint
- 400m/800m
- basketball: fast break followed by a fast recovery.

In rugby, players in a rolling maul set up from a lineout use the lactic acid energy system.

Aerobic energy system
Sports that use this energy system include:
- marathon
- steeplechase
- orienteering.

Participants in a triathlon use the aerobic energy system.

BRONZE

1a) Working in a group of four, take it in turns to sprint and time each other. When it is your turn to sprint, explode as fast as you can from the starting blocks and, at the point when you begin to slow down (even just a fraction), raise your arm in the air. Your partner should stop the stopwatch at this point.

b) Repeat the test but, for the second attempt, try to run at about 80 per cent of your maximum speed for as long as you can. Again, raise your hand when you begin to slow down so that your partner can stop the stopwatch.

c) Look at the data you have collected. What was happening each time you began to slow down?

2. Look carefully at the section on the sporting application of the energy systems and try to come up with a further six activities for each energy system.

SILVER

3a) Create a bar chart showing the results collected by your group during Activity 1 and then compare these with those of the rest of your class.

b) Who has the most efficient anaerobic energy system? Why?

Energy requirements of physical activity

Energy is created from the food we eat, and the amount of energy we take in or use is measured in calories. Put simply, if we eat more calories than we use, we will put on weight; but if we burn more calories than we eat, we will lose weight. The key is in striking a balance between calories in and calories burnt.

BRONZE

4. Collect the wrappers of ten everyday food items and look at the amount of energy that each item provides per serving. Using a sport of your choice, create a graph to show the amount of time you would have to participate in that sport in order to burn off the calories in one serving of each item. For example, a chocolate bar provides 100 calories per serving and you would have to play ten minutes of badminton to burn off this energy.

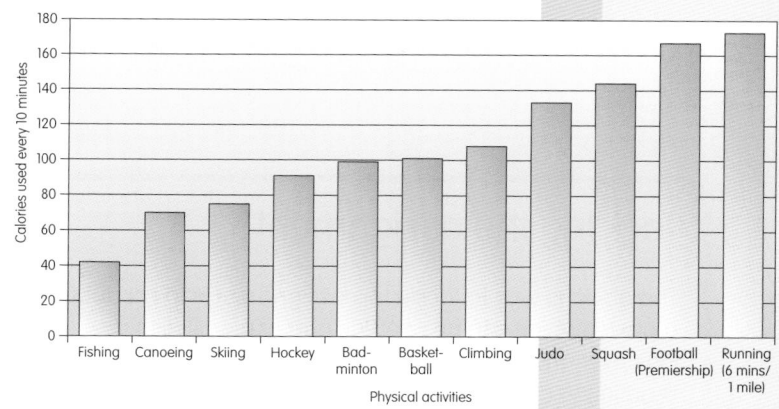

This bar chart shows the calories used every ten minutes by a 20-year-old male weighing 68kg performing a range of physical activities.

Unit 18 assignment, part two

Background

As a fitness consultant, you have been asked by the local hospital to produce a series of leaflets, which can be given away in the outpatient department, showing the benefits of regular exercise and the importance of maintaining the effectiveness of all three energy systems. You have also been asked to give a lecture to point out the potentially harmful effects of taking shortcuts to improve fitness through the use of performance-enhancing drugs. You have been asked to consider all participants, regardless of the sports they take part in.

GRADING CRITERIA
TO BE ASSESSED

P5, P6
M4

Task

Design a leaflet or poster which informs the reader of the difference between aerobic and anaerobic activities, and the relative energy requirements of different sports. You should include pictures, diagrams and/or photographs to show patients how they can investigate the differences for themselves. Your leaflet or poster should:

Describe two types of physical activity that use the aerobic energy system and two that use the anaerobic energy systems (P5).

Investigate different physical activities that use the aerobic and anaerobic energy systems, with tutor support (P6).

Explain the energy requirements of four different types of physical activity (M4).

Tackling the assignment

The obvious way to tackle this assignment is to produce a poster which can be used as part of a wall display. However, many people prefer to take leaflets that they can read in their own time, so you may decide to produce a small leaflet instead. Whichever option you choose, it is important to ensure that the information you include is accurate and presented in an eye-catching way. If your leaflet/poster is dull and boring, patients won't pick it up/look at it in the first place! Pay particular attention to the criteria for P6, because you must ensure that your leaflet or poster shows patients how to investigate different physical activities for themselves.

ANAEROBIC AND AEROBIC SYSTEMS

The aerobic energy system gives us long-term energy. Marathon runners are aerobic athletes because they use oxygen throughout the race, but they are only working at 80 per cent because above this level their body cannot burn oxygen quickly enough to produce energy.

The anaerobic energy system is used when you work without oxygen for a short period of time. Sprinters in the 100m are anaerobic athletes because they are working at 100 per cent effort but only for a short period of time. Therefore, they can complete their event without burning oxygen to produce energy.

The javelin is an anaerobic event because competitors are only working for a very short period of time but are working at their maximum effort level. They burn about ten calories per throw.

Marathon runners are aerobic athletes because they need a constant supply of oxygen to produce energy and they are running for a long period of time. They burn around 416 calories per hour.

Sprinters are anaerobic athletes because they are working without oxygen to produce energy. Also, they are putting in 100 per cent and are only doing it for about 10 to 15 seconds. They burn around 100–220 calories per race.

Football requires a mixture of anaerobic and aerobic activity. Players mainly work aerobically throughout the game (which lasts 90 minutes) because they are constantly moving around the pitch, but most of the time they are jogging or running at 75 per cent of their maximum speed. However, at certain points during the game, they have to sprint, for example, to chase a ball or beat a defender. At these times they are working anaerobically as they are working close to their maximum level and only for a short period of time. Players burn approximately 2000 calories in a full game.

[left margin notes, partially cut off:]

...poster is ...catching and ...se of images ...ttract patients ...d it. The ...nations of ...erobic and ...erobic energy ...ms are very ..., and the ...r would benefit ...more detail ...t how the ...systems work. ...ever, it does ...ribe at least two ...ties that use ...system and, ...ch, has met ...riteria for P5.

...nas has not ...ade any ...ttempt to meet ...e criteria for ...6 and so the ...iece of work ...as not fully ...et the Pass ...riteria.

[right margin note:]

Jonas has made an attempt to meet M4 by showing the amount of calories used in each activity, but this does not explain the energy requirements of these activities. He should have given a more detailed explanation of why each activity is aerobic or anaerobic as well as information about the number of calories each activity burns off. He should also have mentioned the alactic and lactic acid systems in his explanations to show his full understanding of the concepts being examined. The amount of calories burnt off has no bearing on whether an activity is aerobic or anaerobic!

Drugs and sports performance

To compete in the modern Olympic Games, to win gold, and to stand on the rostrum as the flag is raised and the national anthem plays is the dream of many. It comes true for only a few. Only the gifted, dedicated and very best will win. And perhaps a few drug cheats.

Modern sport is plagued by suspicions that many top athletes resort to drug-taking – doping – to enhance their performance. Anabolic steroids, human growth hormone, erythropoietin (EPO), beta blockers, stimulants and diuretics are sometimes used to achieve this effect. While drugs such as these get a lot of publicity, they are not well understood. What do they do? What are the health risks in the short or long term? Can the drugs be detected?

Dwain Chambers was banned from competing for two years, as well as in all future Olympic Games, after testing positive for the anabolic steroid Tetrahydrogestrinone (THG) in 2004.

Anabolic steroids

Anabolic steroids are drugs that resemble testosterone. Some are provided in tablet form and others are injected directly into a muscle. Testosterone is involved in controlling the rates of build-up and breakdown of all human tissue, including muscle. Because testosterone and related drugs affect muscle growth, raising the levels of them in the blood could help athletes to increase muscle size and strength.

Many athletes who use anabolic steroids are convinced that they increase lean muscle mass, and muscle strength and endurance. However, scientific studies have shown that anabolic steroids only enhance physical performance because of the effect on training, diet and motivation which accompany using the drugs. The other androgenic (masculinizing) side effects – such as increased body hair and a deepening of the voice – are not always desirable, particularly in women. Anabolic steroids can be addictive and can also cause aggression, high blood pressure, heart disease, infertility and cancer.

Erythropoietin (EPO)

Erythropoietin (EPO) is a naturally occurring hormone that increases the production of red blood cells, which carry oxygen. By increasing the oxygen-carrying capacity of the blood, EPO improves endurance and can therefore improve an athlete's performance by allowing them to run further or faster. As such, it is of most benefit to endurance athletes. Recombinant (artificially produced) EPO does have a legitimate use in the treatment of some medical conditions, such as cancer-related anaemia, but some athletes misuse it to improve endurance performance.

Dutch cyclist Thomas Dekker was banned from cycling in the 2009 Tour de France after a re-tested urine sample, originally taken in December 2007, was found to contain EPO.

Recombinant EPO (rEPO) is administered by injecting it directly into the blood stream. Unless administered by a medical professional, and even then only after a series of lengthy laboratory tests, rEPO can have very serious consequences. It can lead to a thickening of the blood, which in turn can cause blood clots, thrombosis, heart attacks and strokes. It has been implicated in the sudden deaths of a number of endurance athletes.

Human growth hormone

Human growth hormone (hGH) is a naturally occurring hormone produced by the pituitary gland, and is one of the most important hormones influencing growth and development in humans. It stimulates the production of cartilage cells, resulting in bone growth, and also plays a key role in muscle growth. The reported benefits of hGH include improved brain activity and function, strengthened connective tissue (reducing the probability of injury), weight loss without any loss in lean muscle mass, increased energy levels and improved lung function.

Some individuals use hGH because they think it is as effective as anabolic steroids with fewer side effects, and it is also difficult to detect in a drug test. However, the side effects of hGH misuse are severe. The most common is acromegaly, a disorder that leads to an overgrowth of bones, particularly in the skull, hands and feet, which is irreversible. Other side effects include diabetes, heart growth, increased blood pressure, premature ageing and impotence.

Cannabis

Cannabis is a drug that comes from Indian hemp plants. The active chemical in cannabis is tetrahydrocannabinol (THC). It is a depressant drug, although it does not necessarily make the person using it feel depressed. Rather, it affects the central nervous system by slowing down the messages going between the brain and the body. Small doses of cannabis can have effects lasting between two and four hours, including relaxation and a loss of inhibitions.

Cannabis has no real benefit for sports players, although it is used by some as a recreational drug when they are not playing sport. In the long term, however, there are some serious side effects of using cannabis. It can be very addictive and is thought to lead to confusion, hallucinations, paranoia and respiratory illnesses. It has also been linked to infertility and reduced sex drive.

Amphetamines

Amphetamines are stimulants that speed up the processes of the brain. They work by prompting the brain to release adrenalin, causing an increase in heart rate, stroke volume and blood pressure. These changes combine to give an athlete a burst of energy, which can increase speed and reduce reaction times. Amphetamines can also reduce appetite and, if they are used on a regular basis, this can lead to weight loss.

Amphetamines can damage brain cells and they usually cause mood swings, which can lead to antisocial behaviour. In addition, they can cause hallucinations, paranoia and other symptoms similar to those associated with schizophrenia.

Diuretics

Diuretics help the body to get rid of sodium and water. These can be natural or in the form of medication. They work by causing an increased output of urine and making the kidneys excrete more sodium in your urine. As the sodium is excreted it takes water from your blood with it. Natural diuretics include substances such as coffee, tea and fizzy cola.

Some athletes use diuretics to help them to fall within the required weight categories in sports such as horse racing, boxing and rowing. They are also used by some athletes to dilute their urine to avoid the detection of anabolic steroids. However, athletes using them are at risk of dehydration. This can cause dizziness, headaches, nausea, loss of coordination and balance, cramps, and kidney and heart failure.

The use of diuretics is not banned by the International Olympic Committee, although there are strict rules on which natural diuretics can be used and the allowed quantities of 'legal' diuretics is also controlled.

Beta blockers

Beta blockers slow down a person's heart rate, reducing their blood pressure or the effects of anxiety. They are usually prescribed by doctors to patients who are suffering from certain heart diseases or high blood pressure. Beta blockers may be of use in sports that require steady, controlled movements such as snooker, archery, shooting and gymnastics.

Healthy people who use beta blockers are placing themselves at risk of lowering their blood pressure and heart rate to dangerous levels. Beta blockers also increase the risk of depression and can lead to 'vivid dreams', sleep disturbance and breathlessness.

In October 2009, Uzbekistan international footballer Anzur Ismailov was banned for three months by FIFA after testing positive for cannabis.

BRONZE

1. Using the Internet or a library to help with your research, create a poster showing which drugs are acceptable in sport, and which ones are banned or restricted. Make the poster eye-catching so that it can be displayed in the changing rooms.

2. Choose one sportsperson who has been banned for using illegal drugs and write 500 words about the impact of their drug use on sport, ethics and society.

BRONZE   SILVER

3. 'All sports players should be allowed to take drugs to create a level playing field for athletes.' Discuss this statement.

Unit 18 assignment, part three

Background

As a fitness consultant, you have been asked by the local hospital to produce a series of leaflets, which can be given away in the outpatient department, showing the benefits of regular exercise and the importance of maintaining the effectiveness of all three energy systems. You have also been asked to give a lecture to point out the potentially harmful effects of taking shortcuts to improve fitness through the use of performance-enhancing drugs. You have been asked to consider all participants, regardless of the sports they take part in.

GRADING CRITERIA TO BE ASSESSED
P7, P8 M5

Task

Produce a speech or lecture that could be delivered at your local hospital to inform the audience of the different types of performance-enhancing drugs and the dangers associated with them. You may use visual aids to support your lecture where appropriate. Your speech or lecture will need to:

PASS

Describe four different types of drugs used to enhance sports performance and their effects (P7).

Describe the negative impact of drugs (P8).

MERIT

Explain the negative impact of drugs (M5).

Tackling the assignment

Speeches and lectures can be very boring if they are not supported by other forms of media, such as photographs, diagrams, sounds or videos. Therefore your speech needs to be supported by a series of drawings, photographs or short videos that will capture the audience's attention. You could even use models to show people what various performance-enhancing drugs look like. Using examples of sports players who have been convicted as 'drugs cheats' also helps to keep people interested, because it reminds them of instances they can relate to. The most important thing is to ensure that your speech makes it clear that performance-enhancing drugs are dangerous and in many cases illegal.

Meeting the Pass and Merit criteria

Unit 18:
Effects of
Exercise on the
Body Systems

BTEC Level 2 Firsts in Sport

Unit 18 assignment, part three

Leroy Tomes

DRUGS MISUSED BY ATHLETES

Therapeutic drugs
Diuretics, beta blockers

Performance-enhancing drugs
Amphetamines, ephedrine, caffeine, anabolic steroids, human growth hormone

Drugs typically misused
Alcohol, nicotine, cannabis, cocaine

PERFORMANCE-ENHANCING DRUGS

Anabolic steroids
Reasons for use:
Increases your muscle size and allows athletes to train harder.

Problems encountered:
High blood pressure, heart disease, infertility and cancer. Women can grow increased facial and body hair. Other effects include mood swings, aggression and anxiety.

PERFORMANCE-ENHANCING DRUGS

Human growth hormone
Reasons for use:
To increase muscle mass and decrease fat mass.

Problems encountered:
Gigantism, hyperthyroidism, cardiac disease, arthritis, diabetes mellitus, impotence and osteoporosis.

Many athletes use medication and in the vast majority of cases this is perfectly legal. David Beckham was once caught on camera using an inhaler for his asthma. As long as the substances used are cleared by the relevant sport's governing body as being safe, effective and not performance-enhancing, then it is OK for athletes to use them.

The problem is that some athletes cheat by using drugs to enable them to perform better. There are several problems with this:

- Other athletes who are 'playing fairly' are disadvantaged (cheated).
- Athletes using drugs can become addicted.
- Athletes using drugs can suffer serious side effects and can even die through substance misuse.
- The costs to the sport are huge. Bad press can lead to a loss of sponsorship money throughout the sport, meaning that non-drug-taking athletes suffer too.

The slides I am about to show you contain information about specific performance-enhancing drugs that are used by athletes.

Leroy's speech is informative and engaging. I can picture an audience listening to everything he is saying. His PowerPoint® slides support the speech that he is giving and contain relevant information. The bulleted points in his speech clearly describe the negative impact of drugs (P8) but I would like to see each bullet point developed further to allow Leroy to gain the marks for explaining these effects (thereby allowing him to attain M5).

The slides are clearly on the way to meeting the criteria for P7 but Leroy has only used two examples, and the criteria state that four examples are needed. I am sure that with a little more work Leroy will achieve the Pass criteria (P7 and P8) and with more explanation of the negative impact of drugs, he will achieve M5.

Unit 19: Business Skills in Sport

Business skills

Business skills are needed by many people working in the sport and leisure industry if they are to do their jobs effectively.

Customer information

Information about classes, events and new programmes needs to be communicated to existing customers and potential customers in as many different ways as possible, including leaflets, posters, via a website or even by text and email. A sport and leisure facility should have a marketing plan detailing which of these promotional techniques are most appropriate for their customers and which they can afford.

Booking procedures

Customers can make bookings in many different ways, by telephone, email or face-to-face when they pop in to a centre. Bookings can be made for one-off events, such as a 40-minute squash game on Monday 4 October, for regular events over a specified period, such as a six-week course, or for regular events over a long period, such as a weekly team practice. Staff need procedures for recording all bookings so that facilities aren't double booked. They might use a daily diary, a weekly planner or a database run by a booking software programme.

Customer records

Customer records can be kept on paper or on an electronic database. The minimum information that a sport and leisure business would keep about their customer would be their name, address, date of birth, membership details and information about the exercise programme they are following. More sophisticated records systems might also contain information about the frequency with which a customer visits the centre, the duration of their stays, when their membership runs out and even the amount of money that they spend while they are in the centre. All the information contained in customer records helps a business build a profile of their customers so that it can provide a service which better meets their customers' needs.

Business skills in the sport and leisure industry

Remember:

All information stored about customers is governed by the Data Protection Act 1998. Under this legislation customers have the right to see all the information an organization holds about them, and the information must not be passed to another organization or individual without the customer's permission.

Customer trends

Knowing about customer trends, customers' habits and what they do when, can really help staff to deliver a better service to their customers. They can work out when a sport and leisure facility is busiest, using this information to determine peak and off-peak times and to work out an appropriate staff rota. Because many sports are seasonal and customers tend not to be as interested in sports out of season, businesses can use this trend to buy in stock precisely when customers are going to need it. For example, they might buy in cricket equipment in March, just before the season starts in the UK.

Customer inductions

At an induction session, a new customer is shown around the facility for the first time and is shown how to use the equipment in a safe and sensible manner. A trainer might also put together a training programme for the customer at their induction session. To do this in a business-like way, the customer should complete a Physical Activity Readiness Questionnaire, which is known as a PAR-Q. An example of a PAR-Q can be found on page 263.

Ticketing systems

Ticketing systems are only really needed for large venues, such as stadiums, which hold regular events with seating. Sport and leisure businesses use ticketing systems because of the benefits they bring, including the opportunity for customers to purchase tickets online, the display of reliable and accurate information about the availability of tickets, and fraud prevention. If used effectively, ticketing systems should help a business manage sales, speed up crowd movements, reduce staff time and limit customer service problems. Ticketing systems can also provide managers with valuable data about sales trends, which they can use to help the business grow.

Market analysis

Market trends describe the way a market is developing or changing, and can be influenced by many things including customer preferences, government policy and new technology. For example, there is currently a trend away from squash and many squash courts are being converted into studios that can be used for yoga and Pilates, which are seeing a growth in popularity. Many market research companies, such as Mintel, SIRC and Key Note, publish reports that predict future market trends. However, these reports are expensive to buy and Sport England's website (www.sportengland.org) offers some useful statistics which are easier to access and interpret. Assessing the performance of individual companies and reading market reports in industry magazines are also ways of keeping in touch with trends.

One of the best ways to ensure that a business knows what its customers want is to analyse market trends in order to find out what is happening in specific sectors of the sport and leisure industry. For example, the information can be used to amend the pricing policy in order to attract more customers, to create promotions that entice customers at quiet times of the day or year, or to fill gaps in the provision or product range.

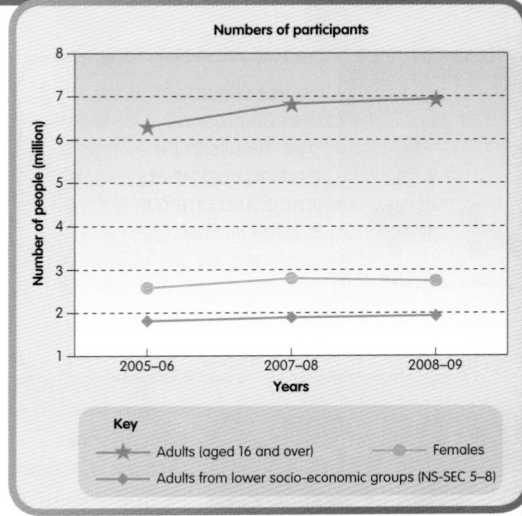

What would this data tell you if you were a sports centre manager or the owner of a shop selling sportswear?

Customer feedback

Feedback from customers is the most accessible source of information an organization has about how it is doing. Customer feedback can be gathered in a number of different ways:

- Asking customers to complete surveys.
- Encouraging customers to share their ideas via suggestions boxes placed at key points around the centre or at reception.
- Employing mystery customers. Mystery customers are specially employed by managers and are unknown to the majority of staff. They pretend to be a customer and then report back to managers on the service they received.

There are two crucial things to remember about customer feedback. Firstly, it is important to ask the right questions and to ask open questions that give customers the opportunity to express their thoughts freely. Secondly, it is vital to analyse and then act on the feedback. Collecting customer feedback is a waste of time if it isn't acted on.

Customer complaints

Having an effective procedure in place for dealing with customer complaints will:

- Help customers to know what their rights are. For example, if they are legally entitled to a refund because the good or service they purchased wasn't as described, wasn't of satisfactory quality or wasn't fit for purpose.
- Help staff to know what to do when confronted with an upset customer.
- Ensure that, as far as possible, customers' complaints can be resolved satisfactorily.
- Help to maintain the image and reputation of the business.

Minor problems can probably be left to staff to sort out but the manager should be called to deal with more serious issues.

BRONZE

1. Make a list of three things that could go wrong if bookings at a leisure centre are not taken and recorded properly.

2. Design a membership application form for a small private-sector gym.

3a) Choose one of the business skills described above, and visit a local sport and leisure facility to find out how it employs the skill you have chosen to support its customers.

b) Prepare and deliver a short presentation to the rest of your class, explaining what you found out during your visit.

Customer types

It is useful for a sport and leisure business to segment its customers – to break its customers down into different types – so that they can offer activities to attract each type of customer and to ensure that all members of a community, including minority groups, feel welcome. Understanding the needs of different types of customers also ensures better customer service (a meditation class for senior citizens shouldn't be arranged in a room next to a rowdy educational group, for example) and better health and safety (because there may need to be extra first aiders on duty when a large school party uses the centre, for example).

Senior citizens: Anyone over 60 is usually classed as a senior citizen. They tend to have retired, have plenty of spare time and can be keen to keep fit. They often visit sport and leisure facilities at off-peak times, and want to meet other people of their own age group.

Children: This type of customer can be further broken down into children and young people of different ages and abilities. Most children are interested in attending clubs in the evening or at weekends, or taking part in activities during school holidays.

Everyone else: Mainly individuals working out, small groups of friends playing recreationally, or clubs and teams practising or playing matches.

Educational groups: These are likely to be school groups or a group of students from a language school or university. Access to sport and leisure centre facilities for educational groups needs to be carefully scheduled, especially if the group is large, so that the impact on other customers is kept to a minimum.

The most common types of customer are …

People with disabilities: Unfortunately, although it is desirable, there are not full facilities for people with all types of disability at all sport and leisure centres. This can be because of a lack of trained staff, suitable equipment or space. However, it is important that every effort is made to accommodate people with disabilities wherever possible.

Mother and baby groups: Pregnant women might want to take part in antenatal exercise classes and mums who have just given birth might want to get back in shape with post-natal exercise classes. New mums and dads might also want to exercise with their babies. These types of classes are common in swimming pools but adapted exercise classes can work well too.

Rehabilitation: Customers who are recovering after injury or are on GP referral schemes, who might need lots of support, encouragement and guidance as they exercise.

BRONZE

SILVER

1. Different customer types have different needs, so a mystery customer has to decide which type of customer they are before they visit a sport and leisure facility. They have to get into character. Working with a partner:

a) Each choose a different customer type and think about the needs of your customer. For example, are they in a hurry or do they have trouble walking up and down stairs?

b) Make a list of everything your mystery customer will be observing and reporting on when they visit a sport and leisure facility. For example, if they are a new mum they might be interested in finding out if the baby-changing facilities are clean.

c) Show your list to your partner and together discuss how the business skill of collecting customer feedback through mystery customers needs to be adapted to support different customer types.

SILVER

2. Look at the business skills on pages 330 and 331. How should each business skill be adapted to support each customer type?

GOLD

3. Evaluate your completed table by placing the skills in order of priority for a business, explaining why you have chosen to put them in that order.

Unit 19 assignment, part one

Background

You are the owner of a newly opened gym and you want to create a pack of information to give to all new employees, which outlines the business skills they will need to be able to do their jobs successfully.

Task

Create an information pack for new employees that outlines the importance of:

- providing customers with information
- taking bookings
- organizing customer inductions
- keeping records
- using ticketing systems

- responding to customer trends
- analysing market trends
- collecting and responding to customer feedback
- dealing with customer complaints.

GRADING CRITERIA TO BE ASSESSED
P1
M1
D1

Your information pack should also:

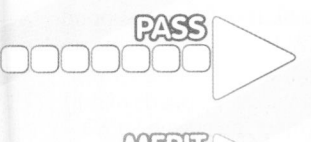

Describe the business skills needed to support customers in the sport and leisure industry (P1).

Explain how business skills differ to support different customers in the sport and leisure industry (M1).

Evaluate the business skills and their role in supporting different types of customer (D1).

Tackling the assignment

This is a research task and there are a number of different sources you can consult to help you with your research. You can:

- Watch films about the sport and leisure industry.
- Visit a sport and leisure facility and observe what takes place.
- Talk to staff working in the sport and leisure industry, or invite someone to come and speak to your class.
- Read magazine articles, leaflets and information on the Internet about the sport and leisure industry.
- Discuss your ideas with your classmates.

As you are carrying out your research, think about how the needs of customers vary and how the business skills required need to be adapted to accommodate these different needs.

Think carefully about the format your information pack is going to take. It can include pictures, diagrams and quotes alongside the text to make it attractive for the end user. Most importantly, remember to describe, explain or evaluate the key points.

Remember:

- When you **describe** something you need to paint a picture in words, making sure you include sufficient detail so that someone else can see the picture you are painting.
- When you **explain** something you need to give reasons why the picture you have painted with your description is as it is. Explanations often contain the word 'because'.
- An **evaluation** requires you to examine strengths and weaknesses, commenting on the quality or importance of something, for example.

Meeting the Pass criteria

BTEC Level 2 Firsts in Sport

Unit 19 assignment, part one   **Mary Becker**

Gathering customer feedback

Gathering customer feedback is important because it helps the business to know preferences and customer needs.

Procedure: This should be done regularly and passed onto the manager.

> Although the information Mary has provided about customer feedback is correct, she has not covered the subject in enough detail to achieve the criteria for P1. She needs to provide more information about the methods that can be used to gather customer feedback – including surveys, suggestion boxes, visits from mystery customers and analysing customer complaints – to ensure her answer is complete.

Meeting the Merit criteria

BTEC Level 2 Firsts in Sport

Unit 19 assignment, part one   **David Bryce**

Customer inductions for Bryce's Gym

Customer inductions need to be carried out the first time anyone visits the gym. This is essential for health and safety purposes. Completing this checklist should ensure all inductions cover everything they need to:
1. Ensure the customer's details are correct in our records.
2. Ensure the customer has completed a PAR-Q.
3. Ensure the customer has an appointment with a personal trainer, who will create a personal exercise programme for them.
4. Take the customer on a tour of the changing area and the fitness suite, and show them the fire exits.
5. Complete the induction by asking if the customer has any questions.

> David has described one of the business skills needed to support customers in the sport and leisure industry and has met the criteria for P1. However, he needs to add more to meet the criteria for M1. How should the customer induction he describes change to support different customers? For example, will a customer in a wheelchair have exactly the same induction as an able-bodied customer? And why would their needs differ?

Meeting the Distinction criteria

Customer inductions for different types of customers

All customers should be given the same induction but the induction procedure needs to be flexible to meet the needs of different customers.

Over-60s

Many over-60s are retired and join a gym as much for the opportunity to meet and socialize with people as they do to keep fit. It is therefore important that the induction is carried out in a friendly, chatty way and that the social aspects of the gym are emphasized. The person having the induction could even be introduced to other people in the gym and the last part of the induction, where the customer is asked if they have any questions, could be completed sitting down in the cafe. It is also important to make sure that over-60s fully understand how the equipment works, particularly if it involves electronic settings, and that they are made fully aware of the dangers of over-exercising. The content of the induction will be standard but the way in which the content is covered must be different to suit the type of client.

If this approach is adopted, the customer should feel very welcome and will look forward to coming back because they know they will have people to talk to when they do. However, it is important to remember that not all over-60s are retired with not much to do. Many still work and/or have a lot of commitments. They may want to slot a visit to the gym into a busy schedule and might be put off by a slow, chatty induction and the idea that they have to talk to everyone when they go to the gym. It is therefore important to recognize the individual beneath the customer type and respond to their individual needs, and not just their exercise needs, accordingly.

> Miriam has evaluated how a standard induction should change for one type of customer, by pointing out the strengths and weaknesses of her suggestions. If she continues in this way, evaluating how the standard induction should change for other types of customers and examining other business skills, such as ticketing and carrying out research, in the same way, I would be happy to award her D1.

Customer service skills

While it is important for a business to employ business skills, such as market analysis and ticketing systems, to make sure it fully supports its customers, the people who use sport and leisure facilities aren't always aware that these skills are being used. What a customer is most aware of is the customer service they receive or, to put it another way, how satisfied they are with their experience of a centre. All staff at a sport and leisure facility have the opportunity to improve customer service, by developing good customer service skills.

Providing information, assistance and advice

The quality of information, assistance and advice employees provide to customers make a big impact on a customer's feelings of satisfaction. So, if you are helping a customer buy a tennis racket, for example, you need technical knowledge to be able to advise them on the most appropriate racket for their height and weight. If you are working on a reception desk you are probably selling services – experiences – rather than products, but the same principles apply. You will need to know all about the different aerobics classes on offer to help the customer choose the right one for them. Similarly, you will need a high level of knowledge if you are going to advise a customer on the safe way to use a running machine that they aren't familiar with.

Passing on messages

People working in a sport and leisure centre will almost certainly be expected to pass on messages. A customer might contact the centre in person, or by telephone, email, letter or fax. If you receive a message, then it is your responsibility to promptly pass it on to the person it is intended for. If the message is given to you verbally, then you must also make sure that you write it down accurately, checking details with the customer to make sure you have got them right.

Maintaining records

Maintaining records is a routine but important task, and must be done accurately. Financial information, such as all tickets or drinks sold, is always recorded because every organization has to keep financial accounts for tax and legal reasons. You might be required to note amounts in a cash book but it is more likely that the till you use will keep a record of most financial transactions. You may also be responsible for keeping records of customers' details on a database or, in a smaller organization, on cards or in a file. Confidentiality is extremely important when dealing with customer records, because all personal information is protected by the Data Protection Act 1998.

When you are confronted with an angry customer, it is time to bring all your communication skills into play. Show that you are actively listening, lower the pitch, volume and tempo of your voice, and make sure your body language shows that you are open to discussing the customer's problem and not defensive.

Dealing with issues

Good customer service doesn't just involve routine tasks like taking messages and providing information. In fact, good customer service is even more important when it comes to non-routine events like dealing with injuries, helping a customer who has had their personal property stolen or responding to complaints. In most cases, there should be procedures in place so that you can deal with the situations confidently and efficiently, and the customer should be content that you did everything you could to help them.

Communication skills

Communication skills are at the heart of good customer service and if you develop good communication skills they will have a positive impact on everybody you deal with, including your colleagues. Follow these tips for success!

Appropriate language

It should be accepted that you never swear at work, because it could lead to disciplinary action if you swore at a customer or colleague; however, appropriate language is much more than not swearing. It is important to try and use language which is suitable for the person you are communicating with. For example, if you are talking to a young person who has come to the leisure centre by themselves for the first time, try to give them specific instructions without too much technical language.

Active listening

Actively listening means showing the person who is talking to you that you really are listening. Maintain eye contact, stop what you are doing and give the person who is talking to you your full attention. Reinforce this by nodding or agreeing from time to time. Don't get distracted by things going on around you, and don't fiddle with anything or continue to work on your computer.

The pitch of your voice

The pitch of your voice is how high or low your voice is. To some extent the pitch of our voices is determined by genetics, but lowering your voice can help you to command more respect from the people you are talking to and this can be used to defuse difficult situations. It can also be useful to reinforce what you are saying with hand gestures.

The volume of your voice

The volume of your voice is very important if you are coaching or giving instructions. Sports halls can be very echoey, so customers might not hear you if your voice is quiet. You can also increase the volume of your voice to control groups, especially if they are in danger, but remember to face your audience for maximum impact. Varying the volume of your voice is also a really useful way to get attention or emphasize a point.

Top tips for successful communication

The tempo of your speech

The tempo of your speech is the speed at which you talk. If you talk too fast the details of your message may be lost or confused, so try to speak at a regular tempo in all situations.

Body language

Body language is a form of non-verbal communication and it is the name given to the messages you communicate with your body while you are talking to someone. Body language is very powerful and people will use your body language to judge how you are really feeling about a situation; if you are, for example, serious, joking, grumpy or not bothered. Your body language needs to match what you are saying and not give people the wrong impression or mixed messages.

Your facial expression especially can reinforce your verbal messages in a very simple way, for example, with a smile to welcome people and signal that you are friendly and approachable. Your posture also says a lot about you. Slouching around, leaning on worktops and generally not looking busy will not be looked on favourably by your boss or by customers. Managers prefer staff to be alert and look it too.

What does the body language of each of these people communicate?

BRONZE

1. Working with a partner, take it in turns to communicate the following with body language only (so no talking!):
- Not understanding an instruction.
- Not being bothered about a situation.
- Actively listening.
- Being frustrated with a customer.

2. Read a short paragraph of text out loud, varying the pitch, volume and tempo of your voice to create emphasis and interest.

3. Design a poster for a ladies only Pilates class, remembering to include all the information that someone who wants to attend the class might need.

Applying customer service skills

Knowing the skills of good customer service is not enough. It is important to be able to apply them, especially in stressful situations.

Dealing with customer complaints

Dealing with customer complaints can be awkward because the customer could be furious and initially you might find it difficult to calm them down. Your organization should train you to deal with complaints and provide you with a procedure for resolving them, but the following sequence is good practice:

- Ask the customer to explain the problem to you step by step. Actively listen to what they are saying, and make sure your body language is friendly and open if you are face to face with them. You could even make some notes.
- Try to agree that the situation is not ideal and reassure them that you are taking their complaint seriously, but do not make any promises to fix the situation or admit liability (that you, a colleague or the organization you are working for is responsible for the problem).
- Consult your supervisor if you do not feel able to resolve the complaint yourself. More serious conflicts may be taken out of your hands and resolved by a manager or even referred to the organization's solicitor.
- Offer a settlement, which might mean making an apology or providing the customer with compensation of some kind.
- Follow up the complaint, to make sure that the customer is happy with the way it was resolved.

Remember that the customer is usually right, but not always! Stand your ground if you are sure you are in the right; however, make sure that the tone, volume and tempo of your voice remain low and that your body language isn't aggressive. Most importantly, be prepared to back down rather than cause an incident. Some people are professional complainers out to get a deal! Always keep in the back of your mind that, if you deal with a complaint effectively, you are more likely to retain that customer.

If the complaint is received in writing, in a letter or an email, it may be appropriate to reply in writing. You may also need to resolve complaints raised face to face in writing. When you are writing to a customer, make sure there are no spelling or grammatical errors (don't forget to run a spell-check) and ensure the customer is addressed appropriately ('Dear Mr Jones' rather than 'Dear Bob', for example). Use a polite tone, restate the nature of the complaint and offer a settlement or explanation. Also state the date by which the customer should reply if they do not feel the complaint has been satisfactorily resolved and thank them for bringing the problem to your attention.

Every organization should have a procedure in place for monitoring complaints. This procedure should record the volume, frequency and nature of the complaints, including detail about who they are made against (if appropriate), what action was taken and whether the customer was satisfied by the resolution. There are a number of good reasons for this:

- This provides an accurate record of what happened if legal proceedings are initiated.
- It helps to identify any patterns that are emerging, such one member of staff or one particular customer involved in a number of problems.
- A company can measure its performance by the number and nature of complaints received (if it collects accurate records).

Dealing with accidents

An accident can be anything from a minor cut to a broken leg in a sporting context. If you are not a qualified first aider, the first thing you should do is contact the first aider on duty, or ask a colleague or member of the public to contact the first aider if you need to stay with the injured person. Keep calm and follow the organization's procedures for accidents. All accidents have to be reported via the accident book, so note down the name and address of the casualty, any witnesses, and the time and nature of the accident while it is all fresh in your memory. If a parent has to be called, ask a senior member of staff to do this.

Dealing with stolen property

Most sport and leisure facilities have a loss book, where all items reported lost or stolen are recorded, along with the details of the incident, and the name and address of the person reporting the loss. If items are stolen, a manager or supervisor should discuss the possibility of calling the police with the customer and, if appropriate, make the call. The loss book will help sport and leisure facilities to monitor any loss or theft and, if a lot of items are being stolen, the management may decide to call the police in to investigate.

Recruitment of members

You may be asked to talk to customers entering or leaving the sport or leisure facility, make telephone calls or even give presentations to try and recruit new members. It is best to prepare a short script before you begin, to get what you want to say clear in your head, but try to sound as if you are talking to a customer naturally and haven't said the same thing lots of times already. Be enthusiastic and friendly and remember to demonstrate your knowledge using appropriate language. The following procedure for selling goods and services can be followed:

- Raise customer awareness by highlighting the benefits of the goods or services that you want to sell.
- Establish a rapport with the customer and find out what their needs are.
- Present your product or services in more detail.
- Answer any questions honestly.
- Try to close the sale, having the form the customer needs to sign near at hand.
- Follow up to make sure the customer is happy.

Customer inductions

Customer inductions are very important because they ensure new customers are aware of all health and safety procedures at the sport and leisure facility, and that the facility is aware of any health issues that might affect the way in which the customer uses the equipment. Procedures for inductions will vary from leisure centre to leisure centre but as a general rule you should:

- Make sure that you are fully informed and have all the support materials you need before you meet the customer.
- Take the customer on a tour to familiarize them with the facilities. Make sure you give them the opportunity to ask questions as the tour progresses.
- Complete membership and/or PAR-Q forms.
- Explain how to use the equipment or follow their programme safely.
- Return the customer to reception.
- Follow up with a courtesy call to ensure that the customer is happy.

Answering the telephone

A sport and leisure facility might have a policy on the maximum number of times a phone is allowed to ring before it is answered, in which case it is important that you answer the phone promptly when it rings. Say the name of the sport or leisure facility you are working at and ask the caller how you can help. You might also be allowed to say your name. For example:

"Hello! This is Falsgrave Leisure Centre. How may I help you?"
or
"Hello, you're through to Naomi at Falsgrave Leisure Centre. How may I help you?"

Listen carefully to what the caller wants and take notes if necessary. Identify exactly what it is the caller needs and decide on your response. Take a message, writing a memo if possible, or connect the caller to the person they want to speak to, if appropriate.

General enquiries

General enquiries often occur when you least expect it. You might be asked a question as you walk through the car park or while you are mopping the floor of the changing rooms. The important thing is to be well-informed about all aspects of the centre and know who can answer a customer's query if you can't. Shrugging, saying "I don't know" and getting on with whatever it was you were doing when you were interrupted is not good customer service! If you want to make a really good impression, ask the customer if they found what they needed next time you see them.

Remember:

Many sport and leisure facilities will ask customers to complete customer satisfaction surveys, so it is important that you employ all your customer service skills to maintain a good image and reputation of the facility in customers' minds. Good customer service might also win you an employee of the month award, so it could benefit you directly too!

You will probably deal with most general enquiries face to face, so remember to be courteous, to actively listen and to smile. Remember to make eye contact with the customer and use positive body language too.

BRONZE

1. Perform a role play to demonstrate the application of good customer service skills in each of the following situations:
- dealing with customer complaints
- dealing with accidents
- dealing with stolen property
- recruitment of members

SILVER

- customer inductions
- answering the telephone
- general enquiries.

2. Include at least two of the following customer service skills in each role play.
- Providing information, assistance and advice
- Passing on messages
- Maintaining records
- Dealing with issues
- Communication skills

BRONZE

3. Create a flow chart detailing an effective procedure for dealing with a customer complaint.

Unit 19 assignment, part two

Background

You work as a receptionist at a leisure centre. Your role requires you to interact with customers a great deal, selling tickets, booking facilities and answering general enquiries. Most of the time, you talk to customers face to face but sometimes you talk to them on the telephone. A new receptionist has been appointed and you have been asked to be their mentor.

GRADING CRITERIA TO BE ASSESSED
P2, P3 M2

Task

Three customer service scenarios have occurred at the leisure centre where you work:

1. A customer telephones to enquire about swimming classes for adult beginners.
2. A customer is very upset. They booked a squash court for today at 12:30pm when they were in the leisure centre last week. They are busy at work but have made the time to take a lunch break, and were looking forward to their game. However, they have arrived at the leisure centre to find there is no record of their booking and that the court is being used by someone else. You didn't make the original booking but you are now on reception.
3. A customer would like to talk to someone about taking out full membership at the leisure centre. It is not your responsibility to deal with membership applications but the person the customer needs to speak to isn't in the centre today.

Role play each scenario to demonstrate best practice in customer service and prepare a booklet for the new receptionist, outlining guidelines for a fourth customer service situation of your choice. You need to:

Demonstrate the use of customer service skills in three different customer service situations (P2).

Produce guidelines for a selected customer service situation (P3).

Demonstrate the integrated use of customer service skills (M2).

Tackling the assignment

Practice makes perfect, and it would be a good idea to practise your role plays before you ask for them to be assessed. If your teacher or tutor agrees, you could even create your own scenarios. To meet the Merit criteria you need to demonstrate the integrated use of customer service skills. This means that you have to demonstrate that you are using more than one skill at the same time. For example, you might take a telephone message while at the same time providing the caller with information they require. Or, you might have to deal with a customer complaint at the same time as providing another customer with some information.

Think carefully through the scenario that you will use to create your guidelines. You might even decide to visit a local leisure centre and talk to the receptionist there about likely scenarios and appropriate procedures. Remember that guidelines are designed to be used by someone who has limited knowledge, so it is important that they are very clear and logical. You could write down a series of numbered stages or you could present your guidelines as a flow diagram to make sure that they are easy to follow.

Skills for effective sport and leisure business operation

Like many other businesses which deal regularly with the public, sports and leisure businesses employ financial, health and safety, and security skills in order to ensure that they run efficiently and effectively.

Financial skills

All businesses need to employ a range of financial skills to ensure that they keep accurate records. Such records help businesses to comply with the law. They also help them to work out if they are making a profit or a loss, which indicates whether the business is efficient or effective (and should continue in the same way), or whether they need to make major changes to ensure that they are successful in the future.

Managing customer accounts creating source documents containing all the basic information about a customer's account, and updating the information as and when things change. Up-to-date customer accounts can help businesses identify fraud and can minimize the impact of customers' debts.

Using billing systems to create invoices that show what a customer owes for goods and services they have received but not yet paid for, and to chase late payments.

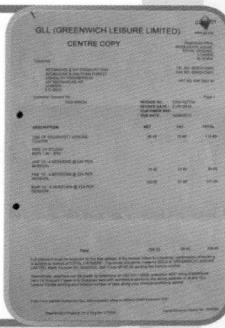

Receiving customer payments in cash, by cheque, debit card, credit card or bank transfer.

Giving receipts giving the various details of sale: time, place, amount, goods and so on.

Purchasing goods and services buying goods and services from suppliers, from the food for the cafe to advertising space in a newspaper.

Using payroll systems to calculate and pay out wages.

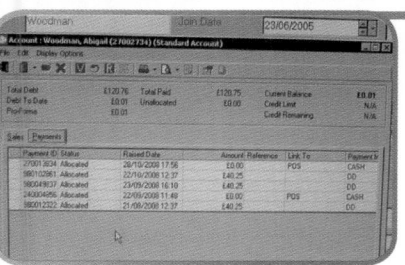

Maintaining sales records to show who has bought what and when. These figures are then used to analyse the success of a business, to work out the profit it has made each year and to predict how much profit it will make in future years.

Controlling stock making sure a business knows exactly how much stock it has, and which goods are selling fast and need to be replaced before they run out.

BRONZE

1. Create an invoice to be sent out by a company called Green Tree Leisure to a customer, John Grainger at Caldecote Rugby Club, who has ordered 15 rugby shirts at £23 each.

2. Create the receipt that John Grainger at Caldecote Rugby Club will receive when he has paid the invoice he received for Activity 1.

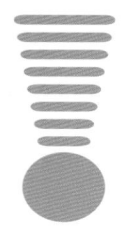

Remember:

When it comes to financial skills, the most important thing to remember is that sums of money must be precise, paperwork should be processed promptly and accurate records should be kept.

Health and safety skills

Having the correct procedures in place to safeguard staff and visitors, and for everyone to follow in an emergency, gives staff confidence and reassures customers. Members of staff must all understand how these procedures work and know how to follow them, even when they are under pressure.

Implementing and adhering to health and safety systems

Assessing hazards and putting measures in place to counteract them is part of the risk assessment process that underpins most health and safety legislation. All businesses must implement health and safety procedures, making sure that these are written up and shared with all members of staff and, where appropriate, with customers. By law, the procedures should cover a range of situations, including lifting, moving and storing equipment, setting up electrical items, and using chemicals. Employees have as much responsibility for ensuring their health and safety as employers do, so ignorance is no excuse. If there is a gap in your knowledge, you should ask your employer for training.

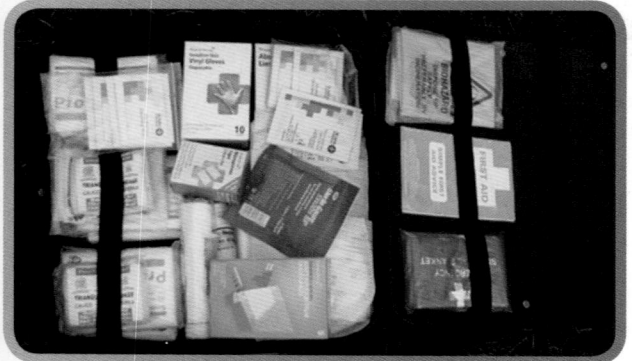

It is important that first-aid boxes are checked after they are used, to make sure that they are always fully stocked.

First-aid training and provision

The Health and Safety (First-Aid) Regulations 1981 state that all employers need to provide adequate and appropriate first-aid equipment, facilities and people to ensure that their staff and visitors can get help if they need it. What is adequate and appropriate obviously depends on the type of business and the number of employees, but for a sport and leisure facility, which members of the public visit, this means having a trained first aider on duty at all times. A trained first aider will be able to deal with minor illnesses and injuries, and know when to call for an ambulance if the injury or illness is serious. Fixed and mobile first-aid boxes must be on display and easily accessible at all times. Most leisure centres have a first-aid room too.

Having an up-to-date first-aid qualification is a must for anyone working, or wanting to work, in the sport and leisure industry these days. These can be obtained by attending various training courses, all of which must be approved by the Health and Safety Executive.

Knowledge of and adherence to emergency procedures

Emergencies are serious situations that require instant action, such as evacuating a building because of a fire or resuscitating someone who has stopped breathing after swallowing water in the swimming pool. All sport and leisure facilities should have procedures in place, which must be followed correctly in an emergency. Staff should remain calm during an emergency and, because it is difficult to remain calm under pressure, it is important that drills are performed so that staff can practise emergency procedures until they know them inside out.

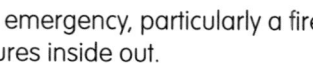

Signs help members of the public to follow emergency evacuation routes, so they need to be highly visible and easy to understand.

Knowledge of and adherence to fire procedures

Knowledge of and adherence to fire procedures are some of the most important health and safety skills there are. Ignorance of what to do in an emergency, particularly a fire, is not an excuse in the eyes of the law and all staff should know the fire procedures inside out.

By law, all sports and leisure facilities must have procedures for:
- evacuating the building in the event of a fire
- running practice fire drills
- checking fire extinguishers
- checking sprinkler systems
- checking escape routes are clear, including fire escapes, fire doors and stairways, as well as evacuation routes for people with disabilities.

BRONZE

3. What should a first-aid box contain?

4a) What do the different colour-coded labels on fire extinguishers mean?

b) Why it is important to use the correct fire extinguisher if confronted with a fire?

Experts, such as consultants, engineers or the fire service, are often called in to check the procedures are satisfactory and that equipment is working properly. Organizations and employees must follow any recommendations made by the experts.

Security skills

Security systems and emergency procedures are designed to keep people and venues safe. They should identify hazards and minimize or eliminate the risk these hazards present.

Emergency procedures protect people or move them away from danger; from fire, flooding, overcrowding, a robbery, a terrorist attack, a structure that is about to collapse, noxious gases or toxic smoke. Alarms may sound to warn everyone at the venue that there is an emergency but staff need to be fully aware of how to lead an evacuation calmly so that panic doesn't set in.

Some security systems and emergency procedures will apply at all times, but others will only apply in certain circumstances, when large crowds attend an event or when vulnerable children are in the leisure centre. Each organization will, for example, have a child protection policy and procedures for staff to follow if they think a child is in danger. There may also be special procedures to protect staff working alone in the venue or late at night. Some employers provide taxis for all staff who do not have their own transport and have to travel home after a certain time at night.

Sport and leisure facilities need security even when they are closed.

Security systems, such as CCTV cameras, alarms and patrolling guards, need to be strategically placed to deter people from committing a criminal act, or breaking into a venue to steal or vandalize the equipment, for example. However, if a crime does take place, they can also help the police to catch the criminals.

Security procedures set down how a building should be locked up and opened. This includes, for example, how to set and deactivate alarms and other security devices, and the appropriate sequence for checking that all windows and doors are shut or locked and all equipment is turned off.

BRONZE

5. Name at least two security measures that would deter each of the following security threats:
- Theft of a tennis kit while its owner is showering after a match.
- Graffiti on the walls of a leisure centre.
- Football supporters abusing staff at a football ground after a match.
- People trying to get into a match without a ticket.
- Ticket fraud.
- Adults interfering with young swimmers.

6. You are caught up in a fire at a leisure centre.

a) During the evacuation your clothes catch on fire. Do you: **A** run faster; **B** stop, drop and roll on the ground; **C** find a sink to cover yourself in water?

b) To leave the building, do you: **A** use the lift because it is the quickest way down; **B** stay where you are; **C** follow the fire exit signs down the stairs?

c) Once you are outside the building, do you: **A** stay close to the building so that you can see if your friends have got out okay; **B** get as far away from the building as possible; **C** go to the designated evacuation point?

d) You suspect that your friend is still in the building. Do you: **A** tell a fire officer that you suspect they are trapped; **B** dash back inside to rescue them; **C** watch at the windows for any sign of them?

e) You have been trapped in a room by the fire. Do you: **A** scream as loud as you can; **B** take some of your clothes off and stuff them around the door; **C** go to a window and jump?

Unit 19 assignment, part three

Background

Staff need to be aware of the financial, health and safety, and security measures that sport and leisure facilities use to make sure that they operate smoothly, safely and securely. Your local leisure centre has recently come under new management and you have been asked to work for the new management team as a consultant, identifying the skills the centre needs to operate effectively as a business.

GRADING CRITERIA
TO BE ASSESSED

P4

Task

Research a sport and leisure centre of your choice. Then, prepare a report which identifies the financial, health and safety, and security skills it uses to ensure that it runs well.

PASS

Identify the skills needed for effective sport and leisure business operation (P4).

Tackling the assignment

You can use textbooks, the Internet and case studies in management magazines to help you with your research. However, the most important thing you can do is visit a sport or leisure facility, and talk to the staff who work there about the systems and procedures that they use, if possible.

To make sure that you meet the Pass criteria, think carefully about how you structure your report, using headings and sub-headings to make sure that you cover everything. For example, you could construct your report in three sections:

1. Financial skills (the skills needed to run a business from day to day).
2. Health and safety skills (the skills needed to ensure staff and customers are looked after and safe in all areas of the facility).

3. Security skills (the skills needed to protect staff and customers as they use the facilities, and to protect the building and the equipment it contains).

You could then break the sections down into sub-sections. For example:

1. Financial skills
   - 1.1 Managing customer accounts
   - 1.2 Billing systems
   - 1.3 Receipts
   - 1.4 Customer payments
   - 1.5 Sales records
   - 1.6 Stock control
   - 1.7 Purchasing
   - 1.8 Payroll systems.

Reviewing the quality of a sport and leisure business

All sport and leisure businesses want their customers to be fully satisfied and, to make sure this happens, many use approaches and procedures that together create a 'quality system'. According to the International Organization for Standardization (ISO), quality is about **all** staff and **all** features of a facility providing customers with a **consistently** good service. This is sometimes called Total Quality Management or TQM, where everything a business does is part of the quality system. Quality in a sport and leisure business is measured using a number of indicators, including meeting the needs of users and maintenance. The higher the standards, the higher the quality of the business and, consequently, the higher the level of customer satisfaction.

Why measure quality?

Quality systems were created by manufacturers who wanted to establish procedures that made sure that the products they produced had no defects. Defective products have to be thrown away and this costs manufacturers money. These principles are now applied in the service industry, including the sport and leisure industry.

Specific quality systems have been developed for the sport and leisure industry, including 'Charter Mark', which has now been replaced by 'Customer Service Excellence', and 'Quest'. More general quality systems, such as 'Investors in People' (which focuses on the quality of training that staff receive) have also been adapted for use. Many businesses also develop their own customer charters which show customers the quality of service they can expect. There are also industry awards, such as the Royal Society for the Prevention of Accidents' Gold award and the Low Carbon Performance Awards from the Chartered Institute of Building Service Engineers (CIBSE), which highlight quality provision in particular areas of a sport and leisure business.

The much coveted Quest award logo and the instantly recognizable Investors in People award are often put on the wall at the entrance to a sport and leisure facility to show that they have been inspected and approved to a high standard.

It is important to measure the level of quality at a sport and leisure facility so that the business can:

- Identify its strengths and weaknesses.
- Compare its performance with similar businesses locally and nationally.
- Improve performance or give rewards to staff when quality is consistently high.
- Achieve awards, which improve its image and increase customer confidence in the services it is offering. In turn, this can lead to more customers visiting the facility. It can even make staff happier, which naturally leads to better customer service.

SILVER

4. Take one 'Weakness' from your SWOT analysis and explain the 'Opportunities' for, and 'Threats' to, future developments to tackle this weakness.

BRONZE

1. Choose one of the aspects of quality described on the next two pages and teach your classmates about it as creatively as possible. You could create a sketch, produce a poster, choreograph a dance or write a rap, but don't forget to include an example of poor quality and high quality in your work.

2a) Design a checklist that could be used to collect information about the quality of a sport and leisure business.

b) Carry out a fact-finding visit to a sport and leisure business, and use your checklist to review the quality of the business.

3. A SWOT analysis is an effective way of processing all the information you have collected about the quality of a business into a manageable format, which will help you to identify the strengths of a business and areas it could improve. Guidance on how to complete a SWOT analysis can be found on page 254. Complete a SWOT analysis of the sport and leisure business you reviewed for Activity 2.

GOLD

5. Justify your reasons for recommending the path for future development that you explained in Activity 4.

How do you measure quality?

Users

To provide quality services to a local community, managers need to have a knowledge of the population they serve. They need to know the age profile of the population; for example, how many people under 16 and how many retired people live and work in the community. They also need to know the gender demographics of the population; how many men and women live in the community. Once managers have this information, which can usually be provided by the local authority, they can compare the information about the community with the information they have about the people who use their facilities. This allows them to assess whether the classes, programmes and facilities they provide are appropriate for the population they serve.

A quality sport and leisure business will have something to offer every member of the community it is targeting. For a public sector business, this will be the whole community. For a private sector business, this will mean a clearly identifiable part of that community. For example, there are many private, women-only gyms around the country.

Affordability

Affordability is closely linked to the population profile. Managers need to know about the incomes of the people living in their community, so that they can ensure that the users they are targeting can afford to make use of the facilities they provide. If they are too expensive then fewer people will come and if they are too cheap then more people than the centre can handle might turn up. In either situation the centre would be missing out on money that it could use, for example, to buy new equipment. However, if the prices are pitched at the right level and people can afford them, the business will be providing a high-quality service to the community.

Private sector facilities usually have more money to spend on their facilities and maintaining those facilities than public sector facilities. This is because private sector facilities are often trying to attract people with more money, so have to look smarter than public sector facilities, but can charge customers more for using them. In contrast, public sector facilities have to be affordable for all and often operate with low budgets.

The local authority might be able to provide managers with information on the income profile of the local population, or the sport and leisure business could carry out surveys amongst people who do and do not visit their facilities in order to discover what prices would be affordable for the community it is targeting.

Maintenance

For a sport and leisure business to provide a quality service, everything must be working as it should. Breakdowns disrupt the quality of service and annoy both staff and customers. Each piece of equipment should have a recommended maintenance schedule, and well-run centres will have a system that records the date of the last inspection and when the next one is due. Telling customers, via notices or a newsletter, that essential maintenance is due or currently underway often helps to increase the patience and understanding of customers, reducing their dissatisfaction. Apologizing to customers if something breaks down and clearly communicating when it will be fixed can also have a similar effect.

Changing facilities

Clean and tidy changing facilities are a sign of a quality sport and leisure facility. Cleaning rotas are therefore very important, as is checking the plumbing.

Marketing

The quality of its marketing activities, measured by their effectiveness, can make or break a business. Managers usually use a range of methods to ensure their message gets out, including:

- Advertising, such as radio and newspaper adverts, posters and leaflets.
- Publicity stunts, such as a demonstration by a gymnastics team in the town square or an appearance by a celebrity.
- Sales promotions, such as offering discounts for short periods to encourage people to take advantage of the classes, programmes and facilities on offer.

In order to assess how effective their marketing techniques are, managers need to review whether they were worthwhile in terms of what was achieved by the amount of money spent. Good quality marketing will give a business a good return on its money.

Customer feedback

Businesses should collect customer feedback regularly in order to ensure quality. There are quite a few methods available for collecting customer feedback, including:

- **Questionnaires:** Customers are asked to answer questions about what they think of the service provided by the business.
- **Focus groups:** Groups of customers discuss their feelings towards the service provided by the business.
- **Suggestion boxes:** Customers can make suggestions about how to improve the service provided by the business.
- **Monitoring enquiries and complaints:** If a business notices it is receiving lots of complaints or enquiries about a particular issue, and can resolve the problem, they should respond to customer feedback in order to improve the quality of the service they provide.

Facility and activity mix

It is important that a sport and leisure business regularly reviews its facilities and the activities it offers to ensure that it meets the needs of its users and provides them with a quality service.

If there isn't another swimming pool nearby, a leisure centre might respond to customer requests for a pool by exploring the viability of building one. The mix of facilities at a centre can also be improved by reorganizing existing spaces, for example, introducing a crèche alongside the soft play area, using an underused squash court for table tennis or Pilates, or setting out the equipment in the gym differently so that there is room to add an extra rowing machine.

Similarly, activities should be reviewed as the seasons change, for example, fixing up cricket nets after Easter or taking down goalposts and reseeding over the summer. Sport and leisure facilities should also ensure that they provide classes and programmes that meet the needs of specialist users, such as people who have been prescribed exercise by their GPs and referred to their leisure centre by the NHS, pregnant women, and parents with babies.

Modernity

Many sport and leisure facilities in the UK are old and some are run-down. A quality business will identify a range of measures that, if implemented, would bring the facility into the twenty-first century. Modernization plans can take many years to complete if they are extensive, and can also require both a lot of investment and planning permission, for example, if a new swimming pool is going to be built. Sometimes, cosmetic changes – such as a new coat of paint, new furniture and equipment, new signs, and new noticeboards – can make a significant difference quickly and relatively inexpensively.

Health and safety, and emergency procedures

Health and safety provision, including risk assessments and emergency procedures, should be checked regularly because:

- legislation changes
- things need replacing, such as items in a first-aid box that have passed their use-by date
- technology develops, for example, better, more efficient smoke or carbon monoxide detectors might come onto the market
- circumstances change, for example, existing evacuation procedures might not work if the number of visitors has increased significantly since they were devised or offering a new activity might introduce new risks that haven't been assessed previously.

Regular surveillance of all facilities is required. Hygiene in the canteen and the pH balance of the water in the pool may change on a daily basis, so it is important for them to be monitored regularly.

Customer information

Providing customers with information is a sign of good customer service and a business that provides good customer service is a quality organization. For example, providing customers with information about opening hours, prices, how to make bookings, and details of clubs and classes makes customers feel welcome. A noticeboard about the management structure of the organization, showing who works there and what they do, also helps customers to feel valued. The noticeboard needs to be updated regularly as staff are promoted, join and leave the organization. An out-of-date noticeboard is worse than no noticeboard at all!

It is also good practice to ensure that signs, particularly signs indicating emergency exits and other emergency procedures, are clearly visible and accurate.

Future development

A quality management team will ensure that all staff are appraised at least once a year. A staff appraisal is an opportunity for each member of staff to talk to their line manager or supervisor about their performance, and to discuss their personal strengths and areas for improvement, setting targets for the coming months.

A good management team will also assess the effectiveness of a business on a regular basis, analysing the strengths, weaknesses, opportunities and threats to the business, producing a strategic plan identifying areas for development and the targets that will need to be met in order to ensure a successful – quality – future.

Disability access

The Disability Discrimination Act 1995 is designed to ensure that people with disabilities have the same rights as able-bodied people and are not discriminated against. This means that, by law, all sport and leisure facilities, including larger private clubs, must ensure that people with disabilities can access their facilities and services. A leisure centre should be accessible via a ramp, for example, and also have toilets and changing facilities that are accessible to people with disabilities. A quality business will also go that step further, reviewing its provision for customers with disabilities regularly in order to identify weaknesses. Consulting with the relevant groups to see what changes could be made to accommodate the needs of customers with different disabilities would be a very effective way to do this.

Information systems

Information systems are usually electronic methods of gathering and reporting data, and include swipe-card systems, smart tills, booking software and software that analyses website hits. The data provided by a good quality information system can be used to inform decision making because it will present an accurate picture of customer and staff activities.

Unit 19 assignment, part four

Background

You are an inspector for a quality award and are visiting a centre that has applied for your award.

<table>
<tr><td>GRADING CRITERIA
TO BE ASSESSED</td></tr>
<tr><td>P5
M3
D2</td></tr>
</table>

Task

Write a report for a sport and leisure business of your choice that the business can use to help it improve, so that it is eligible for your quality award. The report should:

 **PASS**

Review the quality of a selected sport and leisure business, identifying the strengths and areas for future development (P5).

 **MERIT**

Review the quality of a selected sport and leisure business, explaining the strengths and areas for future development (M3).

 **DISTINCTION**

Review the quality of a selected sport and leisure business, justifying the strengths and areas for future development (D2).

Tackling the assignment

First you need to select a suitable facility, probably one you have access to locally and which has links to your school or college. Then you need to make sure that you have the agreement of the centre before you start your research, and that you plan your visit carefully so you know who you want to speak to, what you want to ask them and what you want to see.

Establish a structure for your final report, which could include a SWOT analysis, and use it to keep your research under control and focused. You could use or adapt some of the headings from the last few pages of this book to form sections of your report.

Remember to identify, explain or justify the strengths and areas for future development. When you **identify** something, you state what it is; you describe it. When you **explain** something, you go into more detail about why it is like it is; explanations often begin with the word 'because'. When you **justify** something, you defend or qualify the explanation for it, in this case the explanations for the strengths you have selected and the recommendations you have provided. One way of doing this could be to highlight why alternative options were not suitable.

Meeting the Pass criteria

Review of Lawnsmead Leisure Centre

Section 1: Review of users

Managers should check the age profile and gender demographics of the local community, to make sure that the programmes, classes and facilities they provide meet the needs of that community.

> Josh clearly has a structure in mind for his report, which is good. However, the report would have benefited from an introduction that describes what the review sets out to achieve and gives a brief description of the Lawnsmead Leisure Centre. For example, where is it? What facilities does it have? Are there any other leisure centres nearby?

1.1 Age profiles: The manager found out from the council that there is quite a high population of retired people close to the centre, so he offered mat bowling and badminton for them in the mornings. However, he had never asked them if these were activities they wanted. I thought this was bad.

1.2 Gender demographics: The manager has not had time to do any research on the numbers of women and men that live nearby or use the centre.

> Josh has highlighted a weakness but the language he has used to do this ('I thought this was bad') might offend the manager. It would have been better if Josh had phrased his criticism more positively. He could have identified the fact that the leisure centre manager spoke to the council and consequently offers activities to suit the retired people living nearby as a strength of the centre. He could then have gone on to suggest that the manager improved the quality of provision further by carrying out a survey amongst retired users to find out which activities they would like to do and if the morning is an appropriate time to offer them. If Josh adds to the material here and reviews all aspects of the leisure centre, he would meet the criteria for P5.

Meeting the Merit and Distinction criteria

Review of information systems

Strengths	Weaknesses
The leisure centre has a paper filing system which is contained in one big filing cabinet and seemed to be well-organized, although I was not allowed to look inside to check this. It contains all the membership records, which are easily accessible to all members of staff. The leisure centre has a computerized information system called EZfacility 4.0. This allows staff to view bookings and schedule activities, manage staff rotas, manage membership records, take payments and run reports. This is a system used by a lot of leisure centres and it does its job well.	The leisure centre duplicates all work relating to membership records because changes have to be updated on the paper copy of the records and the electronic copy of the records. All staff should have been trained on the computerized system but many have not and those that have are still not confident about using it. Most can do simple tasks, like make one-off bookings, but can't create regular bookings, so customers still have to book week after week. Only one member of staff knows how to use the system fully and he only works part-time. This means that the benefits of the software aren't being fully exploited.
Opportunities	**Threats**
The leisure centre would benefit from moving all its membership records onto its computerized system. This would save time and make the records more secure, because the filing cabinet is often left unlocked. All members of staff should be trained on all aspects of the computerized system. This would speed up their work and they would be able to use the software to offer their customers a better service, by being able to insert regular bookings just once, for example.	Moving membership records from a paper system to a computerized system takes time and it might be difficult to find the time for someone to do this, because members of staff are already very busy. It costs money to train people, to pay for someone to cover their job while they are training and to pay the person who is doing the training. The leisure centre has a limited budget because it is mainly funded by the local authority, so it might be difficult to find the money to pay for this training.

> By completing a SWOT analysis, Sophie has explained the strengths of the centre's information systems and explained where provision could be developed. To fully meet the criteria for M3 she has to do the same for all other aspects of the quality review but she is well on the way to achieving a Merit.

> Sophie has justified her suggestions. She has said why an effective information system is important and outlined what the consequences of not following her recommendations might be. If she continues like this for all aspects of the quality review she will meet the criteria for D2.

While there are certainly difficulties involved in moving all the membership records onto the computer system and training all staff to use it, I think it is important that the centre spends the time and money on improving their information systems. Having an effective information system can help a leisure centre to offer a higher-quality service to its customers. Waiting while someone rummages in a filing cabinet for your records and not being able to make regular advance bookings will frustrate many customers in the twenty-first century, making the centre look and feel old-fashioned and out-of-date. It might encourage many customers to go somewhere else to exercise.

Unit 20: Planning and Running a Sports Event

Planning and organizing a sports event

Sports events take on many guises, from inter-school competitions to regional and international events. Sports events can also be run for fun or to raise money for charity; a good example of this is Cancer Research UK's Race for Life events that take place every year. In order to successfully plan and run a sports event, many different factors should be considered as part of the planning process.

Types of sports event

The first step when organizing an event is to decide what type of event it will be.

Will it be a school or college sports day?

Whichever type of event is chosen, there is always one burning question: should it take place indoors or outdoors? The advantages of an indoor event are largely weather related because the event can go ahead even in torrential rain. But there are disadvantages to running an indoor event. The main problem with an indoor facility is lack of space for a large number of participants and spectators, something that is rarely a problem for an outdoor event. There is also the cost of hiring an indoor venue, which is often significantly more expensive than hiring an outdoor venue, because there is a higher demand for indoor facilities. If you are planning an outdoor event, consideration must be given to areas for shelter from both the rain and the sun (sunstroke is the most common problem requiring first aid at an outdoor event). Suitable consideration should also be given to a contingency plan in case the weather prevents the event going ahead outdoors.

Will it be a sports activity day run by the local leisure centre to encourage members of the public to try new activities to promote their facilities?

Will it be a sports-themed dinner to raise money for charity?

Will it be a community-based event to raise awareness about an issue or raise money for a c

Customer and participant requirements

Successful sports events don't simply happen. They are the result of weeks, months and sometimes years of organization. However, they all have one thing in common. They begin with someone – let's call them the customer – having an idea and wanting to hold an event. For the event to be considered successful the customer has to be happy with how it went, and this will only happen if the customer is fully consulted at the planning stage.

It is rare for a customer to decide to hold an event without having an idea of what form it should take, who should be involved, and when and where it should take place. It is important that the organizer listens carefully to the customer's requirements, but it is also the organizer's responsibility to identify any potential problems with the initial suggestions and to be able to suggest alternatives. With this in mind, it is vital that the organizer meets the customer **before** any planning takes place, and receives the answers to two key questions:

- What type of event would the customer like? Will it be a competition, a charity event or a community-based event for example?
- What are the aims and objectives of the event? Is the event designed to raise money, provide information, raise awareness and educate people or to improve the health, fitness and well-being of participants?

Bear in mind that some events can be more than one type and have multiple aims and objectives.

You will need to consider who the target audience for the event is and who the participants are going to be, because this will have a big impact on the form your event will take. For example, there is no point playing loud gangsta rap and having lots of energetic activities if your event is aimed at retired people. Similarly, certain activities, such as the London Marathon, are not appropriate for under-18s for legal reasons.

How the success of the event will be measured should also be discussed at this initial meeting. For example, if the aim of the event is to raise awareness then the number of participants and spectators will feature heavily in the success criteria; whereas the success of a fund-raising event is likely to be judged solely on how much money is raised.

Remember:

An aim is something that you intend to achieve by the end of the session or series of sessions and an example of an aim is, 'To raise awareness of the new facilities at an existing sports centre'. An objective is a small step that helps you achieve the aim and an example of an objective is, 'To carry out a poster campaign to showcase the new facilities'.

BRONZE

1. Choose three national or international sporting events and list five things that they have in common that make them successful events.

2. Research a major event, such as the London Marathon, the Great North Run or Cancer Research UK's Race for Life, and find out:

- The aims of the event.
- The target audience for the event.
- How the organizers of the event will measure their success.

Will it be a summer training camp?

The planning process

The process of planning an event can be divided into four sections – resources, participation, health and safety, and contingency planning – and it is best to follow a set programme so you can be sure that all the major items have been covered. If you don't approach the planning logically, you may find problems emerge when you come to use your plan to organize your event.

Resources

- **How much money can be spent on the event?** Before organizing anything you must determine the budget that is available. This will be the biggest constraint on the size, nature and success of the event. One person – ideally the event coordinator – should have control of the budget and keep an eye on it throughout the planning stages. Before any decision is made all the options should be fully costed so that you can work out which is the most cost-effective.
- **Which venue is to be used?** You must book the venue and make sure you have access to it in advance of the event so that you can prepare.
- **Is transport needed for resources, participants or spectators?**
- **How many staff members are needed and how many are available?** You cannot run an event single-handedly so it is important to get other people involved in planning, organizing and running the event.
- **What equipment is needed and what is available?**
- **How will the event be promoted?** Events will only be successful if they are well advertised, so promotional activities should be included at the planning stages. Promotional leaflets and posters, or adverts on the local radio station, are some of the most effective ways of publicizing an event. You must explain clearly who is eligible to join in, when the event begins and ends and where it is taking place (you may want to publish a map of the location and/or the layout of the venue), as well as details of prizes and refreshments etc. You also need to decide whether entrants need to sign up in advance or if they can just turn up on the day.
- **Are caterers or entertainers required?** You must book caterers and entertainers in advance.
- **What is the running order of the event?** This could be a timetable of races, matches or speeches depending on your event.

Participation

- **Does everyone have a role and do they know what it is?**
- **Are people clear on their responsibilities?**
- **Are the staff members working as a one large team, or a series of small teams?**
- **When and where will staff meetings take place?** Meetings should take place on a regular basis. Notes need to be kept of the issues that are discussed, with agreed decisions and actions from the meeting clearly recorded and shared with staff members.
- **How will information be circulated amongst staff members?**

Health and safety

- Has a person or a team been given responsibility for health and safety?
- Has a risk assessment been completed and have potential hazards been identified?
- Has a first aider been arranged? Is one employed by the venue or does one need to be organized?
- Has the location of a first-aid point been considered?
- Has a first-aid kit been borrowed or purchased?
- **Do you need to prepare disclaimer and informed consent documents for volunteers and participants to sign?** An informed consent document (an example of this can be found on page 263) states that anyone taking part in the event is aware of the risks and potential dangers involved, and asks them to agree that they will take all reasonable precautions to ensure that neither themselves nor anyone else is injured. It may also ask for details of a participant's medical history and sporting experience. A disclaimer document states, for example, that the organizers have no responsibility for participants' valuables during the event.

Contingency planning

- Do you have a contingency plan in place for poor weather?
- Do you have a contingency plan in place in case there is an accident?
- Do you have a contingency plan in place in case the number, age or ability of participants changes?
- Do you have a contingency plan in place in case staff are ill or cannot attend due to unforeseen circumstances?
- Do you have a contingency plan in place in case equipment has been damaged, lost or is not delivered in time?
- Do you have a contingency plan in place in case you can't get into the venue or it has been double-booked?

BRONZE

3. Imagine you are producing an outline plan for an inter-form or inter-department competition. Make a list of the things you would need to consider and place them in the order that you would do them.

4. Produce a document that could be used to record what happens at planning meetings. It will need to record the discussions, the decisions made and the actions agreed.

SILVER

5. Explain why you chose the order you did for Activity 3.

Unit 20 assignment, part one

Background

Your local sports centre has been threatened with closure due to a lack of use. You have been tasked with helping to keep the facility open and the manager has suggested four options for raising the centre's profile:

- A charity dinner for local business people, with a special guest speaker from the world of sport.
- A sports holiday camp for children from local primary schools.
- A sports award ceremony with awards for members of local sports clubs, voted for by the local community.
- A multi-sports competition, with teams from the local community entering to try and win a grand prize.

GRADING CRITERIA TO BE ASSESSED
P1, P2 M1

Task

Working in a small group of three to five people, choose one of the four options that have been suggested by the sports centre manager and contribute to the planning and organization of the event. You will need to think carefully about the option you select, because you will have to run the event in part two of the assignment. You will need to:

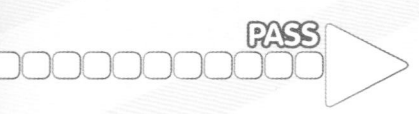

Produce a plan for a chosen sports event, outlining the planning process to meet given participant or customer requirements (P1).

Contribute to the organization of a chosen sports event (P2).

Produce a plan for a chosen sports event, explaining the planning process to meet given participant or customer requirements (M1).

Tackling the assignment

The first thing to do when tackling this assignment is to make sure you work to your strengths and use the facilities that are most readily available. For example, if you have easy access to a running track and have links with school students, then a sports day event is likely to be the easiest option for you. Alternatively, your school or college may organize a charity event on an annual basis, so helping to organize the event might be a good choice. In essence, the secret to this assignment is to keep it simple, because the more simple you make it the more likely you are to succeed.

Once you have decided on your event, you need to set up an initial planning meeting where you'll make most of the major decisions. It may be that you hold a series of meetings throughout the planning stages, checking things out step by step before making any final decisions. Whichever process you follow, be sure to keep detailed records of everything that is discussed and any agreements that are made because these can count as evidence towards meeting the assignment criteria.

Meeting the Pass criteria

BTEC Level 2 Firsts in Sport

Unit 20 assignment, part one   James Taylor

My responsibilities

Before the event:
- Type and print the invitation letters and maps of the venue.
- Check who is paying for the printing costs.
- Post letters to prospective participants.
- Check who is paying for the postage costs.
- Collate the reply slips.
- Make follow-up phone calls for any missing reply slips.
- Inform the rest of the group about participant numbers asap.
- Make phone calls three days before event to check participants are still attending and to sort any issues such as transport, clothing etc.

On the day:
- Meet and greet participants at meeting point.
- Hand out maps.
- Deal with any issues that arise.
- Once all participants have arrived, check if all referees have arrived and step in if needed. If everything is ok, assist with catering.

> James' planning sheet clearly shows that he has taken on significant responsibility for organizing the event. By splitting his responsibilities into two sections – before the event and on the day – he is able to prove that he has had a role in the planning process throughout the course of the event. The responsibilities he describes are consistent with the expectations of a student targeting a Pass, and are in line with the requirements of P2.

> James' evidence would be more substantial if he provided photographs of himself carrying out his role. For example, he could have included a copy of the letter he produced, along with a photo of him posting it to a participant. Alternatively, James could have provided a witness statement from his tutor showing that he had actually carried out his responsibilities.

Meeting the Merit criteria

SPORTS DAY ACTION PLAN
(Janine/Michael/Karl/Kieran)

Area	Task	Responsibility	Due by	Complete ✔	Notes
Volunteers	• Send out invitation to invite volunteers to participate in sports day. Invitation should include reply form. • Letters should include: ☐ times ☐ venue ☐ what the day will include (types of activities) ☐ parking facilities ☐ who's been invited ☐ aim of sports day ☐ contacts ☐ expectations of volunteers ☐ benefits of being involved ☐ cost (buses) ☐ reply form.	Event coordinator	Eight weeks prior		• Reply date should be approximately three weeks from the date the invitation is sent.
	• Follow up with phone call to confirm attendance.	Event coordinator	Four weeks prior		
	• Collate replies to confirm how many volunteers and who will be attending.	Event coordinator	Three weeks prior		
	• Follow-up phone call to confirm attendance.	Event coordinator	One week prior		
	• Organize for backup volunteers, in case of illness etc.	Event coordinator	One week prior		

> Janine and the rest of her group have clearly spent a lot of time planning their event and have made every effort to cover all bases. The planning sheet Janine has provided as her evidence is clearly aimed at meeting the Merit criteria because she has attempted to explain the planning process by adding details in the 'Notes' column. And, by adding 'Responsibility' and 'Due by' columns she is further explaining how the planning process will work within her team.

> However, I am not yet happy to award Janine M1, because she has not made it clear that she is meeting the requirements of the participant or the customer. It may well be that the plan created by Janine and her team is meeting the customer/participant requirements perfectly, but this needs to be made clear in order for her to achieve the Merit criteria for this piece of work.

355

Running a sports event

Once you have planned and organized it, the next step is to run your event. It is at this stage that you will find out how successful your planning and organization has been. The old saying 'fail to prepare and be prepared to fail' will certainly be tested during the event. However, it is important to remember that things rarely run precisely as they were planned, and the real skill is coping with last-minute changes.

Running an event can be broken down into three stages: setting up before the event, the event itself and setting down after the event. The complexity of the event will determine how meticulous the planning for each stage needs to be. Every event will be different, and although the following ideas cover the most common aspects of running a sports event, the list is not exhaustive. You will need to remember this when attempting part two of the assignment.

Setting up before the event

Signs
Participants and spectators will need to know lots of things, and the use of well-written, clear and informative signs is the easiest way to get information across. Signs will be needed to show people the locations of facilities such as car parking, toilets, first-aid points and refreshments. Signs may also be needed to inform competitors and spectators of the timing of events or the order of play.

Other equipment
This includes practically everything else, from seating areas to shelter and transport. As with all aspects of setting up an event, it is important to follow the plan that has been put in place but be prepared to make adjustments on the day if necessary.

Sports equipment
Sports equipment needs to be organized well in advance of the event in case any repairs or replacements are needed. On the day, the sports equipment will need to be readily available, but not left out so that it could cause a hazard, be broken or, worse still, stolen. The sports equipment will also need to be suitable for the age and abilities of the participants.

Food and drink
Food and drink can be provided by outside caterers or prepared in-house by the event organizers. As with the entertainment, someone should be allocated the responsibility of ensuring that the outside caterers have everything they need to set up properly. If you decide to prepare the refreshments yourselves, at least one person should be given the responsibility of doing this. A preparation and service area needs to be set up and you may require an electric socket if you are going to be using a fridge or a cooker.

Entertainment
Any entertainment needs to be booked well in advance and, on the day of the event, one person should be allocated the responsibility of ensuring that the entertainment is set up correctly. This is a relatively easy task in the case of a music player and speakers, but if a live band or sports personality has been arranged, then the person responsible for meeting them and helping them set up will need to know exactly what they require in terms of equipment and space.

During the event

During the event, all members of the team will need to work together to ensure its success. It is unlikely that everything will go smoothly, and so any difficulties should be dealt with quickly and with the minimum of fuss. Event organizers will need to be available to deal with requests from the customer, the participants and the spectators and, for this reason, should not be directly responsible for officiating or instructing. Instead, these tasks should be delegated to willing volunteers or paid personnel. However, event organizers should be responsible for monitoring the overall event and supervising all other employees, regardless of whether they are paid employees or volunteers.

Setting down after the event

Waste disposal
All litter should be collected and disposed of safely, with as much as possible recycled. If you have food and drink left over, perishable items such as fruit should be shared out amongst the organizers and helpers or thrown away and non-perishable items such as wrapped cereal bars or unopened isotonic drinks should be carefully stored ready for the next event.

Sports equipment
All the sports equipment used will need to be collected, checked for damage and returned to storage. Any broken items should be kept separate and a list prepared so that they can be repaired or replaced.

Signs and posters
Signs, posters and similar items should be taken down at the end of the event and stored for future events or disposed of, recycling wherever possible.

BRONZE

1. Refer back to your outline plan of a sports event that you produced for Activity 3 on page 353. Take on the role of event organizer and allocate roles and responsibilities on the day of the event to yourself and four other people. Remember that people can have more than one job to do but, if they do, you will need to list their responsibilities in the order that they should approach them.

Reviewing a sports event

It is important for event organizers to evaluate the events that they have run to provide them with feedback on their performance. If an event is unsuccessful for any reason, the organizers can work on improving things for the next time that they run an event. Equally, if something worked really well, they may want to use this method in the future.

When evaluating an event it is important to gather information from everyone involved, including the customer, the organizing team, the volunteer helpers, the participants and the spectators, to build an accurate picture of how it went. You might want to ask people about:

- **Planning:** How well was the event planned? Were the contingency plans in place appropriate?
- **Content:** How suitable was the content of the event for the participants? Was there enough/too much going on?
- **Organization:** How organized were the leader(s) before the event and on the day? Did they respond to changes from the original plan calmly and efficiently?
- **Health and safety:** Were the participants safe? Were there any incidents? If anyone was injured or ill, were they treated efficiently?
- **Achievements:** Did the organizers achieve the aims and objectives set out for the event? Did the event keep to the budget?
- **Areas for improvement and recommendations for future events:** What could have been done better? What should the organizers do next time to make the event run more smoothly?

Reviewing an event is easiest if everyone involved is asked the same questions in the same format. The most common way of doing this is to use a questionnaire or customer comment cards, which should include a series of simple questions such as those above. It is important to ask open-ended questions, because this allows participants to express their opinions more effectively. However, the most important feedback will come from the customer, and this should always take the form of a face-to-face meeting.

A review of a sports event requires the organizers to get together after the event has taken place.

BRONZE

1. Create a questionnaire or comment card that can be given to participants to review a sports event they have participated in.

Unit 20 assignment, part two

Background

Your local sports centre has been threatened with closure due to a lack of use. You have been tasked with helping to keep the facility open and the manager has suggested four options for raising the centre's profile:

- A charity dinner for local business people, with a special guest speaker from the world of sport.
- A sports holiday camp for children from local primary schools.
- A sports award ceremony with awards for members of local sports clubs, voted for by the local community.
- A multi-sports competition, with teams from the local community entering to try and win a grand prize.

Task

Working in the same group as you did for part one of the assignment, it is time to run your chosen event. In addition, you will need to collect feedback which can then be used to evaluate the success of the event. You need to:

GRADING CRITERIA TO BE ASSESSED
P3, P4, P5
M2
D1

PASS

Contribute to the running of a chosen sports event (P3).

Design and use methods for collecting feedback on the success of a sports event (P4).

Assess feedback received, identifying strengths and areas for improvement (P5).

MERIT

Assess feedback received, evaluating strengths and areas for improvement, and providing recommendations for future events (M2).

DISTINCTION

Assess feedback received, analysing strengths and areas for improvement, and justifying your recommendations for future events (D1).

Tackling the assignment

Achieving a Merit and even a Distinction for this assignment, and for this unit as a whole, is relatively straightforward. The key is to focus on the important parts of each criteria, particularly the differences between P5, M2 and D1. For example, students could simply list strengths and areas for improvement to meet P5, but would need to explain these to meet M2 and justify the explanations to meet D1. Contributing to the running of an event and collecting feedback should both be straightforward tasks, assuming you successfully completed part one of the assignment, and you should now pay close attention to how you use the feedback you received from participants and spectators.

Meeting the Pass criteria

BTEC Level 2 Firsts in Sport

Unit 20 assignment, part two
Michael McMahon

Sports Day 2009

Feedback sheet

(Michael McMahon)

What was good?
The activities were great, lots of fun and very competitive.

What could have been better?
Not enough car parking: quite a few parents came along as spectators and there wasn't enough room in the car park for them. Many had to park on the road outside the school gates.

Your suggestions for next year...
Have someone to greet people as they arrive.
More car parking.
Provide a map to show where the toilets, refreshments and activities are.

- -

Overall the event was a success, and we received lots of positive feedback from people on the day. Each participating school (10 in total) was given a feedback sheet, though only 7 of them replied. The comments were mostly very positive, and tended to concentrate on the activities and how much students enjoyed taking part. There were very few negative comments, although one school was unhappy about the lack of parking facilities available for parents who came as spectators. This is definitely something I would try to change if I was to run the event again in future.

Michael's feedback sheet is very basic, and it doesn't provide many prompts for the person filling it in.

If Michael's event involved ten primary schools I would assume that there were around 250 people involved, yet he received only seven responses using his feedback sheet. He should have handed out more than one feedback sheet per school. I would also have expected him to follow up on the three missing feedback sheets.

Michael has attempted to identify strengths and areas for improvement but I don't feel he has included enough detail to meet the criteria for P5. He needs to look at the feedback more closely, and relate his review to more than just one response sheet.

Meeting the Merit and Distinction criteria

BTEC Level 2 Firsts in Sport

Unit 20 assignment, part two   Jocelyn Brown

Sports Day Feedback Sheet

Your name (optional): _____

School name: _____

Please circle your opinion of each aspect of the event noted below.

Activities	Excellent	Good	Satisfactory	Unsatisfactory
Maps/Letters	Excellent	Good	Satisfactory	Unsatisfactory
Catering	Excellent	Good	Satisfactory	Unsatisfactory
Facilities	Excellent	Good	Satisfactory	Unsatisfactory
Staffing	Excellent	Good	Satisfactory	Unsatisfactory
Prizes	Excellent	Good	Satisfactory	Unsatisfactory
Overall	Excellent	Good	Satisfactory	Unsatisfactory

Comments: _____

_____

_____

_____

The feedback form Jocelyn used has enabled her to make accurate judgements about the success of her event, and is evidence to support those judgements. By evaluating each component of the event and by providing recommendations for the future, I am happy that she has met the criteria for M2.

In places, Jocelyn's review shows an attempt to meet the Distinction criteria. This is evident by her comments which justify her decisions, such as her statement: 'Perhaps next time I would ask people to hand their form to someone, rather than placing them in a box, because this would make it more explicit that a response is expected.'

I handed out my feedback sheet to all participants and to members of staff who accompanied the students to the event. I did not hand out sheets to the spectators, because I felt that they may not have been able to give an objective opinion because they were not directly involved. With hindsight, I believe I should have designed a different feedback form that spectators could have used to give their views on the event from their perspective. I would definitely do this next time.

In total I received 192 out of 256 potential replies (in other words, 64 people did not return their feedback sheets), but as this is a response rate of 75 per cent I am quite happy. Perhaps next time I would ask people to hand their form to someone, rather than placing them in a box, because this would make it more explicit that a response is expected.

As for the event itself, over 90 per cent of the responses rated all components of the event as 'Good' or 'Excellent', and there were only a handful of 'Unsatisfactory' ratings. Of these, the majority related to staffing, and were due to poor refereeing in some cases. I have learnt from this that next time I would try to use fully-qualified officials.

Some of the responses received stated that the catering was good, but not excellent. This was because we had opted to serve cold drinks and snacks, but the weather was cold on the day and some people said they would have appreciated a hot drink of tea or coffee. Again, this is something I would look to improve on next time.

Maps, letters and facilities were rated as 'Good' overall. Next time I would use the same format again.

Overall, I am happy with the feedback I received, and I would look to change very little if I was to run the event again.

To fully achieve the criteria for D1, I would like to see Jocelyn justifying her statements throughout her report. For example, her statement, 'Maps, letters and facilities were rated as 'Good' overall. Next time I would use the same format again', is not a Distinction level answer. My question to Jocelyn would be, if the maps, letters and facilities were only rated as good, what could you do to make them excellent?

Taking all things into consideration, I am happy to award Jocelyn P5 and M2, but there are too few examples of her justifying her recommendations to award her D1 at this stage.

Glossary

A

Abduction   the name given to the movement at a joint, where a part of the body is taken away from the centre line of the body in a sideways motion. It is the opposite of adduction.

Acute injuries   these are injuries which reach a crisis quickly. They often occur as a result of sport and exercise.

Adduction   the name given to the movement at a joint, where a part of the body is moved towards the centre line of the body in a sideways motion. It is the opposite of abduction.

Adhere   when you adhere to something you stick to it, so adherence factors are the things which keep you committed to a course of action and barriers to adherence are the things which get in the way of this.

Aerobic endurance   a measure of how well you are able to keep your muscles supplied with oxygen.

Aerobic energy system   when the energy you are using is created with oxygen present you are using the aerobic energy system.

Agility   the ability of a sports player to move and change direction quickly and under control.

Agonist   when a muscle pulls to create movement it is called the agonist or prime mover.

Aim   the purpose or intention of an event.

Anaerobic energy system   when the energy you are using is created without enough oxygen present you are using the anaerobic energy system. There are two parts to the anaerobic energy system: the alactic/phosphocreatine energy system and the lactic acid energy system.

Antagonist   muscles work in pairs to bring about movement because they can only pull and not push. When the agonist pulls to create movement, the partner muscle is called the antagonist.

Autocratic (command) leadership   a style of leadership where the leader gives out instructions that the group follows.

B

Balance   the ability to keep the body stable, when still or when moving, by keeping the centre of gravity over the base of support.

Balanced diet   a diet that consists of the right balance of the six components of a healthy diet (carbohydrates, fat, protein, water, vitamins and minerals).

Body composition   a measure of how much of your body is made up of muscle compared with how much is made up of fat.

Body language   the way in which your body – how you stand and the gestures you use, for example – communicate non-verbally with your audience.

C

Cardiovascular system   the name given to the body system that comprises the blood, the heart and the blood vessels. The main role of the cardiovascular system is to transport oxygen and nutrients to all the tissues in the body and to remove waste products, such as carbon dioxide, from them.

Circumduction   the name given to the movement at a joint when the bone or bones rotate fully around an axis to complete a full circle of movement.

Concentric contraction   the name given to a muscular contraction when the muscle shortens.

Contingency plan   an alternative plan that can be put into action, if necessary, to ensure that an event takes place safely if something unexpected happens.

Continuing Professional Development   continuing to update and improve your qualifications and skills after you have left formal education.

Coordination   the ability to use two or more parts of the body at the same time.

Customer service   good customer service is an organization's ability to meet the needs and wants of its customers in a positive matter, thereby creating a satisfying experience for the customer.

D

Democratic leadership   a style of leadership where the leader involves the group in the decision making.

Dynamic strength   the amount of force that can be exerted repeatedly by a muscle.

E

Eccentric contraction   the name given to a muscular contraction when the muscle lengthens.

Expiration   the name used to describe what happens when we breathe out.

Explosive strength   the amount of force that can be exerted in one quick, powerful muscular contraction.

Extension   the name given to the movement at a joint, when the joint is fully stretched out or straightened when it is extended.

Extrinsic   the name given to external things that come from outside the performer.

F

Flexibility   a measure of the range of movement possible at a joint.

Flexion   the name given to the movement at a joint, when a joint is bent and the two bones either side come towards each other.

Formative review   a review that takes place while something is going on. Formative reviews provide ongoing feedback that can be used to improve performance to ensure that the desired outcome is achieved.

G

Gaseous exchange   this is the name given to the process that ensures we get the oxygen which feeds our working muscles and organs into our blood, and the carbon dioxide and other waste products produced by the working muscles and organs out of our blood.

Goal   a clear idea of what you want to achieve. A goal can be short-term, medium-term or long-term. Long-term goals can be outcome goals or performance goals.

H

Hazard anything that could cause danger or harm, from a simple pool of water on the floor to a faulty light switch.

Healthy diet there are six components of a healthy diet: carbohydrates, fat, protein, vitamins, minerals and water. However, a healthy diet is not just about eating foods that contain these nutrients. It is also about eating the right balance of those foods; eating a balanced diet.

Hypertrophy muscles adapt to training by increasing in size.

I

Induction a formal introduction to a role or facility, which involves initial training in duties or on equipment, and an outline of health and safety procedures.

Inspiration the name used to describe what happens when we breathe in.

Intrinsic the name given to things that come from within the sports performer.

Isometric contraction these occur when a muscle that is working stays the same length.

Isotonic contraction these occur when a muscle changes length as it works.

L

Laissez-faire leadership a style of leadership where the responsibility for decision making is largely given to the group.

Legislation the name given to rules and regulations that have been made into law by the government of a country.

M

Maximum Heart Rate (MHR) the maximum number of times the heart can contract in a minute.

Motivation the need or desire to achieve a goal or a certain level of success. Motivation can be both intrinsic and extrinsic.

Muscular endurance a measure of how long your muscles can continue to exert force.

Muscular system the name given to the body system that is made up of all the muscles in the body. There are three types of muscle: skeletal muscle, cardiac muscle and smooth muscle.

N

Non-verbal communication this is all the communication that takes place without using words and includes hand gestures, body language, tone of voice and facial expressions.

O

Objective a small step that helps to achieve the overall aim.

Organizational structure the way a company or department sets up its staffing and management arrangements. Organizational structures are usually shown in a diagram, with lines linking roles and showing who everyone reports to.

Outcome what has actually been achieved at the end of an event. An intended or expected outcome is something that you hope to achieve at the end of an event.

Overuse injuries these often occur when a sports performer pushes themselves hard over long periods of time and continuously puts the same muscles, bones and joints under pressure.

P

PAR-Q (Physical Activity Readiness Questionnaire) a questionnaire used to assess a client's current level of activity and their lifestyle to find out if they are fit enough to begin an exercise programme.

Power the ability to combine strength with speed, to perform a strong muscular contraction very quickly.

Procedure an established course of action or method for doing things.

Prime mover when a muscle pulls to create movement it is called the prime mover or agonist.

Private sector this consists of all organizations that exist to make profit.

Public sector this consists of all organizations that are funded by the government.

Q

Quality according to the International Organization for Standardization (ISO), quality is about all staff and all features of a facility providing customers with a consistently good service.

R

Reaction time the time it takes to respond to a stimulus.

Regulations these control how a sport will be played or conducted, including what surface it will be played on and what safety standards need to be met in order to help prevent injuries. There are also regulations that cover how sport and leisure facilities should be run to ensure the health and safety of employees and visitors.

Reliability the degree to which repeated measurements give the same result.

Respiratory system the name given to the body system responsible for bringing about the actions in the body that we call 'breathing'. Breathing is the means by which oxygen from the air is brought into the body.

Responsibility a task that accompanies a specific role.

Risk the combination of the likelihood of a hazard causing harm and the severity of the potential injury. The more likely it is to happen and the more severe the consequences, the greater the risk.

Risk assessment the process of assessing all hazards and the level of risk they pose, and putting in place measures to control and minimize them.

Role a specific part in an organization.

Rotation this is the name given to a spinning or turning movement at a joint, where part of the body rotates around an imaginary axis.

Rules these ensure that a sport is played fairly by all competitors.

S

Skeletal system the name given to the body system that is made of bones and joints. The skeletal system performs five functions: protection, movement, shape, support and blood production.

Skill something that often requires practice in order for someone to be able to carry it out consistently, again and again. Skills can be discrete, continuous or serial.

SMART targets a way of setting out targets, and objectives, for development and improvement to ensure they are specific, measurable, achievable, realistic and time-bound.

Speed a measure of how fast a muscle can contract, once or repeatedly, in a given amount of time.

Strength a measure of the amount of force that can be generated by a muscle when it is contracting.

Summative review a review that takes place at the end of something, to find out if the aims and objectives have been met and to determine strengths and areas for improvement.

SWOT analysis an analysis tool that involves considering strengths, weaknesses, opportunities and threats.

T

Tactic the plan of action used to outwit your opponent and gain an advantage.

Technique the way in which you perform a skill.

Thermoregulation the name given to the process by which the cardiovascular system regulates the body's temperature by regulating the flow of blood to certain blood vessels. Vasoconstriction takes place when the blood vessels contract to keep warm blood deeper inside the body. Vasodilation takes place when the blood vessels relax to stop the body's temperature rising too high.

V

Validity the degree to which an assessment method measures what it is intended to measure.

Verbal communication this is the communication that takes place when people speak to each other.

Voluntary sector this consists of all not-for-profit and non-governmental organizations.

Index